Myrtle Savariau

A World to Love

George E. Knowles

Review and Herald® Publishing Association
Washington, DC 20039-0555
Hagerstown, MD 21740

The author assumes full responsibility for the accuracy of all facts and
quotations as cited in this book.

This book was
Edited by Gerald Wheeler
Designed by Bill Kirstein
Cover art by Warren Rood
Cover photos contributed by: Warren R. Rood, R. W. Pohle, C. L. Thomas,
Joel D. Springer, H. Armstrong Roberts
Type set: Times Roman

PRINTED IN U.S.A.

94 93 92 91 90   10 9 8 7 6 5 4 3 2 1

R & H Cataloging Service

Knowles, George E.
  A world to love.

    1. Devotional literature.   2. Seventh-day
Adventists—Missions.   I. Title.

                242.2

ISBN 0-8280-0565-6

Myrtle Savariau

DEDICATED TO:

My wife, Lillian, my partner in marriage and in ministry for more than 40 years; a loving and lovable Christian who is my constant source of inspiration.

ACKNOWLEDGMENTS

Unless otherwise noted, Bible texts quoted in this book are from The New King James Version. Copyright © 1979, 1980, 1982, Thomas Nelson, Inc., Publishers.

Texts credited to NEB are from *The New English Bible*. © The Delegates of the Oxford University Press and the Syndics of the Cambridge University Press 1961, 1970. Reprinted by permission.

HOW TO USE THIS BOOK

One of the finest ways to use this book is to get an extra copy to share with a friend. In these busy times few people will take time to read a big book, but many could benefit by forming the habit of reading a page a day. This book will be equally beneficial for nurture and outreach.

Many readers already have well established devotional habits. Some will keep this book in the bedroom to be read first thing in the morning. Others will have it close to the breakfast table, and still others will gather in the living room for family worship.

New Christians and newlyweds will have the opportunity of forming their own worship customs. Hopefully the theme of each daily reading and the Scripture text will provide you with food for thought through the day.

The inspirational thoughts are designed for your spiritual growth and nurture. Each day there will be a suggestion of something about which to pray in addition to those items you will already have on your own personal prayer list. Worship would be enriched for a family if one of the children would search out in advance additional information about the country or people group featured in many of the prayer suggestions.

You will gain some new insights on the world mission program as we review how God has led this movement in establishing the church in 186 of the 215 countries listed by the United Nations. As we take a closer look we will discover that each country is made up of different people groups with different cultures and sometimes different languages.

To reach every "tongue [language] and people [people group]" is our challenge. People groups include not only ethnic groups, but the hearing impaired, blind, handicapped, rulers, prisoners, lonely, aged, and many others too numerous to list. Our global strategy must take into consideration all these groups and how to reach them.

As you think of Christians around the world reading a page from this book each day, meditating on the same Bible verse that will occupy your thoughts, and praying for the same needs you will be praying for, it should help you to see yourself as part of a great family. Whether you are at this moment sitting in a family circle or whether there is not another person in sight, you are part of a family. You are never alone.

The model for the daily devotional custom is the example of Jesus of whom we read: "Now in the morning, having risen a long while before daylight, He went out and departed to a solitary place; and there He prayed" (Mark 1:35).

PREFACE

Preparing a book of daily devotional readings has been a rich personal experience. I trust that you will be blessed in reading to the extent that I have been blessed in writing.

In preparing each reading I have prayed that God who knows the personal needs of each one of us, and who can see into the future, will provide for our spiritual needs through these pages. The hours I have put into this manuscript will be rewarded each time a reader finds "just the help I needed for today."

Memory, reading, and notes taken while listening to sermons have furnished the seed thoughts for these pages. I thank all who have had a spiritual influence on my life, and they are many.

Special thanks go to my wife, Lillian, who never once complained about the many evenings and weekends preempted by this project. Thanks also to my former secretary and family friend, Ethel Randall, for assisting with research as well as editing and typing the manuscript.

READINGS FOR SPECIAL TIMES AND NEEDS

A TEXT FOR NEW YEAR'S DAY

A happy and blessed new year on this first day of 1991. And it will be a good year for you if you begin each day with God and His Word.

God's Book has a promise for every need you will meet during this new year. Our text for today contains five promises, and by claiming its assurances we can walk forth into the unknown and untried paths of another year with confidence and trust. Meditate a moment on these five promises:

1. "I am with you." If we walk with God through the next 365 days, we will never be alone. We can expect good things, for He will show us "the path of life," and in His presence "is fullness of joy" (Ps. 16:11).

2. "I am your God." With our God by our side we can face the trials we may encounter with the tread of a conqueror, affirming with Paul that nothing can separate us from the love of God (Rom. 8:35-39).

3. "I will strengthen you." By nature we are morally and spiritually weak, but God has made provision that through His promises we may be "partakers of the divine nature" (2 Peter 1:4) and thus have the strength to resist temptation.

4. "I will help you." With God aiding us, we may turn every trial into triumph, every adversity into achievement, every misfortune into mastery, and every calamity into conquest.

5. "I will uphold you with My righteous right hand." The hand that upholds the worlds in space and guides the planets in their orbits will sustain and direct you and me. The hand that created us and that possesses "all power" has promised to keep us from falling. Isn't that just the promise you and I need?

When Jesus gave the gospel commission He added the assurance "I am with you always" (Matt. 28:20). Always with us, He will help us as we seek to do our part in the church's Global Strategy to fulfill the divine commission to reach everyone, everywhere with the message of His love.

Fear not, for I am with you; be not dismayed, for I am your God. I will strengthen you, yes, I will help you, I will uphold you with My righteous right hand. Isa. 41:10.

Pray for a closer relationship with Jesus and a constant sense of His presence so that He may live out His life through you and draw others to Himself through you.

SEEK GOD FIRST

One of the most important things we can do at the beginning of a new year is to review our priorities. It is the best time to take an inventory to be sure we have them in the right order. What is the number one priority in your life?

Our top priority should be to love God so much that our greatest desire will be to have a part in His kingdom and to help others find their way to it. The only way anyone can enter the kingdom of God is through the merits of Christ's righteousness. When the spirit of Christ's righteousness becomes our spirit, we can't be satisfied to keep the kingdom for ourselves only—we want to influence others to be there too.

When we put God first, spiritual laws come into play that guide us in all our other decisions. Instead of wrestling with the many considerations involved with every decision, we have only to remember that we have already decided to put God first. Then we need to ask ourselves: In the light of that major decision, how shall I decide this secondary issue? When we feel overwhelmed by the countless decisions that we have to make, we need to be sure we have made the all-important basic decision to put God first in our lives. When we put God first in our lives, He has a marvelous way of preventing problems, solving problems, and of providing all the things essential to our well-being.

In our present materialistic age we face a real danger that we will reverse priorities and fall into the trap of seeking material things first and making spiritual considerations secondary. Some people live as if the Bible says, "Seek first all these things, and the kingdom of God will be added to you."

Remember, "Our heavenly Father has a thousand ways to provide for us of which we know nothing. Those who accept the one principle of making the service of God supreme, will find perplexities vanish and a plain path before their feet" (*The Ministry of Healing,* p. 481).

But seek first the kingdom of God and His righteousness, and all these things shall be added to you. Matt. 6:33.

Pray that the kingdom of God and His righteousness for yourself, your loved ones, and all those who come within your influence may always be the most important things in your life.

FAMILY WORSHIP

The cities and towns of medieval times were usually built within a sturdy wall for protection. Gates in the city wall would open onto each of the main roads connecting that city with other cities, just as the Damascus Gate in the wall of old Jerusalem opened onto the road connecting Jerusalem and Damascus.

In England I saw one such gate with a small chapel built above it. I was told that in olden times travelers, before leaving on a journey, would go to the chapel and pray for protection from robbers and other dangers, and for a safe return home.

The hazards of our day might be somewhat different from those of the Middle Ages, but certainly the need for protection is just as great. Every home should be a prayer chapel where family members can seek God's blessing for themselves and for each other before going out the gate.

A family without daily worship is like a family living without a roof over their heads or walls around them, for when the storms come, they have no protection. By sincere, earnest prayer, parents can erect a hedge about their children. Instilling in them the habit of daily worship in the home is worth more than a large bank account, property, or a college education.

When new families unite with the church, it would be helpful to invite them to the homes of members to observe family worship customs and to gain inspiration to enrich their family altar.

A Japanese girl studying in an American college received an invitation to spend the Christmas vacation in the home of one of her classmates. When leaving, she admitted there was one thing she missed. You see, in Japan there is a god shelf in every home where the family gods are kept. "Do not Americans worship their God in their homes?" she asked. Evidently the host family did not have family worship.

"If ever there was a time when every house should be a house of prayer, it is now. . . . And yet, . . . some who profess to be Christians have no family worship" *(Testimonies, vol. 7, p. 42).*

Oh come, let us worship and bow down; let us kneel before the Lord our Maker. Ps. 95:6.

Pray for the work in Costa Rica, where among the population of 2.9 million, one of the largest Protestant churches is the Seventh-day Adventist Church, with 11,572 members.

GLOBAL STRATEGY

It was in 1986 at the General Conference Annual Council in Rio de Janeiro, Brazil, that Seventh-day Adventist Church president Neal C. Wilson challenged the assembled church leaders to develop a global strategy.

Ultimately Global Strategy involves bringing a knowledge of Christ and His message to everyone, everywhere, but it begins with you and me and our personal relationship with Jesus. We can't share with others what we ourselves do not possess. "It is by contemplating Christ, by exercising faith in Him, by experiencing for ourselves His saving grace, that we are qualified to present Him to the world" *(Testimonies,* vol. 5, p. 158).

Global Strategy focuses outwardly on a complex world made up of many different cultural, ethnic, racial, and other distinct people groups. We must first identify the various people groups and then develop a strategy for reaching each one. Specialists in the field of mission estimate that there are 25,000 ethnic people groups in the world, more than 12,000 of which are as yet unreached and have no Christian church accessible to them. And think of other people groups to be reached, including the deaf, blind, prisoners, rulers, entertainers, educators. The list seems endless.

It is no longer true that the mission field is "over there." It is all around us wherever there are people unreached by the gospel of Christ.

Peoples in the 1990s are often a moving target of mission. Asian and African students in North and South America illustrate this point. Koreans, however, are an example of a people who were once an unreached mission field and now form a significant part of the mission force itself.

The tremendous size of the task calls for a redefinition of our mission and a renewed commitment to that mission. We must have a clear sense of the reason for the existence of the Seventh-day Adventist movement.

Global Strategy brings us face-to-face with our total dependence upon the Lord. It drives us to a deeper study of His Word, and to new dimensions in prayer life as we reach out for needed spiritual power. The influence of personal Bible study and a meaningful prayer and devotional experience motivates our outreach.

And He said to them, "Go into all the world and preach the gospel to every creature." Mark 16:15.

Pray that you as an individual or as a member of a family will find that unique area of service where you can fit into Global Strategy.

THE MISSION, THE MOVEMENT, AND ME

This is the first Sabbath of the new year. In many congregations it will be a special day of prayer and spiritual emphasis to launch the outreach thrust for the next 12 months.

Those who are part of it see the Seventh-day Adventist movement as not just another church with a different day of worship. They view it as a special movement that God raised up during the last years of earth's history to prepare people everywhere for the coming of Jesus and for citizenship in His kingdom.

Our unique mission calls for the proclamation of the gospel to every nation, kindred, tongue, and people in the special setting of the messages of the three angels of Revelation 14. In addition to proclaiming, the mission requires leading people out of the world, out of organizations that have fallen into error, and into God's remnant church. The mission involves confronting lost humans with the claims of Jesus Christ, leading them to a decision, nurturing their spiritual growth, and assimilating them as responsible members of the church body. It involves inspiring them to spend the rest of their lives sharing their newfound faith with others as they become coworkers with God in the establishment of His kingdom.

The most difficult challenge in mission today is not evangelizing Africa and Asia, but rather how to proclaim the gospel to the secularized, Western pagan. It is the couldn't-care-less people that churches have the most difficulty in reaching.

There are 90 million unchurched Americans, people who don't belong to any church. Some of these are former church members. Proportionately similar figures might be cited for the countries of western Europe, Australia, and others.

Our denomination has objectives for mission in this new year and hopefully each congregation does too, but what about us individually and as families? What will our mission be? The objectives we choose today will affect what we do for God and our neighbors during the next 12 months.

Also I heard the voice of the Lord, saying: "Whom shall I send, and who will go for Us?" Isa. 6:8.

Pray about the challenge of reaching the multitudes of city-dwellers with Christ's message. According to projections, by the year 2000, figures for metropolitan areas, expressed in millions, will look like this: Mexico City—26.3; Sao Paulo—24.0; Tokyo/Yokohama—17.1; Calcutta—16.6; and Bombay—16.0.

17

PRAY FOR ALL

Notice Paul's words to Timothy: "Therefore I exhort first of all that supplications, prayers, intercessions, and giving of thanks be made for all men, for kings and all who are in authority, that we may lead a quiet and peaceable life in all godliness and reverence" (1 Tim. 2:1, 2).

Here Scripture encourages us to pray for all men and women, beginning first of all with rulers—those in positions of authority. How do we go about praying for all people? Each day we could pray: "God bless everybody in all the world." But I'm sure we would agree that it would be much more meaningful to single out different groups to pray for each day, and that is exactly what we are going to do in our devotional time this year. Each day we will suggest a people group or some particular need to be our prayer focus for that day. The possibilities are unlimited as we think of God's people around the world uniting their prayers for a specific need each day. Each need is in some way related to Global Strategy. Some days we will be praying for people groups who need to be reached, and on other days we will be asking God for victory in our lives so that we will be fit channels to reflect the love and character of God to others.

God's Word says to pray "for all men." He is concerned with all people. Certainly we share that concern, and that is the reason for Global Strategy.

The people group mentioned in today's text are rulers—those involved in government. How faithful have we been in praying for such individuals? Certainly we have a responsibility to pray for these people. God says we do!

Not only should we pray for the government of the country in which we live, but, remembering our brothers and sisters in the faith who live in lands where liberty is restricted, we should pray for the rulers of those countries also.

The next year holds out some exciting possibilities for intercessory prayer on behalf of national rulers and government leaders.

> **Therefore I exhort first of all that supplications, prayers, intercessions, and giving of thanks be made for all men, for kings and all who are in authority. 1 Tim. 2:1, 2.**
>
> *Pray specifically for the rulers and members of government in your country and in other countries that God may lay upon your heart.*

UNCROSSED BARRIERS

Worldwide there is one Seventh-day Adventist for every 1,000 persons in the total population, but there are nearly 1,800 groups of 1 million people that have no Seventh-day Adventist presence whatsoever. A majority of these 1,800 groups are in China and the Middle East, where we have no division organization to assume responsibility, and in northern India. A primary objective of Global Strategy is to organize a concerted movement to establish a witness in each 1 million population segment where presently we have no Seventh-day Adventist presence.

Within every country and within many populations we find "hidden" peoples for whom language or ethnic grouping or socioeconomic level remain as uncrossed barriers as far as the gospel is concerned.

Research in the area of church growth reveals that Christianity usually spreads out within the boundaries of culture and language. Cultural boundaries act as rather formidable obstacles to the spread of the gospel because people are not comfortable with cultural change. It is normal to want to remain within one's culture. For example, a Korean language church in North America will not normally attract Hispanics because of barriers of language and culture.

It is not reasonable to insist that converts to Christianity give up their mother tongue when they become Christians, nor should they be required to drop the various customs of their native culture that do not violate Christian principles.

One of the special needs of our day is to balance the time spent focusing on the internal affairs of the church, with generous amounts of time focusing our thinking on the people of the world as Jesus did. Seeking to understand the needs of each people group and how to reach them for Christ will give real meaning to prayer.

The challenge is for missionaries to learn the language and cultures of unreached people groups, and to live among them until a church has been planted, which should then multiply itself within the boundaries of that particular culture.

To pray for a specific target population expands our sphere of consciousness, creates awareness, and opens the way for God to inspire some kind of appropriate action.

Continue earnestly in prayer, being vigilant in it with thanksgiving. Col. 4:2.

Pray for the more than 28 million people of Kerala, India. Kerala is India's most densely populated state, and most literate.

AN INHERITANCE UNCLAIMED

One of the wonderful things about the Bible is the more than 3,000 promises it contains. You will find a promise to meet every need you will ever encounter. One of the many motivations to Bible study is to know the Word of God so well that you will be able to turn to these promises when you need them. Some people mark them in some special way and others catalog or index them in a notebook.

A visitor in the home of an older Christian noticed t & p by many verses in her well-worn Bible. "What does t & p stand for?" the visitor inquired.

"Tested and proved," the older Christian answered. "For many years now my life has been an exciting series of experiments with the promises of God," she explained. "As I have prayed over them and seen them fulfilled in my life, I have written 't & p' by the specific promise in my Bible."

Why not try this idea yourself? Mark those promises and review them often. "Temptations often appear irresistible because, through a neglect of prayer and the study of the Bible, the tempted one cannot readily remember God's promises and meet Satan with the Scripture weapons" *(The Great Controversy,* p. 600).

The promises are there in God's Word like an inheritance waiting to be claimed. Many years ago an old British sailor was arrested in Savannah, Georgia, for disorderly conduct. Because he could not raise bond, the authorities sent him to jail, and while there he became ill and died. Investigation later revealed that he died before he learned that an aunt in England had willed him several million dollars. He had badly needed money, but he could not make use of wealth he didn't realize he possessed.

Have you ever stopped to think that as you awaken in the morning God presents you a book of signed checks, promissory notes, and negotiable securities, each made out in your name, needing only to be cashed? Such are the promises of God!

Blessed be the Lord, who has given rest to His people Israel, according to all that He promised. There has not failed one word of all His good promise, which He promised through His servant Moses. 1 Kings 8:56.

The Seventh-day Adventist Church is one of the fastest growing churches in Cuba, the largest island in the Caribbean. Pray for the believers in this Communist country.

PEOPLE GROUPS

At first thought we might think of a country as being a single target for gospel outreach. Or we might consider dividing it into mini-targets on the basis of states or counties. However, all countries consist of many varied groups of people. For example, there are socioeconomic groups, and there are racial or tribal groups, to mention some possible groupings.

Nigeria has 466 different tribal groups, and 1,101 different language or dialect groups. Papua New Guinea contains 866 tribal groups and 1,371 different dialects. And Indonesia possesses 752 different tribal groups and 1,413 different dialects. Such information enables us to ask such questions as, Is the Bible available in each language? Is the gospel being preached in each dialect? Is there a church suited to the culture of each tribe?

We define an unreached people group as one that has no group or community of Christians with adequate members and resources to evangelize the people group without outside help. Here are a few examples of unreached people groups: the more than 200,000 pavement dwellers of Calcutta; Muslim students in the United States; the 100,000 Zoroastrian Parsis of Bombay; the more than 40,000 taxi drivers of Hong Kong; or the 17,000,000 members of Sakka Gakkai, a comparatively new religion in Japan.

Remote and isolated tribes far removed from Christian influence are always a challenge to God's people, but we also face frontiers of a different kind that challenge God's messengers today—people groups isolated from God's message by barriers of prejudice, culture, language, or sometimes simply no close acquaintance with someone who knows Jesus and His message. You could be that special friend to someone in your sphere of influence.

The boundary for mission can no longer be set geographically. The only landmark that should determine mission for the church today is the border between belief and unbelief running through every nation, tribe, and tongue. The front line of mission exists wherever people do not know Christ.

Then I saw another angel flying in the midst of heaven, having the everlasting gospel to preach to those who dwell on the earth—to every nation, tribe, tongue, and people. Rev. 14:6.

Zambia, with a population of more than 9 million, is a land-locked, heavily forested country in south central Africa. The Seventh-day Adventist Church has more than 100,000 members. Pray for the unreached groups in this country.

OPEN THE EAST WINDOW

The Old Testament prophet Elisha was a man through whom God changed circumstances. He made the bitter water sweet, multiplied the widow's oil and meal, detoxified the poison pottage, and made the iron axhead to float.

Today God is looking for men and women through whom He can change circumstances—men and women of faith, vision, and enthusiasm. The Lord seeks those who can cause bitter experiences to turn out sweet, who can multiply minuscule resources to meet the needs of a rapidly growing work. He needs those who can counteract poisonous influences, who will serve the One for whom nothing is impossible.

Elisha maintained his courageous spirit in spite of obstacles and adversity. The kings of Israel and Judah for the most part ignored His presence. Some listened to his words, but rejected his counsel. But instead of giving in to discouragement, he continued to point to the true God.

Even on his deathbed, when his body was worn out, Elisha still had the fire of God burning brightly in his militant soul. King Joash came to visit him, and as he entered the sickroom, he cried out, "O my father, my father, the chariots of Israel and their horsemen!" (2 Kings 13:14). In other words, the king of Israel recognized the prophet as a spiritual father in Israel and acknowledged that his presence among them was of more value in time of trouble than an army of horses and chariots.

The dying prophet gave the king some valuable lessons from which we also can benefit. Elisha told the king to take his bow and arrow and take aim at the enemy. "Open the east window" (verse 17), he ordered. Every Christian should open the windows of the soul every morning to receive fresh visions and revelations from the Lord, and a fresh look at the world we have to reach.

We must not give up after two or three attempts (see verses 18 and 19), but must persevere until we have finished the work.

And he said, "Open the east window"; and he opened it. Then Elisha said, "Shoot"; and he shot. 2 Kings 13:17.

Pray for the more than 21 million people of Kansu. Its mountains and its use as a military testing site isolate this Chinese province from the rest of the world.

STRENGTH FOR OUR JOURNEY

The children of Israel had just left the Red Sea, where the Lord had worked a mighty miracle in delivering them from the forces of Egypt. The same means that God had used to deliver the Hebrews became the weapon of destruction of their pursuing enemy. The people of Israel lifted up their voices in a song of praise to God for so great a manifestation of His strength and love for them.

After three days of weary desert travel they exhausted their water supply. We can imagine the shouts that must have gone up when they saw the waters of Marah, but their rejoicing soon turned to complaining when they discovered that the water was bitter. They had already forgotten their marvelous deliverance at the Red Sea.

God, who knows all things, is aware when we complain about the leaders He has provided for us, but He deals patiently with His people. Through Moses God provided another miracle that made the bitter waters sweet. When they journeyed from Marah, God led them to Elim, an oasis with 12 wells of water and 70 palm trees. The joyful voices of the people must have made the barren desert ring when they saw the cool palms and wells of water.

Life's journey has its Marahs of bitter experiences. But we also encounter the Elims of refreshing. As long as we follow the Lord's leading, the bitter experiences as well as the times of refreshing can develop within us strength for our onward journey. In some cases, God may not remove the trial itself, but the sweetening influence from Heaven can either change us or change the circumstances so that we may drink and be strengthened.

Whether we pass through Marahs or Elims, the all-important thing is to know that He is leading. When we find ourselves tempted to complain about God's leaders, let us remember the lessons of the past.

Now when the people complained, it displeased the Lord; for the Lord heard it. Num. 11:1.

Pray for all who are tempted to criticize and complain, that they might look to Jesus and find victory.

A NEW SPIRITUAL ADVENTURE

"The creative energy that called the worlds into existence is in the Word of God" (*Education*, p. 126). Think about the implications in that one sentence! And we have the privilege of free access to the Word of God!

Jeremiah speaks of eating God's Word. He says it was "the joy and rejoicing of my heart" (Jer. 15:16). If you want a new spiritual adventure, think about choosing a book of the Bible, a chapter, or perhaps even one verse as your special portion for this entire year. Should you choose a single verse, you can think of it as your theme text for the year. You might also want to select a short passage or a single sentence from the writings of Ellen White to be especially yours for this year.

Your choices should meet your personal needs and your desires in the Lord's service. There are so many good things to choose from that the choice may not be easy.

Once you have selected, you will think about your special portion every day. You can relate your prayers to your personal theme passage. Soon you will want to share with some of your closest friends the portion you have chosen so they can pray for you in light of the message contained in that part of God's Word.

Only a relative few will adopt this idea, but those who do will be abundantly rewarded. You will begin to experience in your life the creative power that is in the Word of God.

If you don't know where to look for your special text or portion, let me suggest that you consider the books of Ephesians, Philippians, or the Psalms.

Perhaps someone will choose Proverbs 3:5, 6: "Trust in the Lord with all your heart, and lean not on your own understanding; in all your ways acknowledge Him, and He shall direct your paths."

Along with that could go this passage: "Those who decide to do nothing in any line that will displease God, will know, after presenting their case before Him, just what course to pursue" (*The Desire of Ages*, p. 668).

> **Your words were found, and I ate them, and Your word was to me the joy and rejoicing of my heart; for I am called by Your name, O Lord God of hosts. Jer. 15:16.**

> *Pray especially for the* fellakeen *("peasants") in the rural villages of the Nile and oases in largely Muslim Egypt.*

IT IS FINISHED

Matthew, Mark, and Luke tell us that Jesus died with a great shout upon His lips, but they don't tell us what His last words were. John, the writer of the fourth Gospel, does that.

It is really only one word in the original, but what a meaningful word it is—*tetelestai*, It Is Finished.

It was a farmer's word. When inspection of an addition to the herd or flock revealed that it left nothing to be desired, the farmer cried, *tetelestai!*

It was an artist's word. When the painter or sculptor had put the last finishing touches to his masterpiece, he would stand back and survey it. If he saw nothing that called for correction or improvement, he would exclaim, *tetelestai!*

And it was a priestly word. When some devout worshiper with a heart filled with gratitude brought to the temple a lamb as an offering, the priest would carefully inspect the animal. If he found it to be without spot or blemish, he would make the pronouncement, *tetelestai!*

When God completed Creation, He looked upon it and said that it was very good. And when He completed the work of redemption, He cried with a loud voice, *tetelestai!* The expression of divine satisfaction was the same in both the Old Testament and the New.

It was the shout of victory, and the word that John uses is one that we might use when we settle back upon a pillow to rest after concluding a task *tetelestai*

Grasping the significance of *tetelestai*—the finished work of Christ— provides the motivation for a life of dedication and obedience.

So when Jesus had received the sour wine, He said, "It is finished!" And bowing His head, He gave up His spirit. John 19:30.

Pray for the subcontinent of India with an area about one third that of the 50 United States. It has a population of 797 million and an Adventist membership of 160,635.

In 1893 William Lenker and A. T. Stroup, two colporteurs from America, landed in Madras and began selling Seventh-day Adventist publications among the English-speaking.

The first regular missionary sent to India by the Mission Board was Georgia Burrus, a young Bible instructor from California who arrived in Calcutta on January 23, 1895. Georgia Burrus was responsible for winning the first convert from Hinduism.

INTERCESSORY PRAYER

Every believer regardless of age or health can have a part in Global Strategy through intercessory prayer. That means asking God to do something for someone else.

One of my favorite examples of intercessory prayer appears in Daniel 10. For three full weeks the prophet had devoted himself to prayer and fasting because of conditions among his people in Palestine.

It must have seemed to him that nothing was happening as a result of his prayers. But an angel from heaven came to his side at the end of the three-week period and assured him that from the first day of his intercession God had heard his prayers.

For three weeks in response to Daniel's prayers the angel had been working on the heart of the Persian king, but the ruler resisted. Then Michael, who is Christ, came to assist the angel in the spiritual struggle. Can you see the picture? In response to Daniel's prayer heaven dispatches an angel to impress the Persian king, but God does not force the king's will. The king must make the choice. At first the ruler resists, but then Christ Himself joins forces with the angel. Christ also does not force the king's will, but He adds His strong influence to impress the king to decide wisely. Finally Cyrus, the king, makes the decision that provides the answer to Daniel's prayer.

And it all began when one believer engaged in intercessory prayer. "It is a part of God's plan to grant us, in answer to the prayer of faith, that which He would not bestow did we not thus ask" *(The Great Controversy,* p. 525). And we might add, even if it includes a fast trip from heaven to Persia.

Does Daniel's experience give you courage to persevere in intercessory prayer? The leaders of nations need our prayers. Our loved ones who do not enjoy a personal relationship with Jesus need our prayers.

> **Then he said to me, "Do not fear, Daniel, for from the first day that you set your heart to understand, and to humble yourself before your God, your words were heard; and I have come because of your words." Dan. 10:12.**
>
> *Pray for the person the Lord lays on your heart as you think about family members and the rulers of nations.*

MARIE DURAND

The Huguenots were French Protestants of the sixteenth century. The name is believed to come from a root meaning confederates. One writer describes them as "the direct offspring of the Bible."

Most Reformation history tours include a visit to Aigues-Mortes (egg-mort), a medieval town in southern France, where Marie Durand was imprisoned for 38 years for no other reason than she was a Huguenot. Marie was 15 when she crossed the deep moat that led to her prison cell in the massive tower of the ancient fortress that still stands. The walls are 18 feet thick. They have no windows, and narrow slits in the massive masonry permit little light but much wind and cold to enter. In the middle of the floor of the circular room is an opening covered with heavy iron grating through which guards could pass food.

Marie Durand was confined in this tower from 1730 until 1768. On any day of those 38 years she could have had her freedom by saying two words: "I recant." Can you imagine the temptation to say them? Why waste your youth behind these grim walls? Outside you will see sunshine, hear the happy laughter of children, find the love of friends and the comforts of home. Perhaps she visualized herself as a happy mother caring for a helpless baby and being rewarded by its sweet smiles. But she resisted all seductions to purchase liberty at the price of compromise. Into the masonry of her prison cell she scratched the word "Resist."

"To stand in defense of truth and righteousness when the majority forsake us, to fight the battles of the Lord when champions are few—this will be our test. At this time we must gather warmth from the coldness of others, courage from their cowardice, and loyalty from their treason" *(Testimonies, vol. 5, p. 136)*.

One of Marie Durand's letters preserved in the Paris Protestant Library contains the following sentences: "I am in this awful prison 33 years. . . . We must not be Judases by betraying our own consciences. . . . Your humble servant. Marie Durand."

Still others had trials of mockings and scourgings, yes, and of chains and imprisonment. Heb. 11:36.

Pray today for Christians suffering persecution or imprisonment rather than compromise their faith. And pray that God will give you such strength of faith and sense of mission.

NOT TO BE MINISTERED TO

Attitudes are vital. Invariably you will find that happy, well-adjusted people seek opportunities to serve rather than look for others to serve them. When we wait for others to wait on us, we usually find ourselves disappointed that the service is not forthcoming.

This principle applies in many areas of everyday living. For example, we expect compliments that we don't receive, or recognition and don't get it. Demanding appreciation, we get frustrated when the words of appreciation don't come. In each of these cases we had expectations of being ministered to, and we didn't receive it. Many lives experience unnecessary misery because of such attitudes. Self—clamoring for recognition—would rather be ministered to than to minister.

If you focus attention on self—your feelings, your expectations, and your rights—it indicates that you are really wanting others to wait on you. However, God calls us to serve others. Remember, Jesus came to give His life in service to others, and He asks us to follow in His steps.

Many of our problems in interpersonal relationships result from our feeling disturbed or unhappy because someone else is not ministering to our desires, feelings, or expectations. If we will shift our emphasis to ministering to others, our feelings will not be so easily hurt.

Ministry is unselfish. The love of Jesus shining through us, it is thinking more of the needs of others than of our own. Instead of asking "Why don't others do more for me?" we inquire, "What more can I do for others?" Thus ministry comes to life through cups of cold water, visits to hospitals and prisons, and meals for the hungry.

Ministry is words of witness to non-Christians. It is encouragement for the homeless, orphans, singles, aged, lonely, hurting, and any others needing support. Ministry reaches out to persons with fragmented emotions and fractured relationships.

Always ministry helps persons in Christ's name. It is Christ continuing to serve others through us, and is limited only by our vision and the needs of others.

"The Son of Man did not come to be served, but to serve, and to give His life a ransom for many. Matt. 20:28.

Pray for the independent principality of Liechtenstein, situated between Switzerland and Austria. Only 62 square miles in area, the population is 28,000. Seventh-day Adventists living there attend services in nearby Switzerland.

HE WENT ABOUT DOING GOOD

Some years ago when a polio epidemic swept over the city of Chicago and its suburbs, it filled every hospital beyond capacity, including the Hinsdale Sanitarium, which had patients in the halls and classrooms. As soon as the hospital had arrested the acute illness, they had to send the patients home in order to make room for the more seriously ill. One of those who left was a little girl from the community who had won the hearts of the nurses. Two of the overworked nurses, on their own time, went to the little girl's home a few blocks away and gave rehabilitative care, fomentations, exercises, massage, and all the treatment that was needed, day after day, week after week, until finally the young girl was back in school and playing with her classmates.

The nurses refused pay for their labor of love, and the child's parents began to tell the story far and near. One of the families who heard the story was the Eugene Ketterings. Eugene Kettering, the only child of the famous Charles F. Kettering of General Motors, and his wife decided they would visit the Hinsdale Sanitarium. Later, when Charles Kettering passed away, his lawyers found that his will made provision for establishing a medical research center on the family estate in Kettering, near Dayton, Ohio. Eugene Kettering was to be the administrator of the will and the director of the trust. As plans developed for the medical research center and hospital, the son remembered the Hinsdale Sanitarium and decided to ask Seventh-day Adventists to operate the new 420-bed hospital and eventually the Kettering College of Medical Arts.

And it all began because two nurses, back at Hinsdale, gave a practical demonstration of Christianity in action. Little did those two nurses dream of the far-reaching effect of their ministry of love. The Charles F. Kettering Memorial Hospital operates a School of Nursing that constantly prepares large numbers of young people for similar service.

Today it is our privilege as part of this world family to walk in the footsteps of Jesus who went about doing good.

God anointed Jesus of Nazareth with the Holy Spirit and with power, who went about doing good and healing all who were oppressed by the devil, for God was with Him. Acts 10:38.

Pray for our hospitals around the world—the patients and staff.

YOU MUST CARRY ME

Henry Moorehouse was a nineteenth-century clergyman well known both in Britain and the U.S.

Moorehouse had a little daughter who was a cripple from birth. He loved her dearly and claimed that he learned more lessons in faith and simple trust from her than from any other source. In spite of her weakness, the little girl desired to be helpful in every way she could.

One day, Moorehouse returned home carrying a heavy package. His little daughter met him at the foot of the stairs and begged to be permitted to carry the package up the stairs and present it to her mother. Her father kindly pointed out that it was an utter impossibility for her to carry an object of such size and weight.

Eventually by sheer persistence she persuaded her father to let her at least try. He gently placed the heavy package in her arms. "I can carry it easily, Daddy," she said, clutching the burden and smiling up into her father's face, "but now you must carry me."

What an illustration of the provision Jesus has made for each one of us to carry the heaviest burden that will ever confront us in life. Jesus calls upon each one to take up his individual cross and follow Him. But He carries the Christian, cross and all. Apart from this provision we naturally hesitate and tremble as we face the requirements of God's revealed will upon our lives, but strengthened by the strong arms of Jesus and His Spirit dwelling within us, obedience is not merely a possibility, it is a certainty.

"When in faith we take hold of His strength, He will change, wonderfully change, the most hopeless, discouraging outlook. He will do this for the glory of His name" (*Testimonies*, vol. 8, p. 12).

When the way ahead seems impossible, and the load seems too heavy to carry, we will discover that He has not left us or forsaken us. He has made provision for all our needs and "underneath are the everlasting arms" to carry us through.

The eternal God is your refuge, and underneath are the everlasting arms; He will thrust out the enemy from before you, and will say, "Destroy!" Deut. 33:27.

Pray for insight into ways of reaching the handicapped with the Adventist message.

A PERSONAL PRAYER JOURNAL

Do you ever find your mind wandering when you have your private devotions? Did you ever kneel in prayer and fall asleep on your knees? Let me recommend a prayer journal in which you write your prayer each day. You can use a diary or even an ordinary notebook if you can't find a special prayer journal.

You will discover that the exercise of writing your prayer focuses your thoughts. Your prayers become more specific as you record those matters of greatest concern to you.

Like any other worship habit, you must have a regular time for recording your prayer in your journal. Early morning is a good time before you get caught up in the pressures of the day. It will take some time to form the habit. You will miss some days at first, especially when things are going well and you feel no urgent prayer needs. If you have days like that, you can list in your prayer three or four things you are thankful for that day.

The prayer journal will draw you closer to Jesus and strengthen your faith when you look back over your written prayers and discover how many of them have had answers.

In my personal prayer journal I just turned back a few pages and read, "Dear Lord, You know we are planning a baptism on Sabbath. John and Judy both should be in that baptism, but he has not settled his Sabbath work problem, and she does not seem to be convicted about her jewelry. Lord, I've done all I know to do, please convict them and bring them to the baptism."

Three days later I was able to write, "Thank You, Lord, that John and Judy made that total surrender. Their problems are solved. They were baptized yesterday."

Elijah was a man with a nature like ours, and he prayed earnestly that it would not rain; and it did not rain on the land for three years and six months. And he prayed again, and the heaven gave rain, and the earth produced its fruit. James 5:17, 18.

Pray about the matter that is most important to you personally today. Write your prayer request in a notebook or even on a slip of paper until you get a prayer journal. If this plan appeals to you, start right now.

31

GOD IS LOVE

God is love. You've heard it said many times, but have you ever taken time to meditate upon that fact? Think about God's purpose in creating our planet and the people on it. Picture the beauty of God's perfect creation when He pronounced it "very good."

Try to imagine God's anticipation of our perfect planet being peopled with perfect people. Imagine earth's joyful inhabitants with freedom to plan projects and pursue them unhampered by accident, disease, or death.

And then sin entered and spoiled it all. In creating humanity with freedom to choose, God took the risk that in spite of every advantage we would abuse our freedom and make wrong choices.

God as a loving parent did not stop loving man when he sinned. Although God hates sin, He loves the sinner. Jesus died to save us from our sins. It is at Calvary that we find the mightiest manifestation of God's love. Every devoted father knows it would be easier to die than to see a son die.

The words of John 3:16 are so familiar to most of us, and yet, how much do we really understand their meaning? "For God so loved the world that He gave His only begotten Son, that whoever believes in Him should not perish but have everlasting life."

Every individual is responsible for how he uses the gift of free choice. In order to gain eternal life we must choose to accept Christ's sacrifice. But before that we must hear the good news that we have a choice.

Surely this is the great burden of God's heart as He looks upon humanity scattered over the face of our planet—that each person might have a chance to know there is a choice, that there is hope. The question is, How do we let everyone know that there is hope and choice? God has a plan, and He expects His church to have a plan. And that's what Global Strategy is all about.

The earth's population is more than 5.2 billion. More than 1.6 billion are Christians, at least in name, while 6.8 million are Seventh-day Adventists.

He who does not love does not know God, for God is love. 1 John 4:8.

Burkina Faso is a landlocked area of the Sahel of Africa, prone to drought and famine, and one of the poorest states in the world. In a population of 8.3 million, Seventh-day Adventists number 181. Pray for the people of this land, that the good news of the Second Coming may reach them quickly.

CHURCH GROWTH

The very mention of church growth suggests to some a numbers game with heavy emphasis on statistics. However, an understanding of true church growth includes advancement in the experience of the individual believer and in his relationship with his God and with fellow members. It involves first of all spiritual growth. If we only increase numerically, we become an obese church, and obesity is not healthy.

Surveys show that growing churches have three common characteristics: 1. Programs within the church focus on evangelism. 2. The pastor and members share a belief in their ability to grow. 3. The church is alert to all possibilities to reach potential members.

The pastor is an equipper, bringing out the gifts of his people. Ellen White stated this principle many years ago when she wrote: "That which is needed now for the upbuilding of our churches is the nice work of wise laborers to discern and develop talent in the church—talent that can be educated for the Master's use" (*Christian Service*, p. 58).

A growing church will allow nothing in the program that does not have evangelism as its aim. Outreach is the number one priority, and it will eliminate activities that consume time, energy, and resources, but do not contribute to outreach goals.

Goals have the power to lift people's eyes from the earth below to the sky above. They are possibility statements about what could be, should be, and can be. A goal is a statement of what I believe to be God's specific will for this time.

The church exists in order to enlarge God's kingdom and glorify Him. Church growth not only involves methods, but is a philosophy of ministry.

Every growing church has a well-thought-through, carefully-executed master plan for growth.

And the word of God spread, and the number of the disciples multiplied greatly in Jerusalem, and a great many of the priests were obedient to the faith. Acts 6:7.

Pray for the growth of the Adventist Church in Madagascar, which began there in 1927. Ten years earlier a pioneer missionary in Mauritius sent André Rasamoelina's name to the General Conference with the result that someone sent printed material to Rasamoelina, including a package of Present Truth *and a copy of* Steps to Christ, *which Rasamoelina translated into Malagasy for publication in Madagascar. The population of Madagascar totals more than 10 million, and Seventh-day Adventists now number 23,554.*

WHAT IS A DISCIPLE?

A convert is someone who accepts another person's teachings, but a dictionary definition of a disciple is "one who accepts and assists in spreading the doctrines of another." Do you see the difference between making converts and making disciples? Keep in mind that Jesus commands every follower to make disciples (Matt. 28:19). What is a disciple?

A disciple is:

1. One who follows. "Again, the next day, John stood with two of his disciples. . . . One of the two who heard John speak, and followed him, was Andrew, Simon Peter's brother" (John 1:35-40). Jesus said to Matthew, "Follow Me" (Matt. 9:9).

2. One who continues following. Jesus said, "If you abide in My word, you are My disciples indeed" (John 8:31).

3. One who is willing to deny self. Jesus said, "If anyone desires to come after Me, let him deny himself" (Matt. 16:24).

4. One who is a fisher of men. Jesus said, "Follow Me, and I will make you fishers of men" (Matt. 4:19).

5. One who has love for others. Jesus said, "By this all will know that you are My disciples, if you have love for one another" (John 13:35).

6. One who is in the process of growing to be like his Master. As Jesus revealed His Father, so we are to reveal Jesus, for He said, . . . "As the Father has sent Me, I also send you" (John 20:21).

Making disciples implies a relationship. Through a close relationship, Jesus' disciples gradually became like Him and were able to minister as He ministered. In order for us to make disciples, we must be willing to invest our time and means in close relationships with those we would disciple. Christianity is caught more than it is taught. It is by close association that disciples learn to trust, pray, answer questions, share truth, and live the Christian life. As we make someone our disciple we are at the same time turning that person into a disciple of Jesus because by our words and example we are constantly pointing them to Him.

Now I praise you, brethren, that you remember me in all things and keep the traditions as I delivered them to you. 1 Cor. 11:2.

Pray for Tunisia and the challenge of reaching the 7.5 million people of that country, where we have no Seventh-day Adventist church.

MAKE DISCIPLES

A dense fog settled over the California coast on that day in 1952 when Florence Chadwick started to swim from the mainland to Catalina Island. Those with her had to fire rifle shots to scare away the sharks. After 15 hours of swimming, she asked to be taken out of the water. Her trainer tried to persuade her to keep going, but it was no use. When she quit, she was within a half mile of the goal. "If I could have seen the shore," she said afterward, "I might have made it." She gave up because the fog obscured the goal and kept her from seeing her destination. Two months later, on a clear day, she succeeded in reaching the mainland from the island and establishing a new record because the goal was clearly in sight.

Do you have a clear vision of the mission of the church, or is the goal obscured by the mist and fog of uncertainty? What is our mission? Jesus said, "Go therefore and make disciples of all nations." Sometimes we put the emphasis on "go." That can lead to making a Saviour out of activity. Other times we put the emphasis on "teach," and correctness of belief becomes all-important. Or we may put the emphasis on "baptize," and face the accusation of being in "the numbers game." Go, teach, baptize—all are important, but they are not an end in themselves. The mission is to make disciples. Make disciples as you go, as you teach, and as you baptize.

Jesus is telling you to make disciples. Your disciple could be a church member who has never really become involved in Christian service. It could be someone like you who just needs the encouragement of a teammate to share in projects. Or it could be a friend, relative, work associate, or neighbor whom you lead to Christ and then disciple. Whoever they are, encourage your disciples to make their own disciples, and you can go on to choose still others to disciple. This process of multiplication has been the secret of the growth of the Christian church.

Go therefore and make disciples of all the nations, baptizing them in the name of the Father and of the Son and of the Holy Spirit. Matt. 28:19.

Pray that God will lead you to one or two souls whom you can disciple for Jesus. Mention some specific names in your prayer.

ABRAM LA RUE

Abram La Rue was born in New Jersey in 1822 and spent his early manhood in California and Idaho mining gold. It was sometime later, while working as a sheepherder in California, that he became a Seventh-day Adventist.

Soon after becoming an Adventist, La Rue requested a mission appointment to China. At that time there was not one Seventh-day Adventist in all the Orient, and because of his advanced age, the General Conference advised him to go to one of the Pacific islands. He worked his way to Honolulu in 1883. Along with another colporteur, he sold books in the city and on the ships in port, which resulted in the denomination sending someone to establish an Adventist presence in the Hawaiian Islands in 1885.

In 1888, when he was 66 years old, Abram La Rue did go to the Orient, to Hong Kong. For 14 years he sold books, chiefly among the sailors on the ships in Hong Kong harbor. He befriended a colonial court translator who produced two tracts in Chinese for him. In 1902 J. N. Anderson arrived in Hong Kong and baptized seven of La Rue's converts, including six seamen of the British Navy. Fourteen years of tireless labor had produced only seven baptisms. Measured by human standards, some might call that failure, but the territory of the Far Eastern Division today has 730,255 Seventh-day Adventists. Surely this is a testimony to what God can do through one man, although advanced in years, who caught a vision of service.

Like Abram La Rue, many of you reading these thoughts for today, when you came to know Christ and His message, wanted to share it with others, and found an avenue of service.

On April 26, 1903, at the age of 81, La Rue fell asleep in Jesus, and he was buried in Hong Kong. A few days before his death he willed the greater portion of what little money he had to the mission for work in China, thus giving his all to the cause he loved so much. Like Abram of old, he had heard the call of God and responded.

> **Now the Lord had said to Abram: "Get out of your country, from your kindred and from your father's house, to a land that I will show you." Gen. 12:1.**

> *Pray for the people of Hong Kong and Macao, where we operate two hospitals and have 3,631 Seventh-day Adventists among a population of more than 6 million.*

BEAUTIFUL BECAUSE THEY WERE BROKEN

A visitor stepping into the royal palace in Tehran, Iran, is captivated by the sight of the grand entrance resplendent with glittering, sparkling glass. The domed ceiling and majestic columns appear to be covered with diamonds glistening in the sunlight. In reality they are small pieces of mirrors. The edges of the myriad of little mirrors throw out the colors of the rainbow.

When the architects planned the royal palace, they ordered from a firm in Paris many mirrors to cover the entrance walls. When the mirrors arrived, however, the workmen found that they had all gotten broken in transit. There were thousands of pieces of smashed mirror.

The workmen were going to dispose of all the pieces until one creative man saw possibilities in broken mirrors and suggested that perhaps they would be more beautiful because they had been broken.

The skilled craftsman took some of the larger pieces and smashed them also, and then he fitted them together like an abstract mosaic that sparkled like dazzling diamonds.

Can you imagine the great disappointment when the workmen unpacked the smashed mirrors? Perhaps you have had a comparable disappointment. If you are suffering some hurt and perhaps are broken in spirit, turn your shattered condition over to the Master Craftsman, and the Creator of diamonds, pearls, and rubies will skillfully piece together the parts of your destroyed life and make it more beautiful because it was broken.

"In the future life the mysteries that here have annoyed and disappointed us will be made plain. We shall see that our seemingly unanswered prayers and disappointed hopes have been among our greatest blessings" (*The Ministry of Healing*, p. 474).

Remember, "God is too wise to err, and too good to withhold any good thing from them that walk uprightly" (*Steps to Christ*, p. 96).

I will seek what was lost and bring back what was driven away, bind up the broken and strengthen what was sick. Eze. 34:16.

Pray for the people of God and their outreach in Singapore, with a population of 2.6 million and 2,072 Seventh-day Adventists. Although Abram La Rue probably visited Singapore between 1888 and 1903, it was H. B. Meyers, who became an Adventist in India, who brought Seventh-day Adventist teachings to Singapore in 1900.

WHAT MUST
I DO TO BE SAVED?

It was evening worship time, and the family had gathered together in the living room. Father asked 10-year-old Larry to offer prayer at the close. Everyone knelt down, but Larry didn't pray. His father spoke again, thinking Larry might have been preoccupied the first time he asked him to pray. Again there was silence, broken finally by Larry's voice in halting, thoughtful words to God: "Dear heavenly Father, this is the day when I want to make an important decision in my life. My parents have taught me to believe in Jesus, and I have believed in Him for as long as I can remember, but today I want to give my life to Him and promise to serve Him forever."

In his prayer Larry told God about the temptations he had been battling and the struggle he had gone through in coming to this moment of decision. When he finally said amen, that family circle rejoiced over his decision to accept God into his life. Five pairs of knees moved across the carpet as Mom, Dad, and Larry's three brothers made a literal circle of love around the youngest member of the family.

Larry's father told me two of his four boys had chosen family worship time as the occasion to make that all-important decision to give their lives to Jesus and to accept Him as their personal Saviour. Family worship should be a time when the Holy Spirit can speak to the hearts of family members. The atmosphere should be conducive to decision-making. Individual family members should feel the warmth and support of the family in a way that will bring spiritual strength and a desire to be part of the heavenly family.

Every day of our lives we must make decisions. Each person reading or hearing these words is making decisions about some issue confronting him. In some cases it is the most vital of all decisions, to give your life fully to Jesus. If you are struggling with the matter of deciding for Jesus, ask the rest of the family to pray for you. Consider making this your day of decision.

> **And he brought them out and said, "Sirs, what must I do to be saved?" So they said, "Believe on the Lord Jesus Christ, and you will be saved, you and your household." Acts 16:30, 31.**
>
> *Pray specifically for those family members who still need to accept Jesus as their personal Saviour.*

NOTHING IS IMPOSSIBLE

Paul was speaking from experience when he said that he could do all things through Christ. When he was chained to a guard in a Roman prison, his prison became his pulpit, and the guards became his congregation. It was while he was in prison in Rome that he wrote the book of Philippians.

Eight-year-old Walter Davis was playing baseball one day when his legs became as limp as spaghetti and collapsed beneath him on the ground. It was a devastating attack of polio, and the doctors told the boy that he would never walk again.

A visitor from the church knelt by Walter's bed and encouraged him to have faith that God could help him walk again. The child's mother gave him similar encouragement, and she began to work on his legs. Therapy and exercise began to take effect and Walter learned to walk again. He set a goal for himself to break the world record for the high jump. It seemed impossible, but eventually he entered the Olympics and broke all previous records.

William Booth said, "God loves with a great love the man whose heart is bursting with a sublime passion for the impossible."

Andrew Murray said, "We have a God who delights in impossibilities."

Charles Spurgeon said, "One man says, I will do as much as I can. Any fool can do that. He who believes in Christ does what he cannot do, attempts the impossible and performs it."

Is there some sin in your life that you say you cannot overcome? Is there some fault that you say you cannot eradicate? Is there some problem that you say you cannot solve? Claim the promise of Philippians 4:13. Believe in that promise with all your heart and act upon it with all your being, and you will discover that your impossibility has become God's possibility.

I can do all things through Christ who strengthens me. Phil. 4:13.

Pray for the outreach of the gospel in Luxembourg, an independent grand duchy in Western Europe bordered by Belgium, France, and Germany, and having an area of 998 square miles. It has a population of 372,000, and although Adventism has had a few converts through the years, they were never organized into a church. Colporteur work is not permitted.

Seventh-day Adventist programs have for many years been broadcast in many languages from Luxembourg's powerful privately-owned radio station.

MONEY OR MEN?

Which do you care for the most, money or men? One of the miracles of Christianity is that it gives man a higher regard for men and women than for money, and that is contrary to selfish human nature.

When Jesus was here on earth, He healed the poor man who had a whole legion of devils possessing him, but somehow that healing involved the loss of a herd of swine. The owners of the swine completely overlooked the miracle of a fellow human being restored to his right mind because their gaze was only on the pigs.

Is your brother or sister in the human family more precious to you than your bank account?

The rich young ruler faced the choice between men or money. He had many virtues, but he failed the test. Many times Christian service has a monetary price attached to it. To share our time with others may involve a decision whether to use it to make more money or to reach out in caring ministry to others.

What men and women really want is honest interest. Real human brotherly/sisterly interest. They look into your eyes as you take their hand, and they read there whether to you a man is more precious than fine gold or not.

Do you remember the story of how Elisha gave his staff to his servant, Gehazi, and sent him on ahead to restore life to the Shunammite's son? But the miracle did not happen until Elisha himself came, prayed, and raised the lad.

Soul winning can seldom be done by proxy. Our friends, neighbors, and loved ones say in effect, We want you to come, don't send anyone else.

The best use that we can make of money is to employ it for the uplifting of men and women. To the rich young ruler Jesus said, Take your money and go and spend it in helping men and women. But he went away sorrowfully. In which are you really most interested—men and women, or money?

For what is a man profited if he gains the whole world, and loses his own soul? Or what will a man give in exchange for his soul? Matt. 16:26.

Heavenly Father, please dwell within our hearts, and may Your love pour out through us in blessing and service to people near and far so they will be drawn to You.

PARADOXES

If you had seen Pilate on the marble steps of his palace and Jesus standing as a prisoner between two guards in his presence, and someone had asked you, Which name will last, Pilate or Jesus? would you have answered, Jesus? Of course, today you would, but what about back then?

To the people of that day Pilate was the representative of the all-powerful empire of Rome. Jesus was the leader of an insignificant sect. To outward appearance it would seem that the name of Pilate would be the one that would endure, but history reveals otherwise. We probably would never have heard of Pilate had it not been for Jesus.

If you had seen a tentmaker standing on Mars Hill in Athens, the center of the world's culture, and if asked, Which will last, the culture of Athens or the teachings of the tentmaker? what would have been your answer?

An old Roman commented at the beginning of Christianity: This system cannot stand because it is founded upon a cross, upon the death of its own leader, upon a catastrophe; it cannot stand. And yet we know that those are the very reasons that it continues today.

A true Christian is a paradox because a true Christian is a person who believes the unbelievable; bears the unbearable; forgives the unforgivable; loves the unlovable; is perfectly happy not to be perfect; is willing to give up his or her will; becomes weak to be strong; and finds love by giving it away.

A Christian feels supreme love for One whom he has never seen; he talks every day to Someone he cannot see; he empties himself in order to be full; he is strongest when he is weakest; he is richest when he is poorest; he forsakes in order to have; he gives away so he can keep; he dies so he can live.

He who finds his life will lose it, and he who loses his life for My sake will find it. Matt. 10:39.

Pray for the continued blessing of God upon the work of the gospel in Romania, with a population of 23 million and 58,721 Seventh-day Adventists. M. B. Czechowski, a former Polish Catholic priest who, while visiting in the United States, learned of the seventh-day Sabbath and of the soon return of Christ, was the first to preach Seventh-day Adventist doctrines in Romania.

DON'T BE AFRAID

Often we are defeated, not by actual experiences, but by fear of things we think might happen. We weary ourselves crossing bridges that we never reach, by bearing burdens that no one ever asks us to carry, and by attempting to solve problems that never materialize. Fear robs millions of people of contentment, health, and happiness. People fear cancer, heart disease, insanity, AIDS, failure, financial disaster, thieves, war, the dark, the sight of blood, death—the list could go on endlessly.

Fear is perhaps the greatest factor that the devil employs to keep Christians from speaking to others about their faith in Christ. We are afraid of how they will respond. Someone has said, "Fear is faith in Satan." We may be sure that fear does not come from God because the Bible tells us that "God has not given us a spirit of fear, but of power and of love and of a sound mind" (2 Tim. 1:7).

Because of fear Aaron made the golden calf, Jonah started out for Tarshish, Israel spent 40 years in the wilderness, Peter denied his Lord, Pilate passed sentence on the innocent Son of God, and all the disciples forsook Jesus and fled. No wonder Jesus said, "Fear not."

If you have fears that weaken your witness and rob you of joy, identify those fears and then surrender them one by one to the Lord. Believe that He has power to cast them out and to keep them forever out of your life.

Once the servant of Elisha trembled because the king of Syria with "horses, and chariots, and a great army. . . came by night and surrounded the city" (2 Kings 6:14). The prophet reassured him with a message that is true for every generation: "Do not fear, for those who are with us are more than those who are with them" (verse 16).

There is no fear in love; but perfect love casts out fear, because fear involves torment. But he who fears has not been made perfect in love. 1 John 4:18.

Pray for the Lord's work in Turkey where a layman, a Greek shoemaker who had migrated from Turkey to the United States where he became a Seventh-day Adventist, first introduced Adventist teachings in 1889. He returned to Turkey as a self-supporting missionary. Turkey has a population of almost 45 million.

THE MEDIATOR
MAKES THE DIFFERENCE

Today let us take two familiar Bible stories and put them side by side. The first is the story of a man who feels that he is suffering more than his share. In his agony he cries out for one who can mediate between his tortured soul and the God who seems to be so angry with him.

For Job there is a God, but it seems to him that a barrier has arisen between them, a barrier that requires someone else to cross it for him, for he says, "Nor is there any mediator between us, who may lay his hand on us both" (Job 9:33). That is the first story.

The second story is the story of an old preacher whose life work is finished. He writes in a reminiscent vein to a young preacher who is just beginning. Paul tells Timothy that God ordained him for no other purpose than to point men to the Mediator, the One alone who can intercede. Notice Paul's words to Timothy, "For there is one God and one Mediator between God and men, the Man Christ Jesus" (1 Tim. 2:5).

If there are many gods, I can offend one or two of them without involving myself in utter disaster, but if only one exists, everything depends upon my relationship with Him. And there is one Mediator who makes that relationship secure. We need a God and cannot be happy until we find Him and give Him His rightful place in our lives. The instinct to worship is in our blood, and we are ill at ease until we can find the One at whose feet we can lay the tribute of our devotion.

One God, but no mediator, sighs Job. One God, and one Mediator, cries Paul. None means failure; one means hope. None brings despair; one leads to delight. None results in perdition; one gives us paradise.

For there is one God and one Mediator between God and men, the Man Christ Jesus. 1 Tim. 2:5.

Pray for God's work in Grenada, which, along with St. Vincent, the Grenadines, St. Lucia, and Dominica, comprise the Windward Islands. In 1904 W. G. Kneeland pioneered the Adventist Church on Grenada, and in the same year P. Giddings opened Seventh-day Adventist activity on the island of Dominica. Grenada has a population of 98,000 with 5,566 Seventh-day Adventists.

FRUIT BEARING

Before we can have the gifts of the Spirit, we must have the fruit of the Spirit. And before we can have that, we must be able to answer yes to the question "Did you receive the Holy Spirit when you believed?" (Acts 19:2).

The growth of the fruit of the Spirit depends upon our union with Christ. Jesus explains it in John 15:4, 5: "Abide in Me, and I in you. As the branch cannot bear fruit of itself, unless it abides in the vine, neither can you, unless you abide in Me. I am the vine, you are the branches. He who abides in Me, and I in him, bears much fruit; for without Me you can do nothing."

The fruit of the Spirit is eternal, while the gifts of the Spirit are only temporal. "Love never fails. But whether there are prophecies, they will fail; whether there are tongues, they will cease; whether there is knowledge, it will vanish away" (1 Cor. 13:8).

The fruit of the Spirit is the character—the only thing we can take with us from our present life to the next. The gifts of the Spirit might be likened to scaffolding, which is important during construction, but is removed by the builders when they complete the building.

When the body of Christ is perfected, the gifts will no longer be needed. What would a man with the gift of prophecy do with it in heaven? What need would one have for visions of the glories of heaven when one is already there?

What would the discerner of spirits do with that gift in heaven where there is but one Spirit? Of what use would be the gift of tongues or the interpretation of tongues in heaven where all speak one language? What would the evangelist do with his gift where all have found deliverance from sin?

When the fruit, which is eternal, is demonstrated in our lives, we will be entrusted with the gifts.

"By this my Father is glorified, that you bear much fruit; so you will be My disciples." John 15:8.

Pray for the more than 53 million people of the province of Anhui (ahnway) in China. Anhui means peace and honor. It is famous for the production of rice and other crops.

THE FRUIT
OF THE SPIRIT IS LOVE

We need to recognize an important distinction between the gifts of the Spirit and the fruit of the Spirit. The Holy Spirit divides the gifts of the Spirit as He chooses, according to 1 Corinthians 12:11, but God does not divide the fruit of the Spirit. One may have only a few of the gifts of the Spirit, but should have all the fruit of the Spirit.

One cannot say "I am loving, and you are long-suffering and kind." You cannot separate love from long-suffering and kindness, for 1 Corinthians 13:4 declares that "love suffers long and is kind."

Nor can one claim "I have love, and you have meekness," because love is not puffed up; love is meek. It is impossible for a person to possess the love and joy of the Spirit and, in the place of the peace of the Spirit, manifest strife, a fruit of the flesh. Notice that it is the fruit of the Spirit, not fruits. The nine characteristics mentioned as the fruit of the Spirit are inseparable.

Love comes first, and rightly so, for love is the ground in which righteousness thrives. When love takes possession of the soul, all other fruit will appear in the life.

The word used in speaking of the fruit of the Spirit is *agape*, which means "unconditional love, unconquerable benevolence." No matter what a man may do to us by way of insult or injury, we will never seek anything except his highest good.

The love of God manifest in His people draws like a magnet. "The Lord has appeared of old to me, saying: 'Yes, I have loved you with an everlasting love; therefore with lovingkindness I have drawn you'" (Jer. 31:3).

It is the demonstration of God's love that motivates men and women to love God. "We love Him because He first loved us" (1 John 4:19).

Of the early Christians the observing pagans said, "See how they love one another." And the fruit of love in those early Christians created in the pagans a desire for that love until many became converts to the Christian faith.

But the fruit of the Spirit is love, joy, peace, longsuffering, kindness, goodness, faithfulness, gentleness, self-control. Against such there is no law. Gal. 5:22, 23.

Pray for a special group today. For example, remember airplane pilots in a special way.

45

THE FRUIT
OF THE SPIRIT IS JOY

Can you sing "I've got the joy, joy, joy, joy down in my heart" and really mean it? The fruit of the Spirit is joy. And joy dwells in the house of love.

A Hindu once asked an Indian Christian, "What medicine do you put on your face to make it shine so?"

"I don't put anything on it," the Christian answered.

"Yes, you do," the other persisted. "All you Christians do. I've seen it wherever I have met Christians."

The national Christian thought a moment, then said smilingly, "Yes, I will tell you the medicine that makes our faces shine. It is not something we rub on our faces, but a medicine we take inside. It is joy in our hearts."

If you have invited Jesus to dwell in your heart, you have that joy within you, because He is the source. Because Christ lives within us, we have the assurance of salvation as long as we maintain our relationship with Him, and this gives us joy in spite of changing circumstances.

Surrounded by world problems, family problems, and personal problems, it is sometimes difficult to feel joyful. We find ourselves concerned about such things as famine, crime, and the threat of nuclear war. Paul spoke of being "exceedingly joyful in all our tribulations" (2 Cor. 7:4). The joy of the Christian is not the fruit of circumstances, but the fruit of the Spirit.

I like the words of Psalm 16:11: "You will show me the path of life; in Your presence is fullness of joy; at Your right hand are pleasures forevermore."

Jesus told the parable of the vine and the branches, then He gave His reason for giving it: "These things I have spoken to you, that My joy may remain in you, and that your joy may be full" (John 15:11). In other words, the source and secret of our joy is our union with Christ.

Someone has taken the word *joy* apart so that J stands for Jesus, Y stands for you, and O stands for nothing. Jesus and you, with nothing between—that's joy!

And these things we write to you that your joy may be full. 1 John 1:4.

Pray for traffic policemen today, as they may face difficulties at home and on the job. Show them special courtesy and Christian love.

THE FRUIT
OF THE SPIRIT IS PEACE

Christ is the Prince of peace. When the Holy Spirit comes into our lives as Christ's representative, He brings love, joy, and peace.

Peace of mind is one of the most sought-after qualities in the world today. Many have found themselves attracted to Christianity as the result of seeing the peace and tranquility of a Christian neighbor or friend. Multitudes today are desperately searching for love, joy, and peace. When they see what they long for in the life of another, they say "I want what that person has."

The hearts of many are like the troubled sea, which cannot find rest. The fierce waves of temptation sweep over them, and all efforts to stem the tide of evil seem of no avail. Sin has destroyed their peace.

A submarine commander was once asked about a terrible storm that had lashed the Atlantic Ocean for several days. "We didn't even know there was a storm until we came to the surface," the officer replied. The sub had been so far beneath the surface that it had not been affected by the violent storm on the surface.

When Jesus comes into the believer's heart, He brings as a gift His peace, and His peace remains ours as long as we maintain our relationship with Him, the source of peace. Just as a river has a source, so peace has a source. And as a river has a channel, so has peace. We have identified Christ as the source of peace, but the channel is obedience. Isaiah says: "Oh, that you had heeded My commandments! Then your peace would have been like a river, and your righteousness like the waves of the sea" (Isa. 48:18).

In order to experience the peace of Jesus, we must trust Him enough to obey Him. "Many who profess to be His followers have an anxious, troubled heart, because they are afraid to trust themselves with God. They do not make a complete surrender to Him; for they shrink from the consequences that such a surrender may involve. Unless they do make this surrender, they cannot find peace" (*The Desire of Ages*, p. 330).

You will keep him in perfect peace, whose mind is stayed on You, because he trusts in You. Isa. 26:3.

Angola, a coastal nation in southwestern Africa, has a population of more than 9.2 million, with a Seventh-day Adventist member-ship of 102,777. Pray for this land, where there has been much fighting and famine and where many people have fled to surrounding countries.

THE FRUIT OF THE SPIRIT IS LONG-SUFFERING

"Mildness, gentleness, forbearance, long-suffering, being not easily provoked, bearing all things, hoping all things, enduring all things—these are the fruit growing upon the precious tree of love, which is of heavenly growth. This tree, if nourished, will prove to be an evergreen" (*Testimonies*, vol. 2, pp. 134, 135).

The Greek word translated "long-suffering" is *makrothumia*, which means a "conquering patience," and usually denotes patience in regard to people, while seldom in relation to things or events. It is a word very commonly used in the New Testament to describe the attitude of God the Father and of Jesus toward men.

"'Long-suffering' is patience with offense; long endurance. If you are long-suffering, you will not impart to others your supposed knowledge of your brother's mistakes and errors. You will seek to help and save him, because he has been purchased with the blood of Christ" (*My Life Today*, p. 52). The long-suffering of God toward you will be the basis and inspiration for your attitude toward others.

In Paul's famous love chapter, 1 Corinthians 13, he says, "Love suffers long" (verse 4). No matter how much our Christian faith matures, we will still be exposed to opposition, injustice, and contempt from some. What are we going to do under such circumstances? The deeply spiritual person does not get angry because he is opposed, nor does he become sour because of contempt from others. He may be grieved and disappointed, but the Holy Spirit enables him to soar beyond the petty annoyances of life to the heights where the air is pure and ethereal. "To be long-suffering is not to be gloomy and sad, sour and hardhearted; it is to be exactly the opposite" (*ibid.*, p. 52).

The quality of long-suffering places us in the company of Moses, Job, and our Saviour, who said of His crucifiers: "Father, forgive them, for they do not know what they do" (Luke 23:34).

That you may have a walk worthy of the Lord, . . . strengthened with all might, according to His glorious power, for all patience and longsuffering with joy. Col. 1:11.

Think about people in special positions that require much long-suffering and patience. May we suggest judges. As they deal with all kinds of people in trouble, they surely need to have patience that never gives up.

THE FRUIT OF
THE SPIRIT IS GENTLENESS

Yesterday we thought about long-suffering, and today we consider gentleness, or meekness. Long-suffering and gentleness are qualities we find in the lives of Jesus and Moses.

Running through the life of Moses like a golden cord was his unselfish love and utter devotion to God's people, whom he served. "And Moses indeed was faithful in all His house as a servant" (Heb. 3:5).

We recognize Moses as an example of true meekness. In Numbers 12:3 we read: "Now the man Moses was very humble, more than all men who were on the face of the earth."

Too often we associate meekness with weakness, but there was nothing weak about Moses. In fact, it was in this very area that he experienced his great failure, when he became angry and asserted his own will.

But meekness at its best—in all its wonder, strength, and beauty—is demonstrated by the Master Himself as we follow Him from Gethsemane to Calvary. When others reviled, He did not respond in kind. This was indeed strength of character, true meekness.

If we allow Jesus to give us His meekness and gentleness, we will not retaliate when wronged. "We should not allow our feelings to be easily wounded. We are to live, not to guard our feelings or our reputation, but to save souls. As we become interested in the salvation of souls, we cease to mind the little differences that so often arise in our association with one another. Whatever others may think of us, it need not disturb our oneness with Christ, the fellowship of the Spirit" (*Gospel Workers*, p. 475).

The parents of Roland Hayes, the famous singer, had been slaves. Roland's father died when he was just a boy, and the child grew up in poverty, but with the influence of a good Christian mother. Doors began to open to Roland because of his musical talent. When invited to sing for the British monarch, he sent a cable to his mother, which bore a note of pride. She responded with just four words: "Remember who you are."

Remembering who we are apart from Christ should ensure a meek and humble spirit that will not pray "Lord, keep me humble," but rather "Lord, make me humble!"

"Take My yoke upon you and learn from Me, for I am gentle and lowly in heart, and you will find rest for your souls." Matt. 11:29.

Pray for the 100,000 Bedouins of Iraq.

49

THE FRUIT OF THE SPIRIT IS KINDNESS AND GOODNESS

Kindness and goodness are active and busy virtues. Sometimes people refer to them as brother and sister, because, W. R. Nicoll says, "goodness is the more masculine and large-hearted form of charity; and if it errs, errs through blundering and want of tact. Kindness is the more feminine; and may err through exclusiveness and narrowness of view. United, kindness and goodness are perfect."

We can all bear the fruit of kindness and goodness, which will add richness to the lives of others. When Jenny Lind, the Swedish singer, performed in Cincinnati, Ohio, a poor woman, the mother of two young girls, lay near death.

Although they had no money for tickets to the concert, the girls decided to carry to the famous singer their best treasure, a beautiful lily they had grown. They went to the hotel where Jenny Lind was staying. The clerk tried to protect the singer's privacy, but from her nearby room the woman could hear the voices of the little girls pleading for the opportunity to deliver their gift to her.

Jenny Lind invited them into her room and, learning of their wish to hear her sing, gave them each a complimentary ticket and accepted the lily with kind words of thanks.

That evening the large audience noticed that instead of costly floral pieces decorating the piano, the lily given the great singer by the two poor little girls had the place of honor. As Jenny Lind was leaving the platform that night, in a beautiful expression of goodness and kindness she threw a kiss to the two happy girls seated on the front row.

Kindness is love at work, the magic key to every human heart. Inspiration tells us: "If we would humble ourselves before God, and be kind and courteous and tenderhearted and pitiful, there would be one hundred conversions to the truth where now there is only one" (*Testimonies*, vol. 9, p. 189).

How do we gain the qualities of kindness and goodness? They are the fruit of the Spirit.

> **And be kind to one another, tenderhearted, forgiving one another, just as God in Christ also forgave you. Eph. 4:32.**
>
> *Pray for the 20 million people of Inner Mongolia. The rugged Mongolians, descendants of those led by the great Genghis Khan, have been very resistant to the gospel.*

THE FRUIT OF THE SPIRIT IS FAITHFULNESS

Today we will meditate on the fruit of faith, or faithfulness. It is a fruit much needed in our time. One is faithful to a person or a cause only as he or she has faith in that person or cause. Faith holds us steady when earthly foundations crumble all about us; faith gives us a poise that holds us steady when adversities envelop us like a cloud of gloom. Inspiring, uplifting, and energizing, faith is the victory that overcomes the world.

F. W. Robertson said, "To believe is to be strong. Doubt cramps energy. Faith is power." The Holy Spirit produces the fruit of faith in our lives, and the exercise of faith results in faith-full-ness.

Another word for faithfulness is fidelity, and Inspiration tells us: "The approval of the Master is not given because of the greatness of the work performed, but because of fidelity in all that has been done. It is not the results we attain, but the motives from which we act, that weigh with God. He prizes goodness and faithfulness above all else" (*Gospel Workers*, p. 267).

The Creator God who built faithfulness into the fabric of the universe will produce that quality in the surrendered life as the fruit of His Spirit.

The story of the discovery of the planet Neptune illustrates the faithfulness and consequent predictability of the planetary orbits. Uranus, discovered in 1781, had been regarded as the most distant of the planets. But as astronomers studied Uranus, they observed certain deviations for which they could not account by any known laws or theories. They began to wonder if the phenomenon they were observing might be a result of the influence of an unknown planet.

Further research and calculations confirmed their theory. On their charts they located the place in the heavens where that planet should appear and began watching that spot. Finally, after midnight on the morning of September 23, 1846, an astronomy student was the first to see Neptune as it swung into view.

Faith in the fidelity of the laws of the universe led to the planet's discovery. The fruit of faith in your life will lead you and others to limitless spiritual discoveries. God's faithfulness becomes the basis of our faithfulness.

Through the Lord's mercies we are not consumed, because His compassions fail not. They are new every morning; great is Your faithfulness. Lam. 3:22, 23.

Denmark is a wealthy welfare state of more than five million people. Pray for our 3,239 members there and for all evangelistic outreach, including radio.

SPIRITUAL GIFTS

The fruit of the Spirit is the character of Christ that He imparts to us to the degree that we surrender our lives to Him. Like the fruit of the orchard, the fruit of the Spirit grows toward maturity, but can be perfect at each stage of development.

The gifts of the Spirit are ours through spiritual rebirth and are given to equip us for ministry. As we said earlier, they are the scaffolding that enables us to work effectively in His service. The fruit is the building—the character that develops from using the gifts.

A spiritual gift is a special ability that is given to a member of the body of Christ by the Holy Spirit to enable that member to do productive service as a part of the body. "There are many kinds of work to be done by laborers with varied gifts. Some are to labor in one way, some in another" (*Testimonies*, vol. 9, p. 109).

Three chapters of the Bible deal mainly with spiritual gifts—Romans 12, 1 Corinthians 12, and Ephesians 4—but we find scattered references to them elsewhere in the New Testament. As we take a brief look at the major gifts listed in the Bible, you might recognize your gift or gifts.

The gift of *administration* equips certain members of the body to govern the affairs of the church. Those with this gift do well as head elders, deacons, deaconesses, or Sabbath school superintendents.

The Greek word translated *apostle* means "one who is sent." *Missionary* is the term normally used in the church today to refer to one who has the gift to serve in foreign lands or areas far from home and loved ones.

Ministry to children is another gift. The ability to win the confidence of children and to lead them to a relationship with Christ enables members to serve effectively in the children's divisions of Sabbath school and to take part in Story Hours, Vacation Bible Schools, Pathfinders, and other activities designed for children.

There are many more spiritual gifts for us to think about, but space has run out for today. Remember, "to every person is committed some peculiar gift or talent which is to be used to advance the Redeemer's kingdom" (*Testimonies*, vol. 4, p. 618).

Therefore He says: "When He ascended on high, He led captivity captive, and gave gifts to men." Eph. 4:8.

Pray for the 30 million people of Colombia, located on the northwest corner of South America. It is the fourth-largest country on the continent. Seventh-day Adventists number 94,571, one of the three largest Protestant denominations in the country.

FAITH THAT MOVES OMNIPOTENCE

"The unbelief of the professed followers of Christ in the manifestation of spiritual gifts is sufficient reason why they are not more fully manifested. . . . There is an impious unbelief with many at this day. . . . It is humble, confiding faith that moves Omnipotence. Those only who have this faith may expect the manifestation of the gifts" (*Spiritual Gifts*, vol. 3, p. 28).

The apostle Paul stated that he did not want believers to be ignorant concerning spiritual gifts, and with that encouragement we resume our study of the topic, considering first the gift of *discerning of spirits*. This gift enables one to distinguish between the genuine and the counterfeit. Scripture instructs all of us to "try the spirits," and this we can do using the Bible as a test, but those lacking the gift of discernment are more easily deceived.

Empathy, or *mercy*, is the ability to identify with and provide comfort and help to those in trouble or distress. Individuals with this gift are sympathetic listeners who show a compassionate love toward the hurting.

The gift of *evangelism* enables believers to persuasively communicate the gospel through the Holy Spirit's power so that people are led to become His disciples. Research indicates that about 10 percent of believers have the gift, but it is important to remember that God commands all of us to witness, even though we might not have the specific gift.

Exhortation is the ability to go to the side of those who need encouragement and stimulate them to right action.

We all have a measure of *faith* as a gift from God, but He has blessed some with an exceptional measure of faith as a spiritual gift. This gift provides a vision of what God will do for His work and His people. And through the eye of faith the things hoped for become reality. George Mueller, who established the Bristol orphanages in England, certainly must have had this gift.

Now concerning spiritual gifts, brethren, I do not want you to be ignorant. 1 Cor. 12:1.

France is the largest country in Western Europe, with a population of more than 55 million. Pray for France, one of the world's most cultured and sophisticated nations. Pray that the Holy Spirit may use our 8,839 church members to reach the many untouched segments of French society, including the 30,000 Chinese Buddhists in Paris.

KNOWLEDGE PLUS UNDERSTANDING

Some Christians have the special gift of *giving*, and they contribute their material resources joyfully and eagerly in order to advance the work of God.

The gift of *health and healing* is the special ability God gives to certain members of the body of Christ to guide others to the restoration or preservation of physical, mental, and spiritual health.

The gift of *helps,* or helping, enables a person to see practical needs and fill them. It is an especially beautiful gift that aids others to minister more effectively, because someone was there to assist. You can no doubt think of someone you know who has this gift.

Hospitality is another beautiful gift that leads those who have it to graciously open their homes so that guests feel welcome and receive both physical and spiritual refreshment.

You will notice that all the gifts are related to service, and each can be instrumental in revealing the love of God and leading men and women to a salvation experience.

The gift of *knowledge* is the ability to store and recall knowledge from God's Word to meet the need at hand. It has the added dimension of understanding. Near the end of World War II a soldier was seated on a train next to a girl who was also in military uniform, wearing dark glasses and a cape over her shoulder. Fellow passengers became annoyed as the soldier hugged and kissed the girl beside him.

Finally one passenger got up and laid his hand on the soldier's shoulder in protest. Then the serviceman explained: "I was a soldier on the front lines, and this girl was a nurse. She was a ministering angel to the wounded and dying. Then one day a bomb hit the hospital. She lost her sight, and one arm was blown away. Now she's going home to her family, and I'm going with her because she's blind—and then, too, I'm her brother!" Knowledge of the facts gave understanding to those around the couple.

> **"The knowledge of the Holy One is understanding." Prov. 9:10.**

> *Pray for the outreach of the church in the Fiji Mission territory. Out of a population of 758,000, we have 12,230 church members. The islands have such unreached groups as the Hindus and Sikhs, as well as the thousands of Muslims who almost totally resist the gospel.*

TALENTS AND GIFTS

"One worker may be a ready speaker; another a ready writer; another may have the gift of sincere, earnest, fervent prayer; another the gift of singing; another may have special power to explain the Word of God with clearness. . . . To one God gives the word of wisdom, to another knowledge, to another faith; but all are to work under the same Head. The diversity of gifts leads to a diversity of operations; but 'it is the same God which worketh all in all' (1 Cor. 12:6)" (*Evangelism*, p. 99).

The gift of *leadership* is the special talent to inspire and lead others in various ministries within the body of Christ.

The gift of *miracles* permits the member, through the power of the Holy Spirit, to perform acts beyond man's normal and natural capability. The Bible repeatedly warns that Satan can counterfeit miracles, so we must carefully test each miracle and the one performing the miracle by the great standard—the Word of God.

The gift of *music* allows those who have it to express their love for God in music, which in turn draws others to Christ. Perhaps here is a good place to discuss the relationship of spiritual gifts to natural talents.

All people, whether Christian or not, have natural talents or abilities, but only Christians receive spiritual gifts. Talents may come by natural birth as an inheritance from our parents, but spiritual gifts arrive only at the new birth as a gift from our heavenly Parent.

When at the time of conversion and baptism we surrender ourselves to the Lord with all that we have, He might choose to return to us some of our talents as gifts.

One of God's servants, commenting on the parable of the talents, said: "The special gifts of the Spirit are not the only talents represented in the parable. It includes all gifts and endowments, whether original or acquired, natural or spiritual. All are to be employed in Christ's service. . . . These gifts He returns to us purified and ennobled, to be used for His glory in blessing our fellowmen" (*Christ's Object Lessons*, p. 328).

But one and the same Spirit works all these things, distributing to each one individually as He wills. 1 Cor. 12:11.

Pray for our work in Burundi, one of the world's poorest states. The political situation is difficult for Christians, and religious freedom is steadily eroding.

PASTORS AND TEACHERS

The English word *pastor* comes from the Latin for "shepherd." It is a word rich in meaning. The shepherd is responsible for his flock. He cares for them, guards them, provides food for them, defends them from their enemies, and when they stray, he seeks until he finds them and brings them back. If need be, a good shepherd will die to save his sheep.

Jesus called Himself the "good shepherd" (John 10:11, 14), and He did die for us. Peter referred to Jesus as the "Chief Shepherd" (1 Peter 5:4) and the "Shepherd" of men's souls (1 Peter 2:25). The writer of the Epistle to the Hebrews called Jesus the "great Shepherd of the sheep" (Heb. 13:20).

One with the gift to pastor will serve Jesus as an undershepherd. This marvelous gift is not restricted to full-time church employees. Many laypersons have the gift of pastoring. Recognizing this, many fields now have lay pastors who share the ministry under the direction of the full-time pastors, and by doing so bring great strength and blessing to the body of Christ.

Closely connected with the gift of pastoring, or shepherding, is that of *teaching*. It equips the possessor to go beyond relating facts and altering behavior to draw students closer to God by teaching God's Word with clarity and appeal.

Certainly all Christians pray, but some have a special gift of praying, especially *intercessory prayer*, which is interceding with God on behalf of someone else. If we should feel the need of special prayer and anointing, as referred to in James 5:14, 15, we would probably think immediately of certain individuals whose prayers we would especially have confidence in. Probably it would be a special gift of prayer and their devout life that would cause us to think of such persons.

And when the Chief Shepherd appears, you will receive the crown of glory that does not fade away. 1 Peter 5:4.

Pray for Afghanistan. It is virtually unevangelized. Pray that the land may open fully to the preaching of the gospel. Officially there has been religious freedom since 1964, but the authorities forbid proselytizing. It is 99 percent Muslim. The number of Christians is unknown, but it has been increasing since 1979. Seventh-day Adventists have no established work in that country.

STILL MORE GIFTS

We think of the gift of *prophecy* as enabling one to foretell the future, an ability surely included in the endowment. But a prophet does much more than that. The gift of prophecy provides edification, exhortation, instruction, and comfort. God inspires an individual with the gift in order that he or she may speak for Him as His messenger. Scripture mentions prophecy as one of the identifying characteristics of the remnant church. In Revelation 12:17 we read that in the last days the dragon, or Satan, would be angry with the members of the remnant church "who keep the commandments of God and have the testimony of Jesus Christ." And according to Revelation 19:10, "the testimony of Jesus is the spirit of prophecy."

In his attempts to confuse men and women, Satan counterfeits all the gifts, including the gift of prophecy and the gift of *tongues.*

The gift of tongues is the ability to communicate with others in a language not previously learned. The gift of the *interpretation of tongues* is the ability to translate instantaneously from one language to another.

Some see a manifestation of the gift of tongues in the facility that some have in learning foreign languages. Also, there have been many miraculous gifts of language, such as that bestowed on Sekuba of the Kalahari Desert, described in the reading for June 7.

The gift of *wisdom* is the capacity to help care for and nurture the spiritual welfare of a group of believers by imparting wise counsel from the Word of God.

Some authorities classify spiritual gifts as speaking and serving gifts. Others describe them as enabling and serving gifts. The enabling gifts would include faith, discernment, knowledge, and wisdom. Qualities possessed rather than activities performed, enabling gifts make our serving gifts more effective. Thus, God bestows every gift, enabling or serving, for service to Him and others. Let us make this a day when we use our gifts in meaningful service.

Now there are diversities of gifts, but the same Spirit. 1 Cor. 12:4.

One of the largest hidden people groups in the world is the 20 million Muslim Sundanese people of Indonesia. Islam is making a great impact on their thinking. However, there is a strong mixture of other elements in their religious practices. Pray for these Sundanese people, and pray that more Christian missionaries may be willing to work there and find entrance to their hearts with the gospel of Jesus Christ.

THE MORE EXCELLENT WAY

A builder who does not understand and appreciate the relation of tools and scaffolding to the structure being built would not be a competent craftsman. Such a person could not be entrusted with either tools or responsibility.

One who does not understand and appreciate the relationship of the gifts of the Spirit to the fruit of the Spirit cannot be entrusted by the great Master Builder with the gifts of the Spirit for the work of building up the body of Christ.

The individual who seeks to manifest the gifts of the Spirit before he or she bears the fruit of the Spirit thereby shows that he or she is not in a condition to be entrusted with the gifts. Without the fruit of the Spirit, all the gifts are like "sounding brass or a clanging cymbal" (1 Cor. 13:1).

To seek the gift of tongues more intensely than the grace of temperance indicates that one is not using well the one tongue he already has.

Or to go after miracles before meekness shows an unreadiness for the gift of working miracles. Luke 9:51-56 tells the story of two men who wanted the gift of working miracles when they did not yet possess the grace of long-suffering. They went to Christ and proposed a miraculous action of judgment against the Samaritans, but instead of giving them power to work miracles, "He turned and rebuked them, and said, 'You do not know what manner of spirit you are of'" (Luke 9:55).

To covet the gift of healing more than the grace of love proves oneself in need of healing before being entrusted with the gift. Any person possessed of power but devoid of love becomes a tyrant.

The last verse of 1 Corinthians 12, which deals with the gifts of the Spirit, points to "a more excellent way." This more excellent way is revealed in the thirteenth chapter as the way of love. Like scaffolding, the gifts serve their purpose for a time, but the fruit—love—is eternal.

> **Though I speak with the tongues of men and of angels, but have not love, I have become as sounding brass or a clanging cymbal. 1 Cor. 13:1.**
>
> *Remember the victims of natural and man-made disasters today that they may be comforted and strengthened, and that even through adversity they may find the Lord.*

LIFT UP THE FALLEN

"I was bad and I wanted to be good. I wanted to be honest, but I was crooked. I wanted to pray, but I was always cursing. I wanted to be truthful, but I was a liar. I wanted to be sober, but I couldn't stay on the water wagon, and in desperation I cried out, 'What am I to do?' "

Thus Samuel Hadley described himself before he finally found salvation through Jesus Christ and became a mighty apostle to the outcasts of skid row.

When Samuel Hadley was superintendent of the Water Street Mission in New York, a man came on a cold night looking for a bed. He had been a law partner of one of the men in Lincoln's Cabinet. On that particular night Mr. Hadley had no rooms left, and he reluctantly had to turn the man away.

At one o'clock in the morning the individual returned, and once again Mr. Hadley had to turn him down. The old man, leaning on a cane, went down under the Brooklyn Bridge to a spot that would offer a little shelter from the wind, but not from the cold.

Hadley could not sleep that night for thinking about the homeless man. At three o'clock in the morning he went out and found him huddled near one of the piers of the bridge. Mr. Hadley took the individual to his own home, provided him with a warm bath, and put him in his own bed.

Hadley was well rewarded the next night at the service when the man came forward, knelt at the altar, and cried out, "God be merciful to me, a sinner!"

He got up from his knees a new person in Christ Jesus, and before long he was back at his old position—a respected and useful citizen and an active Christian. The Lord, who rescued Hadley, now through him was lifting up others.

It is the task of the church to rescue the perishing and lift up the fallen.

"And the King will answer and say to them, 'Assuredly, I say to you, inasmuch as you did it to one of the least of these My brethren, you did it to Me.' " Matt. 25:40.

Pray for the homeless people around the world, but especially for those within your reach.

FOUR SINS

Four sins that led to the betrayal and crucifixion of our Lord continue as very real problems in our world today. They are envy, avarice, slander, and peer pressure. Have you and I ever been guilty of one or more of them? Whenever we are envious or avaricious, whenever we give credence to scandal or yield to the pressure of evil influence, we are joining the company of those who crucified our Lord.

The simple teachings of Jesus met the needs of the common people, but His popularity became a threat to the pompous pride of the priests. It was out of envy that the chief priests plotted the death of Jesus.

The second sin that led to His betrayal and crucifixion was the love of money. People alone are worthy of being the objects of our love. When a man cares more for money than for men, he joins the company of Judas.

The third sin that contributed to the death of our Lord was slander. Slander is the weapon of those who lack the influence or power to stand up by themselves and strike an open blow on their own responsibility. To repeat an uninvestigated charge, to whisper behind a person's back what we would not have the courage to say to his face, to allow our prejudices to color our interpretation of another's conduct, is slander. Let us beware how we lend our lips to slanderous accusations, which reduce us to a level with the murderers of our Lord.

Peer pressure was the fourth sin that led to the Crucifixion. Pilate did not want to condemn Jesus, but he was not willing to stand up for right against the pressures of the crowd. Nine tenths of all sins committed today have peer pressure involved in them. Youth generally do not want to ruin health, reputation, fortune, and character through indulgence in drugs, drink, and dissipation. But they yield to peer pressure. From these very sins that crucified our Lord, nothing short of the constant presence and power of the Spirit of Christ Himself can keep us.

"The God of Abraham . . . glorified His Servant Jesus, whom you delivered up and denied in the presence of Pilate, when he was determined to let Him go." Acts 3:13.

Pray for victory over the subtle sins of envy, avarice, slander, and peer pressure.

CONTENTMENT

Henry Ward Beecher once said, "We only see in a lifetime a dozen faces marked with the peace of a contented spirit." Perhaps he was exaggerating, but he was more right than many of us might recognize, because the overwhelming mass of humanity who live under otherwise comfortable circumstances are not content. Discontent, like a noxious weed, may grow in the hearts of Christians and non-Christians alike.

It is a human tendency to feel that others are happier than they actually are. The people we resent and envy for having what we lack probably have wounds and scars of their own. They may even envy us. If we knew the facts, we would rarely find someone whose life was to be envied.

Scripture tells of a man who had everything that the heart could desire and still was unhappy. Promotions, honors, even invitations to banquets attended by the king and queen, were not enough to make him happy.

All of his blessings and benefits did not make him happy because he could see Mordecai the Jew sitting at the king's gate, and that made Haman unhappy. He had everything that most people want, but he still was discontented.

Contentment is found only when we learn to be satisfied with where we are and what we have. It is an experience that cannot come to the natural heart, for the natural heart constantly seethes with dissatisfaction. The unconverted heart can never attain peace.

Environment, position, or power will not bring contentment. The Greek word for content indicates that it is a condition wherein we have mastered the situation in which we live. It is the ability to live above circumstances.

God has a purpose in all that befalls us. Our contentment must not depend upon outward circumstances, but rather upon an inner experience. The secret of a truly satisfied and contented life is to be found only in our relationship with Jesus Christ.

But godliness with contentment is great gain. 1 Tim. 6:6.

Pray for the salvation of the checkers at your local supermarket. Pray that God will bless them in a special way. Perhaps a special word of appreciation would be meaningful the next time you go through that checkout line.

61

YOU ARE A PRIEST

Too often we define a layperson in terms of what he or she is not rather than what he or she is. For example, it is a person who is not called to be a minister, not employed by the church, and not trained in theology.

God's definition of His *laos* (the Greek word from which we get the English word *laity*) appears in 1 Peter 2:9—it is a "chosen generation, a royal priesthood, a holy nation." Every person who accepts Christ becomes a priest of God, a royal son or daughter of God, and a part of the royal family of priests. Every believer is a minister. Therefore, we confuse the issue when we use the term *minister* to apply to the clergy only.

The basic difference between clergy and laity is a difference of laboring full-time or part-time—of salaried or nonsalaried positions. Each layperson has a special sphere of influence that pastors do not have, and he or she has the potential of being a self-supporting missionary for Christ.

Individual believers must come to a new sense of their identity and understand who they really are in God's eyes—a minister. All attempts to stimulate outreach activity are going to be unsuccessful unless the laity see who they truly are in God's sight.

William Carey said, "I cobble shoes to pay expenses, but soul winning is my business." God used him to open the continent of India for Christ.

The Bible pictures the pastor as an equipper of the laity for their work of service. It is not God's plan that the laity should support the pastor as the star performer, but rather that the pastor should prepare the laity for their role in service. A pastor may inhibit lay involvement or he may be the one who encourages, trains, and equips the laypeople.

When we realize the large number of people not involved in any soul-winning outreach, we recognize the need for a rediscovery of the biblical theology of the laity—the priesthood of all believers.

But you are a chosen generation, a royal priesthood, a holy nation, His own special people, that you may proclaim the praises of Him who called you out of darkness into His marvelous light. 1 Peter 2:9.

Pray that both clergy and laity will better understand the priesthood of all believers.

SAVED BY SERVING

An old Chinese tale tells about a woman whose only son died. In her grief she went to a holy man and said, "What prayers, what magical incantations, do you have to bring my son back to life?"

Instead of sending her away or reasoning with her, he said to her, "Bring me a mustard seed from a home that has never known sorrow. We will use it to drive the sorrow out of your life."

The woman set off at once in search of that magical mustard seed. She came first to a splendid mansion, knocked at the door, and said, "I am looking for a home that has never known sorrow. Is this such a place? It is very important to me."

"You've certainly come to the wrong place," they told her as they began to describe all the tragic things that had recently befallen them. The woman said to herself, "Who is better able to help these poor unfortunate people than I who have had misfortune of my own?"

The bereaved mother stayed to comfort the family members in the mansion, then she went on in her search for a home that had never known sorrow. But wherever she turned, in hovels and in palaces, she found experiences of sadness and misfortune.

Ultimately she became so involved in ministering to other people's grief that she forgot about her quest for the magical mustard seed. Ministering to other people's grief had in fact driven the sorrow out of her life.

Christ left for us a beautiful example of ministry to others. "Our Saviour went from house to house, healing the sick, comforting the mourners, soothing the afflicted, speaking peace to the disconsolate. He took the little children in His arms and blessed them, and spoke words of hope and comfort to the weary mothers. With unfailing tenderness and gentleness, He met every form of human woe and affliction. Not for Himself, but for others did He labor. He was the servant of all" (*Gospel Workers*, p. 188).

Jesus went. He comforted, soothed, and encouraged. Taking little children in His arms, he spoke to the weary mothers. And we can minister as Jesus did.

But when He saw the multitudes, He was moved with compassion for them, because they were weary and scattered, like sheep having no shepherd. Matt. 9:36.

Pray for someone you know who has recently lost a loved one.

UNUSUAL BABY SHOWER

Portadown is a strong bastion for orthodox Protestantism in northern Ireland, on the banks of the River Bann. In 1895 a Pastor Hutchinson rented the town hall for a series of meetings in Portadown. He caused quite a stir, especially when he preached the Sabbath doctrine. It was common to have a shower of stones come through the windows while the meetings were in progress, but in spite of many difficulties, he ultimately gained four converts—Mr. and Mrs. S. Joyce, Mrs. Keough, and her 16-year-old son George.

When Mr. Joyce closed his bake shop on Saturday, it caused a major sensation in the town. The Joyce family had one child, Rachel, just 2 years old, and a second child was expected. At the time of the baby's birth, the townspeople lit a bonfire in the street and threw pieces of burning peat up at the bedroom window. It was their way of telling Mr. Joyce that they no longer wanted him in the town.

As a result, Joyce gave up baking bread in order to distribute the bread of life as a literature evangelist. It was not long before he became the British Union colporteur leader. In his 90s he could still be seen going from home to home with our publications. The Joyces' daughter, Rachel, became the wife of Arthur S. Maxwell, known around the world as the author of *The Bible Story* and *Uncle Arthur's Bedtime Stories*. The Maxwells' four sons and two daughters all became denominational employees. The little boy who was born to a shower of burning peat became a prominent evangelist and church administrator, as did a younger brother also.

George Keough, another of the first four converts, served as a missionary to the Middle East and an educator. His son Arthur followed in his father's footsteps. Only eternity will reveal the full harvest of Elder Hutchinson's labors in Portadown.

The Pharisee Gamaliel spoke words of wisdom long ago when he said,

"And now I say to you, keep away from these men and let them alone; for if this plan or this work is of men, it will come to nothing; but if it is of God, you cannot overthrow it—lest you even be found to fight against God." Acts 5:38, 39.

Pray for the people of Eire (southern Ireland) and Northern Ireland, where the combined population is 3.7 million and our membership is 293.

RAISE YOUR SIGHTS

Jesus discerned what His disciples failed to see. He saw candidates for the kingdom everywhere He went. In His day, as in ours, obstacles and problems hindered the gospel on every hand, but Jesus' vision reached beyond the obstacles and beyond the problems that faced the infant church.

If you are confronted with prejudice and opposition, remember that Jesus knew a great deal about prejudice and opposition. As a matter of fact, in His day Jesus faced many of the same problems that confront us now. People did not readily accept His message. He had to contend with the forces of nationalism and racism as we do in our day.

In the face of obstacles and opposition, pride and prejudice, wine and worldliness, Christ's message to His followers was "Lift up your eyes; get a new vision; the field is ripe for the harvest."

The words of the Saviour challenged and encouraged. His was a message to challenge His followers' vision and to test their courage in the face of the difficult task.

In the spirit of Jesus we need to raise our sights and roll back the horizon of our vision. It was the burden and the spirit sounded by God's messenger to the remnant church: "Oh, how I seem to hear the voice day and night, 'Go forward; add new territory; . . . give the last message of warning to the world. There is no time to be lost' " (*Evangelism*, p. 61).

We need to ask the Lord to give us vision to see souls being converted in presently unentered areas; vision to see churches and church schools where now there exist only vacant lots.

We need not only to raise our sights, but also to sharpen our focus so that we can see the winnable ones. Look for them today.

Then He said to them, "The harvest truly is great, but the laborers are few; therefore pray the Lord of the harvest to send out laborers into His harvest." Luke 10:2.

Pray for the people in the Islamic sheikhdom of Qatar, occupying the Qatar Peninsula in the Persian Gulf, and the adjacent region, with a population of 369,000. Seventh-day Adventists have been among foreign residents attracted by the oil industry, and they have conducted a Sabbath school there, but there is no Seventh-day Adventist church.

CHRIST'S METHOD

Jesus shared His mission with His disciples and taught them how to witness. He took them with Him into the cities and villages so that they could observe His manner of working. Later He sent them out two by two for personal field experience, allowing them to put into practice what they had learned. Then He evaluated their progress and suggested improvements. They reported to Him, and the learning experience continued as they followed their Master's example. Their witness was by loving fellowship, compassionate service, and faithful proclamation.

"Now as He drew near, He saw the city and wept over it" (Luke 19:41).

Jesus came near. You do not develop a burden for the salvation of others unless you come near to them. Too often our scholastic ivory towers and our affluent homes keep us at a distance from the people.

Jesus beheld the city. He observed carefully and with caring. It was not just a fleeting glance. Instead, He saw the people of the city as individuals with many and varied needs. As He looked upon the city, He wept over it. As we approach the needs of people, our hearts must break.

"Christ's method alone will give true success in reaching the people." What was His method? "The Saviour mingled with men as one who desired their good. He showed His sympathy for them, ministered to their needs, and won their confidence. Then He bade them, 'Follow Me' " (*The Ministry of Healing*, p. 143).

Our Saviour employed relational evangelism—love in action.

He evangelized by serving. When He met a sick person, He provided healing. When He encountered a hungry person, He provided food. To a lonely person, He provided friendship.

Also, Jesus evangelized through His office as a master teacher and preacher.

Above all, Jesus was a friend. His opponents criticized Him for befriending sinners, but He did so first because He loved all men and women, and second, because He knew that it was the most effective way to win sinners. He was able to visualize what they could become through the power of transforming grace.

And when the scribes and Pharisees saw Him eating with the tax collectors and sinners, they said to His disciples, "How is it that He eats and drinks with tax collectors and sinners?" Mark 2:16.

Pray for the untouchables of India and those in our society who might correspond to them.

WAITING

"I was shown God's people waiting for some change to take place—a compelling power to take hold of them. But they will be disappointed, for they are wrong. They must act; they must take hold of the work themselves. . . . The harvest of the earth is nearly ripe" (*Christian Service*, p. 43).

Evidently God's people are waiting when they should be going into action. The Lord wants us to take the initiative in doing the work He has given us to do.

"Christ is waiting with longing desire for the manifestation of Himself in His church" (*Christ's Object Lessons*, p. 69).

He is waiting, and so also is God the Father. "Long has God waited for the spirit of service to take possession of the whole church" (*Christian Service*, p. 11).

Jesus is waiting, God the Father is waiting, and the angels are waiting. "With almost impatient eagerness, the angels wait for our cooperation; for man must be the channel to communicate with man" (*ibid.*, p. 9).

"All heaven is waiting for channels through which can be poured the holy oil to be a joy and blessing to human hearts" (*ibid.*, p. 19).

All heaven is waiting. Think of it! But men and women are also waiting. "All over the world men and women are looking wistfully to heaven. Prayers and tears and inquiries go up from souls longing for light, for grace, for the Holy Spirit. Many are on the verge of the kingdom, waiting only to be gathered in" (*The Acts of the Apostles*, p. 109).

"Many are waiting to be personally addressed" (*The Desire of Ages*, p. 141). If we are willing to let God use us as channels through whom He can communicate His love to a waiting world, we should pray that God will open doors of opportunity. He is able and willing to lead us to those who are waiting for someone to come. One of the greatest thrills in this life is to find yourself keeping a divine appointment.

Now an angel of the Lord spoke to Philip, saying, "Arise and go toward the south along the road which goes down from Jerusalem to Gaza." Acts 8:26.

Pray that God will arrange a divine appointment for you as He did for Philip with the Ethiopian treasurer who was waiting for someone to come.

WHO IS JESUS?

For years a certain pastor fought what seemed to be a losing battle with a troublesome temper. In spite of his best efforts, he experienced one defeat after another. One day after a violent outburst, he buried his head in his arms in absolute despair as he sat at his desk. Emotionally exhausted, he fell asleep.

The pastor dreamed he was in his study, and as he looked out the window, he saw a glorious light. As the light approached him, he realized that it was actually a man who evidently intended to be his guest. The pastor became conscious that his study was untidy and in no condition to receive such a guest.

Frantically the pastor swept and dusted the room, but the more he worked, the worse it looked. As he wondered what to do, he heard a knock at the door. *I can't let him in while the room is in this condition*, the pastor thought to himself. He continued his efforts to improve the appearance of things, and after a time the stranger knocked again. What should he do? All his efforts seemingly were in vain.

When the stranger knocked the third time, the distraught pastor who had exhausted all of his resources flung open the door, saying, "I can't do any more. Come in, if you will enter such a room." As the pastor looked up, he recognized the stranger as Jesus.

The Master entered the room, and strangely, as He did so, the dust seemed to disappear and everything suddenly became orderly. All was bright and clean and joyful. The Master's presence had done in a moment all that his feverish efforts had failed to accomplish.

We can't save ourselves from sin or free ourselves from the habits of sin that hold us in bondage. But we can choose to invite Jesus into our hearts, and when we do, a miracle takes place—a process of change begins that continues as long as we allow Him to control our lives.

"And she will bring forth a Son, and you shall call His name Jesus, for He will save His people from their sins." Matt. 1:21.

Pray that someone you know who has a temper problem might find victory in Christ.

THREE IMPORTANT QUESTIONS

There is theoretical Christianity and there is practical Christianity. We will consider three questions that will help us to know which kind we have. What God really wants to know is that we love Him so much that we trust Him without reservation. In view of this, we might imagine God's first question to be "Will you trust Me with your life?" That, in effect, is what he said to Abraham when He asked him to leave his home and start off on a long journey to an unknown destination.

God didn't inquire whether Mary believed in the doctrine of the Incarnation. He bypassed the theory and went right to the practical application when He asked Mary to be the mother of the Messiah. He was saying, "Will you trust me?"

We might think of God's second question as being "Will you entrust yourself to become a part of My family?" Will you, as a demonstration of your faith in God, turn yourself over to somebody like yourself? That is exactly what is involved in becoming a part of Christ's body, the church. Church membership requires accepting the rest of God's people as our brothers and sisters regardless of race or economic considerations. It means entrusting yourself to their fellowship. Remembering that the church is like a hospital for the spiritually infirm, you can expect to see undesirable symptoms in such people as they may also see them in you. Always keep in mind that the church is not a museum to display perfect specimens, but a hospital for those who are seeking healing.

God's third question might be "Will you get out and be involved someplace in the world?" Are you willing to give of yourself in service to others? Will you let God reveal His love, His Word, and His character through you to others? To say yes to this question involves a commitment to live for Christ and a willingness to give of your time, talent, and means in His service.

When people say yes to all three questions, we have a dynamic, living, growing church.

But when Jesus heard that, He said to them, "Those who are well have no need of a physician, but those who are sick." Matt. 9:12.

Pray for grace to trust God more and for a genuine love for your brothers and sisters in the church—even those who don't seem as lovable as others.

RELEASE BARABBAS

Each year at the Feast of the Passover the Roman governor would release a prisoner chosen by the people. When Pilate offered them the option of either Barabbas or Jesus, they selected Barabbas.

From the four Gospel writers we can glean only a few facts about the background of Barabbas.

The Romans had imprisoned him on charges of robbery, sedition, and murder. They had found him guilty, and he awaited death by crucifixion. For him there was no hope. We can imagine that day when the door of his dark, damp prison cell swung open and the soldiers entered. No doubt he thought the day of execution had arrived, but instead the Romans released him. Someone by the name of Jesus was going to occupy his place on the cross. He deserved to die, but Another was taking his place.

Can you imagine the emotion that must have surged through Barabbas as the soldiers removed his shackles and set him free? We have no record in the Scriptures as to what happened to him afterward. Did appreciation for his undeserved freedom motivate him to learn something about the One who had died in his place? We don't know. The name Barabbas comes from two Aramaic words that together mean "son of the father." Did Christ's death in his place stimulate enough interest in Barabbas that he became a son of the heavenly Father?

Who was Barabbas? He was the guilty one who deserved to die but who was set free because Another died in his place. This leads to another greater question: Who was Jesus? Who was this One who was willing to die for all the guilty of all ages? It would be the greatest ingratitude for the guilty person who lives by virtue of the death of an innocent substitute not to seek an answer to the question Who is this Jesus who died in my place?

Who was Barabbas? In a sense he was you and I—all of us who are guilty before God. All of us for whom Jesus died.

> **But God demonstrates His own love toward us, in that while we were still sinners, Christ died for us. Rom. 5:8.**

> *Pray for those on death row that they might accept the One who died to give them eternal life.*

NEHEMIAH

We observe many parallels between the experience of Nehemiah and that of church leaders in our day. When Nehemiah came to Jerusalem, he found the people of God satisfied to live in the ruins. But Nehemiah made a survey of the work that needed to be done and formulated a definite plan. Then he challenged the discouraged people to become involved in the task of rebuilding the wall.

As soon as God's people began to work, the devil and his followers became active also. Nehemiah and his laborers became objects of scorn and ridicule.

The Judean leader faced a seemingly impossible task. His obstacles included a pagan king; a lethargic, spiritually degenerate nation; fierce Gentile opposition; scant resources; and a discouraged working force. Undaunted, he organized his workers into small groups, assigning each one to a post of duty. His vision became their vision, and his goal became their's.

Nehemiah was a man of high hopes and holy purpose. The people caught the enthusiasm of their leader, and those who came under his influence became Nehemiahs in their own spheres. He reproduced himself in the lives of others. His example inspired in others the courage and determination that he possessed.

In our day the spiritual walls have been broken down, and the needed rebuilding has been delayed by the indifference of the people as much as by the opposition of their enemies.

Prophecy points to a people who will repair the breach in the broken wall. Today we are dealing, not with bricks of clay, but with bricks of truth.

Like the rebuilding of the wall in Nehemiah's day, the task of restoring and sharing truth can be completed through the power of the Holy Spirit in an incredibly short period of time. Inspiration says: "There is need of Nehemiahs in the church today" (*SDA Bible Commentary,* Ellen G. White Comments, vol. 3, p. 1137).

A man of cheerful consecration, purposeful hope, energy, zeal, courage, and determination, Nehemiah's example inspired others. When faced with opposition and conflict, his "strength and courage took the place of feebleness and discouragement" (*ibid.*).

And it happened, when all our enemies heard of it, and all the nations around us saw these things, that they were very disheartened in their own eyes; for they perceived that this work was done by our God. Neh. 6:16.

Pray for your pastor and the lay leaders of your church, that they may be blessed with the spirit of Nehemiah.

71

MIRACLES OF FAITH

When George Mueller felt impressed to establish homes for orphans in Bristol, England, he decided that it would be wholly an act of faith. Never once did Mueller solicit donations for his work. Rather, he talked to God about his needs and let Him impress human hearts to meet them. The result was one of the most beautiful and practical demonstrations of living faith in the history of mankind.

On one occasion George Mueller had 2,000 orphans to feed and no food for breakfast. As the children gathered around the tables, in front of them were 2,000 empty plates and 2,000 empty tin cups. Mueller thanked God for bread and milk, though neither was in sight. No sooner had he offered that prayer of faith than a knock sounded at the door. It was the town baker, who said, "Mueller, you got me up at three o'clock this morning. I woke up and couldn't go back to sleep. The Lord said, 'You had better bake some bread for the orphans.' "

The bread had arrived, but where was the milk? Soon after, there came another knock at the door. It was the milkman. His truck had broken down right in front of the orphanage. He said, "I need to unload the milk so I can take the truck in and get it fixed. Would you help me by taking the milk?"

In a similar manner for 60 years our God miraculously provided for Mueller and his orphans.

When Abraham and Isaac stood on Mount Moriah and Isaac questioned "Where is the lamb?" Abraham answered, "Jehovah-jireh," which in Hebrew means "The Lord will provide."

When we today ask Where is the money for food, rent, or to pay the tuition, remember, "the Lord will provide." In answer to the question Where will we get the money to build the church, the school, and pay the staff, the answer is the same: "The Lord will provide." The Lord will meet our needs when we seek His will, do His will, and trust Him fully.

And Abraham called the name of the place, The-Lord-Will-Provide; as it is said to this day, "In the Mount of The Lord it shall be provided." Gen. 22:14.

Pray for the continued advance of the gospel in the Solomon Islands, where Adventism began in 1914 with the arrival of G. F. Jones and his wife. Population of the islands is 314,000, including 13,632 Seventh-day Adventists.

FIDELITY OR FRIENDSHIP

One day the Honorable Perrin H. Lowrey, circuit court judge in Mississippi, was holding court in Ripley, near his boyhood home. He had to convict and fine the son of a widow who had been his childhood schoolmate.

When the trial ended, the judge received a letter from the boy's mother pleading with him on the basis of their old friendship to remit the fine. She explained that she was now a widow with a number of children. Her son was wayward and lazy, and she herself would have to earn the money to pay the fine by sewing. Her financial burdens were more than she could bear.

Although the plea based on a childhood friendship moved the judge to tears, he still signed the docket and adjourned the court. In a letter to his old friend, he admitted that her letter had greatly affected him and that for a moment he had hesitated between fidelity to duty and his friendship and sympathy for her.

To remit the fine, the judge felt, would violate his oath to uphold and execute the law, and justice would suffer for the sake of mercy. But he enclosed with his letter his personal check to cover both the fine and court costs. Concluding his letter, he said, "I send this check with joy because it gives me the opportunity to be both merciful and just."

"God's love has been expressed in His justice no less than in His mercy. Justice is the foundation of His throne, and the fruit of His love. It had been Satan's purpose to divorce mercy from truth and justice. He sought to prove that the righteousness of God's law is an enemy to peace. But Christ shows that in God's plan they are indissolubly joined together; the one cannot exist without the other. 'Mercy and truth are met together; righteousness and peace have kissed each other' (Ps. 85:10)" (*The Desire of Ages*, p. 762).

Keep justice, and do righteousness, for My salvation is about to come, and My righteousness to be revealed. Isa. 56:1.

Pray for the Maldive Islands, 220 inhabited islands situated in the Indian Ocean, 370 miles south of India. The religion is Islam, and Seventh-day Adventists have no presence there.

THE SEALED BOOK

As the fifth chapter of Revelation opens, the Almighty is seated on the throne. In His hand He holds a closed and sealed book. Someone must open the book. But who? As if to summon the whole universe, a mighty angel cries out, "Who is worthy to open the book?"

No one responds, and John weeps when no one appears worthy, because he believes that the book concerns the destiny of mankind. But then despair turns to hope as One with nail-pierced hands approaches the throne and opens the book.

What's in the book? Church history? Yes, but more than that. It contains the decisions of men and women. "Thus the Jewish leaders made their choice. Their decision was registered in the book which John saw in the hand of Him that sat upon the throne, the book which no man could open" (*Christ's Object Lessons*, p. 294).

It could not have been said that no one could open the seals unless everyone had been given a chance. The event here symbolized takes place at the only time when all who have ever existed are alive at the same time upon the earth—at the end of the millennium, when God raises the wicked dead. At that time the followers of false teachers will step up to those who have led them astray and say, "You promised us an entrance into the city—what about it?" And they will stand there helpless, because only One can keep that promise. There is none other name under heaven whereby men can be saved.

This is the time when every knee will bow, admitting that Christ is Lord. As the controversy between good and evil reaches its climax and God draws down the curtain on sinful history, every question in every mind will be answered, but for many it will be too late. Today is the day of salvation. The decision that will decide our eternal destiny we must make now.

> **"Nor is there salvation in any other, for there is no other name under heaven given among men by which we must be saved." Acts 4:12.**
>
> *Pray for someone you know who is struggling with the issue of right and wrong choices. Pray that they will make the all-important decision to receive Jesus.*

PROVIDENCES IN THE PACIFIC

The United States Trust Territory of the Western Pacific covers 3 million square miles, extending 2,400 miles from east to west and 1,700 miles from north to south. However, the total land area is only about 900 square miles, with a population of more than 123,000. The first Seventh-day Adventist in the Western Caroline Islands was James G. Gibbon, an English sailor who made his home in Koror, Palau. He accepted the Seventh-day Adventist beliefs after reading tracts sent on a merchant vessel in the late 1890s from Hong Kong by the pioneer missionary, Abram La Rue.

Gibbon had no direct communication with Seventh-day Adventists until his son William somehow heard that a man named Armstrong was in charge of the Seventh-day Adventist mission in Japan. In an attempt to make contact with Seventh-day Adventists, William Gibbon wrote a letter addressed to ''Armstrong, Tokyo.'' It was a miracle that his letter reached Elder V. T. Armstrong in Tokyo.

During World War II, Japanese administrators interned two Seventh-day Adventist Japanese missionaries in the Western Carolines for refusal to bear arms, and one of them, Seiichi Yamamoto, succeeded in interesting one of his jailers in Seventh-day Adventist teachings. After the war, the jailer, Toribiong Uchel, was baptized, and in 1956 he became the first ordained Palauan Seventh-day Adventist minister.

The first known Sabbathobserver on Guam was Guillermo Flores, a Baptist pastor who had honored the seventh-day Sabbath since 1926 without ever having seen any other Sabbathkeeper. His church dismissed him for his Sabbatarian views, and in 1948 he united with the Seventh-day Adventist Church and later entered its ministry.

Seventh-day Adventist influence began on Guam on September 9, 1944, when Henry Metzker, of Sutherlin, Oregon, a pharmacist's mate, first class, U.S.N.R., inquired at the home of Guam congressman Manual Ulloa of Dededo about the location of the Seventh-day Adventist church. At that time the island had no church, but Ulloa became interested through Metzker's inquiry, and a year later, in the autumn of 1945, while two officers of the Far Eastern Division were delayed on Guam by typhoon weather, he was baptized together with his wife and a number of their children.

He shall not fail nor be discouraged, till he have set judgment in the earth: and the isles shall wait for his law. Isa. 42:4, KJV.

Pray for outreach of the gospel among the 2,131 islands of Micronesia.

A MAN
WHO WALKED WITH GOD

Of the nine patriarchs before Noah, eight were living at the time of Enoch's translation. Only Adam was not among them.

Death always brings grief, but imagine the grief when Adam, the founder of the human race and one of the only two human beings who had eaten of the tree of life, died. Any hope of ever returning to Eden must have appeared to have perished with him. But Enoch's faith, however, remained strong in the face of death because his confidence rested in God, with whom he walked day by day.

"From the lips of Adam he had learned the dark story of the Fall, and the cheering one of God's grace as seen in the promise; and he relied upon the Redeemer to come. But after the birth of his first son, Enoch reached a higher experience; he was drawn into a closer relationship with God. He realized more fully his own obligations and responsibility as a son of God" (*Patriarchs and Prophets*, p. 84).

The patriarch's faith encouraged faith in the lives of others following the death of Adam. For 57 years after Adam's death, Enoch devoted himself to pleasing God and persuading men.

When it appears that the bottom has fallen out of your life and all seems lost, remember Enoch. That which gives stability is an abiding confidence that comes through a personal relationship with our God.

Whether your problems are personal or marital, at home or in church, community or national, the example of Enoch can provide courage for you.

And Enoch walked with God; and he was not, for God took him. Gen. 5:24.

Pray for the Lord's work in reaching the people on the islands of Trinidad and Tobago, with a combined population of more than 1.2 million, including 36,377 Seventh-day Adventists. Seventh-day Adventist teachings reached the islands through a copy of Ellen G. White's Patriarchs and Prophets, *which someone had sold elsewhere in the West Indies, but which found its way to Trinidad. Through reading it and through correspondence with the International Tract and Missionary Society, several persons became Sabbath observers, even before meeting a Seventh-day Adventist.*

YOUR PERSONAL TESTIMONY

Every Christian needs to develop two basic skills for communicating a knowledge of Christ. One is how to introduce a person to Jesus, and the other is how to share a personal testimony. After Jesus healed the demoniac of Gadara, He instructed him: "Go home to your friends, and tell them what great things the Lord has done for you" (Mark 5:19).

A thought-provoking comment on this story suggests: "This is what everyone can do whose heart has been touched by the grace of God" (*The Desire of Ages*, p. 340). Jesus certainly didn't ask the new convert to go out and argue religion, but simply to relate his personal experience to his friends. Everyone can do that!

Sharing our personal testimony "is Heaven's chosen agency for revealing Christ to the world. . . . These precious acknowledgements . . . , when supported by a Christlike life, have an irresistible power that works for the salvation of souls" (*ibid.*, p. 347).

Your personal testimony is not your life story. It is not about your church—that is a church testimony—but about Jesus and your relationship with Him. You should be able to share it in a few minutes. Write it out to get it well in mind. Your testimony could have three parts: (1) my life before I became a Christian, (2) how I became a Christian, and (3) what Jesus now means in my life.

If you were reared a Christian, your testimony might revolve around an answer to prayer that made Jesus very real in your experience. Or you could share the events surrounding your decision to accept the Christ of your parents as your personal Saviour.

It should not be preachy, but something that non-Christians can relate to. As you in a simple way tell how a relationship with Jesus has given you peace, it will attract many to our Lord.

Remember, your personal testimony has an irresistible power. "This is the witness for which our Lord calls, and for want of which the world is perishing" (*ibid.*, p. 340).

However, Jesus did not permit him, but said to him, "Go home to your friends, and tell them what great things the Lord has done for you, and how He has had compassion on you." Mark 5:19.

Pray that you will have courage to share your personal testimony.

HOW TO BECOME A CHRISTIAN

When you have time, look up the scriptures in today's reading. Then when the Lord provides you with an opportunity to lead someone through this little study, ask them to read these Bible verses, which reveal the simple steps we need to take to become a Christian.

Hebrews 11:6 mentions the first step. We must believe that God exists, otherwise, we can go no further.

Second, we must believe God loves us and wants everyone to be saved (1 Tim. 2:3, 4). What did God do to prove He loves us and does not want us to perish? John 3:16, the most familiar verse in all the Bible, answers that question. I'm sure you can say it from memory.

Luke 15:18 (''I will arise and go to my father'') contains the third step. This means yielding the heart and life to God. It is one thing to know we should turn to God, but another to make a settled decision. Likewise, it is one thing to have good intentions, but another to carry out those intentions.

If you are talking with someone who knows he ought to make a decision to be a Christian but tends to put it off, ask him or her to read Acts 26:27, 28, where King Agrippa admits to Paul: ''You almost persuade me to become a Christian.'' Then invite the person to read the text again, leaving out the word ''almost.'' That one word can mean the difference between being saved or lost, not only for Agrippa, but for you and me.

We need to renew our dedication on a daily basis. Find some time today when you can go to your Father and confess the sins He has been speaking to you about. Ask Him for pardon and claim the promise of 1 John 1:9, which says that if we confess our sinful condition, He will forgive and cleanse us. Then believe that you are forgiven, not on the basis of your feelings, but on the authority of God's Word.

Perhaps someone reading these words has been putting off the matter of baptism. Delay no longer! Heed the apostle Peter in his Pentecost sermon: ''Repent, and . . . be baptized in the name of Jesus Christ'' (Acts 2:38).

> **But as many as received Him, to them He gave the right to become children of God, even to those who believe in His name. John 1:12.**

> *Pray that the light of the gospel may reach the 100,000 nomadic Kababish of Sudan.*

A DOUBLE PORTION

Elijah told Elisha that he would be leaving him soon and asked if he had any requests to make. Now, the young man could have asked for a number of things—Elijah's fame, his honor, or his talent and ability. But instead, he asked for a double portion of the spirit that Elijah had. It might seem rather greedy for Elisha to ask for twice as much of something as Elijah had, but it actually indicated that the younger man sensed his great need.

Elijah responded, in effect, "Son, this isn't for me to give. You have asked for something that comes only from the Lord, but if you see me when I am taken from you, He will grant your request."

Elisha didn't let anything separate him from the man of God. He told the older prophet, "If you're going to Bethel, I'm going too. And if you're going to go to Jericho and to the Jordan River, I'm accompanying you." The younger prophet was determined to stay close to the person of whose spirit he wanted a double portion.

You and I know the source of our power, don't we? It is in staying close to the Lord through a meaningful devotional life, daily study of His Word, constant communion with our Lord, and fellowship with His people.

The miracles Elisha performed were commonplace things—deeds of mercy and kindness. His ministry was very much like that of our Saviour. He received the double portion for which he prayed, and for 50 long years he served the Lord. A double portion awaits you and me in the promised latter rain. This great outpouring of the Holy Spirit without measure will come as the men and women of our churches unite their efforts with those of pastors and church officers. Let us make Elisha's request our request.

And so it was, when they had crossed over, that Elijah said to Elisha, "Ask! What may I do for you, before I am taken away from you?" And Elisha said, "Please let a double portion of your spirit be upon me." 2 Kings 2:9.

Pray for a double portion of God's Holy Spirit and a willingness to meet the requirements for receiving the latter rain.

THE HOLY ANOINTER

The oil from the olive trees of Palestine has become one of the richest symbols of the Holy Spirit to be found in the Bible. The olive crop in Palestine was so basic to the economy that a crop failure was virtually a calamity. And so it is in the Christian church. If we have a dearth of the Holy Spirit, it is a disaster similar to a widespread drought. When experiencing a spiritual dust bowl, we cannot expect a fruitful harvest.

The olive trees in the Garden of Gethsemane bring to mind the prayer life of Jesus. If our Saviour needed communion with His Father, how much more do we! What should we pray about? We should ask for the Holy Spirit in our lives, because "the Spirit awaits our demand and reception" (*Christ's Object Lessons*, p. 121).

"Let Christians put away all dissension and give themselves to God for the saving of the lost. Let them ask in faith for the promised blessing, and it will come" (*Testimonies*, vol. 8, p. 21).

The ancient olive trees, gnarled and twisted by wind and weather, remain evergreen and seem almost indestructible. In human beings the Holy Spirit confronts many gnarled and twisted lives, but His presence keeps the life evergreen, even amid parched surroundings.

Middle Eastern hospitality provided that the guest first be washed with water and then anointed with fragrant oil. The psalmist exclaims, "You anoint my head with oil," symbolic of having the mind or intellect under the influence of the Holy Spirit.

But in the spiritual application we have oriental hospitality in reverse. Instead of the host anointing the guest, it is the Holy Ghost who anoints the host in whose heart He comes to dwell!

The anointing oil was extremely costly, reminding us of the infinite price Jesus paid in order to give us the Holy Anointer.

Reading Leviticus 14 reminds us that cleansing always precedes anointing. When the sinner is saved, the oil is poured out.

The Holy Spirit awaits our demand and reception—today!

"If you then, being evil, know how to give good gifts to your children, how much more will your Father who is in heaven give good things to those who ask Him!" Matt. 7:11.

Pray that God will impress hearts to provide opportunities for the millions of refugees in troubled areas of the world.

LISTEN FOR THE VOICE

The Holy Spirit is like water—cleansing, refreshing, abundant, and freely given. At the same time, He is like fire—purifying, illuminating, searching. Beyond that, He is like the wind—independent, powerful, observable in its effects. Also, He is like oil—healing, comforting, penetrating, reducing friction, quieting troubled waters. Furthermore, He is like rain and dew—refreshing and abundant. He is like a dove—gentle, peaceful, innocent, forgiving; and like a seal—impressing, securing, authenticating.

The Holy Spirit is also like a voice. The Epistle to the Hebrews begins with the declaration that God spoke. The Bible makes it clear that the Holy Spirit communicated to the people through the prophets (2 Peter 1:21). God spoke to Adam, to Moses, and to Abraham.

As Elijah hid on Mount Horeb in a cave, he heard God through a "still, small voice." It was the same mountain on which the Lord had revealed Himself to Moses, and perhaps it was even the same cave.

Elijah experienced an earthquake, a wild, raging tempest, and a sweeping mass of flames. It was reminiscent of the giving of the law, when there was thunder, lightning, the sound of the trumpet, and smoke from the mountain.

The grand display of power impressed the prophet, but it was a "still, small voice" by which the Holy Spirit spoke to him. In our busy schedules we must provide for a daily quiet time during which we can hear that still, small voice, for without it we lack direction and power.

A party of explorers found themselves perplexed by something they found in a remote African jungle. In a clearing they discovered 35 carefully laid fires that had never been lit. They had the appearance of 35 little tepees, with dry leaves surrounded by small, dry twigs, and finally larger pieces of wood arranged in good Boy Scout fashion.

Who built the fires? Why had not even one been lit? The mystery cleared up when the explorers saw dozens of chimpanzees quietly watching from the trees. The chimps had watched campers and copied the art, but they had no fire.

The flame to ignite the fire of global strategy comes from the Holy Spirit—the still small voice.

And after the earthquake a fire, but the Lord was not in the fire; and after the fire a still small voice. 1 Kings 19:12.

Pray for the more than a half million inhabitants of the island of Reunion, in the Indian Ocean, east of Madagascar. There we have more than 1,100 church members in 14 churches.

OUR GREAT NEED

Another beautiful and fitting symbol for the Holy Spirit is the dove. It makes its dwelling place among the rocks (Jer. 48:28).

The Holy Spirit is the one who first leads us to the Rock of Ages. When the Spirit abides in us, He urges us to flee to the "Rock that is higher than I."

Genesis 1:2 pictures the Spirit of God "hovering over the face of the waters." The same word occurs in Deuteronomy 32:11, where it describes a mother bird hovering over its nest of young. The King James Version of the Bible translates the Hebrew word as "fluttereth."

In Genesis 8 Noah releases a dove from the ark, but the waters still lap at the edges of the world, and the dove restlessly hurries back to the ark. We might see here a representation of the Holy Spirit in Old Testament times, resting briefly on certain men and women and then hastening back to the bosom of the Father.

A second time the dove flies forth and returns in the evening with an olive leaf plucked from a tree. We can see in the olive leaf a symbol of peace and reconciliation representative of New Testament times, when the Spirit abode in and on our Lord, the son of reconciliation and the prince of peace.

A third time the dove leaves the ark. This time the dove finds a permanent dwelling place of His own, symbolic of the days since Pentecost, when He stays as an abiding guest wherever He finds the door of a heart open to Him.

At Pentecost the emblem of the Holy Spirit was fire, suggesting the need to burn up sin in the hearts of the disciples. But when the Holy Spirit came upon our Lord, He symbolized Himself as a dove, for our Lord was sinless and had no need of cleansing. But how much we need this cleansing and empowering!

"The inworking ministry of the Holy Spirit is our great need" (*Evangelism*, p. 299). "Oh, how much we all need the baptism of the Holy Ghost" (*ibid.*, p. 369). This is the source of power for global strategy and for daily living.

> **Then Jesus, when He had been baptized, came up immediately from the water; and behold, the heavens were opened to Him, and He saw the Spirit of God descending like a dove and alighting upon Him. Matt. 3:16.**
>
> *Pray for that which is "our great need."*

OVERCOMING ANGER

An English proverb says: "He is a fool who cannot be angry; but he is a wise man who will not." Every minute you are angry you lose 60 seconds of happiness, but you also endanger your health because of the self-destructive nature of the emotion.

Physicians tell us that the influence of anger spreads like poison through the human body. It works upon every nerve, fiber, and tissue—both spiritually and physically. When we give way to temper, we are injuring a part of ourselves that we can never replace. A violent emotion such as anger disturbs the chemistry of the blood. Your blood tends to clot more quickly than normal. This is the body's way of preparing for a fight, caused by your anger, that might result in a wound and bleeding.

Anger makes the muscles at the outlet of the stomach squeeze down so tightly that nothing leaves the stomach, and the entire digestive tract becomes so spastic that many people experience severe abdominal pains either during or after a fit of anger.

The heart rate goes up, and the blood pressure rises. Sometimes a stroke or heart attack occurs during a fit of anger.

John Hunter, one of England's greatest physiologists, had the unfortunate combination of a ready temper and a bad set of coronary arteries. Hunter always said that the first rascal who really got him mad would kill him. His wife came close to finishing him a couple times, but finally it was a colleague at a medical meeting who made him so angry that he dropped dead on the spot from a coronary occlusion.

The anger that we may feel toward someone else is not likely to harm that person—rather, it is much more likely to injure us.

"The depressing and even ruinous effect of anger, discontent, selfishness, or impurity, and, on the other hand, the marvelous life-giving power to be found in cheerfulness, unselfishness, gratitude, should be shown" (*Education*, p. 197).

He who is slow to anger is better than the mighty, and he who rules his spirit than he who takes a city. Prov. 16:32.

Pray for the person who most frequently provokes you to anger.
Pray also for the innocent victims of other people's anger.

THE DAY OF GOOD NEWS

In ancient times the siege of a city meant the cutting off of the food supply, thus resulting in famine, starvation, and death. So it was in the days of Elisha, when Syria laid siege to Samaria.

Four lepers outside the city gate faced starvation if they stayed where they were. But if they went into the city, their own countrymen would kill them. Finally they decided to risk going to the camp of the Syrians.

The four men set out for the enemy camp, expecting to find it full of soldiers from whom they hoped to beg some food. But a surprise awaited them. You can read the story in 2 Kings 7. The lepers discovered that the Syrian camp was deserted. God had caused the Syrian forces to hear the sound of an approaching army, resulting in an immediate retreat.

As the lepers went from tent to tent, they found not only food, but silver, gold, and clothing. As they were eating and drinking, a thought struck them: We rejoice, we eat, we drink, we have wealth, but our countrymen are dying. "Then they said to one another, 'We are not doing what is right. This day is a day of good news, and we remain silent' " (2 Kings 7:9).

We also were lepers, afflicted with the leprosy of sin, and Jesus came and healed us. Through the cross of Christ we have been forgiven. We have found the white clothing of His righteousness and share in the gold of faith and love. Fed with the bread of life, we have also drunk of the water of life, and yet all around us our fellowmen are hungry and thirsty. Because we have the riches of heaven, we must share the good news.

Then they said to one another, "We are not doing what is right. This day is a day of good news, and we remain silent. If we wait until morning light, some punishment will come upon us. Now therefore, come, let us go and tell the king's household." 2 Kings 7:9.

Pray for the Lord's work in Senegal, a country bounded by Mauritania on the north, Mali on the east, Guinea and Guinea-Bissau on the south, and the Atlantic Ocean on the west. It has a population of 7.7 million, 139 of whom are Seventh-day Adventists.

MIRACLES IN MEXICO

In 1891 an Italian-American tailor, S. Marchisio, went to Mexico City to sell the English edition of *The Great Controversy*, and so far as we know, this marked the introduction of the Adventist message into Mexico. Two years later a missionary party of six (including Ora Osborne, a recent convert who had formerly been a missionary for another denomination in Mexico) opened a medical mission and a school in Guadalajara. It seems that it was the first attempt by Seventh-day Adventists to do medical missionary activities outside of the United States, and led to the organization of the first church in Mexico in 1893 or 1894. G. W. Caviness moved to Mexico City in 1899 and organized an English-language school.

The providential leading of God has been most evident in Mexico as in many places in the world. In 1895, far to the south of Mexico, Aurelio Jiménez read of the signs of Christ's second coming from a tract used by a shopkeeper to wrap a loaf of bread. Ten years later some medicine this same man ordered came wrapped in a Seventh-day Adventist missionary journal. Jiménez subscribed, was baptized, and later became a church employee.

The Seventh-day Adventist Church in Mexico has a great sense of mission. Membership has grown from 13,000 in 1950 to 285,524 in 1989. Church leaders there anticipate a membership of 1 million by the close of the century.

After a visit to Mexico, Enoch Oliveira listed the following reasons for the rapid growth of the church:

1. The church is aiming at specific, tangible goals, not merely vague objectives. Every goal is a statement of faith.

2. The church is lay-centered rather than clergy oriented.

3. The church is encouraging church planting rather than the formation of large congregations. There are more than 150 churches and companies in Mexico City alone, the largest of which has a membership of 600.

4. The church members have a consuming love for souls.

So then neither he who plants is anything, nor he who waters, but God who gives the increase. Now he who plants and he who waters are one, and each one will receive his own reward according to his own labor. 1 Cor. 3:7, 8.

Pray for the work in Mexico. Mexico City, with a population of 14 million, is one of the world's most populous cities. It is estimated that by the year 2000 the population will be 19 million, and the metropolitan area, 26 million.

LOYALTY

Love for Christ is the basis for every other loyalty. It's the foundation upon which love for the cause, love for the church, and love for the truth is built.

As you read John 21:15-19, notice the question that Jesus asked: "Simon, son of Jonah, do you love Me?" It was not "Do you love the cause?" or "Do you love the church?" or "Do you love the truth?" but "Do you love Me?" Love demands a personal response. This response to a Person is the foundation upon which love for the cause, love for the church, and love for the truth rests.

What Jesus was saying to Peter, and what He is telling us, is this: "If you really love Me, that love will manifest itself in service to others. It will demonstrate itself in a genuine commitment to advancing My kingdom. And it will show itself in the desire to win others to Me."

How can we say we love Jesus and do little or nothing in the way of genuine service? Peter got the point, and he gave his life in service for others.

It is as if Jesus had said to Peter "I know you love Me, but if you want that love to grow, if you long to experience for Me the same love I feel toward you, enter into the field of service. Love demands growth, and growth comes through service."

Those newly come to faith in Christ need the ministry of those in the church who will feed the lambs. And those of us in the church must have the growth experience that will come to us as we take care of those who are new in the faith.

Two great concerns of many pastors are the idleness of so many Christian people, and the tremendous unfinished task of the church. The challenge of getting the two problems together has been a most serious one. The church should be the pastor's force, not his field of labor.

So when they had eaten breakfast, Jesus said to Simon Peter, "Simon, son of Jonah, do you love Me more than these?" He said to Him, "Yes, Lord; You know that I love You." He said to him, "Feed My lambs." John 21:15.

The Central African Republic, located in the geographical center of Africa, has a population of more than 3 million. It provides freedom of religion. Pray for our Seventh-day Adventist members, who number 1,807.

PLAY WITHOUT RULES?

A rebellious teenage son, growing tired of the rules imposed upon him, asked his father, ''How long before I can please myself?''

''Nobody ever lived that long, son,'' the wise father replied.

''Well, I intend to do exactly that, and very soon,'' the son fired back.

Thoughtfully the father said, ''Then I suppose you will give up your interest in sports. No doubt you will give your tennis racket to your younger brother and resign from the baseball team. And if you really mean to just please yourself, you will not expect me to permit you to have the use of our family car.''

''I'm not giving up anything. Why should I?'' the boy blurted out belligerently.

''But how can you play games without rules? What baseball team would dream of including you if you didn't know the rules and didn't plan to obey the directions of the manager? Neither you nor any other travelers would be safe on the roads unless you stuck rigidly to the traffic laws while driving. You see, in these and many other matters, no man can ever hope to be old enough to please only himself.''

We have here an important fact that even some Christians overlook. The apostle Paul wrote in Romans 15:3: ''For even Christ did not please Himself.''

The life of Jesus was the greatest and most rewarding life ever lived, and yet Jesus lived within the definite and fixed boundaries of His Father's will. He lived not to please Himself, but His Father, and to serve mankind. He said: ''I do not seek My own will but the will of the Father who sent Me'' (John 5:30).

The basic issue in many of our lives that makes the difference between misery and peace is the acceptance of God's will as opposed to self-will. True happiness and peace come at that point in our experience where our will becomes merged with God's will so that His becomes ours, and in pleasing Him we are pleasing ourselves.

For even Christ did not please Himself; but as it is written, ''The reproaches of those who reproached You fell on Me.'' Rom. 15:3.

Pray the prayer that Jesus prayed in Gethsemane and relate it to the major need in your life: ''Not My will, but Yours, be done.''

LOOK ON THE FIELDS

Jesus said: "The field is the world. . . . The harvest is the end of the age" (Matt. 13:38, 39). Many parts of the globe clearly reveal a ripe or ripening harvest. In other areas it is only by the eye of faith that we can see a harvest.

How do we look on the fields? Some would say, With "possibility thinking." Others would say, With "church growth eyes." Certainly we should look on the fields as believers trying to imagine the heart of God reaching out to lost humanity. We should look with the question in our minds, What can I do as my part in the harvest?

First, we should look at the area closest to us—our family, friends, associates, and neighbors. Our greatest influence is naturally on those with whom we are most closely associated. Jesus touched on this principle when He instructed the restored demoniac to go and witness to his friends. And again when He said: "You shall be witnesses to Me in Jerusalem, and in all Judea and Samaria, and to the end of the earth" (Acts 1:8).

Our concern is to reach out in an ever-widening circle until everyone has heard of Jesus' love and special message.

"Not one is made to suffer the wrath of God until the truth has been brought home to his mind and conscience, and has been rejected. . . . Everyone is to have sufficient light to make his decision intelligently" (*The Great Controversy*, p. 605).

Do we really believe that all must have sufficient light to make a decision? What plans do we have to reach every village and city with the three angels' messages? When men and women by the millions are dying in their sins without Christ, are we using our personal assets responsibly? Look on the fields and their potential harvest and see yourself as one of the reapers.

"Do you not say, 'There are still four months and then comes the harvest'? Behold, I say to you, lift up your eyes and look at the fields, for they are already white for harvest!" John 4:35.

Pray for the people of the Seychelles, a group of 86 tropical islands located 700 miles northeast of Madagascar, with a population of 70,000, among whom are 239 Seventh-day Adventists. Seventh-day Adventist work in the Seychelles began in 1930 when an evangelist from Mauritius was sent there.

WAYS AND MEANS

In Luke 8 we have the parable of the sower. Jesus tells why the seed is sown, when, and what will take place afterward. But He doesn't mention how to sow the seed. He leaves the "how" up to us. Jesus is dealing with principles, not methods. The great commission is another example of this.

God allows us to devise methods and approaches of sowing the gospel seed and getting the good news to everyone everywhere. Let's take a closer look at this principle.

"Those who have the spiritual oversight of the church should devise ways and means by which an opportunity may be given to every member of the church to act some part in God's work. Too often in the past this has not been done. Plans have not been clearly laid and fully carried out whereby the talents of all might be employed in active service. There are but few who realize how much has been lost because of this" (*Testimonies*, vol. 9, p. 116).

Undoubtedly one reason why God in His wisdom has left it with believers to choose ways to spread the gospel is that He knew that changing times would require differing methods, and also that varying approaches would have to be used to meet the needs of different cultures.

The gospel commission instructs us to make disciples. In training disciples we should:

1. Major in principles rather than methods.

2. Major in meeting the needs of people rather than on developing and imparting techniques.

3. Major in developing the thought processes rather than skills.

4. Major in learning to trust God rather than teaching theories about God.

You might be wondering why a devotional book is talking about making disciples. The reason is simple—this is what Jesus asks every believer to do, and happiness comes from doing what He invites us to do.

In making disciples, the basic challenge is to develop ways and means that will lead men and women to trust God fully.

"Now the parable is this: The seed is the word of God. Those by the wayside are the ones who hear; then the devil comes and takes away the word out of their hearts, lest they should believe and be saved." Luke 8:11, 12.

Pray that God will guide you and your family in devising ways and means to plant the gospel seed wherever you go.

DESIGN DEMANDS A DESIGNER

We can be thankful for our unique system of Christian education, which, while always upholding the inspiration of Scripture, does not ignore the evidence of scientific research. Indeed, Adventist educators and students are involved in such research.

Speaking of the founding of Battle Creek College, the prophetic voice of one of our pioneers explained: "The great object in the establishment of our college was to give correct views, showing the harmony of science and Bible religion" (*Testimonies*, vol. 4, p. 274).

The beauty and order evident in the universe demand an intelligent Creator. Where there is design, there must be a designer. And the more intricate the design, the more intelligent must be the one who produced it. As the Bible says: "For since the creation of the world His invisible attributes are clearly seen, being understood by the things that are made, even His eternal power and Godhead, so that they are without excuse" (Rom. 1:20).

Many scientists are devout believers in the Creator God. Dr. Edwin Grant Conklin, when biologist at Princeton University, made this frequently quoted statement: "The probability of life originating from accident is comparable to the probability of the unabridged dictionary resulting from an explosion in a printshop."

At one time each one of us was a single fertilized egg smaller than the period at the end of this sentence. Within a half hour 2 trillionths of an ounce of DNA (deoxyribonucleic acid) determines an immeasurable number of traits that characterize the person that baby born nine months later will grow up to be.

Creation, with its teaching of an all-powerful Creator, provides the foundation for true worship. Belief in creation by such a God gives us a basis for true self-worth.

Such belief is the remedy for pessimism, loneliness, and meaninglessness. Belief in a Creator provides moral standards and obligations, and establishes the foundation for the sacredness of life.

By the word of the Lord the heavens were made, and all the host of them by the breath of His mouth. Ps. 33:6.

Pray for the more than 51 million people in the Ukraine, the breadbasket of the Soviet Union. Slightly larger than France, it is home to nearly one fifth of the population of the U.S.S.R.

JOHN BYINGTON

On this very day 139 years ago John Byington made a decision that would affect your life and mine. It was on March 20, 1852, that Byington fully decided to observe the seventh-day Sabbath. It was on this day also that his daughter Teresa was buried. The death of a cherished daughter so touched his heart that he felt that God was speaking to him. John and his wife were baptized in July of 1852.

Byington, first president of the General Conference, had a part in establishing the first Seventh-day Adventist church school and the first church building to be dedicated in our denomination.

He had been a Methodist Episcopal minister and had directed the construction of their first church in Buck's Bridge, New York. But the slavery problem turned him into the ranks of the Wesleyan Methodists, and he then built a church for them. A copy of an early *Review and Herald* called Byington's attention to the seventh-day Sabbath. James and Ellen White visited the Byingtons several times. At the end of a day's work this farmer-preacher would gather his family under the shade of a tree in the garden, and there they would sing favorite hymns, read the Bible, and kneel in prayer.

In 1853 one of the members in Buck's Bridge conducted a home school. Martha Byington, John's 19-year-old daughter, was the first teacher. About two years later the Bucks Bridge Seventh-day Adventist Church was dedicated, the first Adventist church to be thus set apart. The home school was the first Adventist church school. It has multiplied into the largest Protestant parochial school system. From that first church a light has been kindled that will continue to spread until there will be "memorials for Him in every city and village" (*Testimonies*, vol. 9, p. 29).

Perhaps there is a decision you need to make today that will influence many others as did that of John Byington many years ago. Decisions that seem small to us may indeed have far-reaching consequences. John Byington served the General Conference as president from 1863 to 1865, and the next quarter century he spent ministering among the new churches in Michigan.

For who has despised the day of small things? Zech. 4:10.

Pray for Seventh-day Adventist schools around the world—teachers, students, and parents.

HE DIED FOR ME

A pastor saw a man decorating an old grave with beautiful flowers. Thinking he might offer some word of comfort, the pastor inquired, "Is it your wife who lies here?"

After a period of silence, the man explained to the minister, "The man who lies here died in my place. When the war broke out between the states, my name was drawn in the draft. I had a family, a wife, and four little children who were entirely dependent upon me. A young man who lived on the next farm volunteered to go as my substitute, which was allowed in the Civil War.

"His mother was a widow, and he was her only son. He went into the army in my place and was killed in action. She has lived with my family ever since, and it is my privilege to care for her. I support her just as her own boy would have done. He died in my place, and I live in his place."

As we think about this experience from the days of the Civil War, it reminds us of One who died in our place so that we might live. We need to ask ourselves the question Are we living to please ourselves, or are we living to please Him?

It would be extreme ingratitude if the young man did not provide for the needs of the mother of the one who died for him. But what are we doing for the One whose Son died for us? The greatest thing we can do is to tell others of His love.

In the light of what Jesus has done for us, we have no right to live only for ourselves.

For the love of Christ constrains us, because we judge thus: that if One died for all, then all died; and He died for all, that those who live should live no longer for themselves, but for Him who died for them and rose again. 2 Cor. 5:14, 15.

Pray for the work of God in Zimbabwe, with a population of 8.6 million, including 120,859 Seventh-day Adventists. In 1894 Cecil Rhodes, prime minister of Cape Colony, instructed the administrator in Bulawayo to permit Seventh-day Adventist representatives to select whatever land they needed in what was then Rhodesia. On a 12,000-acre site some 30 miles west of Bulawayo, Adventists developed a mission station and school. The school became Solusi College.

A THOUGHTFUL HOUR EACH DAY

We are approaching the week sometimes called Passion Week, or Holy Week—the anniversary of the closing events in the life of our Lord upon earth. At this season each year many Christians find a rich blessing in reviewing these final events in the life of Christ. We trust it will be so for you next week as we attempt to focus on those events.

The limited space in our daily readings provides only for a brief outline of that day's events, but as you try to relive those experiences each day, Christ will become more real in your experience. Those who make time for extra reading in the Gospels or *The Desire of Ages* will find an additional reward.

"It would be well for us to spend a thoughtful hour each day in contemplation of the life of Christ. We should take it point by point, and let the imagination grasp each scene, especially the closing ones. As we thus dwell upon His great sacrifice for us, our confidence in Him will be more constant, our love will be quickened, and we shall be more deeply imbued with His spirit" (*The Desire of Ages*, p. 83).

Although nearly 2,000 years have passed since the Crucifixion, the power of the Christ of the cross is still evident. During this next week more people will attend Christian services than at any other time of the year. It is easy to be critical of those who attend church only on Christmas and Easter, but let's take a positive attitude and recognize that the Holy Spirit will be able to reach some of those who will hear of the birth and death of the Saviour. Many will choose this season to unite with the church. In certain areas Seventh-day Adventist pastors, evangelists, and lay preachers will conduct special services during Holy Week, and many of those who listen to them will decide for Christ and His message.

"And I, if I am lifted up from the earth, will draw all peoples to Myself." John 12:32.

Pray for a mighty moving of God's Holy Spirit during this coming week. Pray for those who will be presenting the message of Christ and for those who will be making decisions for Christ.

TELL IT EVERYWHERE

On this Saturday evening before His triumphal entry into Jerusalem, Jesus attended a feast at the house of Simon, who had been healed of leprosy. It was on this occasion that Mary broke the alabaster box and anointed Jesus with the costly spikenard ointment it contained.

While others criticized her act, Jesus defended her, saying: "Wherever this gospel is preached throughout the whole world, what this woman did will also be spoken of as a memorial to her" (Mark 14:9).

Why did Jesus give such emphasis to her deed? Why did He say to tell about it everywhere? Consider five points: 1. Mary was a sinner who had found forgiveness through Jesus. 2. She loved the Saviour very much. 3. She put her love into action. 4. She had a sense of urgency. 5. And she did what she could.

Imagine what could happen if every believer—every Christian man and woman and child—would put his or her love into action and do what he or she is capable of doing to share with others the fragrance of Christ's love. Think of the transformation it would produce in our own lives, as well as the blessings it would bring to others. Don't wait for some future opportunity, but do what you can where you are with what you have.

Mary displayed the qualities that will make for a finished evangelism—the spirit of Global Strategy. As we are all sinners in need of forgiveness, we love our Saviour and want to put our love into action. As Adventists discerning the signs of the times, we have a sense of urgency. If we will take that one additional step, as Mary did so long ago, our task would soon be finished. What did Mary do? The Bible simply says that she did what she could. Every Christian has spiritual gifts given for service. We cannot all do the same thing because we have different gifts, but we can all do something. If each person who is empowered by the Spirit of Christ would do what he or she can with the gifts he or she has, think what would happen. May He also say of us that we did what we could.

"She has done what she could. She has come beforehand to anoint My body for burial." Mark 14:8.

Pray for our work in Jordan, where the first Arab convert was a teacher baptized in 1930. The population of Jordan is 2.7 million, and the Seventh-day Adventist membership is probably only a little more than 600.

THE TRIUMPHAL ENTRY

Five hundred years before Jesus' birth, the prophet Zechariah foretold His triumphal entry, which took place at Jerusalem the Sunday before the Resurrection. It was the Passover season, and historical records indicate that hundreds of thousands of Jews might have been in Jerusalem at the time.

Jesus came riding on a colt as was the Jewish custom for a royal entry. The people spread their cloaks in front of Him and waved palm branches as a symbol of victory. The crowd shouted Hosanna! which means "save now." It meant different things to different people in that great throng. To many it expressed the hope that Jesus would take the throne and drive the Roman army from Jerusalem.

Unlike the triumphal procession of an earthly conqueror, He had no train of trophies made up of chained captives, but there were captives of Satan set free by a loving Christ. The blind who had received their sight marched behind the resurrected Lazarus, who guided the donkey. The mute whose tongue had been loosed by the Healer's power shouted the loudest hosannas, and the restored cripples waved their palm branches the most vigorously. To all of them, hosanna meant "He has saved us."

When the Pharisees, jealous of His popularity, complained about such noisy demonstrations, Jesus said, "If these should keep silent, the stones would immediately cry out" (Luke 19:40).

When the procession reached the brow of the hill, the Temple came into view, its marble and gold tinted splendidly by the setting sun. Jesus paused and wept for the unrepentant city. The priests complained to the Roman officers about the commotion, and the officers in turn blamed the priests and rulers for the disturbance. It seems that in the confusion Jesus, unnoticed, made His way for a quiet visit to the Temple before returning to Bethany, where He spent the night in prayer.

As the priests complained and the Roman officers blamed, Jesus was lost sight of. This season is an appropriate time to examine our attitudes. May we be found rejoicing because the King has made a triumphal entry into our hearts.

"Rejoice greatly, O daughter of Zion! Shout, O daughter of Jerusalem! Behold, your King is coming to you; He is just and having salvation, lowly and riding on a donkey, a colt, the foal of a donkey." Zech. 9:9.

Pray that the three angels' messages may once again be proclaimed in the People's Republic of the Congo.

PROMISE WITHOUT PERFORMANCE

A fig tree normally has fruit beginning to develop before the leaves appear, but on Monday morning of the Passion Week, as Jesus returned to the Temple, He saw a fig tree with leaves but no fruit. Jesus, the sustainer of life, withdrew life support from the barren fig tree as an acted parable. Unfortunately, that tree, with its pretentious and promising foliage, symbolized many in the Jewish nation. Like the fig tree the Jewish nation was impressive to outward appearance, with its magnificent Temple and solemn ceremonies, but it lacked the spiritual fruit it should have been producing.

On the same day that Jesus cut off life support from the barren fig tree He drove the money changers out of the Temple, just as He had done once before early in His ministry. The priests and money changers were greedily taking advantage of the worshipers' need for Temple coins and animals for sacrifice. They charged exorbitant prices and exploited the pilgrims who had come to worship.

As Jesus forced the money changers out of the Temple, others were entering the Temple in search of the Healer. The presence of Jesus made the Temple truly a house of prayer, and the blind, deaf, and crippled found healing. Those who were guilty of corrupting the Temple had fled, and those who recognized their spiritual needs remained and were blessed.

It was on this Monday, the tenth day of the Jewish month (Ex. 12:3), that the Jews selected the Passover lamb. It was to be a male without blemish, representing Jesus.

As evening came, Jesus once again left Jerusalem and returned to Bethany. Try to imagine His thoughts as He reflected on the events of the day—His people's lack of spiritual fruit, the merciless money changers, the sincere seekers, and the spotless lamb.

> **And seeing a fig tree by the road, He came to it and found nothing on it but leaves, and said to it, "Let no fruit grow on you ever again." And immediately the fig tree withered away. Matt. 21:19.**

> *Pray for the people of Israel, a country with a population of 4.4 million, comprising Jews, Muslims, Druzes, and Christians, all in the small area of 7,847 square miles on the eastern end of the Mediterranean Sea. Abram La Rue visited Jerusalem sometime between 1890 and 1897. In 1904 L. R. Conradi baptized three converts in Jaffa and organized the Jaffa-Jerusalem church.*

96

WE WOULD SEE JESUS

As Jesus and His disciples returned to Jerusalem from Bethany on the Tuesday morning before the Passover, they passed the barren fig tree that He had cursed the previous day. It had dried up at the roots. Jesus proceeded to the Temple and began teaching the people. The Sanhedrin, the chief judicial council of the Jews, had met early that morning to devise a plan whereby they might have Jesus condemned. Now they approached Him in the Temple with the challenge "By what authority are You doing these things?" (Matt. 21.23). Wisely Jesus countered with a question that faced them with a dilemma whichever way they might have answered it.

The parables recorded in Matthew 21-25 were given on this day, including the parable of the two sons, the wicked husbandman, the marriage of the king's son, the fig tree, the porter, the 10 virgins, and the talents.

It was on this Tuesday, Christ's last day in the Temple, that the Greeks came seeking Christ and proclaiming, "We would see Jesus." At the beginning of Christ's life men had come from the East in search of Him, and now at the close of His life men arrived from the West. The Greeks represented the nations and people groups of all the Western world, from which many would eventually come to Jesus. This foreshadowing of the gathering of the Gentiles greatly encouraged our Lord at the very time when so many of His own people were rejecting Him.

It was on this occasion that the voice of the Father was heard from heaven for the third time during Christ's ministry. The first was at His baptism, the second at His transfiguration, and now the Father's voice was heard in the Temple court in the presence of Gentile inquirers.

Although they may not verbalize it, you will meet many today whose heart cry is "We would see Jesus." May they see Him in us.

Now there were certain Greeks among those who came up to worship at the feast. Then they came to Philip, who was from Bethsaida of Galilee, and asked him, saying, "Sir, we wish to see Jesus." John 12:20, 21.

Pray for the United States of America, land from which many missionaries have traveled to all parts of the world, that our members may never lose the sense of mission to all the world.

IN HIS STEPS

On Tuesday afternoon of the Holy Week, after the visit of the Greeks, we find Christ going with His disciples to the Mount of Olives. Tuesday was such an eventful day that we ran out of space even to outline all that happened. (In contrast, Christ evidently spent Wednesday in quiet retirement.)

It was on the Mount of Olives that Tuesday afternoon that Jesus spoke the words recorded in Matthew 24 and 25. We often refer to Matthew 24 as Christ's own prophecy. There He gives a panoramic picture of events from His ascension to His second coming, including many prophetic signs. In Matthew 25 He gives the parable of the 10 virgins and deals with practical Christianity and our preparation for His return.

Reliving these days in the life of our Saviour reminds us that we do not need to take a tour of the Middle East in order to walk in His footsteps.

"Many feel that it would be a great privilege to visit the scenes of Christ's life on earth, to walk where He trod, to look upon the lake beside which He loved to teach, and the hills and valleys on which His eyes so often rested. But we need not go to Nazareth, to Capernaum, or to Bethany, in order to walk in the steps of Jesus. We shall find His footprints beside the sickbed, in the hovels of poverty, in the crowded alleys of the great city, and in every place where there are human hearts in need of consolation. In doing as Jesus did when on earth, we shall walk in His steps" (*The Desire of Ages*, p. 640).

By reliving this last eventful week in the life of our Lord, may we truly experience what it means to walk in His steps.

For to this you were called, because Christ also suffered for us, leaving us an example, that you should follow His steps. 1 Peter 2:21.

Pray for the people of Greece. The first known Seventh-day Adventist convert in Greece was George Brakas, who had become convinced of the Sabbath by studying the Bible. He had no knowledge of other Sabbath observers until he heard of a church in Turkey. Until he finally received a visit, every 15 days he sent a letter addressed to "The Church Which Keeps the Sabbath."

NOT MY WILL BUT YOURS, FATHER

Thursday was Nisan 13 on the Jewish calendar. That morning the disciples asked Jesus where they should prepare the Passover. Jesus told them to enter the city and follow a man carrying a pitcher of water. They were to tell the man, "The Master needs your guest room for the Passover."

After they had eaten the Passover meal that Thursday evening, Jesus instituted the memorial service that would serve as a reminder of His death and a promise of His return. As a preparatory part of this service, Jesus washed the feet of each disciple. After doing so, He explained that He had given them an example that they were to follow.

Next Jesus broke unleavened bread and gave it to them to eat as a symbol of His body, which would be broken. He gave them grape juice to drink as a symbol of His blood, which would so soon be shed. And He gave them hope and assurance when He said: "I will not drink of this fruit of the vine from now on until that day when I drink it new with you in My Father's kingdom" (Matt. 26:29).

Judas got up from this supper and went out for his third meeting with the Jewish leaders. The first was on Saturday night, and the second on Tuesday night. Jesus remained with the eleven in the upper room and shared what we find recorded in John 14. Jesus' parting counsel, begun in the upper room, continued on the way to Gethsemane and climaxed with the longest prayer of Jesus, recorded in John 17.

As He and His disciples approached Gethsemane, He asked Peter, James, and John to join Him in special prayer in the garden. There Jesus felt the separation from His Father, caused by all mankind's sin upon Him. In that last fearful struggle with the tempter, the destiny of the human race was settled. Christ had conquered the enemy.

The three disciples had slept through His agony. The traitor came with the mob and betrayed the Saviour with a kiss.

He went a little farther and fell on His face, and prayed, saying, "O My Father, if it is possible, let this cup pass from Me; nevertheless, not as I will, but as You will." Matt. 26:39.

Pray for the experience of full surrender.

THE SEVEN WORDS

It was after midnight when the mob led Jesus out of Gethsemane and headed for the palace of Annas, the ex-high priest, who in some respects still had more influence than his successor. Next He must go before Caiaphas, the current high priest. The strategy of the priests was to press two charges against Christ—blasphemy, which would bring condemnation from the Jewish authorities, and sedition, which would cause the Romans to find Him guilty. Such were the charges on which the Sanhedrin pronounced Jesus guilty and worthy of death. But only the Roman authorities could sentence a person to death, so Pilate and Herod had to try Him. Neither of these rulers believed Jesus to be guilty, but they lacked the courage to defend Him against the angry mob. Finally, Pilate placed the responsibility upon the mob by giving them a choice between Christ or Barabbas. One would be set free, and the other crucified. The choice was made—Barabbas would go free, and Jesus was led to Calvary.

According to Mark 15:25, it was about nine o'clock in the morning when, after a sleepless night, the Roman soldiers placed Jesus on the cross between two thieves. Seven times He spoke from the cross:

1. Of the Romans and the Jews who condemned Him, He said, "Father, forgive them, for they do not know what they do" (Luke 23:34).

2. To the penitent thief on the cross beside Him, He said, "Assuredly, I say to you, today you will be with Me in Paradise" (verse 43).

3. Speaking first to His mother and then to John, He said, "Woman, behold your son!" Then He told the disciple, "Behold your mother!" (John 19:26, 27).

4. Feeling the separation caused by the sin of the world, He agonized, "My God, My God, why have You forsaken Me?" (Matt. 27:46).

5. In order to fulfill the scripture, Jesus said, "I thirst" (John 19:28).

6. After receiving the vinegar, Jesus announced, "It is finished!" (verse 30).

7. At three o'clock in the afternoon, after six hours on the cross, Jesus said, "Father, into Your hands I commend My spirit" (Luke 23:46).

Just before sunset that Friday Jesus was tenderly laid to rest in the tomb of Joseph of Arimathea.

Then he said to Jesus, "Lord, remember me when You come into Your kingdom." Luke 23:42.

Pray for those who have recently experienced a death in the family.

ACCORDING
TO THE COMMANDMENT

So numerous were the events of the Friday of the Crucifixion that space for yesterday's reading did not permit even a mention of all that happened. There was the supernatural darkness that began at noon and lasted while Jesus hung on the cross (Luke 23:45), and the earthquake and a special resurrection that took place when Jesus drew His last breath (Matt. 27:51, 52).

Joseph of Arimathea, who until then had, like Nicodemus, been a secret follower of Jesus, asked Pilate's permission to care for the burial of Jesus. "The very event that destroyed the hopes of the disciples convinced Joseph and Nicodemus of the divinity of Jesus" (*The Desire of Ages*, pp. 775, 776). Meanwhile, the women prepared spices and fragrant oils to embalm the body, but when the sun set that Friday evening, in obedience to the teaching of Jesus, "they rested on the Sabbath according to the commandment" (Luke 23:56).

Through the years this verse more than any other has been a help to me in deciding what and what not to do on the Sabbath. The action of the women certainly does not imply that to them the Sabbath was more important than Jesus. It was because Christ Himself had blessed that day and made it holy that they rested, and by doing so they were showing the deepest respect to Christ, the lawgiver.

The marvelous part of it all was that the miracle of the Resurrection, so soon to take place, made the anointing and embalming of Christ's body entirely unnecessary. Actually, the anointing had been done in advance of His death by Mary at Simon's house (Mark 14:8).

While the followers of Jesus were quietly resting on the Sabbath, others were going about their usual business. Not even the priests and Pharisees were enjoying the Sabbath rest, for we read that they remembered that Jesus had said He would rise after three days. They went to see Pilate and demanded that he make the tomb secure. The Roman official told them to make it as secure as they knew how, which they did, sealing the stone and setting the guard.

Then they returned and prepared spices and fragrant oils. And they rested on the Sabbath according to the commandment. Luke 23:56.

Pray for those who will be observing their first Sabbath this week, and think back to the first Sabbath you can remember.

HE IS RISEN

Early on Sunday morning the women, who in order to honor the Sabbath, had interrupted their preparation of spices for use in anointing the body of Jesus, came to the tomb bringing them. They discovered the stone covering the entrance to the tomb had been rolled away and the tomb was empty. An angel confirmed that Christ had risen, even as Jesus had predicted.

It was not until Jesus spoke her name that Mary, the sister of Lazarus, really believed that Christ had indeed risen from the dead.

We have no evidence that the women struggled on Friday afternoon to decide whether to anoint the body of Jesus or to keep the Sabbath, but if there was any doubt then, they had no doubt now that they had made the right decision, for now the embalming was unnecessary. If we could see the end from the beginning, we would know that it is always right to obey God's Word.

Jesus had predicted that after three days He would rise again, and that prophecy of His resurrection, the fulfillment of which so many witnesses confirmed, became the theme of the apostles' preaching.

Late on Sunday afternoon two of the disciples were walking to Emmaus, a little town approximately eight miles from Jerusalem. Even though they had heard the report of the women that the tomb was empty, the two men were not convinced of the Resurrection until they had invited Jesus to their home. "Then their eyes were opened and they knew Him" (Luke 24:31).

They hastened to Jerusalem to tell the eleven disciples that they had seen the risen Christ. There they learned that Peter also had seen the resurrected Saviour. As they were excitedly sharing experiences, Jesus suddenly appeared in that upper room, showed them the scars in His hands and feet, and invited them to touch Him. Jesus had risen in triumph over death, and because He lives, we too may live forever!

"Behold My hands and My feet, that it is I Myself. Handle Me and see, for a spirit does not have flesh and bones as you see I have." Luke 24:39.

Pray for many who attend church only two or three times a year that they may have their spiritual interest quickened today and start their journey to the kingdom.

WHO SHALL ROLL AWAY THE STONE?

On the third day after Christ's crucifixion, as the women approached the tomb, the big problem in their minds was "Who shall roll away the stone?" It was a rather large stone, and the Roman and Jewish authorities had taken special efforts to make the tomb secure.

That which was a big problem to the women was no problem at all to God. "An angel of the Lord descended from heaven, and came and rolled back the stone from the door, and sat on it" (Matt. 28:2).

When we place a loved one in the tomb, it seems so final, but our Lord declared, "I am the resurrection and the life" (John 11:25). The resurrection of Jesus is a pledge that all the dead will rise again.

As the angel rolled away that great stone from the tomb of Christ, so Christ's resurrection rolls away the stone of doubt and unbelief from the hearts of men.

The One who gives life to all mankind will restore life in the resurrection. Paul asks, "Why should it be thought incredible by you that God raises the dead?" (Acts 26:8). If God is the life-giver, He can certainly restore life.

Mary failed to recognize the Lord because the tears in her eyes blurred her vision, and her heart was crushed with grief. Often it is the same with us. Our tear-dimmed eyes do not discern Him, though He is right by our side.

Most of us can think of times in our experience when some stone has stood between us and our path into the future. We wanted to move forward, but some boulder blocked the way. The situation appeared impossible as we looked ahead. It seemed we just could not go on. But as we kept moving forward, even though we could not see a solution, God in some marvelous way rolled away the stone.

When tragedy crosses our path—perhaps it is a devastating accident or the death of a loved one—we may not have the power to remove the stone of grief. But God does!

God can roll away the stone of death. Because Jesus lives, our dead, too, shall live.

Jesus said to her, "I am the resurrection and the life. He who believes in Me, though he may die, he shall live." John 11:25.

Pray for our faithful church members in Czechoslovakia that they may continue to win people for the Lord.

CONVINCING EVIDENCE

The very precautions that the enemies of Jesus took to prevent the fulfillment of the prophecy of His resurrection constitute the strongest evidence of its fact.

The Passover season was a great festival among the Jews. Pilgrims crowded Jerusalem, some camping in tents along the streets, and others wandering about all night.

It is absurd to think that 11 disciples could have rolled away the stone and removed the Lord's body without someone seeing them. If they had smuggled His body out of the tomb, several people would have known about it.

Within seven weeks the disciples were publicly proclaiming the fact of the Resurrection. If anyone could have produced the body of Christ, it would have forever silenced their preaching. No Roman soldier and no Jewish priest offered to disprove the fact of the Resurrection by displaying the body of Christ.

The sight of the angels and the glorified Saviour had caused the Roman soldiers to become as dead men. They hurried to the city, telling those they met of the glorious event. The angry priests commanded them to say "His disciples came by night, and stole Him away while we slept." Surely not all of the approximately 100 Roman soldiers guarding the tomb would have been asleep at precisely the same moment.

If the soldiers were asleep, how could they know what happened? Or if the disciples had stolen the body, would not the priests have been the first to condemn them? If the guards had been asleep on duty, would not the priests have been foremost in accusing them to Pilate?

Sleeping at their post was an offense punishable by death, but the priests promised to secure the safety of the guards if they would give a false report.

Dr. J.N.D. Anderson, while dean of the faculty of law at the University of London, was a professor visiting at the Harvard Law School. In a talk given at Harvard he examined many theories of the Resurrection, but concluded, "The most probable account is the biblical one."

To whom He also presented Himself alive after His suffering by many infallible proofs, being seen by them during forty days and speaking of the things pertaining to the kingdom of God. Acts 1:3.

Andorra is a wealthy country located between Spain and France, and is officially Catholic. Pray for a strong Seventh-day Adventist witness in this materialistic land.

104

GET ONTO HIGHER GROUND

One morning the residents of the small town of Fort Morgan, Colorado, woke up to find that they had neither electricity nor water.

During the night a torrential rain had drenched the eastern foothills. Ten inches of rain had fallen in a very short time. Such steep and rocky terrain cannot absorb such sudden downpours.

The immense volume of water drained into the Platte River and began rushing to the plains below. The authorities sent an alarm downstream to the communities in the path of the flood. Fortunately, Fort Morgan is high enough above the river so that there was no threat to its people, but the farmers living in the river bottom faced great danger.

The sheriff organized a telephone brigade, and he and his men raced from farm to farm of those who did not have telephones, arousing them to their peril.

Early in the morning one of the sheriff's deputies banged on the door of a river-bottom farmer, shouting, "A flood is coming down the river! Get onto higher ground as fast as you can!"

It was not the first flood warning in the 17 years the farmer had lived there, and no harm had come to him yet. "I'll believe it when I see it," he grumbled as he crawled back into bed.

About an hour later a deep roar from upriver awakened him. He ran to the door and looked out to see a wall of muddy water 25 feet high moving in his direction, and now he had no time to run. It was not until several days later that searchers found the bodies of the farmer, his wife, and his hired man in the debris downriver

Like the Colorado farmer, we have heard many warnings over the years. But we are still here, and it is easy to become hardened to the appeals to get ready for those things that will come upon the earth. Some will listen and take refuge in Christ, but unfortunately, many others, like the Colorado farmer, will not listen.

"Hypocrites! You know how to discern the face of the sky, but you cannot discern the signs of the times." Matt. 16:3.

Pray that you and your loved ones may heed the call to get onto higher ground spiritually before the coming flood of destruction sweeps over our old world.

VICTORIOUS FAITH

Abdelsai, a Muslim, was born in the slums of a large city. After the death of his mother and the remarriage of his father, the child was treated cruelly, and physically abused by his father. Having to work like an adult, Abdelsai never had play time, but he did enjoy reading. When he was older, because of his self-taught knowledge, he managed to enroll in the university.

He assiduously read the Koran, but curiously he found his attention drawn to the passages about Jesus. By rereading them, he got to know them by heart.

One day at a friend's house, while listening to the radio, he heard the words "This is the Voice of Prophecy . . ." His friend wanted to change the radio station, but Abdelsai insisted that he wanted to continue to listen. Carefully noting the time of the program, he went again to his friend's house when the program came on again and implored him for permission to listen to it. In return, he paid him with some tea for the privilege he was enjoying. And that is how he was able to contact the Seventh-day Adventist Church. He was given Bible studies, and soon he was baptized.

Unfortunately, Muslims of his country are not allowed to practice the Christian religion publicly. Eventually the day came when the police called at his home and took him to prison. Although they released him within a few days, they still carefully watched Abdelsai. He was unable to have any more comforting contacts with his Christian friends.

Abdelsai is now an important teacher of Arabic at the university, and is considered as a living encyclopedia. The pastor who told this story spent an unforgettable evening with Abdelsai and his wife in their home. After a simple but delicious meal, and an evening of conversation about the Bible, the time for prayer came. They took off their shoes, stood, and with hands lifted to heaven, spent a moment in praising the Lord, and then they knelt down and brought their requests before Him.

Choosing rather to suffer affliction with the people of God than to enjoy the passing pleasures of sin. Heb. 11:25.

Pray for the work of God in the Comoro Islands, consisting of four islands and many coral islets, between the northern tip of Madagascar and the African mainland. The religion is Muslim. Population of these islands is 484,000.

MAN'S WAY
VERSUS GOD'S WAY

God gave quite clear instruction as to how Israel should transport the ark of the covenant. It had been constructed with handles or wooden staves that fit into rings along the side so that the hands of the Levites would not touch the sacred chest containing God's holy law. The staves rested on the shoulders of the men who were carrying the ark, and there was something personal about the ark being carried on the shoulders of the Levites. Hauling the ark on a cart lessened the sense of personal responsibility.

It was probably from the Philistines that they got the idea of moving the ark on an ox cart. God expects more of His enlightened people than He does of those who have not had the privilege of His revelation. The Philistines in their ignorance could do things that God would not allow His chosen people to do.

In our day modern technology can be a blessing to the work of God, but we must be careful that we do not allow the Lord's tasks to become impersonal. Fancy new Philistine carts may take a load from our shoulders, but we cannot transfer personal responsibility. God's work must be done by God's people in God's way.

The problem that resulted in the death of Uzzah was not that the oxen stumbled, or that the cart shook, or that the ark lurched. There should have been no oxen and cart to begin with. No matter how many Uzzahs try to steady the ark, we are working on the wrong problem, and we are not going to help matters by making better carts and hiring trained Uzzahs.

The convenient way of transporting the ark on wheels was right in the eyes of all the people, but that still did not make it proper in the sight of God.

And when they came to Chidon's threshing floor, Uzzah put out his hand to hold the ark, for the oxen stumbled. 1 Chron. 13:9.

Please pray for God's blessing to rest upon the Seventh-day Adventist program in Malawi, formerly Nyasaland. Malawi borders Tanzania on the north and east; Mozambique on the east, south, and west; and Zambia on the west.

The first Seventh-day Adventist missionary to Nyasaland was George James of London, England, who arrived in 1891 after attending Battle Creek College. Now there are 84,763 Seventh-day Adventists among a total population of more than 7.7 million in Malawi.

TAKING THINGS FOR GRANTED

For 20 years the sacred ark containing God's holy law remained in the house of Abinadab. We can imagine that at first the family felt great excitement at having in their home such a holy object. But with the passing of time it seems that the sacred ark became just another piece of furniture.

We face the same danger of growing so familiar with the things of God—the gospel, family worship, and the ordinances of the church—that we lose our sense of reverence for holy things. Growing up in a Christian home, we may easily mistake the language of Christianity for its life and become parrots of pious phrases. There is no greater hindrance to genuine spirituality than a superficial familiarity with Christianity—form that has lost its substance.

When we take holy things for granted, nothing worth mentioning happens. And that seems to be the case during the 20 years that the ark remained in the house of Abinadab.

The Bible tells of another house in which the ark of the Lord rested for a much shorter period—only three months—but in that time wonders happened. Because its inhabitants had deep respect for the holy ark, God blessed that house and the people in it.

Uzzah failed to show respect for the ark containing the holy law of God. He touched that which was holy, and even though his motive was good, he died for his disrespect. Perhaps we can understand the story better when we know that he was a son of Abinadab, in whose house the ark rested for 20 years. Uzzah certainly had every chance to know better, but he grew careless and took things for granted. The blessing of God rests upon those who show respect for that which is holy.

The ark of God remained with the family of Obed-Edom in his house three months. And the Lord blessed the house of Obed-Edom and all that he had. 1 Chron. 13:14.

Pray for the advance of the work in Poland, where the Adventist Church began in 1888 as a result of two members leaving the Crimea in Russia and settling in eastern Poland. Within three years the first Polish Seventh-day Adventist church was established as a result of their witness. Today there are 4,743 Seventh-day Adventists in Poland, a country with a population of 37.9 million.

THOSE WHO HOLD THE ROPE

On the road to Damascus Saul saw a great light and heard the voice of Jesus. The experience changed the course of His life, and he became the apostle Paul. The religious leaders turned against him and sought to kill him. The hunter became the hunted. The persecutor became the persecuted. The disciples— the very people whom Saul had gone to Damascus to persecute—saved his life by holding onto a rope and letting him down the city wall in a basket. We don't know the names of those men who held the rope, and they probably didn't know the extent of God's plans for the man in the basket whose life they saved. It was a dangerous thing those men did. If the soldiers on patrol had found them, it would have cost them their lives.

Those disciples who held the rope were willing to risk their lives for the new believer. Having learned the lesson of perseverance, they did not let loose of the rope until Paul was safe.

Thank God for humble Christians who are willing to hold the ropes and work without recognition. Many have given their life savings to the work of God. They have held the ropes that have saved many souls. God may want to entrust a rope into your hand. He needs men and women who will hold the rope even at the risk of their lives. You may never receive any praise or honor or glory from humanity, but there is a God whose eyes see you as you hold that rope.

Too often we let go too soon. We are unwilling to brave persecution. Some are even afraid of criticism or ridicule. No matter how heavy the load or how weary and discouraged we may get, we need to hold on. Like the disciples on that night so long ago, we don't know how much is at stake.

Then the disciples took him by night and let him down through the wall in a large basket. Acts 9:25.

Pray that God will help you to be strong in spite of persecution, criticism, and ridicule. Pray that you will be able through His grace to stand for the right though the heavens fall, and that nothing will cause you to weaken your hold on the rope of right and truth and trust.

WHAT IS A SAINT?

A teacher asked a small boy to define the word *saint*. "Oh, I know," he said, "a saint is a person that the light comes through."

The church that he attended had stained-glass windows depicting the saints of the Bible. He had seen the morning light stream through those figures wrought in the beautiful colored glass, and his mother had explained that they were the saints of God. Thus they were persons the light came through.

In the minds of some, a saint is one who has attained sanctification and been canonized by the church. However, let us notice seven things the Bible tells us about the saints.

1. The saints are those in Christ (Phil. 1:1). Paul addressed many of his Epistles to the saints who were the believers in Jesus Christ.

2. The saints are those who love the Lord (Ps. 31:23). The psalmist, like Paul, addressed his words to the saints who were the living people of God.

3. The saints are a praying people. In Revelation 5:8 we read of the prayers of the saints going up before God.

4. The saints commit themselves to God. Through the psalmist, God says, "Gather my saints together to Me, Those who have made a covenant with Me by sacrifice" (Psalm 50:5).

5. The saints are willing to suffer persecution. Daniel 7:25 speaks of the power of the little horn that "shall speak pompous words against the Most High," and "Shall persecute the saints of the Most High."

6. The saints obey divine commands. Revelation 14:12 describes the people of God: "Here is the patience of the saints; here are those who keep the commandments of God and the faith of Jesus."

7. The saints have the faith of Jesus.

Someone has summed it up well by saying a saint is a sinner saved by grace. Hopefully, these descriptions of a saint fit you and me. And, hopefully, so also does the definition of the little boy, because surely we want to be people the light shines through.

He was not that Light, but was sent to bear witness of that Light. John 1:8.

Pray for the progress of the gospel in troubled Nicaragua, where Seventh-day Adventist church membership now stands at 21,386 in a total population of more than 3.5 million. The first Seventh-day Adventist missionary to Nicaragua was F. J. Hutchins, who arrived in 1892 and began selling Seventh-day Adventist books.

110

MIRAGE OF THE DESERT

Napoleon and his soldiers were crossing the Egyptian desert. The hot sun beat down on the white sands, and the reflected heat made the men pant for water. In their fierce thirst they looked everywhere for some, but the wells were dry.

Then the soldiers scanned the horizon and saw a beautiful lake right there in the desert before them. Lifting up a shout of joy, they started on a run toward the water, but as they did so, the lake seemed to flee from them. It was not a lake of water at all, but a mirage of the desert—a cheat, a delusion, a disappointment.

Life has many mirages. Men look ahead and think they see a lake of joy, an elixir that will satisfy, but as they reach out for it, it fades away.

Some have sought for satisfaction in the world's pleasures, and have not found it. Others have searched for it in acquiring money, land, and houses, but still an aching void troubles the life. Still others have tried to find peace and contentment through alcohol. They have endeavored to drown their troubles, but they remain miserable. There is no lasting refreshing for their souls, just disappointing mirages. The heart cries out for something that can really satisfy.

But there is a joy that will not fail, a refreshing fountain from which men can drink. Its waters will quench their thirsty spirits. That fountain is Jesus Christ.

Jesus can fill empty lives. For the weary, sad, disconsolate, and heartsick, He is the answer. He can satisfy every longing. Our Saviour will meet our every need.

"In that day a fountain shall be opened for the house of David and for the inhabitants of Jerusalem, for sin and for uncleanness." Zech. 13:1.

Pray for the advancement of God's church in New Caledonia, one of the major islands of the South Pacific. It lies about 700 miles east of the Queensland coast of Australia, and has a total population of 158,000. The first Seventh-day Adventist missionaries, Captain G. F. Jones and his wife, arrived in 1925. Now 339 Seventh-day Adventists live on the island.

BAD BOOKS OR BAD PEOPLE?

In the heart of the South American continent is Bolivia. With an area of 424,165 square miles, the country has a population of 6.8 million. It was the last country in South America that Seventh-day Adventists entered.

However, the seed was sown through printed material as early as 1897 when Juan S. Pereira, a former Presbyterian colporteur, began selling Seventh-day Adventist publications. Pereira was discharged for propagating Seventh-day Adventist doctrine, arrested for selling "bad books," and imprisoned and condemned to death. Providentially he escaped the death penalty through the help of a judge who later became interested in Seventh-day Adventist teachings.

The authorities granted Pereira's request that they examine his books, and the officials confessed that the books were not bad, but because of the hostile climate, government officials advised him to leave the country. In 1906 the Bolivian constitution guaranteed religious toleration, and the church made plans to establish our work in Bolivia. Pereira was among the first to volunteer to once again take up selling publications in that country.

One night in 1926 a mob led by religious fanatics made their way to the house of Manuel Quilca, the teacher of the Adventist school at Arca in Inquisivi Province. After beating the teacher and his wife into unconsciousness, they set fire to the house, leaving in it their third victim, the little daughter of the teacher. Although rescued from the flames, she died the following morning from wounds sustained in the beating. Once again the blood of martyrs became the seed of the church, because some members of that mob later became Adventists.

Such was the price paid to establish the Adventist Church in many parts of the world, but they did not die in vain. In the resurrection they will see their harvest.

"In the future life the mysteries that here have annoyed and disappointed us will be made plain. We shall see that our seemingly unanswered prayers and disappointed hopes have been among our greatest blessings" (*The Ministry of Healing*, p. 474).

> **And they stoned Stephen as he was calling on God and saying, "Lord Jesus, receive my spirit." Then he knelt down and cried out with a loud voice, "Lord, do not charge them with this sin." And when he had said this, he fell asleep. Acts 7:59, 60.**

Pray for Bolivia, where we now have 68,361 Seventh-day Adventists.

TIME FOR SALE

A man dreamed that he came to an impressive building somewhat like a bank and yet not a bank, because the brass marker said: "Time for Sale." There he saw a man, breathless and pale, painfully pull himself up the stairs like the victim of some dread disease. "The doctor told me I was five years too late in going to see him," he told the teller. "I'll buy those five years now, and then he can save my life."

Then came another man, older in years, who said to the clerk, "When it was too late, I discovered that God had given me great capacities and endowments, and I have failed to develop them. Sell me 10 years so that I can be the man I could have been."

Then came a younger man who declared, "The company has told me that starting next month I can have a big job, if I am prepared to take it. But I am not prepared. Give me two years of time so that I will be ready to take the job next month."

And so they came in a steady procession—the ill, hopeless, despondent, worried, unhappy—and they left smiling, each man with a look of unutterable pleasure on his face, for he had what he so desperately needed and wanted—time.

When time runs out, people are willing to pay any price to buy an extension of a few months or a few more years.

Someone has said that the greatest tragedy that could befall a Christian would be to come to the end of life and have our Lord say, "Let Me show you what your life could have been if you had been willing to seek and follow My plan for your life." You and I still have time to seek and follow God's plan for our lives, and thus to avoid life's greatest tragedy—the misuse of time and opportunity.

Behold, now is the accepted time; behold, now is the day of salvation. 2 Cor. 6:2.

May this be our daily prayer—that God will help us during this day to use time in a manner that will glorify Him, bless others, and make our own lives joyful and rewarding.

REBUKE THE DEVOURER

From many parts of the world come stories of the crops of faithful tithepayers receiving protection from devourers in harmony with the promise of Malachi 3:11. Grasshoppers, locusts, fire, and hail have come to the very borders of the tithepayer's field and left it untouched, while devastating neighboring fields. The bare acres on one side of a wire fence, and the full crop of healthy grain on the other side, have been an overwhelming evidence of the reality of God's faithfulness.

A farmer in Wisconsin young in the faith had his attention drawn to the tithing system. He was poor and lived on a rented farm. It was a test of his faith to return to God a faithful tithe. But he did. His crops that year were the best in the community, but just before harvest a terrible windstorm brought complete desolation to his fields. The crop was gone, and a period of severe testing followed. But the man remained faithful.

It is relatively easy to trust God when things are in our favor, but it is not so easy in the face of adversity. In this case God did not perform a miracle to salvage the crops, but He did change some other circumstances in the family's life. God opened the windows of heaven and blessed this farmer with a surprising degree of temporal prosperity. He soon became the owner of the farm he was renting, and later God called him into the ministry.

We may not be able to understand all of God's dealings—why one must lose his goods, while divine intervention delivers another. But this we do know: The man whose faith enables him to rejoice in the Lord when the fig tree does not blossom, and when the field yields no corn, is indeed needed as a witness to the world as much as the one who can tell of special deliverance from the devourer.

"And I will rebuke the devourer for your sakes, so that he will not destroy the fruit of your ground, nor shall the vine fail to bear fruit for you in the field," says the Lord of hosts. Mal. 3:11.

Pray that your faith may be unfailing in times of trouble and hardship and, if you are passing through great difficulty now, that you will cling to His sure promises.

CONSCIENCE

The Bible is unique among the writings of the great world religions in that it reveals the fact of the conscience and addresses itself to the conscience. For instance, the Koran does not contain even a word to express the idea of conscience.

There are different kinds of consciences. Paul did not always have the same conscience. After receiving Jesus Christ as his Lord and Saviour, he had a different conscience than he had as a Pharisee.

The words for conscience in Latin, Greek, and other languages indicate something of what unfallen man once experienced with God. It was a sharing of knowledge. In the English word "conscience" one can recognize the word "science."

When the human race fell through sin, the sensitive instrument of the conscience was damaged just as surely as a barometer would be damaged by a physical fall. The New Testament uses four adjectives to describe the fallen conscience: a weak conscience, an evil conscience, a defiled conscience, and a seared, or cauterized, conscience.

We may liken a fallen conscience to a bell buoy that a drunken captain cut away from its moorings many years ago. It was supposed to warn of dangerous rocks, but months later those same rocks destroyed his own ship because the buoy was no longer there to warn him away.

Every natural conscience is imperfect since the Fall, and no two consciences are alike. Each is influenced by environment, heredity, and education. The good news, however, is that a fallen conscience can be regenerated and renewed by the Holy Spirit through the Word of God. The New Testament describes a regenerate conscience by words such as good, pure, and purged. Only the conscience educated in harmony with the Word of God is a safe guide. The function of the conscience is to tell us to do right and not to do wrong.

We must direct the appeal of the gospel to man's conscience if we are to reach the citadel of his soul and have a basis for calling for unconditional surrender.

"This being so, I myself always strive to have a conscience without offense toward God and men." Acts 24:16.

Pray for yourself and those with whom you share the gospel that you and they might have a sensitive conscience, fully in harmony with the Word of God.

VICTORY FROM THE LORD

Amalek was a grandson of Esau, who had sold his birthright for a meal of lentils. Like his grandfather, Amalek manifested an attitude of defiance, arrogance, conceit, independence, and self-sufficiency.

We might think of Amalek as representing the fleshly nature. After conversion the old nature of the flesh tries to rise up again in an attempt to rob the Lord of our usefulness on earth. The fleshly nature wants to hold on to your money, your time, your talents, and your ambitions so that Jesus is robbed of His inheritance in you.

We might see the battle between Amalek and Israel after the Exodus as representing the struggle between the two natures. Moses told Joshua to go fight with the tribes of Amalek, but the outcome had little to do with Joshua other than the fact that he went.

No matter how weak Joshua felt, no matter how he counted the enemy hosts and found their number overwhelming, no matter how inadequate he felt when he went out to fight, so long as Moses kept his hand raised, Joshua won. What is the lesson for us? The victory did not lie in Joshua. It was not dependent on his strength, skill, or bravery—rather the victory lay in God Himself.

It was a God-given victory represented by the rod of God in the hand of Moses, symbolizing the appropriation by faith of a God-given victory.

In Joshua's experience the important thing was that he went. The victory had already been won through the power of God, but Joshua must move forward by faith to claim it. When we go forward in our evangelistic endeavors, the important thing is that we go. The victory might not be evident immediately, but we have success whenever we go forward in faith.

An American admiral used a business card with the words "It can't be done" in gray type. Across them in bold, black type were the additional words "But here it is!"

Man by himself must say, "It can't be done." Christ, however, declares, "But here it is!" The Christian life of faith and obedience is a matter of appropriating a victory already won.

And so it was, when Moses held up his hand, that Israel prevailed; and when he let down his hand, Amalek prevailed. Ex. 17:11.

Pray for faith to accept the victory won at Calvary, and go your way today rejoicing in that victory.

LOST UNTIL WE ARE SAVED

Have you ever been lost in the woods with night coming on or a storm approaching? Perhaps you can remember as a child becoming separated from your parents and lost in a crowd. A sense of lostness produces panic and feelings of desperation.

Many of us who have had the privilege of growing up in a Christian environment can easily conclude that we have never done anything "terribly bad."

Only one who knows the feeling of being lost can truly appreciate what it means to be saved. It is not difficult to think of a brutal murderer or adulterer being lost, but so-called "respectable sins" may not seem so bad in our eyes.

But even the "smallest" sin separates us from God, our source of life, and we are lost. In our natural state we are all lost until we are saved, because "all have sinned."

If I were drowning—going down for the third time—I would be lost, but if you jumped into the water and saved me, when I regained consciousness I would say, "You saved me! You have done something for me which I couldn't do for myself." It was a matter of life or death, and I would owe my life to you as my rescuer.

The danger is that we ignore the seriousness of our situation, or resist the efforts of the One who wants to save us. Frantic efforts to save ourselves can frustrate any attempts at rescue. Surrendering our lives into His hands is essential to the rescue operation.

Imagine the ruler of a far away kingdom in one of the prisons of a remote province a rebel condemned to die. The heart of the ruler moves with compassion, and he longs to provide pardon, forgiveness, and freedom for the prisoner. But the highest law of the land has been broken, and the prisoner must perish unless one equal to the law is willing to die in his place. The ruler has only one son. If that son dies as a substitute, it would prove two things—the unchanging nature of the law, and the supreme love of the ruler for his unworthy subject. This is the experience of salvation. Forgiveness is very costly.

Behold what manner of love the Father has bestowed on us, that we should be called children of God! 1 John 3:1.

Pray for an opening for the gospel in the territory of Lakshadweep, ("a hundred thousand islands"), a group of coral atolls off the western coast of the Indian state of Kerala. The ten inhabited islands have more than 45,000 inhabitants, mostly Muslims.

TO THE JEW FIRST

"It has been a strange thing to me that there were so few who felt a burden to labor for the Jewish people, who are scattered throughout so many lands. . . . There will be many converted from among the Jews, and these converts will help in preparing the way of the Lord, and making straight in the desert a highway for our God" (*Evangelism*, pp. 578, 579).

F. C. Gilbert, a Jew who came to the United States from England, became ill and was taken to a Christian hospital, where he feared they would poison him. After his release from the hospital, he needed an inexpensive room and found one in a Seventh-day Adventist home. There the family treated him with love and kindness.

Gilbert contracted scarlet fever, and being concerned for the health of his landlord's little girl, he suggested that he should move lest she catch the disease. The landlord's wife said, "No, Jesus has assured me that even if she gets it, she will not die. You stay."

Gilbert did, and when his birthday came, something unexpected happened. That night he had to work until 11:00 p.m. When he came home, he found a birthday cake prepared especially for him awaiting him on the table. Such a demonstration of Christian caring and kindness impressed him. Then, as he looked at that birthday cake, he saw on the table what appeared to be letters of fire blazing out the message "You are a sinner." Awakening his landlord, he gave his heart to Jesus.

Jesus and the disciples went first of all to the lost sheep of the house of Israel, and the heart of God still longs after His chosen people. Inspiration makes it clear that many Jews will accept the gospel and will enter into a saving relationship with the Lord. Perhaps the experience of F. C. Gilbert, who became a fruitful evangelist in the cause of God, gives us an important clue as to how we can reach the Jewish people.

For I am not ashamed of the gospel of Christ, for it is the power of God to salvation for everyone who believes, for the Jew first and also for the Greek. Rom. 1:16.

Pray for the Jewish people scattered among all nations, and also for the modern nation of Israel, where 74 Seventh-day Adventists witness to a population of 4.4 million.

HE TOOK MY PUNISHMENT

A rural mountain community had a school that no teacher seemed able to handle. When a young man fresh out of college applied for the job, the school board members laughed. But he begged for a chance, and got it.

On the first day of school the new teacher suggested that the students make the rules. He wrote on the chalkboard as the pupils called out: "No stealing. No cheating. No swearing." Soon they had 10 rules on the board.

"Now," said the teacher, "a law is no good unless there's a penalty attached. What will the penalty be?"

"Ten stripes across the back with no coat on," the class shouted.

All went well for a few days until Big Tom found that someone had stolen his lunch. An investigation revealed the thief to be Jim, a small 10-year-old boy from a very poor home. When the teacher asked him to take his coat off, the boy was very embarrassed. He had no shirt, and only a string held up his trousers over his bony frame.

"Why don't you wear a shirt, Jim?" the teacher asked.

"I have only one shirt, and my mother is washing it today," the boy explained. "My father died, and we are very poor. For two days we have had no food. That's why I stole Tom's lunch. I'm sorry, but I was so hungry."

As the teacher was wondering what to do, Big Tom jumped to his feet and said, "Teacher, I'll take Jim's punishment for him."

The class and the teacher agreed to let Tom take Jim's penalty as a substitute. After five hard strokes, the rod broke. In the quietness the teacher heard the entire school sobbing, and guess what he saw. Little Jim had reached up and put both arms around Tom's neck. "Tom, I'll love you till I die for taking my licking for me! I'll love you forever!"

We have each broken God's rules, but Jesus took our punishment for us. "He suffered the death which was ours, that we might receive the life which was His. 'With his stripes we are healed' " (*The Desire of Ages*, p. 25).

May our response be "I'll love Him forever!"

But He was wounded for our transgressions, He was bruised for our iniquities. Isa. 53:5.

Pray for the work of God in Bermuda, where 2,496 Seventh-day Adventists live among a population of 56,000.

LAY MINISTRY

One of the greatest contributions the rapidly expanding congregations in the non-Western world will make to the Adventist Church as a whole may well be the rediscovery of the church as a lay church. This concept characterized the early Christian church, the early Advent movement, and certain signs indicate that the rediscovery of this biblical concept of the church and its mission has already begun.

"All who receive the life of Christ are ordained to work for the salvation of their fellowmen" (*The Desire of Ages*, p. 822). "All are alike called to be missionaries for God" (*The Ministry of Healing*, p. 395).

To fail to enlist all believers in mission is to retard the work of the gospel.

"If those who claimed to have a living experience in the things of God had done their appointed work as the Lord ordained, the whole world would have been warned ere this, and the Lord Jesus would have come in power and great glory" (Ellen G. White, in *Review and Herald*, Oct. 6, 1896).

The words layman and laity came into our language during the Middle Ages. The New Testament Greek expression *laos* refers to the entire people of God with no distinction between those paid for their service and who work for the institutional church full-time and those who perform their services voluntarily.

"The Christianity that conquered the Roman Empire was not an affair of brilliant preachers addressing packed congregations. . . .When we try to picture how it was done, we see domestic servants teaching Christ in and through their domestic service, workers doing it through their work, small shopkeepers through their trade, rather than eloquent propagandists swaying mass meetings of interested inquirers" (T. W. Manson, *Ministry and Priesthood: Christ's and Ours*, p. 21).

Biblically speaking, the first task of the pastor is not to go out into the world to win unbelievers to the church. The primary role of the pastor is to nourish, strengthen, equip, help, and sustain the laity for its ministry.

> **They were all scattered throughout the regions of Judea and Samaria, except the apostles. . . . Therefore those who were scattered went everywhere preaching the word. Acts 8:1-4.**

Pray for the people of Western Sahara, where there is both physical and spiritual famine.

HIS GLORY WILL BE SEEN

Seventh-day Adventist missions in China began in 1888 as a project of one layman, Abram La Rue, who became a Seventh-day Adventist at an advanced age. Recognizing that the Advent message must go to all the world, La Rue attended Healdsburg College to prepare himself. He requested that the denomination appoint him to China, but because he was 65 years old at the time, the Mission Board suggested that he go to one of the islands in the Pacific Ocean instead. He went to Hawaii, and after creating an interest in the Adventist message there, went on to Hong Kong

The first Seventh-day Adventist baptism in China took place on February 14, 1903, at Sin Yang Chow, and the next day J. N. Anderson organized the first Seventh-day Adventist church in China with eight members. In 1903 Doctors Harry W. and Maude A. Miller, and Doctors Arthur C. and Bertha E. Selmon, went to China to begin medical activities in Central China.

It was characteristic of the early Chinese converts to share their faith with their neighbors immediately, and consequently the church there grew quickly.

In 1904 a young Chinese Seventh-day Adventist, Timothy Tay, who had been baptized in Singapore by R. W. Munson, went to Amoy, a seaport in South China, to perfect his knowledge of the local dialect. There he met Keh Ngo Pit, the principal of a theological seminary. He studied the Bible with Tay in an attempt to correct what he believed to be erroneous beliefs. Instead, Keh Ngo Pit became convinced of Seventh-day Adventist doctrine, and he later became the first ordained Chinese Seventh-day Adventist pastor.

Timothy Tay and Keh Ngo Pit eventually went to Swatow, another large seaport in South China, where they made the acquaintance of a Chinese Christian leader, T. K. Ang, who also attempted to disprove the Seventh-day Adventist message and ended up himself becoming a convert and entering the Seventh-day Adventist work.

For behold, the darkness shall cover the earth, and deep darkness the people; but the Lord will arise over you, and His glory will be seen upon you. The Gentiles shall come to your light, and kings to the brightness of your rising. Isa. 60:2, 3.

Pray for the 50,000 Chinese Muslim Dungans of the Soviet Union. The older generation strictly observes Islamic law, but younger Dungans are often indifferent to Islam.

SPIRITUAL TRANSFORMERS

"Instead of talking of your doubts, break away from them in the strength of Jesus, and let light shine into your soul by letting your voice express confidence and trust in God. . . . Take Christ at His word, and let your lips declare that you have gained the victory" (*Testimonies to Ministers*, pp. 516, 517).

When we talk in a negative, discouraging way, expressing doubts and grievances, we destroy our own faith and jeopardize that of others. It is within the power of each one of us to be spiritual transformers, changing the current of conversation from negative to positive.

"Peace comes with dependence on divine power. As fast as the soul resolves to act in accordance with the light given, the Holy Spirit gives more light and strength" (*ibid.*, p. 518).

We must learn to be dependent upon divine power, which is constant, rather than upon circumstances and feelings, which change from day to day. Satan knows that if he can get people to depend upon feelings and circumstances instead of on divine power, he can impede the flow of light and strength into their lives.

"God's children are not to be subject to feelings and emotions. When they fluctuate between hope and fear, the heart of Christ is hurt" (*ibid.*).

Sometimes you may feel that your prayers don't go any higher than the ceiling, but they don't have to go higher than that because God is present everywhere.

Satan knows that if he can bring us to a point of discouragement where we will cease to pray and read the Bible, he will have us as helpless victims. But remember:

"Never a prayer is offered, however faltering, never a tear is shed, however secret, never a sincere desire after God is cherished, however feeble, but the Spirit of God goes forth to meet it" (*Christ's Object Lessons*, p. 206).

Let the words of my mouth and the meditation of my heart be acceptable in Your sight, O Lord, my strength and my redeemer. Ps. 19:14.

The country of Gabon, 80 percent dense tropical rain forest, is located in West Africa. The nation maintains its freedom of religion, and Seventh-day Adventists already have 109 members in a population of 1.2 million.

HAND ON MY SHOULDER

It was April 21, 1855, 136 years ago today, that Edward Kimball, the teacher of a young men's Sunday school class, started down the street to Holton's shoe store in Boston, determined to speak to one of his class members (who worked there) about Christ and his soul. He was nearly at the store when he began to wonder whether he ought to contact the young man during working hours. When he actually passed the store, he still felt the irresistible urge to speak to that young man, so he turned back and went in. There he found the young man in the back part of the store wrapping shoes in paper and putting them on the shelves. Kimball walked up to the class member and put his hand on his shoulder.

In a simple way, Kimball told the young man of Christ's love for him, and evidently the timing was right, because there in the back of that shoe store, D. L. Moody gave himself to Christ. To the end of his life, Moody bore the testimony, "I can feel his hand on my shoulder yet!" Describing his conversion experience in later years, Moody said, "The morning I was converted I went outdoors and fell in love with everything. I never loved the bright sun shining over the earth so much before, and when I heard the birds singing their sweet songs, I fell in love with the birds. Everything is different."

Moody's Sunday school teacher said, "I can truly say . . . that I have seen few persons whose minds were spiritually darker than was his when he came into my Sabbath school class, or one who seemed more unlikely ever to become a Christian of clear, decided views of gospel truth."

What a loss it might have been to the cause of Christianity if Kimball had not made that visit that day. When the Holy Spirit speaks to you, encouraging you to present the claims of Christ to someone, remember the experience of Edward Kimball, and don't give up on unpromising prospects!

In the morning sow your seed, and in the evening do not withhold your hand; for you do not know which will prosper, either this or that, or whether both alike will be good. Eccl. 11:6.

The Ivory Coast is on the West African coast between Liberia and Ghana. This French-speaking country of 11.1 million people presents a great challenge to the Seventh-day Adventist Church. Pray for our leaders and members there.

A LITTLE RED PURSE

One Sunday morning in Philadelphia a father and his 8-year-old daughter walked to Sunday school. When they arrived, they discovered the door shut with a notice on it that said, "Room for no more."

Sadly, they turned around and walked home. On the way they met the preacher, who saw the little girl crying. He picked her up in his arms and carried her into the church saying, "Someday, Hettie, we will have a church big enough for all the boys and girls, and no one will be turned away."

Hettie went home and asked her parents for things to do to earn money. She worked for the neighbors and saved what they paid her. After a time, Hettie became ill and had to go to the hospital. She never went home again.

The child had a little red purse in which she saved her money for the church. On the day of the funeral, the pastor asked her mother for that little red purse. In it were her savings—57 cents.

When people began to learn about her story, funds came from all over the city as a result of what she had done.

The foyer of the new Temple Church in Philadelphia contains a plaque in honor of Hettie. But that is not all. Behind the church is Temple University, and down the street is Temple Medical Center. In both buildings you will find plaques in memory of the child.

In the resurrection Jesus and Hettie will meet. I can imagine the girl saying, "Thanks for dying for me." And I can imagine Jesus saying, "And thanks for the church you built, and the hospital, and the university."

But Hettie might reply, "There must be some mistake." And then I imagine Jesus telling her the story you have just read.

The following passage would have been appropriate words of comfort for Hettie's parents, as they are for us: "Whatever may arise, never be discouraged. The Lord loves us, and He will perform His word. . . . Though some of His followers may fall in death . . . theirs will be a joyous awakening in the resurrection morning" (*Selected Messages*, book 1, p. 85).

> **Then I heard a voice from heaven saying to me, "Write: 'Blessed are the dead who die in the Lord from now on.' " "Yes," says the Spirit, "that they may rest from their labors, and their works follow them." Rev. 14:13.**

Pray for children in developing nations who do not have a shelter where they can gather to worship God.

THE RED-FACED MONKEY

Sin thrives on attention, even negative attention. It is like the Indian wonder-worker who came to a village declaring that he would demonstrate how to make gold.

The villagers gathered around as the mystic poured water into a huge caldron, put some coloring matter into it, and began to repeat magic words as he stirred. When he had the attention of the people diverted for a moment, he let some gold nuggets slip into the water. Stirring a little more, he poured off the water, and there everybody could see gold at the bottom of the caldron. The villagers' eyes bulged. The moneylender offered 500 rupees for the formula, and the wonder-worker sold it to him. But before he left, the mystic said, "You must not think of the red-faced monkey as you stir. If you do, the gold will never come." The moneylender promised to remember what he was supposed to block out of his mind. But try as hard as he might, the red-faced monkey kept flashing into his mind, spoiling all his gold.

When we pray, it is important to focus not on the problem, but on the solution, who is Jesus Christ. Concentrating on our sins and problems will get us into trouble, but focusing our eyes on Jesus will keep us out of trouble.

Therefore, watch the focus of your prayers. If you find yourself rehearsing your problems and defeats, beware. Briefly confess the problem, but then fill your prayers with praise and thanks to Jesus, the solver of problems and the giver of victory. Thank God in advance for the things prayed for. Turn your attention away from the problem and look to Jesus.

Looking unto Jesus, the author and finisher of our faith, who for the joy that was set before Him endured the cross, despising the shame, and has sat down at the right hand of the throne of God. Heb. 12:2.

Pray for the people of Japan, a nation with a population of 122 million, and 12,415 Seventh-day Adventists. The total land area of the islands of Japan is slightly smaller than the state of California.

Abram La Rue made a number of trips to Japan and distributed Seventh-day Adventist publications in Yokohama and Kobe in 1889. S. N. Haskell visited Japan in 1890 and baptized one convert. The first Seventh-day Adventist resident missionaries arrived in 1896, and the first Seventh-day Adventist church was organized in Tokyo on June 4, 1899, with a membership of 13.

THE PRIVILEGE OF PRAYER

Many Christians overlook the privilege of prayer. But every believer has the invitation to come boldly to God's throne—into the very presence of the Ruler of the universe.

For the Christian, prayer is simply talking with God. The Christian can pray in any language and does not need to memorize any special phrases. Since the highest goal of the devotional life is to strengthen the relationship between God and man, prayer is the vital contact we need. Answers to prayer are most meaningful when we dwell on them least, while prayer itself is most meaningful when we think of God most.

Prayer brings power. Days of soul winning have usually been preceded by nights of prayer. The evangelistic ministry of Charles G. Finney would begin with the prayer ministry of a humble Christian known as Father Nash. Three or four weeks in advance of Finney's crusades Nash would move to town and find a place of prayer. After revival came, he would quietly leave town to prepare the city chosen for the next crusade.

The mind that has experienced the joy and delight of true communion with God will turn its thoughts as naturally to God as the flower turns to the sun. The one who prays without ceasing is likely to rejoice evermore.

Years ago the emperor of Ethiopia held court on certain days at the palace gates. Large crowds of people took advantage of the opportunity to present their problems personally to their king. At other times regularly appointed judges settled grievances, but on these special occasions they could directly approach the emperor himself. The great King of the universe invites us to come to Him not only on special occasions, but as often as we please.

Let us therefore come boldly to the throne of grace, that we may obtain mercy and find grace to help in time of need. Heb. 4:16.

Pray for the rapidly expanding Seventh-day Adventist Church in Nigeria, where D. C. Babcock first introduced its teachings in 1914. The son of a local chief who was his language teacher soon began to observe the Sabbath, and before the end of 1914 three schools were in operation and seven persons had accepted the Seventh-day Adventist message.

Nigeria is a large country of 115 million people, with 59,966 Seventh-day Adventist Church members.

DIGGING FOR DIAMONDS

The first Seventh-day Adventist in South Africa was William Hunt. A miner from Nevada, he went to dig diamonds, and took with him a supply of tracts and papers. As early as 1878 Hunt had convinced some South Africans of Seventh-day Adventist doctrine.

In 1885 G. J. VanDruten, a Beaconsfield businessman, remarked to his wife that people claimed Hunt was lazy because he kept two Sundays. The wife replied, "He looks like an old saint to me." Her reply aroused VanDruten's curiosity, and he visited Hunt in his little backyard room and began to ask questions. Hunt's answers convinced VanDruten of the Sabbath.

In that same year (1885) young Peter Wessels began observing the Sabbath, not knowing of another Christian in all the world who was doing so. In poor health, he had thrown himself on the mercy of God and pleaded for forgiveness and healing. The Lord miraculously answered his prayer. Arising the next morning, he dressed and left the house eager to tell everyone what God had done for him. Peter tried to persuade his brother John, a deacon in the Dutch Reformed Church, that a man ought to rely wholly on God for healing. John contended that the Bible was not to be taken so literally and pointed out that if Peter really intended to follow the Bible exactly, he would have to observe the Sabbath. When Peter protested that he was, John pointed to the calendar. Peter began to search the Bible, and soon became convinced that he should keep the seventh day holy.

Not long afterward, Peter Wessels and G. J. VanDruten met at the Dutch Reformed Church in Beaconsfield. When they discovered that both were honoring the seventh-day Sabbath, they went together to visit William Hunt. Peter Wessels was happy to learn that there was a worldwide church teaching the Sabbath doctrine. Filled with enthusiasm, the two men began to propagate their newly found faith among their relatives, friends, and neighbors.

"Again, the kingdom of heaven is like treasure hidden in a field, which a man found and hid; and for joy over it he goes and sells all that he has and buys that field." Matt. 13:44.

Pray for the continued expansion of the work of God in the Republic of South Africa, where we have 50,643 Seventh-day Adventists in a population of 35 million.

SEEING THE INVISIBLE

Moses had trained to be a pharaoh, but he found himself caring for sheep. He had been educated to rub shoulders with VIPs, but now he rubbed shoulders with sheep. Once accustomed to fine marble floors, he now walked on desert rock. The hand that had once held a scepter now grasped a rod. Once formal gardens had surrounded him, now he was surrounded by desert bushes.

But Jesus walked with Moses, and in His presence common sand became holy ground, and the dry, ordinary bush ignited with His holy fire.

The question is, is God's holy fire burning within you? God wants you to give Him the rod, or whatever might be the tools of your trade, and He will make them into a scepter of power. He wants to dwell in you and do His work through you and for you.

The book of Hebrews portrays Moses as rejecting the throne of Egypt and turning down the offer of a crown because he saw the invisible. He could see beyond the brickmaking to the land of Canaan.

In the wilderness when things appeared dark to most people, he looked ahead over 1,000 years and caught a vision of the Christ who was to come. He recognized symbols of the coming Redeemer in the smitten rock, the daily sacrifice, the falling manna, the holy sanctuary, the guiding cloud and pillar of fire. Seeing the invisible, he saw the future.

Faith is like radar. It sees in the dark, looks through clouds, is unaffected by storms, and makes spiritual navigation safe.

At every turn of the road we will find something that will rob us of peace of mind and victory if we let it. But faith reaches to the invisible to give us peace and victory. There is no explanation for the mysteries of our existence if there is not an invisible God ruling the universe, and faith based on reason and revelation sees Him. It is when we look to God in faith that our eyes open to the invisible.

By faith he forsook Egypt, not fearing the wrath of the king; for he endured as seeing Him who is invisible. Heb. 11:27.

Pray for the Islamic sultanate called Oman, situated on the southeastern part of the Arabian Peninsula. It covers an area of 82,030 square miles, has a population of 2 million, and yet has no Seventh-day Adventist presence.

MUCH MORE THAN THIS

Amaziah, the ninth king of the southern kingdom of Judah, was planning a military campaign. He had 300,000 men, but thinking he needed more, he hired 100,000 men from the northern kingdom of Israel. With a total of 400,000 men he was ready to go to battle, but just then the prophet of the Lord came and said, "O king, do not let the army of Israel go with you, for the Lord is not with Israel—not with any of the children of Ephraim."

Now Amaziah faced a dilemma. He had paid 100 talents of silver for those 100,000 men, and the contract had no provision for a refund. It seemed he would lose a hundred talents of silver and 100,000 soldiers whom he felt he needed to win the battle. Desiring to be assured of God's blessing, and yet not wanting to lose the money he had paid, King Amaziah asked the prophet, "But what shall we do about the hundred talents which I have given to the troops of Israel?"

Several years ago I visited several countries in the Far East in company with Dr. M. T. Bascom. Many times since then I have found practical help from a sermon Dr. Bascom preached on the prophet's answer to Amaziah's query, "But what shall we do about the hundred talents which I have given to the troops of Israel?" The prophet replied, "The Lord is able to give you much more than this."

When tempted to grieve over losses, or when it seems that the cost of living the Christian life is a price higher than you are willing to pay, remember, "The Lord is able to give you much more than this."

Are you facing financial problems? Do you need wisdom as you wrestle with some perplexity? Are you struggling with family difficulties? Are you worried about your health? Does following Jesus seem to jeopardize your social standing, your employment, and your circle of friends? Remember, "The Lord is able to give you much more than this."

Then Amaziah said to the man of God, "But what shall we do about the hundred talents which I have given to the troops of Israel?" And the man of God answered, "The Lord is able to give you much more than this." 2 Chron. 25:9.

Pray about the promise in today's text as it might apply to some current circumstance in your experience.

APRIL 28

FOLLOW JESUS

Some people find themselves greatly troubled by the words of Jesus in Luke 14:26, "If anyone comes to Me and does not hate his father and mother, wife and children, brothers and sisters, yes, and his own life also, he cannot be My disciple."

The word "hate" is not used here in the sense of to detest or abhor. It simply means to love less. In the language of Jesus' day, it was a method of emphasizing that we should love Him supremely.

Should we love ourselves or anyone else more than we love Jesus, we will surely find ourselves diverted from following Him. We must put obedience to God above the cravings and desires of the flesh and above all the opposition of loved ones. Jesus knew that when people were about to step out and fully follow truth, opposition would often come from their own family. Those closest in the family would try to dissuade them from going forward in obedience to Jesus.

Jesus was simply saying that those who face such a test must love God supremely. When a person chooses to obey God rather than be persuaded by family members, it might seem to those family members that the one who is choosing to obey God hates them. By words and action we must help them to see that this is not the case. As they see the transformation and joy that following Jesus brings, they will want the same experience.

Many people will actually lose an eternal, happy home in heaven because they listened to close members of the family more than they did God. Others will forfeit eternity because they allowed some friend or loved one to hold them back from walking in the light of truth. The decision to follow truth is an individual matter, and each person will be accountable before God.

> **"The soul who sins shall die. The son shall not bear the guilt of the father, nor the father bear the guilt of the son. The righteousness of the righteous shall be upon himself, and the wickedness of the wicked shall be upon himself." Eze. 18:20.**

> *Pray for family members or friends who might be jealous because of your supreme love for Jesus. Pray that God will help you to live in such a way that they will see that your love for them is greater because of your love for Jesus.*

130

REPRODUCTIVE FAITH

The parable of the sower illustrates four responses to God's Word.

1. No faith. Birds picked up the seed that fell on the hardened path. There was no soil preparation, no receptivity, and consequently no germination, and certainly no harvest.

2. Faith without conviction. Some soil did not have enough depth of soil to provide stability for the tender plants. They never became firmly rooted. This represents those who give mental assent to the Word, but when the time comes that it costs something to believe, they give up the faith. They lack the conviction that it is worthy of the cost.

3. Faith without perspective. This group of hearers represents those who entertain competing interests in their lives. They lack commitment and singleness of purpose. After receiving the Word, they turn around and give their lives to insignificant matters.

4. Reproductive faith. Here, those who respond have a high degree of receptivity. The soil is good, and it has been prepared. The rocks have been removed and the weeds eradicated. Under these circumstances the gospel seed reproduces itself many times, and the kingdom of God enlarges.

The four types of soil represent four degrees of receptivity that we encounter in the world today. Some have no faith and find themselves unable to receive the Word of God. Others have faith without conviction, and it does not stand the test of real-life situations. Still others lack perspective. Material interests crowd out the degree of faith they do possess.

But faith that takes root and trusts the Object of faith in spite of changing circumstances is reproductive faith that yields an abundant harvest. Remember that faith is only as good as its object. If the Lord is the object of your faith, He will give you increase, and you will be fruitful.

"But the ones that fell on the good ground are those who, having heard the word with a noble and good heart, keep it and bear fruit with patience." Luke 8:15.

Pray for the farmers who provide food for the multitudes. Grant them bountiful harvests, but also that as they sow seed they might remember that Jesus made seed a symbol of the Word of God.

131

HE SAVED A LIFE

As my wife and I waited for our train at the railway station in Edmonton, Alberta, we noticed a small boy was excitedly telling something to one group of people and then another in the station. When the train arrived, it was our good fortune to find a seat next to the boy and his parents. Here is the story we heard:

Four-year-old Steve Campbell had gone out to play with a 3-year-old neighbor. Suddenly the family dog, barking and pawing at the back-door screen, caught his mother's attention. It was clear the animal was trying to tell her something. The dog ran out into the farmyard, raced in circles at a certain spot, and continued his barking.

Mrs. Campbell discovered that Steve and his playmate had fallen through the boards covering an abandoned well. Frantically she called the neighbors who came with ropes. The rescue team found the 4-year-old with one hand clutching an old rope dangling from the top of the well. With his other hand he managed to hold the head of his smaller friend above the water for approximately 45 minutes. Steve insisted that the younger boy be rescued first.

For his act of bravery, Steve was decorated with a medal bearing the inscription "He Saved a Life." His story appeared on the front page of the newspaper that day, and television covered the presentation, but the joy that the boy felt was not primarily because his picture was on the front page of the newspaper or because he had been on television, but rather because he had saved the life of his friend.

There is a great rescue operation going on, and each of us may have a part. "He who becomes a child of God should henceforth look upon himself as a link in the chain let down to save the world, one with Christ in His plan of mercy, going forth with Him to seek and save the lost" (*The Ministry of Healing*, p. 105).

"For the Son of Man has come to seek and to save that which was lost." Luke 19:10.

Pray that today God will use you as a link in that chain reaching from heaven to earth.

THE SMOKE
OF A THOUSAND VILLAGES

David Livingstone, missionary, physician, and explorer, was the son of a Scottish itinerant merchant and colporteur of religious tracts. Because money was scarce in the Livingstone home, David went to work in a cotton factory when he was 10 years old. He labored at the factory from 6:00 in the morning until 8:00 at night, with only short breaks for breakfast and dinner.

Afterward he spent from 8:00 until 10:00 each evening in the room of the schoolmaster getting his lessons. Then he would go home and eat the dish of porridge his mother had waiting before working on his lessons until midnight.

At the age of 12 David asked to join the church. He wanted to devote his life to alleviating human misery and had decided to become a medical missionary.

The young man remained at the factory until he was 23 in order to save enough money to attend the university. When he heard missionary Robert Moffat say, "I have seen in the morning sun the smoke of a thousand villages where no missionary has ever been," young Livingstone felt challenged, and determined that he would go to those villages.

Livingstone hated the slave trade and repeatedly risked his life in order to rescue Africans from the slave masters. Chuma, one of Livingstone's two faithful traveling companions, was one whom the missionary doctor had rescued from his captors.

After 30 years of service to God in Africa, Livingstone died on his knees in prayer on May 1, 1873. A British cruiser took the body to England for an honored burial in Westminster Abbey.

On the day of the burial a boyhood friend who had ridiculed Livingstone for throwing his life away in Africa was among the crowd. The man had chosen to stay in London and become rich. He had lived for self and few had ever heard of him. Livingstone on the other hand was the best known and most loved man of his day.

Global strategy has new frontiers to challenge today's Livingstones:

No weapon formed against you shall prosper. Isa. 54:17.

The Seventh-day Adventist Church is the second-largest Protestant church in Venezuela. Pray for continued evangelization by our church in that country, and for the opening up of the remaining unevangelized people groups.

IN SPIRIT AND IN TRUTH

God selected Israel as His chosen people. He committed to them His truth and made provision for them to be possessed by His Spirit. The search for truth would be much easier if the custodians of truth were always foremost in manifesting Christ's spirit. But it is not always so today, and evidently it was not always so in Bible times.

The Jews had the true temple, the right Scriptures, and the proper mountain on which to worship. The religion of the Jews and Samaritans was very similar, but the Samaritans built their own temple on Mount Gerizim, and they accepted only the first five books of Moses as their scriptures.

The Jews had more truth than the Samaritans, but at least one Samaritan in Christ's day had more of the spirit of Christ than many Jews. He is the one we know as the good Samaritan. Perhaps it will help if we define *spirit* as sincerity, loyalty, love, and devotion. The priest and the Levite had a theoretical understanding of truth, but they closed their eyes to the needs of one who had been left to die by the roadside. It was the Samaritan who manifested the true spirit of love and devotion, and at personal risk and expense ministered to the suffering victim.

Spirit and truth must never become separated. When that happens, we are left with the husk of outward forms and ceremonies but lacking the inner kernel of the life-giving Spirit. The Seventh-day Adventist Church has a message of truth fully in harmony with the Bible. What we also need is the Holy Spirit. "The inworking ministry of the Holy Spirit is our great need" (*Evangelism*, p. 299). It is God's desire that spirit and truth be united in each individual. This combination of the Holy Spirit and truth is essential because "It is the Holy Spirit that makes the truth impressive" (*Testimonies,* vol. 6, p. 57). Only then will the message have power.

As a representative of Jesus Christ, may you manifest His truth and His Spirit in your life so that seekers might more easily find Him.

God is Spirit, and those who worship Him must worship in spirit and truth. John 4:24.

Pray for Saudi Arabia, with a population of 13.6 million and no Seventh-day Adventist Church. Our temperance program provides one area of common interest with this Islamic kingdom.

PEOPLE WHO KNOW THEIR GOD

Daniel tells us that the people who know their God shall be strong and will do great exploits. He was such a person. So, also, were Moses, Paul, and Peter. Can you think of some persons you know who know their God; are strong spiritually and do exploits for God? Such strength does not come simply from knowing about God. Instead it is a matter of a personal acquaintance with Him.

A well-known pastor visited a prisoner on death row. The prisoner asked the clergyman to introduce him to Jesus. As the pastor talked about the theology of justification, the condemned man interrupted, "Sir, what I really want to know is how to meet your Christ. Can't you tell me in simple terms how to get acquainted with Him?"

The now-frustrated pastor left that cell convinced that he had been preaching and writing about a Christ whom he did not know sufficiently well to introduce Him to a man doomed to die.

Not all of us have the gift of evangelism, but most of us could learn to present a simple study to answer life's greatest question, "What must I do to be saved?" We would want to include some of the following facts: God is love. He created us with freedom of choice. All have sinned, and sin separates us from God and causes death. God gave His Son in response to man's sin problem, to provide forgiveness and to restore our relationship with Him, that we might live. Salvation is a gift of grace, and we can do nothing to earn it. We may be assured of salvation as long as our relationship with Christ is intact.

When Jesus is our best friend, it will be a joy to introduce Him to other friends, relatives, and neighbors who recognize that we know Him and indicate that they would like to know Him too. Knowing Him will enable us to do exploits for Him.

You will gain encouragement as you think of humble men and women whom God has used in a mighty way. They were persons who really knew their God.

Those who do wickedly against the covenant he shall corrupt with flattery; but the people who know their God shall be strong, and carry out great exploits. Dan. 11:32.

Pray that you will know God so well you will find it natural to introduce Him to your friends as you have opportunity.

COMMUNICATING

Too often we assume that the non-Christian would not be interested in what we have to say. If that is our attitude, it is no wonder we feel uncomfortable in sharing spiritual things. We need to develop positive mental attitudes.

As the message itself increasingly transforms us, our lives will be living gospels. Evangelism will not be a program, but a fire burning in our hearts.

Often when non-Christians seem embarrassed, apologetic, and defensive, it is because they are picking up our attitudes. If we assume they will be absolutely fascinated to discover the true nature of Christianity, they probably will. We should project enthusiasm, not defensiveness. And we need to find the point where God is currently working in the life of each individual.

When missionaries go overseas, the church spends large sums of money on them for language school and cross-cultural studies. How many of us who stay in the homeland take the trouble to learn the vocabulary and thought forms of our non-Christian neighbors around the corner? We tend to develop an insider's vocabulary, but Jesus went to the people with words they could understand.

Dr. Eugene Nida of the American Bible Society said, "The best modern translation of the Scripture is the one which communicates the truth most effectively to the constituency in question." And we might add that the best translation of the gospel in flesh and blood is "a loving and lovable Christian."

You are manifestly an epistle of Christ, ministered by us, written not with ink but by the Spirit of the living God, not on tablets of stone but on tablets of flesh, that is, of the heart. 2 Cor. 3:3.

Pray for the work in Hungary, where there are now 3,599 Seventh-day Adventists. Pray also for the 10.6 million people.

L. R. Conradi visited Transylvania, in Hungary, in 1890 with the result that a woman convert went to the Hamburg Publishing House and translated several Bible readings into Hungarian and took charge of their distribution throughout Hungary. Three years later the church had 30 small tracts published in the language. By 1904 membership in Hungary had grown to nearly 200.

IN TOUCH WITH THE PEOPLE

Adoniram Judson and his wife, Nancy, were the first Protestant foreign missionaries to set sail from America. They arrived in India in 1812, but, forced from there, headed for Penang on the Malay Peninsula. In Penang the threat of deportation resulted in the Judsons sailing for Rangoon, Burma.

Secluded in their mission house, they felt too separated from the Burmese people. They noticed that Rangoon had many Burmese zayats—shelters for resting, discussing the day's events, or listening to Buddhist lay teachers.

The Judsons became convinced that living in a zayat would put them in touch with the people. So they built one complete with Burmese seating patterns and other elements familiar to the people. The concept worked Almost immediately visitors who had never come to the mission house began stopping by, and only one month after the Judsons opened their zayat the first Burmese made a profession of faith.

As we reflect upon the experience of the Judsons, what lessons can we learn that will help to remove barriers and establish common ground between us and the people we are trying to reach for Christ in the family, in the neighborhood, or where we work?

When Adoniram Judson went to Burma as a missionary, he had such a strong desire to preach the gospel before he had learned the language that one day he walked up to a Burmese man and embraced him. The man went home and reported that he had seen an angel.

The radiant joy of Christ's presence was in Mr. Judson's very countenance. So much so that men called him Mr. Glory Face.

To the weak I became as weak, that I might win the weak. I have become all things to all men, that I might by all means save some. 1 Cor. 9:22.

Pray for our work and workers in Burma, where we have a church membership of 12,315 in a population of 39.4 million. Seventh-day Adventist work began in 1902 when Herbert Meyers and A. G. Watson entered the country to sell Seventh-day Adventist books. Soon after his arrival, Meyers met a Christian Burmese woman whose mother Adoniram Judson had baptized. Through reading the Bible, the woman had become convinced some two years previous that the seventh-day Sabbath is the true day of worship. She and her brother became Seventh-day Adventists.

OTHERS MAY, YOU CANNOT

"Others May, You Cannot" is the title of a little leaflet written by an unknown author long ago.

God has called you to be like Jesus. He will draw you into a life of crucifixion and humility, and put upon you such demands of obedience that you will not be able to follow other people, or measure yourself by other Christians.

Other Christians and ministers, who seem to be highly religious and useful, may promote themselves, pull wires, and work schemes to carry out their plans, but you cannot do it.

Others may boast of themselves, of their work, of their success, of their writings, but the Holy Spirit will not allow you to do any such thing.

Others may be allowed to succeed in making money, or have a legacy left them, but God wants you to have something far better than gold—namely, a helpless dependence on Him.

The Lord may let others be honored and put forward, and keep you hidden in obscurity, because He wants to produce some choice, fragrant fruit for His coming glory, which can only develop in the shade.

The Holy Spirit will put a strict watch over you, with a jealous love, and will rebuke you for little words and feelings, or for wasting your time and money, which other Christians never seem distressed over. So make up your mind that God is an infinite Sovereign, and has a right to do as He pleases with His own.

Settle it forever, then, that you are to deal directly with the Holy Spirit, and that He is to have the privilege of tying your tongue, or chaining your hand, or closing your eyes, in ways that He does not seem to use with others. Now when you are so possessed with the living God that you are, in your secret heart, pleased and delighted over this peculiar, personal, private, jealous guardianship and management of the Holy Spirit over your life, you will have found the vestibule of heaven.

Oh, the depth of the riches both of the wisdom and knowledge of God! How unsearchable are His judgments and His ways past finding out! Rom. 11:33.

Pray that God will give you peace as you surrender completely to the leading of the Holy Spirit in your life and let Him mold you as the potter shapes the clay.

SEEDS OF TRUTH

The seeds of Adventism first reached Russia through the influence of German colonists who settled there and received exemption from military service. Some of these families migrated to America in the 1870s, and after becoming Seventh-day Adventists, sent tracts and books in German to their families and friends back home in Russia. Through these publications, Russians also became interested.

Leaving the state church was punished by banishment to Siberia. One of the early Seventh-day Adventists told how her father, a Russian army officer, discovered from his study of the Bible that the seventh day was the Sabbath. He taught his children to observe it, and for doing so the authorities exiled him to Siberia.

At about the same time, in the middle 1870s, Theophil A. Babienco assisted an Orthodox priest in the church services by reading the psalms. Obtaining permission to take the Bible home, he gathered his neighbors in the evenings and read to them from it. Through such readings he learned that many doctrines believed and taught by the state church were not scriptural. When he asked the priest about this, the clergyman asked him to return the Bible, but later at Kiev he purchased a copy of his own. Several others obtained Bibles and began to share Babienco's views. Babienco went to the governor in Kiev to obtain the necessary permission to erect a church building for his group of Bible-believing Christians, but instead, the authorities arrested and exiled him to a remote area. While in exile he secured a Bible, and after two years of study he began to observe the seventh-day Sabbath and to expect the soon return of Jesus to earth. At this time he had not heard of Seventh-day Adventists and was not aware that there was a world church which believed and taught as he did.

L. R. Conradi organized the first Seventh-day Adventist Church in Russia in 1886.

"For the eyes of the Lord run to and fro throughout the whole earth, to show Himself strong on behalf of those whose heart is loyal to Him." 2 Chron. 16:9.

Pray that the honest in heart throughout the vast Union of Soviet Socialist Republics will have an opportunity to know Jesus. The Soviet Union has a population of 287 million, with an estimated 32,400 Seventh-day Adventists.

LONELINESS

Loneliness is one of the great challenges of our day. It leads to drugs, immorality, and suicide. A widow who leaped to her death from her twelfth-floor apartment in Chicago left this note: "I can't stand one more day of this loneliness. I have no friends. I receive no mail. No one calls me on the telephone. I can't stand it any longer."

After hearing of the tragedy, her neighbors said, "We didn't know she felt that way." Her story is a sober reminder that loneliness exists even among crowds of people.

Perhaps one of God's suicide preventatives appears in this instruction: "Wherever a church is established, all the members should engage actively in missionary work. They should visit every family in the neighborhood and know their spiritual condition" (*Testimonies*, vol. 6, p. 296).

As we learn the spiritual condition of those we meet, we will in some instances recognize suicidal tendencies, and by the grace of God we may help spare a life. God has entrusted His church with a work upon which hangs human destinies.

There are many kinds of loneliness. One is the loneliness of solitude, or just being physically alone. An extreme example is a prisoner in solitary confinement. But we also find loneliness in the midst of society, as in the case of the Chicago woman who jumped to her death although surrounded by apartments filled with people.

Many experience the loneliness of suffering. You can find examples in hospitals and nursing homes. Related to it is the loneliness of guilt. More people than we can imagine are waiting for one of God's messengers to come with the good news "You are forgiven."

You can also find the loneliness of mental anguish in an unhappy marriage. An increasing number suffer the loneliness of old age and the loneliness of being far from home.

We can thank the Lord that there is also a loneliness for God that draws us to Him. Every life has a God-shaped vacuum, and we are restless until we find rest in Christ. An awareness of Christ's presence in our lives is the ultimate answer to loneliness.

"They should seek the Lord, in the hope that they might grope for Him and find Him, though He is not far from each one of us." Acts 17:27.

Pray for the thousands of church members in the 30 inhabited islands of the Bahamas, that they may reach those who do not know Jesus.

WORRY CAN MAKE YOU ILL

More illnesses result from worry than germs. Prolonged worry can affect the working of all the organs of the body. Dr. W. C. Alvarez, a stomach specialist at the Mayo Clinic, said, "Eighty percent of the stomach disorders that come to us are not organic, but functional. Wrong mental and spiritual attitudes throw functional disturbances into digestion. Most of our ills are caused by worry and fear, and it is my experience that faith is more important than food in the cure of stomach ulcers."

The devil is robbing many Christians of victorious living because they do not realize that worry is one of his devices. Worry is looking into the future without God in the picture. Missionary and author E. Stanley Jones went so far as to say that worry is actually atheism, because it is the opposite of faith.

The key to the cure for worry is in the hand of God. When the sinister shadows of worry threaten our lives, we are to turn them over by faith to our all-wise heavenly Father, who cares for us and wishes to relieve us of our burdens of anxiety. Counting our blessings will cause worry to melt like icebergs floating in tropical seas.

A woman who was a chronic worrier sat in her doctor's office more disturbed than she had ever been before. "What's the problem?" the physician asked.

"Well, Doctor, you know how through the years I have worried about everything. I worry about the weather, I worry about the economy, I worry about my family, I worry about my work—I worry about everything! The first thing when I wake up in the morning, I start worrying about something. But, Doctor, this morning when I woke up, for the first time that I can remember, I wasn't worried about anything. Now I'm worried about this radical change in my behavior pattern."

Often when we stop to look at the things we worry about, it becomes evident that our anxious thoughts cannot possibly help matters. Many times the things we spend so much energy being concerned about never happen. In many cases worry has simply become a habit, and like all bad habits, it needs to be overcome.

Commit your way to the Lord, trust also in Him, and He shall bring it to pass. Ps. 37:5.

Pray for Barbados, which, in a population of 256,000, has 9,349 Seventh-day Adventists.

LIFE'S IRRITATIONS

Life's irritations often come in the form of people. To describe the effect such people have on us, we use such expressions as: "He gets on my nerves" or "He gets under my skin."

When a grain of sand invades an oyster, the oyster makes a pearl out of it. With God's help, we too can turn every irritant that comes our way into a pearl for His kingdom.

"If we keep uppermost in our minds the unkind and unjust acts of others we shall find it impossible to love them as Christ has loved us" (*Steps to Christ*, p. 121). Step 1 in dealing with those who irritate us is to stop focusing on their negative qualities.

Step 2 is to center our thoughts on the love of Christ. "If our thoughts dwell upon the wondrous love and pity of Christ for us, the same spirit will flow out to others. We should love and respect one another, notwithstanding the faults and imperfections that we cannot help seeing" (*ibid.*).

Step 3: "Cultivate the habit of speaking well of others. Dwell upon the good qualities of those with whom you associate, and see as little as possible of their errors and failings. When tempted to complain of what someone has said or done, praise something in that person's life or character" (*The Ministry of Healing*, p. 492).

The prayerful practice of these three steps will ease irritations and might even produce some pearls. Praying for the persons who provoke us will bring freedom from such exasperations.

Edwin Markham set forth the principle in verse when he wrote:
"He drew a circle that shut me out—
Heretic, rebel, a thing to flout.
But Love and I had the wit to win:
We drew a circle that took him in!"

The world needs people who will lift others up, encourage them, inspire them, and build them.

The most glorious victory you can have over an enemy is to turn him into a friend!

Finally, all of you be of one mind, having compassion for one another; love as brothers, be tenderhearted, be courteous. 1 Peter 3:8.

Pray for the advance of the gospel in the extremely dry country of Botswana, especially for evangelistic work among the 50,000 Bushmen of the Kalahari.

142

A MOTHER'S INFLUENCE

H. C. Mabie was a contemporary of D. L. Moody. Something his mother did when he was about 4 years old eventually shaped his entire life.

Mabie was sitting on his mother's lap at a missionary meeting. As the medical missionary made his appeal and the offering plate came by, Mabie saw his mother slip a prized keepsake gold ring from her finger and drop it into the plate in place of money. The little boy saw his mother wipe the hot tears from her face. He sensed that something significant was going on, and his heart joined her tears of emotion as she gave her gift.

When Mabie was a college student, his pastor gave him a list of nearly 200 young people, challenging him to find them and lead them to Christ. He visited them one by one, and by the end of the summer virtually each one had been converted.

Dr. Mabie believed that the real secret of evangelism was to lead an individual into the practice of following whatever light he had.

When Dr. Mabie was pastoring in Minneapolis, Dr. Ivan Panin, a Russian lecturer, came to town to speak on atheism, and Dr. Mabie went to hear him

In the lecture the man declared himself to be an honest atheist. It encouraged Dr. Mabie to make an appointment to visit him at his hotel, where he challenged the atheist on the basis of John 7:17. The text says that if a man will do God's will, he will know the doctrine. Mabie presented his challenge so convincingly that Panin canceled his lecture engagements and left the city. Two years later he returned to Minneapolis, where he had last lectured against Christianity, and there he made his public confession of faith in Christ and was baptized.

Just as Mabie's life was influenced by the sacrificial gift of his mother, your life might be influenced by Mabie's example in witnessing so that you will begin doing as he did—simply encourage persons to put into practice whatever light they have. Persevere in this practice, and you will see results.

"If anyone wants to do His will, he shall know concerning the doctrine, whether it is from God or whether I speak on My own authority." John 7:17.

Pray for our expanding church in Kenya, where, in a population of more than 23 million, there live 263,211 Seventh-day Adventists.

A TRIBUTE TO MOTHERS

Susanna Wesley was the twenty-fourth or twenty-fifth child of an Anglican clergyman. She married Samuel Wesley, who was also an Anglican clergyman and a scholar, but a rather impractical man, unable to cope with the everyday duties of life. He spent time in debtor's prison because of unpaid bills.

In spite of her responsibilities as a preacher's wife and the mother of a large family, Susanna safeguarded three periods a day for her own solitary prayer and devotions. Praise and thanksgiving constantly characterized her life.

On one occasion Susanna started worship meetings in her kitchen. When her husband heard of this, he sent word to her to stop them immediately. She sent word back that she would not stop unless he sent her a written command to stop, so that when each of them should stand before the final great tribunal, her conscience would be clear in the matter. The written command never came, and the meetings continued. Such small group meetings for Bible study and testimonies became an important part of early Methodism.

Susanna set aside time every week for each of her children. Thursday night was her son John's time, and he remembered those appointments fondly to the end of his life. A born teacher, she spent six hours a day educating her children, in addition to all of her other duties. Years later her children talked of how she gave them a love for learning. She had the ability to react to adversity in positive ways because she had a sense of self-worth. Her trait of self-discipline and her orderly methods show up in early Methodism and its emphasis on disciplined, methodical, orderly worship.

John Wesley, the most famous of her children, was the product of a Christian home and the dedication of a mother who invested her life in the training of her children.

Let's show appreciation to our mothers. Let's express that appreciation today and every day by word and action.

> **Her children rise up and call her blessed; her husband also, and he praises her. Prov. 31:28.**
>
> *Pray for mothers, who have the potential of being the most important of all missionaries. Pray that they will give top priority to their role in parenting.*

ARE YOU HURTING?

Are you hurting? Does it seem that everybody and everything are against you? Perhaps you feel as the psalmist did when he wrote: "For I was envious of the boastful, when I saw the prosperity of the wicked." "They are not in trouble as other men, nor are they plagued like other men." "For all day long I have been plagued, and chastened every morning." "Behold, these are the ungodly, who are always at ease; they increase in riches" (Ps. 73:3, 5, 14, 12).

The psalmist felt greatly perplexed by the apparent lack of justice in the world: "Until I went into the sanctuary of God; then I understood their end" (verse 17). The sanctuary is the great object lesson of the plan of salvation. There the justice of God stands revealed. Those who have been unfairly treated in this life will receive the justice they deserve.

Many times we become unhappy and disgruntled when we attempt to be conscientious yet observe that the careless appear to be rewarded and we deprived. It seems unjust, and we get to the place where we envy those who prosper.

Don't let envy rob you of your peace of mind. Trust the justice of God that assures everyone ultimate fairness. It is God's task to keep score and settle accounts, not yours or mine.

A Christian accompanied a non-Christian friend on a duck-hunting expedition. When the Christian spoke of his faith in Jesus, his friend challenged him with a question: "Why do you have more trouble in life than I do when you are the one who claims to be a Christian?" Moments later the hunter shot at some ducks. Some fell dead into the water, but one fell wounded. The hunter's dog immediately went after the wounded duck.

"Why did your dog go after the wounded duck?" asked the Christian. When the hunter answered that there was no need to try to catch the dead ducks, the Christian applied the illustration: "The devil doesn't bother going after you because he's already got you, but he goes after me because he's still trying to get me!"

Beloved, do not avenge yourselves, but rather give place to wrath; for it is written, "Vengeance is Mine, I will repay," says the Lord. Rom. 12:19.

Pray for the 4.5 million people of the People's Republic of Benin, a long, narrow country wedged between Nigeria and Togo. It is the least evangelized of all the non-Muslim countries of Africa. We have 316 members there.

PRAY FOR GOOD JUDGMENT

An appropriate prayer for each of us to pray daily would be "Dear Lord, please give me good judgment."

Judgment affects many areas of our lives, including the sometimes controversial question of how we dress. Let us agree that God is more concerned with our hearts than with our outward appearance, but He could well be interested in both.

Peter says: "Do not let your beauty be that outward adorning . . . but let it be the hidden person of the heart, with the incorruptible ornament of a gentle and quiet spirit, which is very precious in the sight of God" (1 Peter 3:3, 4).

Paul, writing on the same subject, specifically mentions gold and pearls (1 Tim. 2:9). By the way, "braided" hair apparently refers to the custom of braiding gold or silver strands into the hair.

Our God is a lover of beauty and is, of course, the Creator of precious minerals and jewels. Revelation's description of the New Jerusalem mentions a street of gold, gates of pearl, and walls of jasper.

Gold, silver, and precious stones are not wrong in themselves. It is the heart motive that matters with God. We cannot read motives, nor do we know the thinking or moral values of another, and therefore we should not judge. But some will judge us, and we don't want to be a stumbling block to anyone. In view of this, and considering what the Bible says on the subject of ornaments, it seems appropriate to invest in souls rather than adorning our mortal bodies.

Princess Eugenie of Sweden sold her diamonds to build a home for the incurably ill. On one of her visits to the institution, she met a patient who had lived an extremely wicked life. The princess talked to the woman about Christ and His love, and asked the matron to follow up the contact.

On a later visit the princess found the invalid with a bright and radiant face because a new hope was in her heart. Upon returning to the palace, the princess said to her husband with tears in her eyes, "I saw the glitter of my diamonds today!"

"Therefore give to Your servant an understanding heart . . . that I may discern between good and evil." 1 Kings 3:9.

Although Seventh-day Adventists are the largest Protestant denomination in Belize, a former British colony in Central America, please pray for the many groups as yet unreached with the gospel.

THE POWER
OF THE PRINTED PAGE

In 1889 a colporteur by the name of William Arnold, who was selling publications on the island of Antigua, sold a book to a Mr. Palmer. Palmer sent the book he had purchased to his son James, who lived in Kingston, Jamaica. James liked what he read and wrote to the International Tract Society, requesting more literature.

The society sent a supply of tracts to James Palmer, and he distributed them in the city of Kingston. One of the recipients was a physician who was not particularly interested in reading the material, but passed the tracts to a British woman, Mrs. Margaret Harrison. As she read the tracts, she became convinced of the Sabbath, but did not begin immediately to observe it.

One Sunday the pastor of Mrs. Harrison's church preached a sermon on the Ten Commandments. During the sermon the Holy Spirit called her attention to the Sabbath of the fourth commandment, and right there in the Sunday service she decided to honor God's holy day.

She learned that the Palmers were studying with several people who were interested in Seventh-day Adventist teachings, and she opened her home for the group's meetings.

In 1893 Mrs. Harrison went to Battle Creek, Michigan, for medical treatment. While there she attended the General Conference session and asked that the church send a missionary to Jamaica. A. J. Haysmer and his family went in answer to her plea. In March 1894 the first church in Jamaica was organized with 37 members. That congregation today has a membership of about 6,000.

Today one in 24 inhabitants of the small island of Jamaica (150 miles long and 50 miles in width) is a Seventh-day Adventist, but the government census bureau lists a much higher number of persons giving a Seventh-day Adventist denominational preference. Our membership now is 130,853, and it all began through a colporteur, a book, and some tracts.

So shall My word be that goes forth from My mouth; it shall not return to Me void, But it shall accomplish what I please, and it shall prosper in the thing for which I sent it. Isa. 55:11.

Pray for the work in Jamaica. Include the name of at least one literature evangelist in your prayer today, and pray that God's Holy Spirit will this day bless the message in the form of books, tracts, and Bible lessons.

WHAT WOULD JESUS DO?

What does it really mean to be a Christian? Charles M. Sheldon, in his religious classic *In His Steps,* tells of a group of Christians who pledged themselves for an entire year not to do anything without first asking the question "What would Jesus do?"

The book traces the experience of a newspaper editor, a college president, a wealthy heiress, a brilliant opera singer, and a young couple in love, each making every decision of his or her life on the basis of the question "What would Jesus do?"

What happens when business and professional people make every decision on the basis of such a question? Isn't this what it means to be a Christian? But is it really practical? Will it really work as we approach the twenty-first century?

Think about the last time someone asked you to give time or money to some needy cause. How did you relate to the last person who irritated you? Consider the last time someone mistreated you. How did you react on each occasion? What would Jesus have done?

If you should decide to do nothing without first asking "What would Jesus do in this situation?" would it alter your way of life?

Perhaps we are afraid of what might be the consequences if we should do as He would have done. However, God wants us to leave the consequences with Him. He wants to know that we love Him enough to trust Him. And remember: God gives the best to those who leave the choice to Him.

We must trust the Lord enough to believe that when we do as Jesus would have done, we are doing all He requires.

A United States senator was visiting Mother Teresa's work among the poor of India. When he saw the magnitude of the need and the little that one individual could possibly do, he asked her, "Don't you get discouraged when you see how little one person can do when the need is so great?"

"No," she replied, "because God does not require success, but He does require faithfulness." And faithfulness is what it really means to follow in the footsteps of Jesus.

He who says he abides in Him ought himself also to walk just as He walked. 1 John 2:6.

Pray for our work in Guinea-Bissau, wedged between Senegal and Guinea. The church has unprecedented opportunities for evangelization and church planting, for the majority of the people have never heard the good news of the gospel.

CAMPUS MINISTRY

A Christian engaged in campus ministry decided to use something other than the usual approach of logic and argument. Simply describing what Jesus was like as a person, he talked about the things He valued, especially people. He spoke about the quality of relationships that Jesus desired and enabled His people to have.

In response, the students freely revealed how competitive and insecure they felt, how much they abhorred phoniness and elitism, and how surprised they were that Jesus was concerned with such things. The speaker was delighted to find that the atmosphere among the students was one of beauty and grace, of openness, love, and acceptance.

We too need to be able to communicate Jesus in fresh and descriptive ways to make our sharing more effective. Whereas our human tendency is to preach to people, to give answers to questions people are not yet asking, Jesus Himself always seemed to be either asking questions or telling stories. Everybody loves a story, partly because it utilizes both sides of the brain, sparking our creative, imaginative side as well as the conceptual, rational part of us.

A New York lawyer said that he would be a Christian if somebody could prove to him that Jesus really rose from the dead. A clergyman provided him with a manuscript containing factual arguments on the subject, but a week later the lawyer admitted, "I have found out that my chief trouble is not with my head, but with my heart."

Christian writer Josh McDowell says that often more people on university campuses are willing to consider truth than in any other segment of society. International students are especially receptive, and often they are the future leaders of their countries. The frontiers of foreign missions are in our own neighborhoods and on our campuses.

And I, brethren, when I came to you, did not come with excellence of speech or of wisdom declaring to you the testimony of God. For I determined not to know anything among you except Jesus Christ and Him crucified. 1 Cor. 2:1, 2.

Pray for students on secular campuses, that they might have a chance to hear Christ's message.

A LIVING BRIDGE

In one of the large cities of the eastern United States a multistory apartment house in the poorer section of town caught fire. A father and three boys aged 3, 5, and 7 years were trapped on the top floor. The lower stories were already ablaze, and there seemed to be no way of escape.

Looking out the window, the father saw a window at the same level in the building next door. And that window was open! The two buildings were a little more than three feet apart.

The father explained his plan of action to his three boys. He would make of his body a living bridge to span the gulf between the two buildings. The oldest boy would cross first and would then be able to reach out and steady his two younger brothers as they passed over.

The plan worked, and the three boys crossed over to safety, but the father did not have strength left to pull himself to safety. Losing his grip, he plunged to his death. He saved his boys, but it cost him his life.

Sin has created a gulf that separates man from God. When the fires of the last days ravage the earth, we need to escape the burning, and God has prepared a way. Only Jesus can bridge the gulf caused by sin. He said, ''I am the way, the truth, and the life. No one comes to the Father except through Me'' (John 14:6). Like the father of the three boys, Jesus gave His own life in order to save us.

Jesus is the only way—the only bridge—but we can be the ramp to the bridge. Think of the many different kinds of ramps that lead to Jesus. It could be a book, a sermon, a Christian message on radio or TV. Or it could be a Christian neighbor, physician, businessman, or tradesman. You or I could be the ramp that will guide the footsteps of some wayfarer to Jesus, the only bridge from this world to the next.

Jesus said to him, ''I am the way, the truth, and the life. No one comes to the Father except through Me.'' John 14:6.

Pray for Italy, where 5,000 Seventh-day Adventists represent the church among a population of 57.4 million. Pray for the personal outreach of believers as well as our radio and TV ministry there.

THE CALLED-OUT ONES

A typographical error turned up in some kindergarten material. A flower vase was to be used for an illustration, and the author instructed the leader to fill the vase with *followers*—"real or artificial are all right."

The church consists of followers of our Lord. Ideally, all followers should be real, but some are artificial. The artificial might look like the genuine, but they are man-made while the genuine are the work of God.

Ekklesia, the Greek word translated "church," means "a calling out." The message of the gospel summons people out of confusion and worldliness into the fellowship of the church. The church is made up of called-out ones, those who respond to God's call.

The Bible pictures the church as a body, a bride, a family, an army, a temple, and a city—"Jerusalem above." Believers are portrayed in group settings: a limb in a body, a sheep in a flock, a soldier in an army, and a stone in a building.

Sometimes a person will say, "I want to be baptized, but I don't want to join the church." But that is an impossibility, because "by one Spirit we were all baptized into one body. . . . For in fact the body is not one member but many" (1 Cor. 12:13, 14).

"And the Lord added to the church daily those who were being saved" (Acts 2:47). A newborn Christian needs the warmth of the church as much as a newborn baby needs the warmth of its mother's arms. "God requires His church to nurse those who are young in faith and experience" (*Evangelism*, p. 352).

Sometimes we speak of the invisible or universal church made up of all true believers, many of whom have not had opportunity to learn all the doctrines but who have a personal relationship with Jesus. Who these believers are only God knows, but as greater enlightenment becomes available, leading them to the remnant church, these sincere people will walk in the light and become part of the visible organized church.

The church bears responsibility for nurture and outreach, and God's plan is to equip the members so that each will in some way minister to others and share the good news (see Eph. 4:11-13).

And He is the head of the body, the church, who is the beginning, the firstborn from the dead, that in all things He may have the preeminence. Col. 1:18.

Pray for the more than 63 million people of Guangdong (gwong-doong), meaning "wide east." This province, with Canton as its capital city, is located on China's south coast.

151

THE BLESSING OF FORGETFULNESS

Have you ever heard anyone say "I don't remember as well as I used to"? Someone else has commented: "There are three signs of old age. The first is forgetfulness. And the other two I can't remember!"

While forgetfulness can be frustrating, the inability to forget could be an even greater problem. Wisely the Creator formed the brain with the ability to store memory in more than one place. Each time we recall the same thought, the brain will place a record of it in a slightly different place. Another way of visualizing it is to think of strings attached to thoughts we want to remember. The more strings, the better chance of retrieving a thought or memory when we need it. Continuing to recall or study a thought increases the number of strings leading to it. But if we seldom recall the thought or memory, the strings unravel or get tangled.

To forget the unpleasant experiences and sorrows of life is a natural and instinctive tendency, and what a fortunate tendency it is! A healthy mind will dwell on the happy and pleasant events of life. Those who have witnessed great suffering in time of war know the blessing of forgetfulness as those haunting memories become less vivid. The apostle Paul also knew the blessing of forgetfulness. As a persecutor of the Christians, he had been responsible for many atrocities. And then his life miraculously changed on the Damascus road when he had an encounter with Jesus.

Try to imagine Paul's experience in those early years as a Christian. Many times he must have faced congregations that included wives and brothers and sisters of Christians whom he had caused to be put to death. Only a miracle of grace made it possible for those surviving family members to forgive and forget, and accept him as a brother in the faith.

He had to accept the fact that God had forgiven him, and he had to accept that forgiveness and try to forget the past. Paul was speaking from deep personal experience when he said:

Brethren, I do not count myself to have apprehended; but one thing I do, forgetting those things which are behind and reaching forward to those things which are ahead, I press toward the goal for the prize of the upward call of God in Christ Jesus. Phil. 3:13, 14.

Portugal, Europe's southwesternmost state, has faced many political and economic upheavals. Pray for our 6,960 members there, for there are many new opportunities for evangelism in this country of more than 10 million.

FROM SMALL BEGINNINGS

We need to restudy the history of the beginnings of the Advent movement and feel anew the warmth of the fire that burned in the pioneers. God repeatedly warned the Israelites not to forget the past. He had them build memorials to great events so that when the children should later ask what the memorial meant, they could be told the story of God's leading in earlier days.

It was on May 21, 1863, 128 years ago today, in Battle Creek, Michigan, that the General Conference of Seventh-day Adventists first organized and adopted a constitution. In 1844 the first Sabbath-observing Adventist group came into being, and the publication of the *Review and Herald* began in 1850. By 1863 Adventism had 125 churches and a total of 3,500 members.

By 1990 the world membership had grown to 6.8 million. The 125 churches have multiplied to become 29,039, and the 30 salaried evangelistic workers of 1863 have grown into a force of 123,694.

From that small beginning 128 years ago, a worldwide movement has developed. Think of what a challenge it was to the vision of the pioneers when Ellen White said: "I looked intensely over the world, and I began to see jets of light like stars dotted all through this darkness; and then I saw another and another added light, and so all through this moral darkness the starlike lights were increasing. And the angel said, 'These are they that believe on the Lord Jesus Christ, and are obeying the words of Christ. These are the light of the world; and if it were not for these lights, the judgments of God would immediately fall upon the transgressors of God's law.' I saw then these little jets of light growing brighter, shining forth from the east and the west, from the north and the south, and lighting the whole world" (*Selected Messages*, book 1, p. 76).

What a privilege it is to be a part of the fulfillment of this thrilling prophecy.

Arise, shine; for your light has come! And the glory of the Lord is risen upon you. For behold, the darkness shall cover the earth, and deep darkness the people; but the Lord will arise over you, and His glory will be seen upon you. Isa. 60:1, 2.

Pray for the people in Suriname, a republic and former Dutch colony located on the northeast coast of South America, where the population of 400,000 includes 2,097 Seventh-day Adventists. Seventh-day Adventist evangelism began there in 1894.

DIVINE NATURE

The corruption that is in the world is all too evident. Some have moved to isolated areas, trying to get away from physical and moral corruption. Others have retreated to monasteries only to discover that the cancerous corruption is actually a part of our very nature.

We can escape the corruption that is around us and part of us in only one way, and that is by becoming partakers of a new divine nature, the result of the new birth.

It is by acting upon the promises of God's Word that we experience the new birth and receive a new nature. One biblical promise tells us that by receiving Jesus we become sons and daughters of God (John 1:12). As members of the family of God, we partake of the divine nature.

Another promise assures us that if we are in union with Christ, we are new creatures (or new creations) with a new nature (2 Cor. 5:17).

Meade MacGuire, in his book *Lambs Among Wolves*, tells an imaginary story of a little wolf that tried to become a lamb by associating with a flock of sheep and imitating them. Do you think a wolf who really tried hard could become a lamb? No, of course not! Can a leopard change his spots by diligent effort? No. Can a human being alter his corrupt nature into the divine nature by his own efforts? No. But God can give us a new nature if we will believe His promises—promises that will never fail.

"What God has promised, He is able to perform" (*The Desire of Ages*, p. 98). The supreme proof of the dependability of God's promises is the fact that He fulfilled the most costly promise He ever made when He gave His Son to die for our sins.

With unfaltering confidence, Paul writes of the "hope of eternal life which God, who cannot lie, promised before time began" (Titus 1:2).

If you are battling with a bad temper, pride, dishonesty, evil thoughts, or any other temptation, God's Word contains a promise exactly suited to meet your need. Claim it today.

> **His divine power has given to us all things . . . by which have been given to us exceedingly great and precious promises, that through these you may be partakers of the divine nature, having escaped the corruption that is in the world through lust. 2 Peter 1:3, 4.**

> *Pray a prayer of faith, claiming a Bible promise to meet some need in the family or in your own life.*

PEOPLE PROBLEMS

In order to have friends, we must be friendly and willing to give of ourselves. And in order to make friends, we must take some initiative. However, many well-meaning people with habits that repel others wonder why they don't have more friends. Some people with socially unacceptable habit patterns include: the critic or gossip who tears down other people, leaving the impression that when you are not present, you might well be one of his victims; the person who talks continuously about himself, boasting of his ideas, exploits, and plans; the individual who lacks the good judgment to respect the privacy of others, asking questions that are none of his business; the argumentative person who is always right; the chronic complainer; and the person who gives the impression that he is using people to his own personal advantage.

The sad part about those who repel rather than attract others is that they often have many wonderful qualities, but they lack the sensitivity to discern what is socially acceptable and what is not.

The Scottish poet Robert Burns expressed a sentiment that we might do well to echo when he said:

> "O wad some Power the giftie gie us
> To see oursels as ithers see us!
> It wad frae monie a blunder free us, and foolish notion."

At the end of the first hour of driving lessons, the learner said to his instructor, "This is easy! There really isn't anything to it." The instructor didn't comment, but simply suggested they go from the quiet country road into the rush-hour traffic. In a few short minutes beads of perspiration were rolling down the student's brow as impatient drivers honked and pulled around him. When he finally returned to the country road, he said to his instructor as he mopped his brow, "It would be OK if it were not for the other people!"

And often that's the way it seems in life. Most of our problems are people problems, but let us try to be part of the solution rather than the problem. Where we are wrong, may God make us willing to change, and where we are right, may He make us easy to live with.

If it is possible, as much as depends on you, live peaceably with all men. Rom. 12:18.

Pray for our believers in Bulgaria, a Balkan state.

HOW CAN WE KNOW GOD?

John Wesley had been studying and preaching the need for a closer relationship with God for at least nine years, and yet he had not gained more than 30 followers. One day a friend asked him the penetrating question: "John, do you know God?"

Can you imagine the impact of such a question on Wesley, who for nine years had been advocating a closer relationship with God?

Whatever he replied, the questioner persisted: "But John, do you know God?" The conversation ended with those words echoing and reechoing in his ears: "John, do you know God?"

On his way back to England from America, Wesley said, "I went to America to convert the Indians; but, oh! who shall convert me?" Wesley saw in the lives of some Moravian missionaries a peace that he did not possess.

It was on May 24, 1738, 253 years ago today, that John Wesley attended a meeting in Aldersgate Street at which someone was reading Luther's preface to the Epistle to the Romans. In his diary Wesley wrote: "About a quarter before nine, while he was describing the change which God works in the heart through faith in Christ, I felt my heart strangely warmed." From that time on, he could say with confidence that he knew God. A new power came into his ministry. Now that his life was truly changed, the lives of others were being changed through him. Wesley had studied deeply and systematically. He knew a great deal about God and His Word, but the peace and power came when he found that personal relationship with Him.

How do we come to know God personally? Here are some steps:

1. Make the definite choice to know God personally.

2. Admit our need for such an experience.

3. Have an intense desire for such an experience.

4. Read the Bible devotionally, not just for information.

5. Establish meaningful communication with God through prayer.

6. Meditate on God's love and goodness. Count our blessings with gratitude.

7. Share with others the spiritual blessings He bestows upon us.

> **"And this is eternal life, that they may know You, the only true God, and Jesus Christ whom You have sent." John 17:3.**
>
> *Pray that you will know God so well that you will feel His concern for a lost world. Then knowing God will mean eternal life to you and those whom you reach for Him.*

THE ARMS OF THE CHURCH

"God's Spirit convicts sinners of the truth, and He places them in the arms of the church. . . . God requires His church to nurse those who are young in faith and experience, to go to them, not for the purpose of gossiping with them, but to pray, to speak unto them words that are 'like apples of gold in pictures of silver' " (*Evangelism,* p. 352).

How wide and warm are the arms of your church? The following should be considered minimum requirements of a church body that hopes to attract and hold new members.

1. Love all who enter so that their expectations will not meet with disappointment. A soldier lay mortally wounded in one of the trenches on a battlefield. Knowing the danger involved, his friend jumped up and ran through a rain of mortar fire to reach the side of his companion. He made it, but he himself was mortally wounded. The tide of battle turned, and other soldiers managed to get to where their two buddies lay. "Why did you do it when you knew you would be shot?" a soldier asked the one of the two who was still alive. "I got here in time to hear his dying words, and I'm still glad I came, because he said, 'I knew you would come.' "

2. Accept those who come just as they are. Some fear that such acceptance and confidence will cause the standards of the church to go down, but experience has shown that the confidence demonstrated by such an attitude actually motivates the standards to rise. Acceptance is just as essential to the survival and growth of a new Christian as it is to a newborn baby.

3. Demonstrate unconditional forgiveness. Perhaps you have visited a tourist attraction at which someone has a photograph or painting with space cut out for tourists to poke their heads through so that their faces will appear to be part of the picture. When you think of your church as the body of Christ, it is good to ask yourself the question Would Christ as the head look fitting joined to my church as the body, or would it be something grotesque that would cause people to turn away in disgust at the incongruity of it all?

And the Lord added to the church daily those who were being saved. Acts 2:47.

Pray for your church that it will be loving and warm.

LIKE CHILDREN

An increase in the family calls for some preparation, and it involves some expense and inconvenience. When the baby finally arrives, the parents experience more expense and inconvenience. Children need attention, protection, and a lot of care. Above all, they need love. Like children, new converts come into the church requiring care and attention and love, and we must realize that it will take time for them to mature spiritually.

Can you imagine a couple bringing a new baby home from the hospital and saying "Help yourself to food in the refrigerator, and if you need anything when we are both away, call one of the neighbors." You say, "That is ridiculous," but it is no more so than the way we often treat new members. Too often the attitude at the time of a baptism is that a year from now, 75 percent of these people will be out of the church. And our very attitude makes it a self-fulfilling prophecy.

Children sometimes stray into dangerous places. Imagine a father coming home from work and asking his wife "Where is little Danny?" And she replies "I don't know. I haven't seen him for a couple days. He has probably fallen into sin. In fact, he may be moving into another family. You know, we really don't need him. He's always messing up his room and is just a lot of trouble."

Do you really care for the people in your fellowship? What happens when somebody leaves your church? If you go after them and get them back, you'll be more excited about the fact that they returned than about all those who never left. God and the angels are concerned about every straying child, and we should share that concern.

Some years ago I visited an orphanage in Vietnam that had 1,800 children ranging in age from a few days to 18 years, with virtually no paid staff. As I watched the older children caring for the younger, I felt it was a good demonstration of the love and caring that should characterize every congregation of God's church.

> **"Assuredly, I say to you, unless you are converted and become as little children, you will by no means enter the kingdom of heaven." Matt. 18:3.**
>
> *Pray that God will make you a caring big brother or sister to those who are younger in the faith.*

KEYS CALLED
PROMISE AND PRAYER

In John Bunyan's immortal *Pilgrim's Progress*, Christian and Hopeful, falling asleep on the grounds of Giant Despair, were captured by the giant and thrown into the dungeon of Doubting Castle. For four days and nights they languished in the foul atmosphere of their dark cell, beaten and abused at intervals by their captor. Finally, when death itself stared them in the face so that all hope seemed lost, they began to pray, and throughout the fourth night they kept vigil with God.

Early the next morning Christian began to chide himself for having forgotten that he had a wonderful magic key in his possession called "Promise," which, he felt sure, would open any door of the castle. When he put the key in the lock of their dungeon, the door readily opened, admitting them into the outer corridor. To their great joy, the same key opened the door from the corridor into the courtyard.

When they came to the main gate of the castle, Christian found that his key moved with great difficulty. However, the lock finally opened just in time for the two men to escape the pursuing giant.

Bunyan's allegory is rich with practical lessons for us. Too often we find ourselves suffering torment as prisoners in dungeons of doubt and despair. And too often we forget the keys called "promise" and "prayer" that have power to set us free. So many pilgrims on the Christian way have let their keys become so rusty from lack of use that they find them turning the locks to liberty only with great difficulty.

"Why should the sons and daughters of God be reluctant to pray, when prayer is the key in the hand of faith to unlock heaven's storehouse, where are treasured the boundless resources of Omnipotence?" (*Steps to Christ*, pp. 94, 95).

When you find yourselves tossed by temptation into seeming dungeons of doubt and despair, remember the keys of promise and prayer that will set you free or enable you to bear it.

No temptation has overtaken you except such as is common to man; but God is faithful, who will not allow you to be tempted beyond what you are able, but with the temptation will also make the way of escape, that you may be able to bear it. 1 Cor. 10:13.

Pray today for the southeast African state of Mozambique. Pray that this Communist land may open up for the preaching of the gospel.

SEEK AND YOU WILL FIND

Prospectors exploring for precious metals have no guarantee that their quest will be rewarded, and yet many have spent a lifetime at it. Those who hunt for the spiritual treasure of truth have the sure promise that their search will not be in vain if they persevere with sincerity. "And you will seek Me and find Me, when you search for Me with all your heart," we are promised in Jeremiah 29:13.

A man was telling his friend how he had struck it rich. "Gold?" the other asked eagerly. "No, God," he replied. And he was right, for to find God is the greatest riches of all.

In 1864 Charles Breyfogle went to Death Valley in search of buried treasure. He wandered so long across the desert in his quest that he felt he would have given a fortune in gold for a cup of water to quench his desperate thirst. But he had neither gold nor water.

In the distance Breyfogle caught sight of something green. As he trudged up a reddish hill, he kicked a rock that sparkled in the sunlight. It was yellow with gold! As he excitedly explored the area, he found evidence of gold all around him—enough gold to make Breyfogle the richest man in the world.

But the poor man was near death for lack of food and water. He had no way of transporting it or marking the location. There was no water near the green bush he had seen. What could he do? Picking up a few rock samples, he wandered almost in a stupor for many days, sustaining himself on bunches of grass and brackish water. He walked some 200 miles before he was rescued by a rancher, who nursed him back to health.

On repeated expeditions Breyfogle attempted to find again that rich deposit of gold by a reddish hill. Countless others have searched for it also, but no one has found it. A prospector will spend his last dollar and his last ounce of strength to make one more expedition because he has hope—but no promise. In the spiritual realm we have hope *and* a promise.

And you will seek Me and find Me, when you search for Me with all your heart. Jer. 29:13.

Pray that a revival may come to the materialistic, permissive segments of the population of beautiful Sweden, where in a population of more than 8 million, Seventh-day Adventists number 3,295.

BIG MEN AND WOMEN

Colonel George Boone, a descendant of the great Daniel Boone of pioneer Indian war days in the United States, was elected to the office of state senator. He was six feet eight inches tall and a man of striking appearance. At the same time he was also an extremely able debater.

One day Colonel Boone's opponent on an issue that came to the floor of the state senate was a man with a very thin, high-pitched voice and a height when standing erect of four feet ten inches.

Senator Boone would make an assertion, and his little opponent would shout at the top of his squeaky voice, "That's a lie! That's a lie! That's a lie!"

Unperturbed, Senator Boone would continue calmly: "As I was saying, Mr. President." Boone acted as though he were not even aware of the little man who kept insisting "It's a lie!"

Finally, in sheer desperation and in a futile attempt to get attention, the little senator sprang from his seat, rushed over, and pounded the big senator on the back.

Senator Boone completely ignored the little man until he closed his speech. Then turning around with curiosity, he looked down and asked, "What are you doing here?"

"What am I doing here?" snapped the angry little man. "I'm fighting!"

"Fighting whom?"

"I'm fighting you," his exasperated opponent gasped.

"Me!" exclaimed the big senator as though completely surprised.

By that time the little man with the shrill voice had reached a state of emotional exhaustion, and someone had to assist him to the cloak room.

Someone said, "A church member cheated me out of $40 ten years ago, so I stopped going to church." Another claims, "A church member circulated an untrue story about me in the community, so I dropped out."

We must be too big to spite, or we shall be too small for heaven. Above all, we must be too big to let little grievances separate us from the Lord.

Great peace have those who love Your law, and nothing causes them to stumble. Ps. 119:165.

Cameroon is a country on the continental hinge between West and Central Africa. It has a population of almost 11 million, with 39,279 Seventh-day Adventists. Pray for the 400,000 Fulbe in Cameroon and widely dispersed from West Africa to Sudan. Ninety-nine percent Islamic, they are somewhat open to Christianity.

ATMOSPHERE OF GLOOM

An elderly widow was the terror of her household. She had made life miserable for her husband until the day of his death. Now she was living with her son and daughter and was treating them the same way. An unhappy, discontented woman, she always created an atmosphere of gloom and dissatisfaction about her. Her conversation centered on the past. But it was always the sordid events of the past—injustices done to her, painful experiences rehearsed in all their morbid detail.

She talked of her illnesses and operations—much of which she blamed on childbirth—and you can imagine how that made her children feel. Every symptom of a possible disorder she magnified into a matter of life-threatening magnitude. She didn't know that "it is a positive duty to resist melancholy, discontented thoughts and feelings—as much a duty as it is to pray" (*The Ministry of Healing*, p. 251).

The family had as little to do with her as possible. Her children and grandchildren came less and less frequently to see her because it was so depressing. She had created an atmosphere that kept them away—an atmosphere that no one enjoyed being in. In time she became full of self-pity.

Eventually something happened. It seemed as though her whole personality changed—her whole attitude toward life.

One day one of the family members dared to ask her what had happened. "Well," she said, "for the first time I have seen myself as others see me. All my life I have been discontented and unhappy. No matter how I tried not to be, I was still that way. Finally it bothered me so much that I said the only thing I can do is just to be content with my discontent."

She found that when she took that attitude, her discontentment disappeared.

Her family discovered something else had happened. For the first time in her life she had given her heart fully to Jesus Christ. Like the apostle Paul, she had discovered that we can do all things through Christ.

Not that I speak in regard to need, for I have learned in whatever state I am, to be content. Phil. 4:11.

Pray for the more than 7.3 million people of the Dominican Republic, the eastern two thirds of the island of Hispaniola, shared with Haiti. The Seventh-day Adventist Church is the largest Protestant church, with a membership of 63,893.

THINK BIG

"We are altogether too narrow in our plans. We need to be broader minded. . . . His work is to go forward in cities and towns and villages. . . . We must get away from our smallness and make larger plans" (*Evangelism*, p. 46).

The foundation of all church growth is God's love for mankind and His desire to save the lost. Witnessing is a biblical doctrine. It is a command of God to proclaim the good news of God's love to everyone everywhere, but when we view our mission in the perspective of Calvary, it is transformed from an obligation into a delight, and sharing becomes natural. We cannot accomplish the great commission in our own strength, but we have the guarantee of His accompanying power.

The expression "all nations" in the gospel commission includes every caste, every language group, every city, every community, and every person in every house in every neighborhood.

Furthermore, we must never separate the great commission from the great commandment, which is to love the Lord with all our hearts and our neighbor as ourselves. Love is the motivation and the means of fulfilling the great commission.

Rebecca Manley Pippert, in her book *Out of the Saltshaker*, tells of a new Christian who finally got up the courage to speak to a close friend about the Lord, but then nervousness overcame her, and her carefully prepared approach completely vanished from her mind.

Embarrassed by her inability to remember what she had planned to say, she broke into tears and blurted out, "I came to talk to you about the Lord."

Her friend replied, "I was prepared to give you a really bad time. But I wasn't prepared for this. I didn't know you cared so much." Then the author makes the point that we transmit dynamic Christian truth relationally rather than propositionally.

Remember, the most winnable people groups, in prioritized order, are friends, relatives, associates, and neighbors. At first thought, those in these groups may seem unreachable, but keep in mind the power of God and think big! Expect miracles and miracles will happen.

"Is anything too hard for the Lord?" Gen. 18:14.

Pray that we may establish the church in San Marino, a tiny enclave on the Adriatic coast of Italy. It is probably the oldest state in Europe, with an area of only 24 square miles. The population is 23,000, with no Seventh-day Adventists. However, colporteurs go there regularly to distribute publications.

163

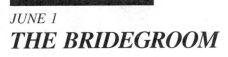

JUNE 1

THE BRIDEGROOM

The famous Indian poet Kalidasa tells the story of an Indian prince who desired to marry a beautiful and gentle Persian princess. The king organized a party of trusted servants to make the long journey, arrange the marriage, and bring the beautiful princess to the young prince.

In the caravan party that was returning to India with the princess was a handsome young man, the overseer of a small band of servants, who began to pay special attention to the princess. At first the girl was unresponsive, but slowly the overwhelming charm and politeness of the young man began to steal her affections.

It was first an approving glance, then a smile, and then secret meetings outside the tent after nightfall. They shared many moments together, and soon the princess realized that she, for the first time in her life, had fallen deeply in love.

The last evening was indeed a sad one as the princess and her suitor met for what she thought would be their final time together. Her heart was inextricably bound to the young servant, and now she must wrench her love from him and give it to an unknown prince. They wept, and with broken hearts they parted.

The next day servants took the princess to the court to meet the prince who would become her husband. There was a rustle as he entered the room, but she did not even look up until a familiar voice called her name. It was a glorious moment when she raised her eyes and saw the form of her lover in princely attire, the very servant who had courted her all along the way.

The Lover of our souls came first as a servant, but today the church waits eagerly for the appearance of the Bridegroom as a prince. The church has known Him, for it is He who has led her all along the way. As you reflect on the many ways the Prince of heaven has wooed you and won your love, it will intensify your desire for His coming and will inspire you to share this love with others.

And as the bridegroom rejoices over the bride, so shall your God rejoice over you. Isa. 62:5.

Iran, formerly Persia, has a population of 51.2 million, with 60 Seventh-day Adventists. The Adventist Church began in Iran in 1911 when two Americans, F. F. Oster and Henry Dirksen, entered the country. Pray for its progress in this country.

164

GLUED TOGETHER

A little girl who was attending a church wedding for the first time whispered to her mother, "Did the lady change her mind?"

"No, dear," her mother answered. "What makes you think that?"

"Well, she went up the aisle with one man and came back with another."

With an understanding smile, the mother explained to her daughter that the bride entered with her father, who was to give her away, and left with her husband.

But too many men and women do change their minds. One of the social concerns of the twentieth century has been the constantly rising divorce rate. The insecurity and emotional upset imposed on children by the divorce of their parents is a handicap more damaging than even the victims themselves fully realize. Children of divorced parents subconsciously tend to blame themselves for their parents' problems.

Sometimes parental interference destroys a marriage. Parents need good judgment to accept their new role after the marriage. If they do not accommodate to the changed relationship, there will unavoidably be conflicts of loyalty.

The newly married couple, along with the parents on both sides, will have a wonderful opportunity to demonstrate practical Christianity in terms of interpersonal relations. Each should try to put himself or herself in the other's shoes and then practice the golden rule. Resist every temptation to speak critically or sarcastically of other family members. Look for the strengths and not the weaknesses in each other.

God said, "Therefore a man shall leave his father and mother and be joined to his wife" (Gen. 2:24). Here the Hebrew word has the connotation of being joined as with glue. God's intention was that marriage should be a lifelong relationship.

"Around every family there is a sacred circle that should be kept unbroken. Within this circle no other person has a right to come. Let not the husband or the wife permit another to share the confidences that belong solely to themselves" (*The Ministry of Healing*, p. 361).

Every person reading these words can contribute to the success of a Christian marriage, either your own or someone else's.

Be kindly affectionate to one another with brotherly love, in honor giving preference to one another. Rom. 12:10.

Pray for those who are afflicted with leprosy in the slums of Calcutta, that they may know the joy of receiving Jesus as Saviour.

PRAYING HANDS

It was about 1490 that 19-year-old Albrecht Durer and another young man slightly older served as apprentices in a wood-carving establishment in Nuremberg, Germany. Both men came from homes of poverty, so they shared a room to save expenses as they pursued their common ambition to become master artists.

Frustrated by their lack of money, they hit on a plan—one would study while the other worked and supported both of them, then the other would study while the first worked. Each was willing to yield first benefits to the other, so they finally tossed a coin, and the decision was made that Durer would go first.

Durer left Nuremberg and went to Vienna to study under the greatest painter of his time. The other young man went to work first in a restaurant and then in a blacksmith shop. No toil was too menial or hard because he was helping his friend to receive the training he himself also desired and looked forward to.

Durer returned to Nuremberg with a large sum of money from the sale of one painting. Now he would do for his friend what his friend had done for him.

Arriving unannounced and unexpected at the room of his friend, Durer recognized the voice of his friend in prayer. He entered the room quietly and saw his friend kneeling in prayer, with his hands uplifted. Durer stood spellbound, gazing intently at those toilworn hands with enlarged joints, twisted fingers, and stiffened muscles.

Instantly Durer realized that the toilworn hands of his friend could never become the hands of a master artist. Durer made a brush drawing of those praying hands, and no doubt you have seen a copy of this famous work, which for nearly 500 years has inspired men and women around the world and told the story of devotion and friendship.

Durer's friend and benefactor, whose faith in God was far stronger than any disappointment in life, took this experience as one of the blessings handed him from the all-loving Father who knows what is best. He found satisfaction in knowing that he had helped Durer to be what he wanted to become.

"Greater love has no one than this, than to lay down one's life for his friends." John 15:13.

Please pray for students who desire and long to reach their goal but have no funds to pursue their formal education.

SIGNS OF THE TIMES

The first issue of the Signs of the Times was printed in Oakland, California, on June 4, 1874. The idea for the publication came to James White as he spent a few days of rest and relaxation in the Rocky Mountains.

The June 11, 1874, issue stated the periodical's objective: "The Signs of the Times is designed to be not only an expositor of the prophecies, a report of the signs of our times, but also a family, religious, and general newspaper for the household." The unique subscription policy was explained in these words: "The *Signs* is offered without money or price to all who do not object to receiving it on such terms. Two dollars a year to those who choose to pay a subscription price, and free to all others."

Before the *Signs of the Times* had its own printing facilities, the employees had to transport the heavy bundles of paper and typeset copy down the street to the printing office, and in order to cut down on expenses, William C. White, son of James White, hauled the heavy materials in a wheelbarrow. Although the pay scale for employees ranged from 7 to 11 cents an hour, no financial inducements could lure the faithful young people into more lucrative work.

It was James White who urged that a publishing enterprise be established to print the *Signs of the Times*. When someone read White's message at a camp meeting in Yountville, California, in 1874, the congregation of 400, plus many weekend visitors, responded liberally with an offering of $19,414.

Many reading these words received the Adventist message through the *Signs of the Times*. Many of us send subscriptions to prejudiced relatives who never read it, but finally some do and are converted. Greater results in terms of numbers would occur if we offered the journal to those who want it. This can be ascertained by sharing copies with friends, relatives, neighbors, associates, by visiting door to door, or by using a direct mail plan to locate receptive and interested people.

"But others fell on good ground and yielded a crop; some a hundredfold, some sixty, some thirty." Matt. 13:8.

Pray for those who receive our evangelistic journals, and for those who would benefit by receiving a subscription, that many more may be able to trace their conversion to them.

THE PRICE OF SERVICE

One foggy morning in 1955 John Napolii, an Italian fisherman, returning with his catch, piloted his boat beneath the Golden Gate Bridge, into San Francisco harbor. He was surprised to see people in the water. The hospital ship, Netherlands, had collided with an oil tanker.

Everywhere people shouted, "Help me! Save me! I'm drowning!"

Carefully the fisherman guided his fishing vessel to a cluster of drowning men. Quickly he began to pull them aboard one by one. Soon the small fishing boat was overcrowded. John Napolii made one of the hardest decisions of his life. He knew that the lives of those men were more important than his small fortune of fish. Within minutes he unloaded his entire cargo of 2,000 pounds of fish, worth thousands, into the waters of San Francisco Bay and pulled more than 70 people aboard his boat.

Do you think John Napolii was ever sorry for his decision? Do you think he ever regretted placing top priority upon people and not things? For years after, he met those whom he had saved and rejoiced with them. If you want to know that joy, commit your life to saving others.

As we individually determine our priorities, we must decide whether the souls of men or the things that can be bought with gold are more important to us. John Napolii made his decision. He paid a price to save 70 lives. What are we willing to give for a soul?

"I will make a mortal more rare than fine gold, a man more than the golden wedge of Ophir." Isa. 13:12.

Pray for the advance of the church in Malta. The little nation consists of three inhabited and three uninhabited islands located about 60 miles south of Sicily. The population is 358,000, and no Seventh-day Adventist church yet exists there. The official religion is Roman Catholic.

When Giuseppe Catalano, then publishing department secretary for southern Italy, learned that Malta, where Paul had been shipwrecked, had never been visited by Seventh-day Adventist missionaries, he laid plans to go to the island as a colporteur in 1957. He returned the next year with another colporteur and received permission for Seventh-day Adventist literature evangelists to work three months each year. We now have a church there.

PEBBLES ALONG THE PATH

When I was a small boy, my mother used to tell me a story about a child who dropped pebbles as he walked along a path through the forest so he would be able to retrace his steps and keep from getting hopelessly lost.

Have you ever searched for a Bible promise or a text to support some cherished belief only to find yourself hopelessly lost in the Bible?

When I was a new Seventh-day Adventist trying to share my faith, someone gave me a copy of the little book *Helps to Bible Study*, by J. L. Shuler. The book described a simple system for chain-marking texts in your own Bible on the basic doctrinal subjects.

You use a flyleaf at the front or back of your Bible as the index page on which you write (or better yet, neatly print) your list of topics. After each topic you put the first Bible verse in that particular study with code letters to identify the subject. For example, the topic on the Second Coming might be listed: Second Coming of Christ—1 SC John 14:1-3.

The numeral 1 indicates that it is the first text in this study. John 14:1-3 tells you where to turn for your first text. Across from John 14:3, in the margin of your Bible, you will write 2 SC Acts 1:9-11 or whatever reference you choose as your second text.

You can get your sequence of texts from a set of Bible lessons or from a book such as *Bible Readings for the Home*. The time required to mark your Bible will be one of the best investments you have ever made. Proof of the value of this system is the fact that the little book by J. L. Shuler has remained in print for more than 40 years!

Not only is a marked Bible a valuable tool for sharing your faith, but it is a source of personal encouragement as you review the "pebbles" you have dropped along the way.

"Whom will he make to understand the message? . . . For precept must be upon precept, . . . line upon line, . . . here a little, there a little. Isa. 28:9, 10.

Pray for the more than 4.2 million people of Ningxia-hui (Ning-she ah), meaning "serene summer." The word "hui" (whey) attached to the original name means "Islam." Two thirds of the people of this province are Muslims.

THE PEOPLE WITH THE BOOK

On the day of Pentecost God manifested the gift of tongues for the purpose of communicating the gospel. One such example of the gift in modern times is the experience of Sekuba, an African Bushman of the Kalahari Desert, in what is now Botswana.

One night a shining being appeared to Sekuba and told him to travel eastward and search for the people who had the Book and could tell him about the true God.

The Bushman told his family about the strange dream and then, with a sense of urgency, began his eastward journey. He walked 150 miles across the desert before he came to a village.

For Sekuba, with absolutely no formal education or any language skills, to communicate with any people other than the Bushmen would have been a miracle. And that miracle happened! Sekuba was able to speak the Tswana language, which he had neither heard before nor studied.

He inquired for the people with the Book, and someone took him to the pastor of the church to which the chief belonged. Deeply moved by Sekuba's story, the pastor brought out a large Bible, which Sekuba recognized immediately as the book he had seen in his dream. Satisfied, Sekuba fell asleep that night, but during the night the angel told Sekuba that he must continue searching until he found a church that practiced everything taught in the Book, including the observance of the seventh-day Sabbath.

In the morning the pastor became angry when Sekuba insisted he must continue his search. Arrested for defying the chief's church, he was tried in an outdoor court. But the British commissioner was so impressed by Sekuba's story that he released him.

The next morning a small cloud hovered close to the ground, and Sekuba followed it until he came to the Seventh-day Adventist mission. He became a believer and took the third angel's message back to his family.

Until his death in 1957 Sekuba retained the ability to speak, read, and write the Tswana language—truly a gift of tongues that led him to the people with the Book.

> **Blessed is he who reads and those who hear the words of this prophecy, and keep those things which are written in it; for the time is near. Rev. 1:3.**

> *Pray for the more than 14 million people of Xinjiang (shin-jee ong), meaning "new frontier." This desolate region, the largest province of China, borders Russia, Mongolia, Tibet, India, and Afghanistan.*

170

DO NOT TOUCH ME

People movements caused by persecution, war, drought, economic conditions, or whatever reason have played a vital role in the spread of the Adventist message.

German immigrants moving to Brazil were an important part of the spread of Seventh-day Adventist teachings in that country. One such family, the Kumpels, fled from Sao Pedro city to the jungle because of a revolution in the south of Brazil. They found refuge in a place called Nao-me-Toque.

The Kumpels began a home Sabbath school and were able to interest other families in joining them each week for Bible study and worship. Soon a company formed that later became a church. The baptism of the Kumpels' converts was one of the first baptisms conducted by an Adventist pastor in Brazil, and the church in Nao-me-Toque was one of our first churches in that country.

Though the name of the city, Nao-me-Toque, means "do not touch me," the Adventist message touched many honest hearts in that place. And through the influence of that first church and school, other lives are being touched in many places, because that church and school have produced scores of pastors, missionaries, medical personnel, and church administrators.

Think of the exciting possibilities for growth if every isolated individual or family in the Seventh-day Adventist Church around the world would start a small Sabbath school and invite friends and neighbors to join them for Bible study, fellowship, and worship.

The Sabbath meeting in your home could be a care support group for those who are experiencing bereavement, terminal illness, divorce, or other traumatic experiences. It should be a time of warm fellowship suited to the needs of those present, with opportunity to express needs and time for prayer and singing.

God's messenger says: "Invite your neighbors to your home, and read with them from the precious Bible and from books that explain its truths. Invite them to unite with you in song and prayer. In these little gatherings, Christ Himself will be present, as He has promised, and hearts will be touched by His grace" (*The Ministry of Healing*, pp. 152, 153).

"For where two or three are gathered together in My name, I am there in the midst of them." Matt. 18:20.

Pray for the more than 3 million Lambadi people located throughout much of south central India. Living in isolated groups, the majority are animists and are extremely cautious toward Christianity. Only 5 percent are Christians.

171

PRAYER IDEAS

John Fletcher, who was intimately associated with John Wesley, was known for his life of unceasing prayer. People said of him that the very walls of his room were stained by the breath of his prayers.

Martin Luther was also a man of prayer. He said, "I have so much work to do that I cannot get along without giving three hours daily of my best time to prayer." His everyday motto was "He that has prayed well has studied well."

George Mueller said, "I went to my God and prayed diligently and received what I needed." It was the story of his life.

Sometime try the experiment of a continuous chain of intercession, letting those whom you know pass before your mind as one suggests another and praying for each in turn.

The church's most vital resource is prayer, and its greatest lack. Without increasing the number of Christian workers or their financial support, we could see multiplied results if we would only multiply prayer. And if we did increase prayer, we would discover that people and funds would expand in effectiveness also.

Christ rules the world through prayer. As God's royal priesthood we are to share this rule by intercession for others even as Christ constantly intercedes for us.

We have been given access to heaven's throne room so that we may join our intercession with that of Christ.

Sir Thomas Browne, a beloved English physician of the 1600s, was an example of constant prayers of blessing. He prayed for the occupants of the houses that he passed as he made house calls. As he encountered a church building, he would send up a prayer for the people who worshiped there, asking that souls might be saved there. Constantly he prayed for his own patients and those of other physicians. After hearing a sermon, he prayed for a blessing on God's truth and upon the messenger. When he would see a handicapped person, he would pray that God might give him wholeness of soul and physical wholeness in the resurrection.

Pray without ceasing. 1 Thess. 5:17.

Pray for Paraguay, where the first Seventh-day Adventist missionary, a colporteur by the name of Lionel Brooking, arrived in 1892. An interest that led to the first five baptisms in Paraguay resulted from someone sending a German missionary magazine from Uruguay to his brother in Paraguay.

CHECKBOOKS DO TELL TALES

The stubs of a person's old checkbooks provide reliable information about what that person considers to be most important. They reveal where a man is putting his treasure and what he loves most, the value placed on the cause of Christ, and his faithfulness or unfaithfulness in stewardship.

What story do the checkbook stubs tell of the balance between temporal and spiritual interests? Study carefully what you did with the money you earned over a period of time. A sizable chunk of earnings goes into the automobile, an even larger piece into the house, and various amounts into the wardrobe. Can you detect love of self? It is a universal blight that attacks saints as well as sinners. Devastating in its effects, it eats out a person's soul, leaving a hollow, empty shell. Covetousness binds a man in clanking chains of slavery to things.

"As the people of God approach the perils of the last days, Satan holds earnest consultation with his angels as to the most successful plan of overthrowing their faith. . . . Says the great deceiver: . . .'Go, make the possessors of lands and money drunk with the cares of this life. Present the world before them in its most attractive light, that they may lay up their treasure here and fix their affections upon earthly things. . . . Make them care more for money than for the upbuilding of Christ's kingdom and the spread of the truths we hate. . . . Every selfish, covetous person will fall under our power, and will finally be separated from God's people" (*Testimonies to Ministers*, pp. 472-474).

What does my checkbook tell of my commitment to God's church? How much of what I have earned have I translated into tithes and offerings? How much has gone as help for the poor? How do my earthly securities balance with my "treasure in heaven"?

Covetousness is as sinful as idolatry, for it is worship at the shrine of self.

As we reflect on our checkbooks, let's resolve to convert more of what God has entrusted to us into investments that promise eternal benefits.

"Do not lay up for yourselves treasures on earth, where moth and rust destroy and where thieves break in and steal." Matt. 6:19.

The explosion of evangelism that has rocked Seoul, the capital of South Korea, has not yet penetrated many towns. Farther to the south and on South Korea's scattered islands, many people are either Buddhists or spirit worshipers. Pray for the nearly 6 million Buddhists of South Korea.

WHERE ARE YOU?

When God asked Adam the question "Where are you?" the question was for Adam's benefit rather than God's. God knew where the first man was, but He wanted to be sure that Adam knew where he was.

Where was Adam? He was trying to hide from God because of a sense of guilt. The first man was living in a state of disobedience because he had made a decision on the basis of what seemed right to him in spite of the fact that God had said not to do it.

When God asks us the question "Where are you?" does it embarrass us to give an honest answer? Have we really stopped to consider where we are living spiritually? Some of us who cherish honor and recognition would have to admit we are living on Popularity Plaza. For those of us who hunger for recognition and the applause of the multitude, our address might be somewhere on Achievement Avenue.

The desire to move in high social circles and to be looked upon as experienced in the ways of the world might mean that we have landed on Sophistication Circle. To live for clothes, cars, furniture, boats, and silver and gold shows that we dwell on the Thoroughfare of Things. When we get caught up in the pursuit of pleasure and spend our time hunting thrills to lift us from our boredom, we frequent Entertainment Expressway. Or when resentment or revenge festers in our souls, we have settled in a haunted house on Hate Highway.

As we said yesterday, your check stubs might give you a clue. The way you spend your money tells a lot about where you live, for "where your treasure is, there will your heart be also" (Matt. 6:21).

Do you recognize any of these as the street on which you live? Where do you live? The way you spend your time—especially your free time—is an indication of where you live. To answer the question "Where are you?" find the street on which your imagination drives most frequently. Examine the motives that prompt your daydreams. What decides your selection of reading material? Would you feel comfortable to invite Jesus to move in where you live?

"For in Him we live and move and have our being, as also some of your own poets have said, 'For we are also His offspring.' " Acts 17:28.

Pray for students from unentered countries who are attending Western universities, that Christian witness might reach them.

DWELL IN SAFETY

Toward the end of the Mau Mau uprising in Kenya in 1960, a missionary couple was returning one night to Nairobi through the heart of Mau Mau territory, where Kenyans and missionaries alike had been killed. Seventeen miles outside of Nairobi their Land Rover stopped. The missionary could not restart it. They spent the night in the car, claiming the promise of Psalm 4:8. In the morning they managed to repair the car and continue their journey.

A few weeks later the couple received a visit from a local pastor. He told them how a member of the Mau Mau had confessed that on the night of March 23 he and three others had crept up to the car to murder its occupants. But when they saw 16 men surrounding the car, they left in fear.

During their furlough the missionary couple met a friend who provided another link in this thrilling story. He told them that God had placed a heavy prayer burden upon his heart for them on March 23. Calling the men of the church, he assembled a group of 16 men and prayed until the burden lifted.

"How graciously and tenderly our heavenly Father deals with His children! He preserves them from a thousand dangers to them unseen and guards them from the subtle arts of Satan, lest they should be destroyed. . . . We do not . . . appreciate the ever-watchful interest that our kind and benevolent Creator has in the work of His hands" (*Testimonies*, vol. 3, p. 373).

"Every redeemed one will understand the ministry of angels in his own life. The angel who was his guardian from his earliest moment; the angel who watched his steps, and covered his head in the day of peril; . . . what will it be to hold converse with him, and to learn the history of divine interposition in the individual life" (*Education*, p. 305).

Heaven will reveal many wonderful accounts of how God has used special prayer burdens to advance His cause and protect His people.

I will both lie down in peace, and sleep; for You alone, O Lord, make me dwell in safety. Ps. 4:8.

Martinique, an overseas department of France, is an island in the West Indies. The Seventh-day Adventist church began there in 1919 when Philip Giddings, a Seventh-day Adventist missionary from Guyana (formerly British Guiana), visited Martinique, won one convert, and interested another man. In 1924 Giddings moved to Martinique, organized a Sabbath school in his house, and baptized the first four converts.

PRAYER AND FASTING

Immediately after his first encounter with Christ on the Damascus road, Paul spent the next three days without food or drink (Acts 9:9). From that time on fasting was a regular part of his spiritual discipline. In 2 Corinthians 6:5 Paul mentions "sleeplessness" and "fastings." Sleeplessness signifies going without sleep, and fasting means abstaining from food.

"It is true that there are unbalanced minds that impose upon themselves fasting which the Scriptures do not teach, and prayers and privation of rest and sleep which God has never required. . . . They have a pharisaical religion which is not of Christ, but of themselves. They trust in their good works for salvation" (*Testimonies*, vol. 1, p. 556).

We need to avoid the extremes of going without sleep and food from spiritual pride. There are times and circumstances, however, when it might be appropriate to spend a night in prayer alone or with others. And sometimes fasting can bring both spiritual and physical benefits. But there are other times and circumstances when our greatest need is for a good night's sleep or a healthful meal.

In the first verses of Acts 13 we read of five leaders in the church at Antioch praying and fasting together. According to Scripture, they "ministered to the Lord" (verse 2). Through such ministry to the Lord, the Holy Spirit provides the direction and power needed for effective ministry to others. We might consider this an important part of the global strategy in the early church. It was during this experience that the Holy Spirit revealed that He had a special task for two of the men—Barnabas and Saul. Again followed praying and fasting and the laying on of hands before the church sent them forth to fulfill their mission.

As new congregations rose under the ministry of Paul and Barnabas, they prayerfully selected new converts to be ordained as elders in every church, and through the ministry of prayer and fasting, they commended them to the Lord (Acts 14:23).

As they ministered to the Lord and fasted, the Holy Spirit said, "Now separate to Me Barnabas and Saul for the work to which I have called them." Then, having fasted and prayed, and laid hands on them, they sent them away. Acts 13:2, 3.

Pray for the elders in your congregation that God will strengthen them spiritually so that they in turn may strengthen others.

THE UNCHANGING THEME

John 3:16 is probably the best known and the most loved verse in all the Bible. Someone has called it "everybody's text," and "the gospel in a nutshell." This verse shows us God acting, not for His own sake, but for ours. It tells us that no one is excluded from God's love, even the one who spurns it. Augustine said, "God loves each one of us as if there was only one of us to love."

Henry Moorehouse, the English preacher who so mightily influenced D. L. Moody through his sermons on the love of God, began preaching at the age of 16. Like his Master, Moorehouse died at the age of 33, and during his entire ministry of 17 years he only had one text. The text for his first sermon was John 3:16, and the text for his last sermon was John 3:16. The text for all his sermons in between was John 3:16. Of course, he preached different sermons, but he always used the same text.

Moorehouse received an invitation to preach in Moody's tabernacle in Chicago during the great evangelist's absence. When Moody returned, he found that by popular demand Moorehouse was preaching every night. Moody sat in the back of the packed tabernacle and listened as Moorehouse spoke, always using the same sermon text.

At his last meeting Moorehouse said, "My friends, for a whole week I have been trying to tell you how much God loves you; but I cannot do it with this poor stammering tongue. If I could borrow Jacob's ladder, climb up to heaven, and ask Gabriel, who stands in the presence of God, to tell me how much God loves sinners, all he could say would be"—and Moorehouse concluded by quoting John 3:16.

"For God so loved the world that He gave His only begotten Son, that whoever believes in Him should not perish but have everlasting life." John 3:16.

Pray for the church in the great country of Australia, with a population of 16 million and an Adventist membership of 45,738.

The first Sabbath school in Australia was held on July 4, 1885, in a suburb of Melbourne. Alexander Dickson, of Melbourne, first preached Adventist teachings on the island continent. He came in contact with the Adventist message while serving as a missionary of another denomination in Africa. There he met Hannah More, another missionary who had become a convert to Adventism. When Dickson returned to Australia, he published tracts and traveled about preaching the Adventist doctrines.

177

THE SEEKING FATHER

The night that followed the last day of the battle of Gettysburg left thousands dead and wounded strewn over the battlefield. About 9:00 that evening a little spot of light appeared. It was an old Quaker with his lantern, hunting for his boy who was in the Union Army.

As the Quaker father went along with his lantern, he looked into the faces of the dead and wounded, crying out, "John Hartman, thy father calleth thee."

Some poor boy nearby would say to himself, "Would to God that it was my father."

The father pursued his relentless search, with his voice piercing the night air: "John Hartman, thy father calleth thee." He heard men groan and curse, but then in the distance he detected a voice, weak but familiar. The ears of love are keen. They pick up the words: The ears of love belong to the father: "Here, Father; here, Father. This way, Father."

At last the seeking father finds his wounded and bleeding son. He lifts him to his shoulder and carries him home and to healing. What a beautiful portrait this is of our loving heavenly Father. Another picture is found in the story of the prodigal son.

When the prodigal returned, "still a great way off, his father saw him and had compassion, and ran and fell on his neck and kissed him" (Luke 15:20). That father was never able to forget his wayward boy. We can imagine that every day the old man's eyes focused on that spot on the horizon where he had last seen his boy.

Even when rumors indicated that the boy had turned to a life of debauchery and disgrace, that father still loved his son and longed for his return. What a joyful moment it was when the son and father were reunited.

Many sons and daughters have been wounded in the battle with sin and Satan, but the heavenly Father never gives them up. Day and night He is calling them home, and His eyes eagerly search the horizon for evidence that one is returning.

Your name may not be John Hartman, but whatever it is, your heavenly Father is calling you.

Have you accepted His call?

As a father pities his children, so the Lord pities those who fear Him. For He knows our frame; He remembers that we are dust. Ps. 103:13, 14.

Pray for those who have been wounded in the battle with Satan, to whom the loving Father seeks to bring healing.

FATHER'S DAY

The third Sunday in June is Father's Day—a day to honor fathers, and a time for fathers to take a personal inventory and be sure they have shown themselves worthy of honor and respect.

Fathers have the tremendous privilege of representing the heavenly Father. Here is the story of one who did. This father was about to administer necessary punishment for his daughter's disobedience. "If you spank me, I'll run away from home and I won't come back," the little girl threatened. But the threat did not deter the father.

After receiving the punishment, which she deserved, the little girl removed her dirty clothes from the clothes basket, made a small bundle of them, tucked them under her arm, and slipped out the back door into the night.

The father saw the little girl's head as she passed the window near where he was sitting. Waiting until she reached the front sidewalk, he followed her, keeping out of sight behind the trees.

When the child came to the first corner, she paused to consider which way to go. From behind a tree the father watched her. Suddenly she turned and retraced her steps toward home. When she passed the tree behind which her father was hiding she was whimpering to herself. As she neared home, she began to run—across the lawn and through the rear door by which she had left. The father entered the house by the front door and resumed sitting by the window.

Hearing a feeble knock, he opened the door, and the little girl leaped into his arms, crying, "Oh, Daddy, if you'll let me come back, I'll never run away again."

The beautiful part of the story is the fact that there was not a single moment when the father was not watching over his child. And it's that way with God! He does not forsake us, even when we rebel against Him. At the farthest point from home the little girl would have received an instant response if she had called. Lovingly the father watched over her each step of the way. Lovingly he stood by, ready to help if called upon. Lovingly he received her into his arms and forgave her.

His name shall be called . . . The everlasting Father. Isa. 9:6.

Pray for fathers that they may be faithful in representing the heavenly Father to their families.

GOD IS WITH US

John Wesley is a good example of a man with a clear sense of mission. From dawn to dusk he galloped on horseback over the rough roads of England, leaving the hoofprints of his horses on about 220,000 miles of British soil, an average of 4,000 miles a year. Most of his reading he did while riding on horseback. During all those years he preached some 40,000 sermons.

At 51 Wesley almost died of consumption, but at 86 he was still galloping to his appointments. At 83 he confessed sheepishly in his diary that he was unable to write more than 15 hours a day without tiring his eyes.

A woman once asked him, "Suppose you knew you were to die at midnight tomorrow. How would you spend the intervening time?" Without a moment's hesitation he explained that he would keep his appointments, including a sermon that night and one at 5:00 the next morning. Then he would ride to another town for afternoon and evening meetings. "I should then go to friend Martin's house, who expects to entertain me, converse and pray with the family as usual, retire to my room at 10:00, commend myself to my heavenly Father, lie down to rest, and wake up in glory." Such was the spirit of a man with a clear sense of mission.

England of Wesley's day was steeped in immorality, and the church was asleep. There was desperate need for revival and reformation, and God used him as His instrument for awakening a mighty revival in the dead pulpits of a slumbering church.

Wesley was born 288 years ago today, on June 17, 1703. The June 17, 1739, entry from his diary reads in part: "I preached, at seven, in Upper-Moorfields, to (I believe) 6,000 or 7,000 people." "At five I preached on Kennington Common, to about 15,000 people."

He rests in Westminster Abbey, and there you can read three of his great sayings:

"I look on all the world as my parish."

"God buries His workmen, but His work goes on."

"The best of all is, God is with us."

Wesley had a world vision and, in a sense, a global strategy. We can share his confidence that "God is with us."

The Lord of hosts is with us; the God of Jacob is our refuge. Ps. 46:11.

Pray for a world vision and a sense of mission for yourself.

A LITTLE BIT OF HEAVEN

Marriage was divinely established in Eden and affirmed by Jesus to be a lifelong union between a man and a woman in loving companionship.

God's final message before the great day of our Lord's return is to have the effect of strengthening families. This "Elijah message" calling for decision and repentance "will turn the hearts of the fathers to the children, and the hearts of the children to their fathers" (Mal. 4:6).

Certainly we need the influence of such a message today both in the church and in the world. Marriage and the Sabbath are the two institutions that have come to us from the Garden of Eden, and Satan violently attacks both of them in our day.

Knowing that the strongest witness for Christianity is the consistent testimony of the lives of God's people, the devil makes strong efforts to make us so much like the world that others will see no appreciable difference.

Marriage is a love relationship that should provide an ideal atmosphere in which to rear well-adjusted children with positive and wholesome attitudes toward life. No other influence can equal that of a happy Christian home to make children favorably disposed to following in their parents' footsteps.

The Christian home is an ideal place for family members to grow in all Christian graces. We learn lessons in kindness, sympathy, forbearance, forgiveness, and how to say "I'm sorry."

Many a nonbelieving spouse has been won for Christ by the changed life of a believing husband or wife. A family made up of those who truly reveal Christ in their lives will be a light in the community that will point others to the Saviour.

In addition to what we usually think of as a family, there are extended families. The church is an extended family that embraces singles, the elderly, and those far from home.

God's plan seeks for our homes to be a little bit of heaven to go to heaven in.

"So then, they are no longer two but one flesh. Therefore what God has joined together, let not man separate." Matt. 19:6.

Pray for the second-smallest state in the world—Monaco, with a population of 29,000. The Roman Catholic Church is the state religion. The authorities permit no open evangelism, and the evangelical presence is extremely small. Pray that the Seventh-day Adventist Church may be established there.

MATERIALISM DESTROYS ITS WORSHIPERS

Material improvements promise faster travel, bigger cities, a more abundant diet, and wealth for all. Many have become convinced of the supposed supremacy of material things, forgetting that wealth has its limitations. It can give you doctors, but not health (often it seems as if the more money people have, the more doctors they need); a good table, but not appetite; houses, but not homes; followers, but not friends; and envy, but not love. Materialism places far too much emphasis on having and far too little emphasis on being.

As one approaches the sunset years of life, it becomes evident that an abundance of things becomes a useless burden. You can use only a few of them, and the rest are a care and a snare.

Jesus calls that man a fool who neglects the spiritual in his pursuit of material things. The one who makes money his god becomes its slave instead of its master. Pitiful is the hunger of the one who seeks to satisfy his soul with gold instead of bread. Selling true riches for glittering tinsel, he barters God and heaven, salvation and peace, for things that perish. When he dies, he leaves the gold that has damned him to be a curse to those of his own household.

The Bible speaks of the street of gold, reminding us that the right place for gold is not in the heart, not in the fist, but under our feet.

Men turn away from God that they may become rich, because they believe that money will do more for them than God can. Money rivals God. Covetousness is idolatry, and like any false god, materialism destroys its worshipers.

For the love of money is a root of all kinds of evil, for which some have strayed from the faith in their greediness, and pierced themselves through with many sorrows. 1 Tim. 6:10.

Pray today for the work of the church in Belize, formerly British Honduras. About the year 1885 a woman from the republic of Honduras, who had joined the Adventist Church in California, distributed publications in her home area and also in British Honduras. The pastor from New Orleans visited Belize in 1887 and placed a reading rack on one of the principal streets. He arranged with one of the interested readers to keep the rack supplied with tracts. By 1891 a small group of converts resulted from this distribution of publications.

SUICIDE PREVENTED

A literature evangelist in Lahore, Pakistan, hailed a horse-drawn taxi to take him to his territory. Strangely, though, they went in the opposite direction, for the driver couldn't get his horse turned around. The animal seemed determined to go straight ahead. Finally the literature evangelist said, "Maybe this horse knows something we don't. Give him his head and see where he takes us."

Finally the horse stopped in a residential neighborhood. In that neighborhood was a family experiencing a severe trial. Only one daughter still remained at home, and the father had made marriage arrangements with a man twice her age, a man she did not love. He had done so without the consent of the mother or the daughter. Every night the daughter and mother pled with the father not to go through with the marriage contract. But the father always answered, "The man is wealthy, he is influential, and I've already made the decision. The matter is final."

It was to this home that the literature evangelist came that morning in the horse-drawn taxi. He sold the woman a book and arranged to deliver it some days later. The book was delivered, but left unopened on a shelf. The situation in the home became so desperate that the mother decided to end it all by committing suicide. She tied a rope around one of the rafters. Standing on a chair, she made a noose, but found that the rope was too short, and she couldn't get her head inside the noose. Looking around for something on which to stand to make her a little taller, she spied the book the literature evangelist had delivered a few days before. It was just the right size for her to reach the noose.

As she picked up the book, a voice seemed to say, "Why don't you unwrap the book and read it before you kill yourself?" She sat on the chair with the noose hanging over her head and read the book during the entire morning, and it changed her plans. Hope came into her heart, and eventually she became a faithful Seventh-day Adventist.

To everything there is a season, a time for every purpose under heaven. Eccl. 3:1.

Remember the 8 million people of the Baltic Soviet Socialist Republics of Estonia, Latvia, and Lithuania, where we have a church membership of around 3,000.

ALL THAT IT CONTAINS

A wealthy man became ill and died. When the lawyer read his will, the man's favorite daughter was disappointed to learn that her inheritance was her father's Bible. Specifically, the will read: "My Bible and all that it contains."

She put the Bible away in an old trunk and went on living as before. During a prolonged period of adversity in her life, she turned to the almost-forgotten book in the trunk. Can you imagine her surprise when she discovered that between many of the pages of her father's Bible were valuable bank notes?

This daughter had lived ignorant of her wealth because she had failed to explore her inheritance. Your Bible might not contain bank notes, but it does contain a lot of love notes from your heavenly Father, and promises more valuable than earthly treasure.

After the death of his wife, a husband found in the family Bible an envelope with his name on it. His wife, sensing that her illness was terminal, had written him a message: "Thank you for being such a good husband. You have made our years together happy for me. Virtually everything my heart desired you got for me. There is just one more thing that I want, and that is for you to meet me in the resurrection morning."

Here was a Bible that contained a powerful appeal to the heart of a lonely husband.

Once when I was visiting in a home, a man told me how a message written in the flyleaf of the family Bible by his mother before her death had a significant influence in turning his heart to the Lord. He let me read those words from a loving and concerned mother: "The Lord and His Word have meant much to me. Now I don't have much longer in this world. My great desire is for each one of my children and grandchildren to give their hearts to Jesus and be part of that great family reunion."

What an inheritance each of us has in the Bible "and all that it contains"!

> **"You search the Scriptures, for in them you think you have eternal life; and these are they which testify of Me. But you are not willing to come to Me that you may have life." John 5:39, 40.**

Pray for the Kurds in Iran, a group of people who have never had the gospel preached to them.

YOU CAN TRUST THE BIBLE

As a young pastor, the well-known British Congregationalist G. Campbell Morgan experienced a time of confusion and perplexity resulting from the many conflicting beliefs and theories of his day. He came to the place where he doubted the truth of the Bible, so he decided to put Scripture to the test.

He took all the books about the Bible, with their conflicting ideas, and locked them in a cupboard. Describing this episode in his life many years later, he said, "I can hear the click of that lock now."

Then he went down to a bookshop and bought a new Bible. "If it be the Word of God," he told himself, "and I come to it with an unprejudiced and open mind, it will bring assurance to my soul of itself." It did just that, and Morgan's faith was revived.

Satan has many strategies to deprive us of the faith-building influence of the Bible. He has attempted to destroy the Bible by undermining confidence in it. To deceive others, he has promulgated false interpretations, and still others he tries to keep too busy to spend time with the Bible. Some he attempts to confuse with pseudointellectual doubts regarding the reliability and authority of the Bible.

Early in his ministerial career Billy Graham went through a period of confusion. Scholars suggested that Graham's faith was too simple. He struggled over whether he should spend his life trying to understand things that were obscure or preaching the things that were clear. On a moonlit night he knelt down by a stump on which he had placed his Bible and made his decision to accept by faith what he could not prove, and devote his life to preaching the simple gospel.

"Instead of questioning and caviling concerning that which you do not understand, give heed to the light that already shines upon you, and you will receive greater light. By the grace of Christ, perform every duty that has been made plain to your understanding, and you will be enabled to understand and perform those of which you are now in doubt" (*Steps to Christ*, p. 111).

The entirety of Your word is truth, and every one of Your righteous judgments endures forever. Ps. 119:160.

Pray that God will help you to commit all your life, all your prayers, all your time, all your talent, and all your treasure to evangelizing the world.

AN INSTRUMENT OF PEACE

One reason that the prayer of Saint Francis of Assisi has been preserved through the centuries is that it expresses in a beautiful way the thoughts that so many of us feel:

"Lord, make me an instrument of Thy peace.
Where there is hatred, let there be love;
Where there is injury, pardon;
Where there is doubt, faith;
Where there is despair, hope;
Where there is darkness, light;
Where there is sadness, joy.
Oh, Divine Master, grant that I may not seek
So much to be consoled as to console;
To be understood as to understand;
To be loved as to love.
For it is in giving that we receive;
It is in pardoning that we are pardoned;
It is in dying that we are born to life eternal."

"God is too wise and good to answer our prayers always at just the time and in just the manner we desire" (*The Ministry of Healing*, p. 231).

Elizabeth Yates described how the French voyageurs who explored the inland waterways of North America prayed for each other on their journeys. As they paddled their canoes through the dangerous waters of the Great Lakes, or portaged across difficult terrain, each man prayed, not for himself, but for the man ahead of him and the man behind him. Prayer linked them together.

"Only the work accomplished with much prayer, and sanctified by the merit of Christ, will in the end prove to have been efficient for good" (*The Desire of Ages*, p. 362).

Then another angel, having a golden censer, came and stood at the altar. And he was given much incense, that he should offer it with the prayers of all the saints upon the golden altar which was before the throne. Rev. 8:3.

Pray for the Indonesian island of Sumatra, the world's sixth largest island, with a population of approximately 30 million, and 23,861 church members. South and central Sumatra have at least 38 unreached people groups.

186

HALF AWAKE, BUT HALF ASLEEP

A modern writer compared our time to an elephant hanging from a cliff with its tail tied to a daisy.

When the ship is sinking, what do we do? Paint the boat? Discuss theories of navigation? Call a committee?

No, we sound an alarm. We launch the lifeboats and help as many as possible to escape. When the world is sinking, we must have our priorities in order, and as we approach midyear, it is a good time to check them.

Today we are living in a time when civilization reminds one of an ape with a blowtorch playing in a room full of dynamite.

We face anarchy in the world, apostasy in the professing church, and apathy in the true church.

The woman in Song of Solomon 5:2 says: "I sleep, but my heart is awake." This reminds us of when we are caught napping and we manifest our embarrassment by saying, "I had my eyes closed, but I heard everything that was going on."

Here's a church that is half asleep and half awake, and therefore is only halfhearted in serving her Lord.

This maiden in Old Testament times had gone to sleep one night, worrying about losing her Lord. When the Lord knocked at the door, her comfortable, drowsy state kept her from opening it. By the time she responded to the knock of the Lord, the Lord had gone. Finally, after much searching, she found her Lord, and there was a joyful reunion.

God's messenger pleads with His church to wake up: "Wake up, brethren and sisters, wake up. Sleep no longer. . . . This death stupor is from Satan.

"What shall I say to arouse the remnant people of God? I was shown that dreadful scenes are before us; Satan and his angels are bringing all their powers to bear upon God's people. He knows that if they sleep a little longer, he is sure of them, for their destruction is certain" (*Christian Service*, pp. 80, 81).

"But while the bridegroom was delayed, they all slumbered and slept." Matt. 25:5.

Pray for the inhabitants of the 1,000 small islands comprising Maluku in Indonesia, with a population of more than 1.5 million. The inhabitants consist of more than 100 language groups, which once again present a challenge for Scripture translation.

HE HAS DONE MARVELOUS THINGS

Haiti occupies the western third of the large island of Hispaniola that Columbus discovered in 1492. The rest of the island is the Dominican Republic. In 1820 Haiti became the first Black republic in the world, with 95 percent of the people of pure Negro stock.

Seventh-day Adventist doctrines first reached Haiti in 1879, when John N. Loughborough, then living in Southampton, England, and William Ings sent a box of books and tracts to Cap Haitien. They did not address the box to anyone specifically, and the steamship company delivered it to the Episcopal missionary stationed in the city. He in turn distributed its contents among other Protestant missions nearby. On the following Sunday the Baptist missionary gave the publications to his congregation, two of which studied the tracts and began to observe the Sabbath. More than 10 years later, in 1892, they met a Seventh-day Adventist for the first time.

In 1904 Michel Nord Isaac, a Methodist preacher and teacher who was longing for more spiritual light, knelt one day in a corner of his office and asked the Lord to help him find the truth. While he was praying, someone knocked on the door. It was one of his pupils, who said, "Teacher, I have found among my father's books at home one entitled *The History of the Sabbath*. Would you like to read it?" To Isaac it seemed a direct answer to prayer. As he studied the scripture references he soon became convinced that all he learned from that book was the truth. Determined to live up to what he had learned, he began at once to preach his new beliefs. He published and circulated a tract in order to share these teachings with others. Because of his work, when the first Seventh-day Adventist evangelist went to Haiti in the fall of 1905, he found several groups of Sabbath observers waiting for him, including an entire congregation from one of the Protestant churches.

Oh, sing to the Lord a new song! For He has done marvelous things; His right hand and His holy arm have gained Him the victory. Ps. 98:1.

Pray that miracles of God's grace will continue in Haiti. Thank God for the more than 30 congregations that in recent years have changed affiliation and become Seventh-day Adventist.

NOT EASY, BUT RIGHT

In 1884 Henry Clay Trumbull discovered and identified the remains of ancient Kadesh-barnea. He also authored 38 books, but his greatest contribution was in the area of personal evangelism. At the age of 21 Trumbull accepted Christ as the result of a personal appeal made by a friend in a letter. The experience resulted in an urge to win others to the Lord.

Trumbull's first effort was to speak about Christ to a fellow employee in the office in which he worked. The other person had been a secret follower of Christ for years, and he felt guilt-stricken when this new Christian witnessed to him.

The incident motivated Trumbull to resolve that whenever circumstances provided him with the opportunity of choosing the subject of conversation, he would testify of Christ's goodness. For a half century he shared Christ with thousands, but it never became easy. Satan continued to cause feelings of nervousness and uneasiness, insinuating that the timing was not good or that Trumbull might harm personal relationships by speaking of Christ.

Trumbull, however, had the conviction that it was better to make a mistake and correct that mistake later than not to make any effort at all. He concluded that Satan works especially hard to discourage people's efforts at personal evangelism because he knows it is the most effective and productive of all methods.

Looking back on a half century of ministry, Trumbull said he could see more direct results from personal efforts with individuals than from sermons preached to multiplied thousands or from all the words written in his books and articles. He summed it up by saying, "Reaching one person at a time is the best way of reaching all the world in time."

Evangelist Leighton Ford, who has been witnessing since the age of 14 and who has preached to crowds of more than 60,000, says he still gets nervous when talking to an individual about Christ. The devil would win the day if all of us who find it difficult would withhold our witness.

And many of the Samaritans of that city believed in Him because of the word of the woman who testified, "He told me all that I ever did." John 4:39.

Pray for the 692,000 people of East Timor, a former Portuguese colony now part of Indonesia. The more than 20 languages present an urgent need for Bible translation.

SURRENDER

A story tells about a man who fell over a cliff but managed to break his fall by catching hold of the limb of a bush. In his precarious position he cried out for help, and a voice from above replied, "If you have faith, let go of that limb." As the frightened man looked at the sheer drop below him, he cried out in desperation, "Is anyone else up there?"

Of course, this is just a story, but it is true to life. When God asks for full surrender, many look around for some other god to worship—for a faith that doesn't require that kind of total commitment.

"Self-surrender is the substance of the teachings of Christ" (*The Desire of Ages*, p. 523). Surrender is the most difficult thing in the Christian life. It seems to involve risk, and that's why we fear it.

Surrender involves our acknowledgment that we are sinners, that we can't save ourselves. But God can, and if a person will surrender completely and depend on the Spirit of Christ, his life will be righteous. It is the work of the Holy Spirit to change and empower the surrendered life.

Surrender happens when we look at Calvary and see Jesus dying there in our place on a cross that should have been ours. It takes place when that cross becomes more important than our pride and when we decide once and for all that we don't want to wound our Saviour again.

Surrender happens when we reach the point at which we know that God loves us so much that we can safely trust Him with all that we have and are. It results when we die to sin and self and yield the control of our life into the hands of Jesus to let Him live out His life in us. Surrender is to trust Him fully.

For to this end we both labor and suffer reproach, because we trust in the living God, who is the Savior of all men, especially of those who believe. 1 Tim. 4:10.

Pray for the people of Swaziland and the influence of the Seventh-day Adventist Church there, where several members of the royal family are Adventists. The beginnings of the church in Swaziland can be traced to veteran American missionary J. C. Rogers in 1920. Present Seventh-day Adventist membership is 1,532 in a country of 757,000.

GOD'S CHOSEN FAST

There are different kinds of fasts. Some people abstain from all food and drink, some drink water, and others drink fruit juices. During partial fasts a person may eat modest quantities of plain food and lay aside luxury items.

Isaiah 58 is the great Old Testament chapter dealing with fasting. In verses 3-5, Isaiah describes the kind of fast unacceptable to God—a mere religious ritual without any true repentance or humility. Verses 6-12 describe the type that He does approve of. It was designed to purify the motives and reform the life.

In verse 6 Isaiah defines the motives behind acceptable fasting: "To loose the bonds of wickedness, to undo the heavy burdens, to let the oppressed go free, and that you break every yoke." There are many bands that cannot be loosed, many burdens that cannot be lifted, many yokes that cannot be broken, and many oppressed who will never go free until God's people obey God's call to fasting and prayer.

Verse 7 describes the attitude toward other people, especially the needy and oppressed, that is part of the kind of fasting God seeks. "Is it not to share your bread with the hungry, and that you bring to your house the poor who are cast out; when you see the naked, that you cover him, and not hide yourself from your own flesh?" Fasting of this kind must go hand in hand with sincere and practical sharing with those who are in need of material or financial help. In some cases food and money saved by fasting will provide the means to feed the hungry.

Isaiah indicates a close connection between fasting and the work of restoring truth committed to God's people. He closes his message on fasting with a reference to building the old waste places, raising up the foundations of many generations, repairing the breach, and restoring truth. In other words, the climax of God's work in the earth is closely associated with prayer and fasting.

"Is this not the fast that I have chosen: to loose the bonds of wickedness, to undo the heavy burdens, to let the oppressed go free, and that you break every yoke?" Isa. 58:6.

Pray for the oppressed and the hungry. Try to think of specific people in the world today who fall into these categories.

191

WHY DON'T I GO?

The shift that has taken place that has brought the main field of mission closer to home calls for some changes in strategy. One of the greatest needs in mission today is the need for dedicated Christians who will serve Christ in the marketplace.

A young artist in London, England, was painting a picture that would later find its place in a famous art gallery. It depicted a young woman struggling up a street on a wild, stormy night, trying desperately to shield the face of the little baby in her arms from the sharp bites of sleet driven by an angry wind. Along the street all doors and windows were closed to her need and desperate condition. He called the painting Homeless.

As the artist continued painting, the scene on the canvas seemed to become a living reality, until, putting down his brush, he exclaimed, "God help me! Why don't I go to lost people themselves, instead of painting pictures of them?" He gave himself to God, and the love of Jesus filled his heart. Then he prepared himself for ministry with the thought in mind to go to that part of the world where men seem to be most lost. The Lord led him to Uganda, where he became a mighty missionary.

Today many areas of North America and Europe are more a mission field than parts of Africa, Asia, and Latin America. In New York City we have 1 Adventist to every 533 non-Adventists, and in Rwanda the ratio is 1 Adventist to every 33 non-Adventists.

Logically our field of Christian mission should be where we spend most of our time—in the home, on the campus, on the job, and in our social and professional circles. Every Christian has a holy vocation.

It is in the secularized Western nations where we will likely find the people who are most lost today. Some of them may be our neighbors or the people we work with. Let's not be satisfied with painting pictures of them or even with praying for them when we can actually go to them, befriend them, and let the love of Christ touch them through us.

Jesus said to him, "Let the dead bury their own dead, but you go and preach the kingdom of God." Luke 9:60.

Pray for the person of your acquaintance who seems in your judgment least likely to become a Christian.

ACCEPTED IN CHRIST

Today's reading in its entirety is excerpted from an article by Ellen G. White in *Signs of the Times*, July 4, 1892:

"All who look unto Jesus, believing in Him as their personal Saviour, shall 'not perish, but have everlasting life.' . . . The intercession of Christ in our behalf is that of presenting His divine merits in the offering of Himself to the Father as our substitute and surety; for He ascended up on high to make an atonement for our transgressions. . . . It is evident that it is not God's will that you should be distrustful, and torture your soul with the fear that God will not accept you because you are sinful and unworthy. . . . Present your case before Him, pleading the merits of the blood shed for you upon Calvary's cross.

"Satan will accuse you of being a great sinner, and you must admit this, but you can say: 'I know I am a sinner, and that is the reason I need a Saviour. Jesus came into the world to save sinners. . . . I have no merit or goodness whereby I may claim salvation, but I present before God the all-atoning blood of the spotless Lamb of God, which taketh away the sin of the world. This is my only plea.' . . .

"It is the righteousness of Christ that makes the penitent sinner acceptable to God and works his justification. However sinful has been his life, if he believes in Jesus as his personal Saviour, he stands before God in the spotless robes of Christ's imputed righteousness. . . . Then shall we permit ourselves to have a vacillating experience of doubting and believing, believing and doubting? Jesus is the pledge of our acceptance with God. We stand in favor before God, not because of any merit in ourselves, but because of our faith in 'the Lord our righteousness.' . . .

"Perfection through our own good works we can never attain. The soul who sees Jesus by faith repudiates his own righteousness. He sees himself as incomplete, his repentance insufficient, his strongest faith but feebleness, his most costly sacrifice as meager, and he sinks in humility at the foot of the cross. . . . In amazement he hears the message, 'Ye are complete in Him.' "

Therefore, having been justified by faith, we have peace with God through our Lord Jesus Christ. Rom. 5:1.

Pray for the gospel outreach to tradespeople like carpenters, plumbers, electricians, and mechanics.

WHAT HAVE THEY SEEN?

During the vacation months many of us will have friends and relatives visiting in our homes. Consciously or unconsciously we will be witnessing to them. What will they see? What will they hear? The searching question that Isaiah asked King Hezekiah might well be asked of us: "What have they seen in your house?" (2 Kings 20:15).

Will the visitors in your home see a demonstration of practical Christian living that will make them want to know more about your faith? Will they observe happy, well-disciplined children, or will they encounter quarreling and strife?

Will your guests notice that you are putting the things of God first in your life, or will it be evident that your major interests center around material things? Hezekiah showed off his "silver and gold, the spices and precious ointment" (2 Kings 20:13). He missed a great opportunity to be a true witness for the Creator-God.

Actually Hezekiah did many good things during his reign. The king had a good record up until his last years. But his love for material things above the things of God caused him the loss of his children. He was too busy to give them proper companionship and training.

Hezekiah should have been able to share a wonderful testimony of the healing power of God, but there's no indication that he did. I wonder if the Judean ruler showed his visitors the family altar in his house? What will your guests see in your home?

It would be interesting someday in the kingdom to conduct a survey to determine how many men and women first learned of God by coming in contact with the altars that Abraham established in his travels. The Bible says that wherever he went, he built an altar to God.

People would inquire about those altars, and men would say, "Oh, Abraham built that as a place to worship Yahweh."

"Who is Yahweh the God of Abraham?" they would ask. And a knowledge of God spread.

What will they see in your house?

And he said, "What have they seen in your house?" So Hezekiah answered, "They have seen all that is in my house; there is nothing among my treasures that I have not shown them." 2 Kings 20:15.

Pray for the more than 58 million people of the province of Hunan in China, which borders on Lake Tungting, the second-largest lake in China.

194

A MESSAGE FROM THE MUD

In southern Yugoslavia in what was once the Roman province of Macedonia there came heavy rains and serious flooding. A shepherd noticed his dog digging in the mud, and from the mud it managed to retrieve a book, which it brought to its master.

The book was torn and plastered with mud, but he could see that it was about God. That evening the shepherd took the book to two brothers and their sister, whom he knew to be very pious people.

The unusual way in which he had discovered the book interested them, and they were happy to have it. They had never read such a book before. It reminded them of an old man they knew who seemed to be well informed about religious matters. They took the book to their friend, who immediately recognized that it was a portion of the Holy Bible. Explaining that the Bible is the Word of God and a revelation of His will for our lives, he also told them how they could obtain one for themselves.

Within weeks the two brothers and their sister had a Bible of their own. As they read it they immediately began to put into practice all that it told them to do. Among other things, they began observing the seventh day of the week as the Sabbath, they gave up eating pork, and they began preparing for the return of Jesus.

That same year an Adventist woman went to this resort area for her vacation. Hearing about this family of Sabbathkeepers, she made it a point to meet them. Describing to them the love of God and the plan of salvation, she led them to accept Jesus Christ as their personal Saviour.

"Whoever is with singleness of purpose seeking to do God's will, earnestly heeding the light already given, will receive greater light; to that soul some star of heavenly radiance will be sent to guide him into all truth" (*The Great Controversy*, p. 312). God gives more light to those who walk in what they now have, even if He must use a dog to deliver His Word.

Teach me Your way, O Lord; I will walk in Your truth; unite my heart to fear Your name. Ps. 86:11.

Pray for the 1.4 million people of the United Arab Emirates. Islam is the official religion. Non-Muslims are not allowed to proselytize.

I AM A DEBTOR

The apostle Paul looked out upon the world and saw it filled with racial hatred, immorality, hypocrisy, and wars and rumors of wars. He saw multitudes of unhappy, hopeless, and confused people, and he said, "I am in debt to all these people."

Paul felt no debt toward people until that day when on the way from Jerusalem to Damascus he had a very real encounter with Jesus. In that experience he saw the heavenly light that transformed his life. He caught a heavenly vision of God's mission for him that remained clear to the very end of his days.

Prior to his Damascus road experience Paul was a zealously religious man. A proud Pharisee convinced that he was right and the Christians were wrong, he carried papers of authority stating that wherever he found a Christian he might accuse him, have him thrown in prison, or even have him put to death.

Paul's encounter with Jesus dramatically changed the direction of his life. His new call brought him deliverance from envy, hatred, and bigotry. The Holy Spirit came into his life and filled him with such a love for others that it nearly broke his heart.

Peace of mind, purpose for living, and the assurance of eternal life were overwhelming benefits to Paul. He realized that he had received something so wonderful and of such great value that he felt himself a debtor to all mankind. He was indebted to the Christians for accepting him as a brother. And he was a debtor to the non-Christians who had never had a chance to experience the riches of God's love in Christ Jesus.

An insatiable urge to share the spiritual wealth he had gained by receiving Jesus now motivated him. He felt he owed it to every person to share what God had given him. From the moment of his encounter with Jesus he felt himself a debtor to all men and women.

Friend, do you know that feeling? Do you feel yourself a debtor to your fellowmen? That is the motivation for mission.

I am a debtor both to Greeks and to barbarians, both to wise and to unwise. Rom. 1:14.

Pray for the more than 2 million Anatolian Turks in Turkey, one of the least Christianized countries in the world. Most of the Turks are Muslims, or Muslim-animists, while others are secularists. They all feel superior to Christianity.

NEW CLOTHES FOR OLD

In vision Zechariah saw "Joshua the high priest standing before the Angel of the Lord, and Satan standing at his right hand to oppose him" (Zech. 3:1). This conflict between Christ and Satan for the control of the minds of men repeats itself in the experience of every person.

The Angel, or messenger, of the Lord was none other than the Son of God. It was the same one who appeared to Moses in the burning bush—the great I AM. He had appeared to the wife of Manoah and spoke with her about the birth of Samson.

"Now Joshua was clothed with filthy garments, and was standing before the Angel" (verse 3). Two hundred years earlier Isaiah had written, "But we are all like an unclean thing, and all our righteousnesses are like filthy rags." The symbolism was familiar. The filthy garments represented human righteousness in contrast to Christ's righteousness.

Christ commanded, "Take away the filthy garments from him." And then to Joshua Christ said, "See, I have removed your iniquity from you, and I will clothe you with rich robes" (verse 4) "This covering, the robe of His own righteousness, Christ will put upon every repenting, believing soul" (*Christ's Object Lessons*, p. 311).

Notice that the robe of Christ's righteousness is not a cover-up for a filthy robe. The child of God does not wear the spotless robe over a filthy one. It is a *change* of raiment. We must surrender the soiled robe, must recognize that it is unfit. Each one of us must have a desire for something better.

God takes away the old garment, a mixture of man's best efforts plus sin and guilt. He removes it, not hides it. "The righteousness of Christ will not cover one cherished sin" (*ibid.*, p. 316).

As the vision of Zechariah 3 closes, God promises to send His Servant, the Branch—Christ. He alone can keep us from falling back into sin and enable us to walk in His ways.

Praise God for the gift of His righteousness to fit us for our global task.

Then He answered and spoke to those who stood before Him, saying, "Take away the filthy garments from him." And to him He said, "See, I have removed your iniquity from you, and I will clothe you with rich robes." Zech. 3:4.

Pray for the gospel outreach to the unemployed and the disabled.

THE ARMOR OF GOD

The Lord has honored us by choosing us as His soldiers. Soldiers? Yes, for whether we are new Christians or have been Christians all our lives, we come to the point where we recognize the cosmic as well as the personal struggle and battle taking place. Serious thought as well as life's experiences will reveal to us that we are engaged in no mock battle, or make-believe war. The conflict we are engaged in is the most crucial battle ever fought.

We need to identify the enemy. The Bible tells us that we are up against all the trickery of the devil. Is the Christian soldier defenseless in this battle for his soul? Thank God, we do not have to fall prey to the devil's assaults, but we need to put on the armor God has provided.

Because we wrestle not against flesh and blood, we must make every preparation in our power to resist the enemy of souls, and every provision has been made for our success in this mighty warfare.

The more we know of ourselves, our motives and desires, the greater will be our consciousness of our utter inability to fight the battle in our own strength. Am I clothed with the whole armor of God—*truth, the breastplate of righteousness,* feet shod with the *preparation of the gospel of peace,* the *shield of faith,* the *helmet of salvation,* and the *sword of the Spirit?*

How do we get this all-important armor? God wants us to stand with all of it on, every piece. When we have on the armor, the assaults of the enemy will have no power over us, and angels of God will be round about us to protect us.

During the next few days we will be thinking more about each part of this armor that God has provided. Let us remember that we cannot battle successfully against our spiritual enemies in our own strength. Rather, we need the Lord and His strength and power.

For we do not wrestle against flesh and blood, but against principalities, against powers, against the rulers of the darkness of this age, against spiritual hosts of wickedness in the heavenly places. Eph. 6:12.

Pray for the 6.5 million Shi'a Muslims in the U.S.S.R.

THE BELT OF TRUTH

In Ephesians 6:10 Paul writes about the spiritual conflict in which we are all involved. He says, "Be strong in the Lord," and then he proceeds to talk about armor.

Our strength depends upon our being "in the Lord," as the Roman soldier was clad in his armor. What does it mean to be "in the Lord"? We are in the Lord when our wills are in harmony with His. Deliberate rebellion on any issue puts us outside the will of the Lord and unprotected by the armor that He provides.

Paul places truth first in his description of the Christian armor because it is basic and all-embracing. Truth is personified in Christ, and falsehood in Satan. A prophecy of Christ made 700 years before His first Advent spoke of His belt of righteousness (Isa. 11:5).

As Christian soldiers we must gird ourselves with the belt of truth. Truth accepted in our minds is an important part of our armor, which will protect us from the devil's darts. 1 Peter 1:13 speaks of the loins of the mind. The mind of the Christian operates within a girdle of truth, and he lives and acts in conformity to God's will as revealed in His Word. The belt or girdle also holds the sword and gathers up the clothing to unencumber the warrior and free him for action.

In Roman military attire almost every other part of a soldier's armor depended upon the belt for security and usefulness. Loose armor was hazardous and made the soldier feel awkward, so the belt bound the various pieces together, providing greater security against the enemy's attacks.

As we read the Bible we find some who are victorious in their spiritual battles because their belt of truth is secure. Joseph in Potiphar's house and Daniel in Nebuchadnezzar's palace are examples. Others, like Jacob and Samson, were careless about the belt of truth. Let us today secure the belt of truth around our minds.

Therefore gird up the loins of your mind, be sober, and rest your hope fully upon the grace that is to be brought to you at the revelation of Jesus Christ. 1 Peter 1:13.

Pray for the 14.25 million Hindus of Nepal, where Hinduism is the state religion and anyone who changes his faith to Christianity goes to jail. Far less than 1 percent of the Nepalese population is Christian.

THE BREASTPLATE OF RIGHTEOUSNESS

When we put on the whole armor of God, we are admitting our insufficiency and our need of something outside ourselves. At the same time we show our desire to be overcomers. What does the overcomer subdue? Have you ever thought about it? Primarily, the overcomer conquers his dependence upon his own strength.

The righteousness of the breastplate is not a human product. It is a provision of God's grace through Jesus Christ. The breastplate is the part of the armor that covers the heart and the other vital organs. The suggested symbolism here is certainly significant because the enemy will aim to strike the head or the heart with a fatal blow.

Righteousness is an affair of the heart. Receiving the righteousness of Christ results from a love relationship. In 1 Thessalonians 5:8 Paul speaks of the "breastplate of faith and love."

When we put on the whole armor of God, the righteousness of Christ covers us. "If you give yourself to Him, and accept Him as your Saviour, then, sinful as your life may have been, for His sake you are accounted righteous. Christ's character stands in place of your character, and you are accepted before God just as if you had not sinned" (*Steps to Christ*, p. 62).

The good news of the gospel is that by faith we are justified before we are qualified; accepted before we are acceptable; trusted before we are trustworthy; and declared perfect in Christ before we are perfect in ourselves.

A. G. Daniells wrote: "Justification by faith is God's way of saving sinners. . . . It is also God's way of canceling their guilt, delivering them from the condemnation of His divine law, and giving them a new and right standing before Him and His holy law. Justification by faith is God's way of changing weak, sinful, defeated men and women into strong, righteous, victorious Christians" (*Christ Our Righteousness*, pp. 64, 65). This is what the breastplate symbolizes.

Stand therefore, having girded your waist with truth, having put on the breastplate of righteousness. Eph. 6:14.

Pray for the 37,865 Seventh-day Adventists in Canada as they reach out to a population of 25.6 million spread across 3,223 miles from east to west. Students and others from many unentered areas of earth also form part of Canada's population.

GOSPEL SHOES

If the feet or legs suffer injury, it will seriously handicap the soldier. He cannot move quickly, and he cannot stand to resist his foe, being able neither to pursue nor to flee. A soldier must be ready to march at a moment's notice. All governments in all ages have been particular about the footwear of soldiers. Even today's mechanized warfare still trains soldiers to endure long and rapid marches.

The feet represent the foundation and are symbolic of firmness and stability. Putting on shoes is an act of preparation and indicates resolution—a decision to act. Shod feet suggest a readiness to serve in God's cause by spreading the good news of victory and peace. Paul apparently borrowed this symbol from Isaiah, who wrote: "How beautiful upon the mountains are the feet of him who brings good news, who proclaims peace, who brings glad tidings of good things, who proclaims salvation, who says to Zion, 'Your God reigns!' "

In the midst of the apostle's illustration of armor and weapons we find mention of the footwear of peace, implying the good news of victory. And how true it is that although the enemy continues his warfare relentlessly, he has already been defeated. Christ won the ultimate victory at Calvary. We need to be reminded of this!

Is victory over the forces of spiritual wickedness an accomplishment or a gift? If we look to the Word of God, the answer is clear and plain: "But thanks be to God, who gives us the victory through our Lord Jesus Christ."

Victory is a gift from God, and it is impossible to experience it on any other terms. Nor is it something we can gain wholly by human effort. We are as dependent upon Jesus for victory day by day as we are upon Him for pardon for sin. The armor teaches us that only Christ's righteousness will save us, and only His victory will guarantee our victory and give us peace. But Christ's righteousness and Christ's victory are available to all who will accept the gift. This is the good news we are privileged to share, symbolized by the sandals of peace.

Stand therefore, . . . having shod your feet with the preparation of the gospel of peace. Eph. 6:14, 15.

Pray for those who go forth to share the gospel whose only means of transportation is their feet.

THE SHIELD OF FAITH

Paul employs the emphatic expression "above all" as he introduces the shield of faith. It seems to indicate that the shield is more necessary than any other piece of the armor. Perhaps it is because the shield is a universal means of protection. The soldier can turn it in any direction to protect any exposed part of the body. A shield is constructed in such a way that it will deflect the deadly darts and render them ineffective.

Fiery darts were arrows with a special tip soaked in pitch and set ablaze before the soldier shot them. We might think of them as the incendiary (fire) devices of ancient times. They could set buildings on fire and also clothing not covered by metal armor.

What is this shield of faith that protects us against enemy weapons? Faith is belief, trust, and confidence in the Word of God. The protecting shield, then, is our confidence in His Word.

The shield of faith turns aside the devil's darts of hate, lust, revenge, and despair. Faith is the victory that overcomes the world (1 John 5:4). It is by grace through faith that we are saved (Eph. 2:8). We receive the Holy Spirit by faith (Gal. 3:14).

The Christian life is a walk of faith, not of sight (2 Cor. 5:7). Faith comes to us as a gift from God. We can increase our faith by exercising it, but the original measure of faith began as a gift from God (Eph. 2:8, 9). It is not just an abstract and vague belief in God, but rather, love for and trust in a Person and in the promises that He has given in His Word. "Put away the suspicion that God's promises are not meant for you. They are for every repentant transgressor. . . . With the rich promises of the Bible before you, can you give place to doubt? . . . As you read the promises, remember they are the expression of unutterable love" (*Steps to Christ*, pp. 52-55).

Luke describes Stephen as a man "full of faith and power" (Acts 6:8). Fullness of faith is impossible for one with an unforgiving, impenitent, or unconsecrated heart. We must lay aside all these things as we take up the shield of faith.

Above all, taking the shield of faith with which you will be able to quench all the fiery darts of the wicked one. Eph. 6:16.

Pray for the people in a country presently being ravaged by war. You select the country and name it in your prayer.

THE HELMET OF SALVATION

The helmet protected the soldier's head which can be used as a symbol of the mind. The helmet of salvation safeguards the Christian soldier from the domination of the carnal mind and from human reasoning that exalts itself against God.

We greatly need the helmet of salvation in our day when carnal thoughts constantly bombard our minds. This is an area where the spiritual warfare is intensely real. Radio, TV, billboards, newspapers, and magazines seek to reach and influence our thoughts. And what we think determines our characters.

An ever-increasing number of people are making a god of their own intellect, exalting human reasoning above the authority of God. The helmet of salvation guards against such dangers.

The psalmist said, "O God the Lord, the strength of my salvation, You have covered my head in the day of battle" (Ps. 140:7). In our battle against the devil, human reasoning is not enough. We need the covering for our heads that God provides, the helmet of salvation, which is the mind of Christ.

In writing to the Thessalonians, Paul speaks of it as "a helmet the hope of salvation" (1 Thess. 5:8). This gives us a clue that the helmet is "Christ in you, the hope of glory" (Col. 1:27). We put on the helmet of salvation when we "let this mind be in [us], which was also in Christ Jesus" (Phil. 2:5).

Hope is an indispensable quality in our present age of doubt and skepticism. We have a glorious hope, and it is our privilege to share it with others. Men and women today feel a desperate need for hope.

Some years ago a submarine went down off the coast of Massachusetts near Cape Cod. Divers descended to the sunken vessel. As they circled the wreck lying on the ocean floor they wondered if any of the crew had survived. Then they heard persistent tapping coming through the hull. They recognized Morse code hammering out a question, "Is there any hope?"

The helmet of salvation keeps hope alive. When hope dies, the enemy has won.

But let us who are of the day be sober, putting on the breastplate of faith and love, and as a helmet the hope of salvation. 1 Thess. 5:8.

Pray for the thousands of mainland Chinese students in the United States.

THE SWORD OF THE SPIRIT

"Take . . . the sword of the Spirit, which is the word of God," says Paul. He calls it the "sword of the Spirit" because the Holy Spirit gives it, and it receives its fulfillment in the Christian's life through Him. A two-edged sword, it cuts both ways, smiting some with conviction and conversion, and others who resist conviction with condemnation.

The sword is the only offensive weapon in the armor. The Christian can use it both as a weapon of attack and as a defense against sin. The psalmist said, "Your word I have hidden in my heart, that I might not sin against You" (Ps. 119:11). It is also our weapon for attacking the strongholds of sin with the gospel of salvation.

There is no weapon more effective against temptation than the Word of God. Jesus met Satan's tests with an "It is written." But we must receive the Word of God into the mind and life. One cannot say, "It is written," unless one knows what is written. And it is only by diligently searching and studying the Word of God that one learns what Scripture teaches.

"Temptations often appear irresistible because, through neglect of prayer and the study of the Bible, the tempted one cannot readily remember God's promises and meet Satan with the Scripture weapons. But angels are round about those who are willing to be taught in divine things; and in the time of great necessity they will bring to their remembrance the very truths which are needed. Thus 'when the enemy shall come in like a flood, the Spirit of the Lord shall lift up a standard against him' " (*The Great Controversy*, p. 600).

When John G. Paton was a missionary to the New Hebrides, the islands experienced a great drought. He found a group of natives pleading to God for rain. Paton called to them and told them to use their shovels and dig deep into the earth until they found fountains of water beneath their feet. Like underground springs, we should hide the Word of God deep within us.

And take the helmet of salvation, and the sword of the Spirit, which is the word of God. Eph. 6:17.

Pray for the 300,000 Muslims in Australia.

PRAY ALWAYS

After mentioning each part of the Christian's armor, Paul speaks of the need for constant prayer as part of the believer's protection. Without prayer we can have no victory. You have heard it said that in time of war there are no atheists in foxholes. When the battle is raging, every soldier prays. Yet we are engaged in a spiritual battle, and prayer is one of the great defensive weapons the Lord has provided to protect us from the powers of darkness.

We might view prayer as that which buckles on all the other parts of the armor. Prayer cannot be separated from any part of the armor because it relates to truth, righteousness, resolution, faith, salvation, and the Word of God.

Thus prayer becomes more than merely a spiritual devotional exercise. Walking with God day by day, clad in the armor of light, one finds that prayer becomes a relationship, an attitude of heart and mind keeping a person in the atmosphere of heaven.

Enoch, the man who walked with God, was a type of the righteous in the last days. It is said of him, "To him prayer was as the breath of the soul; he lived in the very atmosphere of heaven" (*Patriarchs and Prophets*, p. 85).

Coupled with Bible study, prayer represents our line of communication with heaven. No soldier is safe when he has no two-way communication with his command post.

Now do you see why we need "the whole armor"? We must have the belt of truth around us as a safeguard against deception and error. The breastplate of righteousness supplies our lack of righteousness of our own so that we can stand up to the accusations of Satan or the requirements of a holy God. The armor protecting our legs and feet enables us to stand resolutely for truth and travel with the good news of victory and peace. The shield of faith gives us the faith without which we cannot please God or overcome the enemy. The helmet of salvation guards our minds from doubt and unholy thoughts. And we need the sword of the Spirit—the Word of God—and prayer to keep us in contact with our heavenly Commander.

Praying always with all prayer and supplication in the Spirit, being watchful to this end with all perseverance and supplication for all the saints. Eph. 6:18.

Pray for our work in Norway, where in a population of 4.2 million, Adventists number 5,378.

YOU SHALL NOT BE AFRAID

Seventh-day Adventist outreach in Panama began when missionaries from the Bay Islands of Honduras visited the area in the 1890s. In 1897 a schooner, *The Herald*, built by and under the command of F. J. Hutchins, a preacher-colporteur-dentist, served as a floating base along the coast from Honduras to Colombia.

In the early days the mission leaders chose a pastor named Chavanz to labor among the Guaymi Indians who live in the mountains of western Panama. It was not an easy matter for him to convince the Indians that he had come to help them. He had been there only a few days when the tribe selected one of their members to kill him. The Indian appointed for the act set out to commit his wicked deed. But as he observed the kindly face and pleasant manners of the Adventist, he thought to himself, *I can't do it while I am looking at the man*. So he tried to sneak around the back through some low brush, but before he could carry out his intentions, a snake bit him. When he cried out in anguish, Chavanz, unaware of the plot, rushed over to help. He brought the wounded man to his home and gave him all the help and attention he could. At the same time he spoke to him about the love of Jesus.

The Indian remained for a week. Then, when he was finally well enough to leave, he confessed what his real motive had been, but hastily added, "Now, I don't want to kill you. I want you to baptize me."

Seventh-day Adventists were the first Christian group to enter this area, and are now among the four largest Protestant churches in Panama. In a population of 2.3 million the nation has 24,364 Seventh-day Adventists.

You shall not be afraid of the terror by night, nor of the arrow that flies by day, nor of the pestilence that walks in darkness, nor of the destruction that lays waste at noonday. Ps. 91:5, 6.

Pray for the continued success of the church in Panama, a Central American country located in the isthmus linking North and South America. It is almost as large as South Carolina. Spanish is the official language of this country that Columbus claimed for Spain in 1502.

LET GO OF IT

Moses had almost forgotten what he had in his hand, it had been there so long. For 40 years he had been a shepherd in the wilderness, and all the time he had with him his shepherd's staff, or rod—just an old stick of wood.

"Cast it on the ground," God said. When Moses obeyed, the rod became a serpent, and he fled from it. The Lord then instructed him to take the serpent by the tail, but that would leave the dangerous end free to strike with its poisonous venom. God wanted Israel's future leader to trust Him to take care of the problems and the poison. At the same time He wanted to impress upon the man the lesson of Genesis 3:15—that the head of the serpent has already been bruised.

When by our actions and attitudes we depend upon something other than God for our security, we are in danger. That is why God says, "Let go of it!" The material things upon which we place our trust, like the rod, have within them the potential for good or evil. When we surrender all that we are and have to God, He takes away the hidden danger—the serpents—and gives back to us that which is for our best good.

What have you got in your hand? Perhaps it's some talent that you have almost forgotten. It could become a source of pride and self-glorification, or you could let go of it, and God could return it as a gift to employ for His glory. God can use what you have in your hand as a miracle-working instrument to lead others to salvation. It may be something perfectly harmless, such as a cherished possession, some consuming ambition, or a cherished human relationship. Whatever it is, God says, "Let go of it. Trust Me with it, and if it is according to My will, I will return it to you."

Nothing will ever legitimately be ours until we have dropped it, and God has given it back again.

So the Lord said to him, "What is that in your hand?" And he said, "A rod." And He said, "Cast it on the ground." So he cast it on the ground, and it became a serpent; and Moses fled from it. Ex. 4:2, 3.

Pray for the Bedouin peoples of the Middle East, many of whom are nomads.

A FORMER MISSIONARY?

Hubert Mitchell was a former missionary in his 60s who had memorized the entire New Testament. He spent his days going from one office building to another in downtown Chicago. Mitchell would confidently ask the secretary for five minutes with her boss to talk about a personal matter.

When ushered into the boss's office, he would say, "I only have five minutes, but I want to ask you, 'Did you read your Bible before you came to work this morning?' "

The man behind the big desk would look at him as if he were crazy and say, "No."

With a warm and winning smile Hubert would respond, "Sir, you sure missed a blessing, didn't you? I'd like to share with you what God spoke about to me in the Bible this morning."

Then he would open the Bible to a New Testament passage and hand it across the desk with the suggestion "Let's start right here." Sitting back, he would start quoting word for word as the executive followed the text in the open Bible amazed.

After five minutes the former missionary would say, "My time is up, and I've got to go. Wasn't that a blessing?" On most occasions the man behind the desk would ask Hubert to stay longer. In this way Mitchell led many men to Christ in downtown Chicago.

Would you say Hubert Mitchell was a former missionary? Or was it just that he was now laboring in a mission field closer to home? Did he and others benefit from the time he invested in memorizing Scripture? Could God give you the same holy boldness it took to confront busy businessmen with the Word of God?

One of God's gifts is "holy boldness." "He gives His chosen messengers a holy boldness, that those who hear may fear and be brought to repentance" (*Prophets and Kings*, p. 105).

"Not all can go as missionaries to foreign lands, but all can be home missionaries in their families and neighborhoods" (*Testimonies*, vol. 9, p. 30).

"Do not be afraid of their faces, for I am with you to deliver you," says the Lord. Jer. 1:8.

Pray for the Danakil people of Djibouti. Better known as Afar, they are considered to be unreached by the gospel. The Afars also live in Ethiopia and Somalia. They are a nomadic people, and are mainly Muslim.

THE MARKED BIBLE

Harold Wilson was the rebellious son of a widowed mother. To get away from his mother's Christian influence, he decided to go to sea. His mother bought the finest Bible available and marked from Genesis to Revelation those texts she thought might someday appeal to the heart of her son. On the flyleaf she wrote a message that ended, ''Its promises are all sure; and as you take them into your heart, they will make you new and clean and strong and victorious. You will then be supremely happy; you will be a blessing to others; you will rejoice the heart of the Friend who died; and someday not long hence, you will meet me where there will be no more parting. Lovingly, Mother.''

Mrs. Wilson hid the Bible in the trunk her son had packed to take with him. When he discovered the Bible with his mother's message, he found himself haunted by memories of a better way of life symbolized by that Bible. In an angry moment of conflicting emotions he threw the Bible into the ocean.

After many years at sea Harold was returning home when word reached him from a friend that his mother had died. His grief drove him deeper into a life of sin, and he obtained a position on a ship sailing from San Francisco to Yokohama. The day before the ship departed, through most unusual circumstances he came into possession of his mother's marked Bible!

On board the ship were some Seventh-day Adventist missionary families. Harold was finally receptive to the impressions of the Holy Spirit, and through the influence of that marked Bible and the missionaries he and several others were converted. To get the full story, read *The Marked Bible*, by Charles L. Taylor, available at your Adventist Book Center.

If you have not experienced the benefit of marking your study Bible, you have a rich experience in store. Not only will the markings be a blessing to you, but as long as that Bible remains in readable condition it has the potential of leading others to Christ and His message.

For who has stood in the counsel of the Lord, and has perceived and heard His word? Who has marked His word and heard it? Jer. 23:18.

Pray for the 2.3 million inhabitants of the Indian state of Tripura, where Christians have suffered persecution from animists and extreme Hindu groups.

IDENTIFICATION BY ELIMINATION

While taking a class in zoology I became fascinated by a book that gave a method of identifying birds through the process of elimination. It started out by giving characteristics common to many birds. Progressively it moved on until it came to extremely rare characteristics possessed only by the unknown species.

This same principle of elimination can also enable a person to identify the Christian movement in our generation most clearly resembling the original apostolic church.

First, we must catalog the characteristics of the apostolic church: (1) It recognized Jesus Christ as Lord and God (John 20:28); (2) The church was built upon the Rock, Christ Jesus (Eph. 2:20); (3) It realized that there is no other way of salvation than by grace through faith in Jesus Christ (Eph. 2:8, 9); (4) The original church recognized sin to be the breaking of God's moral law, or Ten Commandments (Rom. 7:7); (5) Jesus and the apostles taught a literal, visible second coming of Jesus that would be manifest by sight and sound (1 Thess. 4:16); (6) Believers held that man's immortality was conditional upon a personal saving relationship with Jesus Christ (1 John 5:11-13); (7) They believed in and prayed for the coming of Christ's kingdom on earth (Matt. 6:10); (8) Entrance into the apostolic church was by baptism by immersion, signifying that the believer had found new life in Christ and was burying the past life of sin (Rom. 6:4); (9) The church had the identifying combination of obedience to the commandments of God and adherence to the faith of Jesus (Rev. 14:12); (10) Those early believers accepted the Scriptures as the inspired Word of God constituting the only rule of faith and practice for the Christian (2 Tim. 3:16).

In addition to these doctrines, we also find important lifestyle characteristics such as mutual love between believers (John 13:35).

Many denominations claim the above characteristics, but they would be eliminated if they lacked even one of the distinctive marks of apostolic Christianity. No wonder the enemy attempts to minimize the importance of these distinctive characteristics!

"But why do you call Me 'Lord, Lord,' and do not do the things which I say?" Luke 6:46.

Pray for the more than 42 million people of the Zhejiang (juh-jee-ong) province in China. Zhejiang, which means "river revival," is one of the richest and most beautiful provinces in China.

AFTER MANY DAYS

In 1886 Ellen White visited the Waldensian valleys of northern Italy. She held meetings with Pastor A. C. Bourdeau as her translator. Among those who attended were 9-year-old Elias, his 14-year-old brother David, and their parents. When the parents detected some of Mrs. White's teachings were different from the doctrines of the Waldensian church, they lost interest and refused to attend any more meetings, but the two boys continued to attend.

After Mrs. White left Italy, they kept up their studies with Pastor Bourdeau. The Adventist teachings concerning the Sabbath and the nature of man especially captivated them. When Elias reached the age of 21, he married, and he and his bride joined the thousands from the Alpine valleys who were migrating to the fertile farmlands of Uruguay and Argentina.

Several years after settling in Uruguay, Elias stepped into a wholesale house one day and discovered a magazine entitled *El Atalaya* lying on the counter. Waiting to be served, he idly picked up the journal and paged through it. When his eye caught an article on the seventh-day Sabbath, his heart began to beat faster. Here was a magazine with the same message about Jesus, His rest day, and His soon return that he had heard in the meetings presented by a little woman from America. The young Waldensian farmer read and reread the article about the Sabbath.

July 18, 1915, was a Sunday. Elias and his wife and 12 children went to Sunday school and church as usual. After a quiet day together, he gathered his family for evening worship and told them of his study of the Sabbath and his determination to keep it holy from then on. The following Sabbath he started a Sabbath school in his home, although he had never attended such a service.

By 1980 there were 260 living descendants of Elias Cayrus and his wife, and all but five of them were Seventh-day Adventists. Fifty-one of them have dedicated their lives to full-time denominational service. What a marvelous harvest has resulted from the seed sown in the heart of a 9-year-old Waldensian boy so many years ago.

Cast your bread upon the waters, for you will find it after many days. Eccl. 11:1.

Pray for our work in Uruguay, with a population of more than 3 million, and 6,013 Seventh-day Adventists.

BITTER OR BETTER

It is not so much the misfortunes that befall us as our attitudes toward them that shape our lives. The poet said it well: "One ship drives east and another drives west/With the selfsame winds that blow,/ 'Tis the set of the sails and not the gales/which tells us the way to go."

Perhaps we can't help it when the hurt comes, but we can help it if the hurt lasts. When hurts come, don't curse them, don't rehearse them, don't nurse them, but disperse them and reverse them, and under the miracle-working power of God the hurts may become halos, and scars may turn into stars.

Many hurting people do not know how to use the inner resources of mind and spirit that they possess.

A young woman left her home in the East to be near her husband who was stationed at a military outpost in California's Mojave Desert. Heat, sand, and loneliness were for her an unbearable combination until two lines in a letter from her father caused her to change her attitude: "Two men looked out from prison bars; one saw mud, the other saw stars." She learned to appreciate the desert and finally wrote a best-selling book about her experiences.

"What have you to live for?" A prominent psychologist asked 3,000 people this question. To his shock and disappointment he found that the great majority—94 percent—were "simply enduring the present while they waited for the future, . . . waiting for tomorrow without realizing that all anyone ever has is today because yesterday is gone and tomorrow never comes."

The present meant little because their lives were empty. In contrast to such persons are those who lead purposeful, constructive lives, sometimes in spite of privation, hardships, and pain. Their lives are full because they use their inner powers and because they give themselves unselfishly and joyously to the pleasure of bringing happiness to others.

We must refuse to become embittered by hurts and disappointments. Instead, we must forget self in dedication of our lives to unselfish service to others. Always keep in mind these words:

> **You will show me the path of life; in Your presence is fullness of joy; at Your right hand are pleasures forevermore. Ps. 16:11.**

Pray for the work in Rwanda with a population of 7 million. Seventh-day Adventist missions began there shortly after World War I, and now we have 188,202 members.

MY FATHER'S BUSINESS

Bible commentator William Barclay said there are two beginnings in the life of every person who has left a mark on history. There is the day when one is born into the world, and there is the day when one discovers the purpose of that event.

At the age of 12, when Jesus visited the Temple during the Passover and saw the white-robed priests and the bleeding victim upon the altar, inspiration tells us, "The mystery of His mission was opening to the Saviour" (*The Desire of Ages*, p. 78).

Our Lord's first public sermon reveals His sense of mission. He knew without any doubt that God had anointed Him to preach the gospel, to heal the brokenhearted, to restore sight to the blind, and to offer freedom to the captives of sin. At the well in Samaria His own physical hunger could not make Him forget His mission. When death was approaching, He reaffirmed that He had come to seek and save the lost. After His resurrection He made it clear that His mission was now to become the mission of His disciples as He said, "I also send you" (John 20:21).

His disciples today, members of a last-day movement that will restore lost and neglected truth, have the same commission.

God has much more effective means at His disposal for the spreading of the gospel than to use you and me, but He gives this privilege to us because He knows fellowship with Him in service will be the source of our greatest joy and fulfillment.

Do you have a clear sense of mission? Do you have a real purpose in life? Do you know why you are here? "In a special sense Seventh-day Adventists have been set in the world as watchmen and light-bearers. To them has been entrusted the last warning for a perishing world. . . . There is no other work of so great importance. They are to allow nothing else to absorb their attention" (*Evangelism*, pp. 119, 120).

And He said to them, "Why is it that you sought Me? Did you not know that I must be about My Father's business?" Luke 2:49.

Pray for the work of the Lord in Tanzania, where the first Seventh-day Adventist missionaries arrived from Germany in 1903. Tanzania has a population of 23.2 million, with 88,281 Seventh-day Adventists.

THE GENIUS OF ADVENTISM

The genius of Adventism is its sense of mission to the world. Mission is always incarnational, and that in a double sense: Christ in us, and we in the people for and with whom we work. All members of Christ's body by virtue of baptism are alike ordained as missionaries and have the privilege and the obligation to share in His ministry to the world.

We must have two factors in focus: a sharp vision of what the mission is, and a clear conception of who has been entrusted with the task. We must frequently refer back to the Guidebook to be sure that our work reflects the biblical view of the task of the church.

To the Navajos of Monument Valley, Utah, Seventh-day Adventist means the patient ministry of the medical staff at Monument Valley Hospital.

To unnumbered thousands along the Amazon River system of Brazil, the name Seventh-day Adventist symbolizes the periodic visits of one of the many medical launches.

To victims of earthquake, flood, and fire, the name Seventh-day Adventist stands for food, clothing, medical help, and people who care. To the millions of many lands who receive the Adventist message by way of radio or television, it expresses hope and a clearer understanding of the Bible.

To Seventh-day Adventists themselves, this name epitomizes the message to which they have committed their lives and that God would have them proclaim to all men everywhere.

God led the movement to its foundation of beliefs. It was necessary also that the believers should have a responsible organization and a system of finance that could sponsor a world program. Until these steps had been taken, the church was not ready to take up world outreach. But now the time was ripe for the believers to begin on the great world mission foretold in Revelation 14. The words "To every nation, tribe, tongue, and people" became their guiding force.

The mission program that began in 1874 has now extended into 186 countries of the world. The message is preached in more than 650 languages and dialects, and Adventist publications now circulate in 187 languages.

Then Jesus said to them again, "Peace to you! As the Father has sent Me, I also send you." John 20:21.

Pray for the more than 24.2 million people of Jilin (jee-lynn) province in China, a name meaning "magic forest." This province has forests, rivers, and vast prairies.

MONTHS OR A MOMENT

When Jesus multiplied the five loaves and two fish so that food still remained after feeding the crowd of 5,000, there was no doubt about it being a miracle. When He changed water into wine instantaneously, that was undeniably a miracle.

However when we drive past a vineyard, we don't think about the miracle that's going on as root systems draw water and chemicals from the soil and defy gravity by forcing the water through the branches to the uppermost leaves of the vine.

The leaves of plants and trees are nature's manufacturing centers, assimilating carbon dioxide, water, and light to make carbohydrates in the form of sugar, starch, and cellulose. In a large tree the process will require the pumping of many gallons of water up the trunk of the tree every day.

No pump devised or designed by man could force that amount of water through the dense wooden trunk of a tree. The tree must exert a working pressure of more than 3,000 pounds per square foot just to move the water up to the leaves!

Every seed is a miracle as it germinates and a tender shoot forces its way through the ground to eventually become a plant or tree.

Some people question whether miracles still take place in our modern times, failing to recognize the multiplied examples taking place around about us every day in the natural world.

When Jesus turned water into grape juice instantly, we all agree it was a miracle, but that same transformation occurs in the vineyards every summer as the grapevine takes water from the soil and transforms it into grapes filled with luscious juice. The only difference between what Christ does in the vineyard and what He did at the wedding in Cana was the time element. One miracle took months, the other moments!

The greatest miracle of all is the transforming power of love on the human heart. Like other miracles of Jesus, the miracle of the new birth can take place in a moment.

Then the chief priests and the Pharisees gathered a council and said, "What shall we do? For this Man works many signs." John 11:47.

West Germany has a population of more than 61.1 million and 11,732 Seventh-day Adventists. It is 92 percent Christian, but the nation has many unreached groups including immigrant workers and refugees. Pray for the witness of the Seventh-day Adventist Church.

CROSSING MOUNTAINS

Sometimes in the Christian life we face mountains of difficulties with no apparent way through. In such times in our experience the thing to do is to keep going forward by faith, a lesson demonstrated in the experience of ancient Israel. "Often as they had traversed the sandy wastes, they had seen before them rugged mountains, like huge bulwarks, . . . seeming to forbid all further progress. But as they approached, openings here and there appeared in the mountain wall, and beyond, another plain opened to view" (*Patriarchs and Prophets*, p. 301).

The children of Israel were following the Lord's leading, and that was all that mattered. And so it is in our lives today—the all-important thing is to know we are following His guidance. He knows the way across deserts and through mountains.

How can we discover God's will for our lives and be sure that He is in charge of them? George Mueller, the founder of the Bristol orphan homes, said, "I never remember, in all my Christian course, a period now of 69 years and 4 months, that I ever sincerely and patiently sought to know the will of God by the teaching of the Holy Ghost, through the instrumentality of the Word of God, but I have been always directed rightly. But if honesty of heart and uprightness before God were lacking, or if I did not patiently wait upon God for instruction, or if I preferred the counsel of my fellowmen to the declarations of the Word of the living God, I made great mistakes. The Spirit and the Word must be combined. If I look to the Spirit alone without the Word, I lay myself open to great delusions also. If the Holy Ghost guides us at all, He will do it according to the Scriptures and never contrary to them."

God has given us His Holy Spirit and His Word as two great guides and safeguards against deception and error. God's Spirit makes it possible for us to understand His Word, and the Bible enables us to test the spirits.

Study to know the will of God in your situation, and then go forward in faith.

"And the Lord spoke to me, saying: 'You have skirted this mountain long enough; turn northward.' " Deut. 2:2, 3.

Pray for the opening of all of Sudan for the preaching of the gospel. Many areas have never been evangelized. In a population of 2.5 million, we have 1,932 Seventh-day Adventists.

THE SPIRIT-FILLED LIFE

The Spirit-filled life is not an attainment, but an obtainment. Romans 12:1 tells us to give our bodies as a living sacrifice, but it does not explain to us to which member of the Godhead we should give them.

Jesus has a body of His own, but there is One who has come to earth without a body. God the Father could have made a body for the Holy Spirit as He did for Jesus, but instead, at Creation He made man to be the dwelling place of the Holy Spirit. He gives you and me the honor of presenting our bodies to the Holy Spirit to be His dwelling place on earth.

As sin led to the expulsion of man from the Garden of Eden, it also caused the driving out of the Spirit from within him, but the Holy Spirit was still present to the extent of man's surrender. Christ's victory at Calvary followed by Pentecost made possible the Holy Spirit's coming in His fullness, but still in relation to our surrender.

If we think of the Holy Spirit as a mere influence, we will try to use "it" as a willing servant to help us in self-appointed tasks. But if we recognize Him as a divine person, our thought will be, *How can He get hold of me and use me?*

To offer the sacrifice of Romans 12:1, we will give ourselves to the Holy Spirit without reservation—our hands, our feet, our eyes, our lips, and our brains—so that He can live out His life within us.

Once I have made this sacrifice, I need never again ask Him to help me as though He were one and I another, for we dwell together, and He is free to do His work and His will in and through me. He can use my hands to write a check on *our* bank account. The Holy Spirit can employ my tongue to share His message with my neighbor.

As I present my body as a living sacrifice, I realize that nothing but the fire of the Holy Spirit of God can make the offering holy, unblamable, and acceptable in God's sight. And when the offering is on the altar, that fire will fall.

I beseech you therefore, brethren, by the mercies of God, that you present your bodies a living sacrifice, holy, acceptable to God, which is your reasonable service. Rom. 12:1.

Pray for the outpouring of the Holy Spirit in the latter rain.

HOW MUCH LONGER?

A little Indian girl was dying. "Father," she cried, "where am I going? What lies before me in the darkness? Oh, Father, I am frightened. Help me! Help me!"

"My little girl," groaned the stricken man, "I cannot tell, for I do not know. There are other lives beyond, though the body decays in the grave, but—"

"Oh, Father, are they happy lives? Or will I suffer there? Can you not give me hope? What do your books say? Tell me! Help me!"

But the poor father knew nothing more to tell. In the darkness the slender fingers tightened upon the father's hand until they grew cold in death. The child of his love had passed into the darkness without a ray of light or hope.

From the icy shores of the Northwest Territories an Eskimo, whose rugged countenance bore evidence that he had braved the elements for many winters, challenged the bishop of Selkirk with these words: "You have been many moons in this land. Have you known the good news since you were a boy? Did your father know? Then why did you not come sooner?"

This cry was echoed from the great subcontinent of India as an aged woman of Bengal asked, "How long is it since Jesus died for sinful people? Look at me, I am old. I have prayed, given alms, gone to the holy shrines, become as dust from fasting, yet all this is useless. Where have you been all this time?"

From the snowy heights of the Andes the cry was heard: "How is it that during all the years of my life I have never before heard that Jesus Christ spoke those precious words?"

"Why do you not run everywhere with this Book? Why do so many of my people not know of the Jesus this Book proclaims? Why have you hoarded its truths to yourselves?" a man asked a seller of Bibles in the city of Casablanca on the shores of the Northern Atlantic in North Africa.

How much longer? Our answer is Global Strategy—not a promotional program, but an individual commitment, yours and mine.

> **"And this gospel of the kingdom will be preached in all the world as a witness to all the nations, and then the end will come." Matt. 24:14.**
>
> *Pray today for changed lives, revived churches, and a vision for evangelism.*

GATHERED AND DISPERSED

Gottfried Oosterwal points out that the Bible contains two views of the church. The Old Testament especially pictures the church as God's fortress in a revolted world. Jerusalem is the city on a mountain, the citadel built on the foundation of the prophets and apostles. Such a church calls converts out of the world into the safety of the city of God. Characteristic of this concept is the expanding of institutions, the strengthening of administration, the perfecting of the citizens, and the keeping of the walls safe and secure.

The New Testament, however, portrays the church not as a walled city in isolation, but as salt and yeast, servants, ambassadors, and pilgrims. In this view the church exists in dispersion rather than as a cloistered community. Every believer is a minister, and there is meaningful involvement in the world's activities. This is in contrast to an overemphasis on the "set apart" ministry concept that tends to turn the worship service into entertainment and the churchgoers into mere spectators.

The Bible holds both views in balance, in creative tension. They correct and complement each other. When they become isolated from each other, the balance is lost, and the result is two opposing views.

No cloister is to be built on the Mount of Transfiguration as long as people on the plain still need the healing touch. The first concern of the scattered saints of Peter's time was to minister "the manifold grace of God" (1 Peter 4:10). They went to those among whom they resided.

God has gathered His own people from all nations, cultures, and countries. He has cleansed them and made a new nation out of them which the Bible calls the "laos." But God called His people into existence for a particular purpose, namely, to proclaim what they have heard and seen and experienced in their own lives.

The role of the laity, then, is characterized by a continuous pendulum movement, withdrawal and return, gathering and dispersal, calling out and scattering abroad.

This is the heartbeat of the church. If one of its strokes fails, the heartbeat stops.

"You are the salt of the earth." Matt. 5:13.

Pray for the more than 35 million people of Heilongjiang (hay-loong-jee-ong) province, meaning "black dragon river." This Chinese province, bordering Siberia, has been the scene of many violent border clashes between the two countries. It leads in the production of lumber and soybeans.

219

A VERSE OR A VOICE

The Great Commission that Christ gave to His church provided authority and promised power for the accomplishment of its mission. At Pentecost the members experienced the promised power.

Something happened in an upper room in Jerusalem nearly 2,000 years ago that launched the outreach of the message to Jerusalem, Judea, Samaria, and the uttermost parts of the earth. With Pentecostal power the early church carried Christ's gospel to all of the then-known world, so that Paul could say the gospel has been preached "to every creature under heaven" (Col. 1:23).

Centuries later the next great surge of Christian conquest occurred. This thrust originated from Europe, the birthplace of the Reformation. The impetus came from the rediscovery of the great biblical truths of salvation, justification, and righteousness by faith.

Two centuries later came what historians call the Great Awakening and the nineteenth-century missionary movement.

Another great moving of God's Holy Spirit is promised and has been described in these words: "I have been deeply impressed by scenes that have recently passed before me in the night season. There seemed to be a great movement—a work of revival—going forward in many places. Our people were moving into line, responding to God's call" (*General Conference Bulletin*, May 19, 1913).

No significant missionary stride has been made in the past 20 centuries apart from the "enduement of power from on High." When the church relies on human plans apart from divine power, a voice can be heard saying, "Not by might, nor by power, but by My Spirit, says the Lord of hosts" (Zech. 4:6). When dedicated men have taken themselves to upper rooms, the miracle of Pentecost has been repeated, and the cause of Christ has moved forward.

"If Christians were to act in concert, moving forward as one, under the direction of one Power, for the accomplishment of one purpose, they would move the world" (*Christian Service*, p. 75).

A command constitutes a call, and a verse has the authority of a voice. He needs no call who has a command. Why should he wait for a voice when he already has a verse telling him what to do?

"But you shall receive power when the Holy Spirit has come upon you; and you shall be witnesses to Me in Jerusalem, and in all Judea and Samaria, and to the end of the earth." Acts 1:8.

Pray for the more than 109 million people of Sichuan (ssu-ch-wan) province in China, a name meaning "four rivers."

I HAVE FOUND THE BOOK

From 2 Chronicles 34 and 2 Kings 23 we can trace the story of Josiah, king of Judah, who began to reign when he was eight years old. Although his father, Amon, and his grandfather, Manasseh, were wicked kings, Josiah "did what was right in the sight of the Lord."

The boy had a poor spiritual heredity, but "Christ has given His Spirit as a divine power to overcome all hereditary and cultivated tendencies to evil" (*The Desire of Ages*, p. 671). How wonderful it is to know that we do not have to be marked for life because of the sins and mistakes of our ancestors.

In the eighth year of his reign, when he was just 16 years old, Josiah "began to seek the God of his father [ancestor] David." When he was 20, "he began to purge Judah and Jerusalem of the high places, . . . and . . . images."

During his eighteenth year the Temple staff found a copy of the Book of the Law. Judah had neglected God's laws during the wicked reigns of Manasseh and Amon, and the book had been lost.

The discovery and reading of the book brought revival. Josiah had paved the way for it by personally seeking the Lord and by leading the people to put away the strange gods and serve the Lord only. In response, the people gave up their idols, did away with the pagan altars, and turned to the living God. And as a result they were victorious over their enemies.

The Bible contains the Book of the Law and so very much more. Our great need is to find the Book that can make God a living reality in our lives and bring us victory over our enemies—habits and attitudes that would destroy us.

Then Hilkiah answered and said to Shaphan the scribe, "I have found the Book of the Law in the house of the Lord." And Hilkiah gave the book to Shaphan. 2 Chron. 34:15.

Mongolia is a People's Republic in central Asia bordered on the north by the U.S.S.R. and on the east, south, and west by China. It covers an area of 604,095 square miles. Seventh-day Adventist work for the Mongols began about 1926 when Russian missionaries printed a hymn and four small tracts in Mongolia. Remember Mongolia today in your prayers.

221

EFFECTUAL FERVENT PRAYER

A young boy, ready for bed, interrupted a family gathering in the living room by stating, "I'm going up to say my prayers now. Does anybody want anything?" One definition of prayer is that prayer is asking, but prayer is much more. Prayer is making contact with the Creator of the universe, the Source of all power. Through its medium we enter the very throne room of heaven. The prayer life of Jesus illustrates the fact that prayer is communion with our heavenly Father. No wonder the disciples requested, "Lord, teach us to pray."

Dr. Wilbur Chapman wrote to a friend, "I have learned some great lessons concerning prayer. At one of our missions in England the audience was exceedingly small; but I received a note saying that an American missionary was going to pray God's blessing down upon our work. This man was known as 'Praying Hyde.' Almost instantly, as his intercession began, the tide turned. The hall became packed, and at my first invitation 50 men accepted Christ as their Saviour. As we were leaving, I said, 'Mr. Hyde, I want you to pray for me.'

"He came to my room, turned the key in the door, dropped to his knees, and waited five minutes without a single syllable coming from his lips. I could hear my own heart thumping, and his beating. I felt the hot tears running down my face. I knew I was with God. Then, with upturned face, down which tears were streaming, he said, 'O God.'

"Then for five minutes at least he was still again; and then, when he knew that he was talking with God, there came up from the depths of his heart such petitions for men as I had never heard before. I rose from my knees to know what real prayer was. We believe that prayer is mighty, and we believe it as we never did before."

"Family prayer and public prayer have their place; but it is secret communion with God that sustains the soul-life" (*Gospel Workers*, p. 254).

> **Therefore I desire that the men pray everywhere, lifting up holy hands, without wrath and doubting. 1 Tim. 2:8.**
>
> *Pray for the more than 38 million people of the province of Liaoning (lee-ow-ning), "distant tranquillity." This province is perhaps the most cosmopolitan in all of China, and its educational level is one of the highest. Gospel broadcasts from nearby Korea penetrate this area.*

CHAIN REACTION

John Eliot was among the Puritan pilgrims who came to this country. For 50 years he preached to the Indians, translated the Bible into the Indian language, and founded at least a dozen religious communities among the Indians.

A hundred years later someone wrote his story, and a young man in Connecticut, reading the book, felt the missionary fire burn on the altar of his heart. He felt the call to preach to the Indians. That young man was David Brainerd.

Jonathan Edwards wrote the biography of David Brainerd, and a copy fell into the hands of Henry Martyn when he was at Cambridge. He read the story of David Brainerd, and he too felt the missionary fire burn within him. God led him to India, where he gave the Bible to the people in their own tongue.

After the death of Henry Martyn, a young man read the story of Martyn's life, and he in turn felt the missionary fire burn within him. This man, Horace Pitkin, went to China and labored for four and a half years before being murdered during the Boxer Rebellion. He had time to write a note to his wife. "Tell my boy, Horace, that when he grows up and receives the proper training, it is the request of his dying father that he come out here and take up the work which I must lay down."

F. B. Meyer was preaching in Moody's school in Northfield, Massachusetts. A young man in the back row heard Meyer say, "If you are not willing to give up everything for Christ, are you willing to be made willing?"

Those words transformed the ministry of the young man, J. Wilbur Chapman. Chapman, in turn, influenced Billy Sunday, and John L. Shuler was converted in a Billy Sunday crusade in Farmington, Illinois. Shuler became a successful Adventist evangelist and a prolific writer who remained active well into his 90s.

The influence of a dedicated life or a Spirit-directed word can start a chain reaction that will reach into eternity.

And the things that you have heard from me among many witnesses, commit these to faithful men who will be able to teach others also. 2 Tim. 2:2.

Pray for the union territory of Pondicherry, formed in 1962 out of four former colonies of French India. It has 300 villages and hamlets, and three major languages. Hindus form the majority in all four regions.

WHAT DOES THIS MEAN?

The full history of how God uses the prayers of His children to prepare for revival is little known in this world.

Two elderly women in the village of Barvas on the island of Lewis in the Hebrides began nightly prayer times when they agreed to pray for God to send revival to their community. After some months, unknown to them, a group of young men began to meet nightly on the other edge of the village to pray for revival.

In December 1949, Duncan Campbell began a series of meetings in the Hebrides. Revival spread from village to village. Many people, suddenly convicted by the Holy Spirit as they sat in their homes, fell on their faces before God and were powerfully converted. Others, seized by the Spirit as they walked down the street, dropped to their knees to pray.

Similar manifestations of the Holy Spirit's power occurred during the early days of the Adventist movement.

During a visit to London, England, D. L. Moody received an invitation to speak at a morning and evening service in a large church. Although the church was packed at the morning service, the people did not appear to respond. Moody said, "They seemed as though carved out of stone or ice." He found himself wishing he had not promised to speak again that evening.

The church was filled again for the evening service, but again without any apparent interest until about halfway through the sermon things began to change. At the close of the message Moody gave an invitation, and the response was spontaneous. People got up in groups and came forward. Moody turned to the host pastor and whispered, "What does this mean?"

The reaction had been so overwhelming that Moody thought the people had misunderstood his invitation. He made a careful announcement about an after-meeting, and all those who had come forward stayed. It was the beginning of a genuine revival.

Moody's question, "What does this mean?" had its answer when he discovered that an invalid member of the congregation had been praying for two years that God would send Moody to their church in London.

Will You not revive us again, that Your people may rejoice in You? Ps. 85:6.

Ethiopia has many unreached people groups, one of which is the Burji. The Burji, known also as Bambala, are also located in Kenya. Pray for the Burji people today.

JUDAISM

The roots of Judaism take us back some 4,000 years to the time when God called Abraham to be the father of His chosen people. The scriptures of Judaism are identical with the Christian Old Testament, but the Hebrew scriptures are divided into three parts: The Law, or Torah, the first five books of the Bible; the Prophets, which include the historical books as well as the prophetic writings; and the Writings, comprising the remaining books of the Old Testament and including Daniel, which Christians would classify as a prophetic book.

Other Jewish writings include the Targum, the Aramaic translation of the Old Testament together with commentary; the Mishnah, a long series of expositions of scripture accumulated through many centuries, forming the first part of the Talmud. The Talmud itself is the great collection of Jewish law, both civil and religious.

Judaism has three main branches today: Orthodox, Reformed, and Conservative. The Orthodox seek to keep their religion true to the traditions of the past. The Reformed Jews, however, are liberals who believe that the only hope of the race and the religion is to admit frankly that changes must be introduced and that Judaism must accept the obligation of interpreting itself in the light of modern knowledge.

Christianity emerged out of Judaism. Christians, of course, accept Jesus as the promised Messiah, but Judaism still looks forward to the coming of the Messiah at some time in the future.

Our plans for Global Strategy must take into consideration our obligations to the Hebrew people. "It has been a strange thing to me that there were so few who felt a burden to labor for the Jewish people, who are scattered throughout so many lands" (*Evangelism*, p. 578).

"In the closing proclamation of the gospel, when special work is to be done for classes of people hitherto neglected, God expects His messengers to take particular interest in the Jewish people whom they find in all parts of the earth" (*The Acts of the Apostles*, p. 381).

For I am not ashamed of the gospel of Christ, for it is the power of God to salvation for everyone who believes, for the Jew first and also for the Greek. Rom. 1:16.

Pray for the Hebrew people that they might recognize that Jesus is their Messiah. Pray for those among them who have given up their faith in the Creator-God.

TRIBAL RELIGION

Tribal religion is sometimes referred to as primitive religion or animism. It is a form of spirit worship that attributes feelings, personality, and consciousness to all animate and inanimate objects. Such tribal religion is characterized by superstition and nature worship. To the animist, evil spirits cause sickness and adversity.

The prayers of primitive people seldom rise higher than purely material needs and physical desires. Think about those words in relation to your own prayer life.

Not so long ago many anthropologists described the development of religious thought as an evolution starting from magic, to spirit worship, to the worship of many gods, and finally to the worship of one god. But now further research has shown that what they earlier thought to be developmental stages are inextricably interwoven. Even among the most remote and primitive tribes we find a concept of one supreme god. It is thrilling to discover that in this field, as in so many others, advanced research has brought scientists back closer to the position of Scripture. Many scholars now see evidence of a universal knowledge of one god. In the traditions of many tribal religions we observe remnants of belief in the Creator-God. Many of these people respond warmly to the gospel of Jesus Christ.

In the modern world in which we live there remain many evidences of superstition, such as good-luck charms and other fetishes. A fetish is any object thought to be inhabited by a spirit and that will bring good luck or benefit to its possessor. Carrying a rabbit's foot, or nailing a horseshoe over the door, would be illustrations of this.

Among the many things that Christianity has to offer the animist is the love and security that come through a personal relationship with the Creator-God.

In Romans 1:18-32 Paul explains that we can understand the attributes of God through the things that He has created. The apostle then describes those peoples who chose to put a knowledge of the Creator-God out of their minds, and he explains the sad consequences.

For since the creation of the world His invisible attributes are clearly seen, being understood by the things that are made, even His eternal power and Godhead, so that they are without excuse. Rom. 1:20.

Pray for the believers in tribal religions that the love of God and the light of the gospel will dispel their superstitions and fears.

TAOISM

Taoism was founded by Lao-tzu who was born in China in the sixth century B.C., about a half century before Confucius. The Latin form of Lao-tzu is Laocius, just as Confucius is the Latin form of K'ung Fu-tzu. Tao means the "way" or "process." As Laocius looked out on nature, he saw quietness, humility, self-effacement, placidity, emptiness, and freedom from effort. The passivity of the processes of nature impressed him, and according to his teachings, man was to follow nature as closely as he could. He must not even teach his doctrines but must let them shine for themselves. Some Christians in our day reflect this philosophy when they take the position that the witness of a virtuous life is sufficient without a verbal witness. Such people say, "I just live my religion."

The teachings of Confucius, the apostle of strenuous endeavor, were more attractive to the Chinese people than those of Laocius. Some Taoists made their way to lonely mountain retreats where they devoted themselves to contemplation and fasting, believing that a saint needed no food. Unfortunately they became sadly emaciated, and when this did not have the desired effect, they sought drugs and elixirs to induce the spiritualized condition they searched for. They thought that by absorbing the good in nature they might live long and even achieve immortality.

For nearly 2,000 years Taoism has had a line of so-called popes and a priesthood that deal in many forms of magic. The Taoist "pope" dwells in an inaccessible mountain retreat in the province of Jiangxi (jee-ang-she). He does not have the great authority that the designation pope might suggest, but he is the spiritual father of a loose-knit religious system.

Taoism suggests that man control his environment by cooperating rather than fighting, just as a sailor uses the force of the wind to move him in the direction of his choice.

Think how Taoism contrasts with Christianity. For instance, Taoism means "the way," but Jesus said, "*I* am the way." What aspects of Adventism might appeal to a Taoist? How can we reach these people?

Do not be overcome by evil, but overcome evil with good. Rom. 12:21.

Pray for the more than 35 million people of the province of Jiangxi or "river west." This province in the southeastern part of China, where the Taoists live, has the largest freshwater lake in the country, and is often called the Rice Bowl of China.

THE RELIGION OF ZOROASTER

The traditional date for the life and work of Zoroaster, the Persian, is the sixth century B.C. It was the time of the Buddha in India, Confucius in China, Pythagoras in Greece, and Jeremiah in Judea.

When he was 30 years old, Zoroaster left home to attend a religious festival. During it he experienced a vision in which he claimed that an archangel led him into the presence of God Himself. He began to preach and spent 10 years developing a distinctive doctrinal message. To his discouragement a cousin was his only convert. Then Zoroaster went to the court of the king, and he succeeded in converting the king, the queen, and finally the entire court. From that time on his work was relatively easy until his death at the hand of an enemy in a "holy war" in defense of the faith.

The two great teachings that Zoroaster emphasized were that God is one and that He is holy, and that the powers of good and evil are ever struggling for mastery in the world.

At the beginning of the Christian Era, Mithraism, with its origin in Zoroastrianism, spread west. In the seventh century A.D., when the armies of Islam swept over Persia, many of the Parsis who were Zoroastrians escaped to India where they settled.

Zoroastrianism shares some teachings in common with Christianity, including a high system of ethics, belief in a final judgment, and a clear promise of a blessed hereafter. However, Zoroaster was a stern prophet, unmellowed by the thought of God's love and mercy. The Zoroastrian believer has nowhere to look for salvation except to himself. Everything depends upon the purity of his own thoughts, words, and actions. Certainly it is evident that we as Christians have much to offer to the followers of Zoroaster—the Parsis of Iran and India.

Now after Jesus was born in Bethlehem of Judea in the days of Herod the king, behold, wise men from the East came to Jerusalem, saying, "Where is He who has been born King of the Jews? For we have seen His star in the East and have come to worship Him." Matt. 2:1, 2.

Pray for the approximately 2 million Parsis of India who have descended from five Persian families who migrated into the Indian subcontinent about the time of the reign of King Ahasuerus and Queen Esther. They have retained their ancient form of worship.

BUDDHISM

Buddha, a title meaning "the enlightened one," lived in India some 500 years before Christ. His family name was Gautama.

According to tradition, Gautama was a prince in a small kingdom who at the age of 29, without announcement, left his sleeping wife and child at midnight to seek for enlightenment. That enlightenment came one day as he meditated under the bo tree. His discovery was that the cause of human suffering is ignorance, and that self and the craving for self-satisfaction is merely a delusion.

The end and object of the Buddhist religion is nirvana, a state of nothingness. The appeal of such a belief can be understood when we think of the long series of reincarnations, some of them as animals, they believe one must live through. Buddha taught nothing concerning the assurance of a happy life after death such as the Christian faith provides.

Over the centuries Buddhism has had more adherents than any other religion in history. Although not the dominant religion in India (where it began), Buddhism is the leading religion today in Sri Lanka, Burma, Tibet, Thailand, China, Vietnam, Korea, and Japan. Wherever Buddhism has spread it has incorporated into its teachings the many beliefs and customs of the religions with which it has come into contact. In China, for example, Buddhists are usually Confucianists or Taoists, as well as Buddhists. In our day more than a quarter of a billion people seek to find the answers to life's ultimate questions in the elaborate rituals of this meditative and passive religion.

Until he died at the age of 80, Buddha would rise at dawn and would walk 15 to 20 miles a day, teaching without recompense and without distinction of class or caste all who would listen. He lived for the purpose of sharing with others the enlightenment that he had found. Certainly his example is a challenge to us as Christians to share the enlightenment the Holy Spirit has given us. Buddhists generally are reasonable, peace-loving people with whom we can freely share a knowledge of Christ, the Prince of peace and ever-living Saviour.

Surely these shall come from afar; Look! Those from the north and the west, And these from the land of Sinim. Isa. 49:12.

Pray for Buddhist people around the world, that they might respond to the enlightenment that comes through a personal relationship with Jesus, the Light of the world.

SHINTOISM

Shintoism is the ancient ancestral religion of Japan. The term Shinto is of Chinese origin and means the way of the gods. Dating from about the seventh century B.C., Shintoism combines nature worship with reverence for ancestors.

It was almost absorbed by Buddhism when that religion reached Japan from China by way of Korea in the sixth century A.D. For long centuries the two religions mixed, and then after the seventeenth century there came a revival of Shintoism.

According to revived Shinto doctrine, the emperor exercised his sovereignty by divine right through his reputed descent from the sun goddess, the traditional founder of the Japanese nation. This led to the belief that the Japanese were superior to other races because of their descent from the gods, and that the emperor was destined to rule over the entire world.

The defeat of Japan in World War II resulted in the elimination of government financial support for State Shinto, and the emperor issued a statement renouncing all claims of divinity.

Some of the weaknesses in Shinto include:

1. A polytheism lacking even one deity worthy of veneration as a moral ideal.

2. No high moral code for human beings.

3. No historic founder to standardize and inspire.

4. No intrinsic value in a human individual.

5. No magnificent goal for human society.

6. No glorious hope of a future life.

Some of the strengths in Shinto include:

1. An enthusiastic, unifying patriotism.

2. Emphasis on cleanliness and purity.

3. Reverence for the beautiful as a vital part of religion.

4. A strong emphasis on loyalty to the superior.

In relating to adherents of Shinto, we can look for beliefs that we share in common and build on these in seeking to introduce Jesus Christ.

> **"I have raised up one from the north, And he shall come; From the rising of the sun he shall call on My name; And he shall come against princes as though mortar, As the potter treads clay." Isa. 41:25.**

Pray for sincere believers in Shintoism, that they might come to know and to worship the King of the universe.

HINDUISM

Hinduism is the oldest of the organized world religions and the largest. It presents no universal moral standard, no moral responsibility to a supreme being, and no outstanding admirable historic figure in the Hindu scriptures. Rather, Hinduism is a religion of many gods.

It has been said that Hinduism is absolutely indefinite. Many Hindu teachers teach that the world and all things in it are an illusion. Perhaps the most distinctive characteristic of Hinduism is the caste system.

The religion has an unending list of sacred objects. The cow is holy and must be treated with reverence. Even monkeys are sacred with temples erected in their honor.

In the earliest days the father was the priest in the Hindu family, but with the passage of time the ceremony and ritual of the religion became so complicated that the services of a professional priest became a necessity. The priests, or Brahmans, became the mightiest power in the land. Doctrines came into Hinduism by degrees, some from primitive religions. One of these may have been belief in the transmigration of the soul—the theory that when a man dies his soul leaves the body and enters the body of some animal or human being to begin another life cycle. This process repeats itself indefinitely. The law determining the operation of transmigration is that of Karma, which means action or deed. These actions or deeds of the present life build up as rewards or penalties that decide one's fate in the next incarnation. The belief is that according to our Karma we are born into a new life well or sickly, good or bad, rich or poor. To be saved from the endless succession of births and deaths is what religion is all about for Hindus. The ultimate goal is to be absorbed into the divine essence.

You can imagine the joy that the gospel of Jesus Christ holds for the Hindu who finally comes to understand that repeated life cycles are not necessary in order to atone for the mistakes of the past.

If we confess our sins, He is faithful and just to forgive us our sins and to cleanse us from all unrighteousness. 1 John 1:9.

Pray for the millions of Hindu people in India and around the world, that they might find new life in Christ Jesus.

OTHER RELIGIONS OF INDIA

Mahavira, a contemporary of Gautama Buddha, founded Jainism in India during the sixth century B.C. The religion has as its basis the principle of two opposing forces in the universe—good and evil.

The Jains practice severe asceticism and have made the prohibition of killing any single living creature, large or small, a cardinal doctrine. While Buddhism has virtually ceased to exist in the land of its birth, Jainism survives even though its adherents are small in terms of numbers compared to the masses of Hindus.

The founder of this religion was a somewhat legendary character. Mahavira, a name meaning "a great man" or "hero," is said to have sacrificed everything in order to follow austere Brahman asceticism. He also provided for a lay order of persons who could join Jainism and yet carry on their married life and follow occupations in the everyday world, relationships denied the monks and nuns.

The lay order furnished Jainism with its power and resulted in its continuity. It gave the religion an influence far beyond what secluded priests and nuns could have exerted. Many of the lay people were wealthy traders who provided contacts and funds for promulgating their faith.

Sikhism is a Hindu sect founded by Guru Nanak in the early 1500s in the Punjab. The name Sikh means "a disciple." The Sikh religion involves belief in one god, prohibits idolatry, abolishes caste, and refuses to recognize the supremacy of the Brahmans or priestly class. Sikhism combines features of Hinduism and Islam.

The millions of followers of these religions include many noble, high-principled persons reaching out for the finer things in life and searching for life's meaning. These people need more than ritual and philosophy—they need the Saviour.

> **Beware lest anyone cheat you through philosophy and empty deceit, according to the tradition of men, according to the basic principles of the world, and not according to Christ. Col. 2:8.**

> *Pray for the people of the Punjab, with a population of 18 million comprised of 40 languages and over 30 small minority tribal groups. Known as the "breadbasket" of India, Punjab is a fertile wheat-growing area, and is the only state in India where Sikhs form the majority. There are 45 caste groups that are untouched by Christianity, and only two of the 30 tribal groups have Christian churches.*

ISLAM

Of all the great world religions Islam is the most recent in its origin. While we have little historical documentation for the beginnings of some of the world religions, Islam arose in the full light of history. It spread more rapidly than any of the other great religions.

Muhammad, who was born in Arabia, lived from A.D. 570 until 632. Afflicted with epilepsy, he was brought up without formal education. He came into close touch with Christianity and Judaism. Muhammad claimed to receive messages from God through visions and through the angel Gabriel. After experiencing his call as a prophet, he spent his first three years working for the conversion of family and friends.

In 622 the wrath of the pagan Arabs forced Muhammad to flee from Mecca to Medina where multitudes accepted him as a prophet. Within two years Muhammad had resolved to subdue the world to his monotheistic faith. He gathered together an army and his motto soon became "Islam, tribute, or the sword." Islam spread rapidly by military conquest.

Within 100 years of Muhammad's death Islam had subdued Persia, Syria, Egypt, Jerusalem, Afghanistan, Cyprus, Tunisia, Algeria, Morocco, Spain, and Turkey. Finally, by 732 Charles Martel stopped the Muslim armies in France at the Battle of Tours.

Today Islam is the dominant religion in 50 countries, claiming approximately 1 billion adherents.

Abstinence from pork and alcoholic drinks and a general commitment to a healthy lifestyle provide common ground between us and the followers of Islam. Muslims have a strong sense of community and respond to genuine hospitality. They enjoy discussing religion, and among the beliefs we hold in common are views on the resurrection, the return of Jesus, a new earth, and a Creator-God.

Although Muslims claim to believe the Bible, they consider the Koran their final authority. Muslims believe in verbal inspiration and accept every word in the Koran as the word of God. Five times each day, from the minarets, or mosques the world over, the followers of Islam prostrate themselves in prayer facing Mecca. Certainly this is a challenge to us to be faithful in prayer.

Evening and morning and at noon I will pray, and cry aloud, And He shall hear my voice. Ps. 55:17.

Pray for the multitudes of sincere people among the 1 billion adherents of Islam.

THE PROMISE OF POWER

The early disciples took the gospel commission seriously. The command of Jesus to go everywhere with the message of good news was paramount in their thinking. Their Leader had promised power, and they tarried according to Jesus' instruction until they received that power from above.

The contrast between the Peter who stood in the palace of the high priest with the cock crowing in his face and the Peter on the day of Pentecost, the mouthpiece of the Holy Spirit, is the difference in the life of any man when he goes to his task in his own power as opposed to when he works empowered with the wisdom and power of God's Holy Spirit.

In spite of the most adverse circumstances, including fierce persecution, between 5 and 6 million people embraced Christianity during the lifetime of the original apostles.

The Holy Spirit in the lives of the apostles gave them a combination of power with a sense of divine mission and urgency. Those early believers knew they were God's servants with His message for a desperately needy world.

Moody had that sense of urgency combined with a clear view of mission. Looking upon our world as a wrecked vessel, he saw himself as a man with a lifeboat with God shouting in his ears, "Moody, save all you can!"

The powerful evangelist said that the greatest danger facing God's people was not opposition but their own conformity to the world. He said, "If you have any friends on this wreck unsaved, you better lose no time in getting them off!" We need his sense of urgency, and we need the promised power.

For many years visitors to Yosemite National Park watched the famous Fire Fall. About nine o'clock in the evening the crowd's attention would focus on a great fire burning on Glacier Point. Piercing the stillness of the evening, a voice would cry out, "Let the fire fall!" At that moment rangers pushed the great bonfire over the cliff and let it plunge from those dizzying heights like an illuminated waterfall.

Our prayer today should be "Lord, let the fire fall!"

> **Behold, I send the Promise of My Father upon you; but tarry in the city of Jerusalem until you are endued with power from on high. Luke 24:49.**
>
> *Pray for the promised power of the Holy Spirit in your life to make you a soul winner.*

COME

Wherever you find man, you find him worshiping something or someone. Our Creator has placed this instinct to worship within each of us as a means of drawing us to Him.

Religion has been defined as man seeking after God. That is what is back of all the ceremonies and rites of religion on every continent. It is the great search of the soul for rest, the attempt to placate the gods and to soothe the conscience. That is what is back of fasting, penances, and pilgrimages. But we do not find rest in ceremonies alone.

Millions are vainly seeking to quench their thirst at the broken cisterns of pleasure and the other gods of this world. Some seek rest and satisfaction in society, achievement, wealth, or fame. But such things alone cannot satisfy. There's only one place to find rest, and that is at the feet of the Saviour, our Creator.

Even among professed Christians many have not yet found rest. The most painstaking study of bare doctrines or prophecy, or the most careful observance of the law will never bring rest. We find rest in coming to Jesus.

The gospel invitation is so beautifully simple, and yet we often make it appear so involved. Jesus says, "Come unto Me." One of the first words that a baby learns from its mother's lips is *come*.

Our Saviour invites us to come with our sins, burdens, anxieties, and restlessness. He urges us to leave them with Him and find rest.

One man said, "I'd come, but I operate a tavern. When I get rid of my tavern I'll come."

Jesus would reply, "Come as you are with your tavern and your liquor. Leave all these problems with Me, and I will help you the rest of the way."

Another protests, "I have to overcome my bad temper before I can come." Jesus would tell him, "Come as you are, and in Me you will find victory and rest."

"I must give up my smoking first," still another says. Jesus would answer, "Come, and I will give you rest—rest from enslaving habits, rest from the burden of sin; but first, come."

Religion is man seeking God, but Christianity is God seeking man.

Come unto Me, all you who labor and are heavy laden, and I will give you rest. Matt. 11:28.

Remember in prayer the 5 million Muslim Balochs of Pakistan, a land with a population of more than 100 million, in which there are only 6,579 Seventh-day Adventists.

FIVE THINGS WE CANNOT DO

Are you where you want to be in your relationship with Jesus today? If your answer is no, do you know how to get there?

Perhaps there is someone reading these lines who is struggling with some secret, hidden sin. You recognize the problem, but lack the power to overcome, or perhaps you just don't know how to overcome.

Desires for goodness and purity are a good beginning on the path toward victory, but that alone is not enough.

"We cannot change our hearts, we cannot control our thoughts, our impulses, our affections. We cannot make ourselves pure, fit for God's service. But we can *choose* to serve God, we can give Him our will; then He will work in us to will and to do according to His good pleasure" (*The Ministry of Healing*, p. 176). (Italics supplied.)

Here are five things we are powerless to do: (1) We cannot change our nature; (2) we cannot control our thoughts; (3) we cannot control our impulses; (4) we cannot control our affections; and (5) we cannot make ourselves pure. If we were to stop here, we would find ourselves saying with the disciples, "Who then can be saved?"

"But we can choose to serve God, we can give Him our will; then He will work in us to will and to do according to His good pleasure." Herein lies our hope and the answer to our deepest needs.

We are born with a carnal nature, but when we are born again we receive a spiritual nature, and the two natures struggle with each other. Even after conversion the old carnal nature remains, but it is now in subjection to the spiritual nature. The person with only a carnal nature may experience less conflict than the Christian.

Does it sometimes seem that you have had more trouble in your life since becoming a Christian? Do not be discouraged. You have chosen to serve God and the devil is angry and will not easily give you up. This conflict is real and will continue until God redeems our bodies at the second coming of Jesus.

Remember, we can choose to serve God, we can choose to feed the spiritual nature and starve the carnal nature.

For the flesh lusts against the Spirit, and the Spirit against the flesh; and these are contrary to one another, so that you do not do the things that you wish. Gal. 5:17.

Pray for the 120 million non-Christian Japanese of Japan.

I DON'T WANT
TO BE A HYPOCRITE

There's an oft-used story that illustrates a point so well I dare to use it again. The parents of a healthy little boy became greatly concerned because their little son did not walk at an age when even younger children were doing so. What concerned the parents even more was the fact that their child did not even try to walk.

The little fellow learned to talk and frequently assured his parents that he believed that walking was a good thing and someday he planned to walk, but he didn't want to be rushed into walking.

One day when the boy was about 5 years old he and his father were having a serious talk. "Why don't you at least try to walk?" the father asked.

"Dad," the boy said, "I've seen little kids try to walk. They take a few steps, and then they fall on the floor and make fools out of themselves. I don't want to be a hypocrite. If I'm going to walk, I want to walk properly and not fall on the floor."

But of course, those little leg muscles gain strength only when they get used. A toddler develops a sense of balance only by trying to walk. No baby learns to walk without some falls.

In the Christian life, if we make no commitment until we are sure we will never fall, we will never make a start. Making the commitment gives us a sense of obligation and provides motivation to succeed.

Failure to make a commitment leaves the door ajar so it will be easy to slip back to the old habits. To delay commitment once the path of duty has become clear is to make provision for failure. The Bible says, "Let us walk properly. . . . Put on the Lord Jesus Christ, and make no provision for the flesh, to fulfill its lusts" (Rom. 13:13, 14).

We will never be strong enough to walk the Christian way in our own strength. It is only possible through the power of Christ. His power is available whenever you are ready and willing to ask for it.

If you know the truth and believe the truth, the next step is to act upon the truth. Make your commitment today.

But put on the Lord Jesus Christ, and make no provision for the flesh, to fulfill its lusts. Rom. 13:14.

Pray for our work in Togo, a tiny nation wedged between Ghana and Benin in Africa. In a population of more than 3 million, we have 1,036 members.

A WORLD CONSCIOUSNESS

For many decades Christians in developing nations have watched missionaries come and go. But now they are sending their own missionaries. There are more than 300 Third World mission agencies born, based, administered, and funded primarily in the Third World. Mission fields are transforming into mission forces.

Christian education must be mission-centered. One researcher says that 85 percent of the missionaries serving today first started thinking about mission service when they were in the fifth or sixth grade. Usually because they had seen and heard a missionary share his/her experiences. Think about the implications if today's children do not have the opportunity to see and hear real live missionaries.

One kindergarten leader features a different country each month in order to help the children develop a world consciousness. When it is "God Loves Japan" month, the children remove their shoes before entering the room and place them with the toes pointed toward the door. The leader may dress in a kimono and will greet the children with *"Ohio gozimas,"* "Good morning" in Japanese.

For "God Loves the Philippines" month, the children hear Filipino songs and see a Filipino flag as they enter their classroom. During the program they view slides depicting people, places, and the way of life in the Philippines. The teacher greets the class with a hearty *"Mabuhay!"* which in the Tagalog language of the North Philippines means "Welcome!"

In each case the class discusses the progress of the work and its needs in the specific country. Children pray for specific needs and perhaps for specific persons by name. Writing letters to a person in the country to be featured that month will provide a source of names and places to pray about.

We need to keep mission emphasis needs before children from their youngest years. It should be prominent in the books they read and the classes they attend.

Children must learn the lessons of going, giving, and praying. They must have a world perspective.

But Jesus said, "Let the little children come to Me, and do not forbid them; for of such is the kingdom of heaven." Matt. 19:14.

Pray for the more than 51 million people of Hubei (hoo-bay). The name means "lake north" because it is situated on the north of Tungting Lake. Like its sister province, Hunan (hoo-non), to the south, Hubei is a land of lakes and rivers.

MAKE YOURSELF AVAILABLE

"Consecrate yourself to God in the morning; make this your very first work. Let your prayer be, 'Take me, O Lord, as wholly Thine. I lay all my plans at Thy feet. Use me today in Thy service. Abide with me, and let all my work be wrought in Thee.' This is a daily matter. Each morning consecrate yourself to God for that day. Surrender all your plans to Him, to be carried out or given up as His providence shall indicate. Thus day by day you may be giving your life into the hands of God, and thus your life will be molded more and more after the life of Christ" (*Steps to Christ*, p. 70).

At the beginning of each day we should make ourselves available to the Lord for service. If you do this, it will make Him even more real in your experience, because He will present you with many opportunities.

Sometimes we get so involved with the cares of this life that we fail to see the openings that the Lord presents us to share His love with others. If we consciously make ourselves available to Him, we will be more alert to these opportunities. Only in eternity will we really learn all that has happened because we have let God work through us.

A young woman who was a complete stranger called at the home of one of our pastors to ask how she could become a member of his church. Curious as to what had prompted her desire for membership, the pastor inquired how she became interested. She told this story:

"I am a telephone operator, and I work the night shift. People ask for a doctor at all hours of the night, and some of the calls are often quite unreasonable. But your Seventh-day Adventist doctor in this city has always been so patient and kind and thoughtful that he led me to realize that there is something different about your people. They have a kindness that is needed in the world today. I want to join a church where people make Christianity a part of their daily lives."

So, "consecrate yourself to God in the morning." Make practical Christianity a part of your daily life.

Who then is willing to consecrate himself this day to the Lord? 1 Chron. 29:5.

Pray that God's love may reach the hundreds of thousands of pavement dwellers of Calcutta, India.

THE GIFT OF PROPHECY

The entrance of sin made it impossible for human beings to continue enjoying face-to-face communication with God, so He gave the gift of prophecy to bridge this gulf. The New Testament also speaks of the gift of prophecy as the spirit of prophecy and the testimony of Jesus. According to Revelation 12:17 and 14:12 it is to be one of the identifying characteristics of Christ's remnant church, convincing evidence that the gift of prophecy will remain in the church until Jesus' return once more makes face-to-face communication possible.

When the time came for the remnant church to appear with the gift of prophecy, God called two young men, William Foy and Hazen Foss, and later He chose "the weakest of the weak"—a 17-year-old girl named Ellen Harmon.

At the age of 9 Ellen and her twin sister were walking home from school in Portland, Maine, when a girl behind them shouted angrily and threw a stone. Ellen turned around, and as she did, the stone hit her face, breaking her nose as she fell fainting to the ground. The accident resulted in an extended period of illness that severely limited her formal schooling.

Ellen's initial reaction to the call of God was "Lord, I cannot," but she did not say she would not. Married to James White, she was never ordained and never held a church office, but for 70 years she served as a messenger of the Lord.

The writings of Ellen White have always served to point men and women to the Bible as the authority in all matters of doctrine. In one of her last public messages she said, holding up the Bible, "I commend unto you this Book."

The fruitage of God's activity through her appears in the way her writings have stood the test of time and the attacks of critics, and in her ability to choose the good from the writings of others without borrowing their errors. It is seen in the Adventist educational system, our health message, and a world movement exalting Jesus and the Word of God.

Believe in the Lord your God, and you shall be established; believe His prophets, and you shall prosper. 2 Chron. 20:20.

Pray for the more than 7.6 million people of Kampuchea (Cambodia), where Seventh-day Adventists have no organized activity, and pray for the Cambodian believers in refugee camps.

BREAKING BAD HABITS

A wise old professor was walking through a forest with a pupil by his side. When they came to a clearing in the woods, the teacher stopped and pointed consecutively to four objects. The first was a seedling just forcing its way through the ground, the second was a sapling about 1 year old, the third was a small shrub, and the fourth was a mighty tree.

"Pull up the seedling," said the professor to his student. With ease the young man yanked the seedling out of the ground. It took more effort to uproot the sapling at the professor's command. The shrub presented an even greater challenge, but finally yielded to his youthful energies. But not so the mature tree. The young man was powerless to dislodge the roots that were firmly anchored in the earth.

From this object lesson the professor illustrated the point that habits are most easily uprooted before they become deep-rooted. It was Benjamin Franklin who said, "The chains of habit are often too weak to be felt until they are too strong to be broken."

A friend of mine recommends the WDA method of dealing with bad habits. W means you must want to break the habit. D stands for deciding you will stop it. And A is for asking God to help you be true to your decision and give you power to overcome the habit.

You will never win over a bad habit until you admit it is bad, wrong, or harmful. You must want to change. It's human nature to excuse ourselves. We say "It's my only vice" or "He does it, so why can't I?" or "I can quit any time I want to."

One can summarize the key to dealing with bad habits in the following words: "God has given us the power of choice. . . . We can *choose* to serve God, we can give Him our will; then He will work in us to will and to do according to His good pleasure" (*The Ministry of Healing*, p. 176). (Italics supplied.)

Let the wicked forsake his way, and the unrighteous man his thoughts; let him return to the Lord, and He will have mercy on him; and to our God, for He will abundantly pardon. Isa. 55:7.

Pray for someone you know who is trying to break a bad habit, or someone who needs to be convicted of a habit that he or she must overcome.

THE MESSAGE OF THE CROSS

There have been many momentous happenings since the dawn of human history. But no event approaches in significance and influence that greatest of all—the Crucifixion of the Son of God on Golgotha that fateful day so long ago.

The theme of the cross has absorbed the minds of men and women, and crowded all else into a secondary place. They pondered it; they lived it; they felt compelled to share it with others. As a result, they crossed seas, penetrated jungles, and laid their loved ones to rest on distant shores in order to proclaim its message.

The gospel has been the most powerful force in the world for transforming lives. And it still is, but unfortunately for many it has become common-place. It is difficult for us to understand Calvary because we know so little of sacrifice.

The disciples who stood near the cross were transformed by that experience into tireless emissaries of the gospel. Succeeding generations, including our own, have witnessed the repeated miracle as unbelievers have become missionaries, timid followers have become heroes, and sinners have become saints through the influence of the cross.

What is the message of the cross for our generation? It teaches us that what we are powerless to do for ourselves Christ has done for us. The cross is God's involvement in our salvation. He is not a severe tyrant, but a compassionate Father who was in Christ reconciling the world to Himself. And Christ would have died for you alone.

Rembrandt, the seventeenth-century Dutch painter, chose the Crucifixion as the central theme for several of his pictures. The artist included his own face in one of these scenes, signifying that in a sense each one of us was part of that picture.

The cross tells us what it cost God to forgive our sins. Loving us with an unconditional love, He gave Himself to save us. That is the message of the cross.

God was in Christ reconciling the world to Himself, not imputing their trespasses to them, and has committed to us the word of reconciliation. 2 Cor. 5:19.

Known as the Phoenix Islands, Canton and Enderbury are coral islands located about 1,650 miles southwest of the Hawaiian Islands. The size of these islands is only 11 square miles, and Seventh-day Adventists have no organization there.

THE OLD LANDMARKS

Soon after the historic 1888 meeting in Minneapolis, the Holy Spirit prompted Ellen White to speak out against calling human concepts and interpretations "old landmarks of the faith." It seems that some were endeavoring to add their own landmarks to those divinely established. She wrote:

"There was much talk about standing by the old landmarks. But there was evidence they knew not what the old landmarks were" (*Counsels to Writers and Editors*, p. 30). Then she mentions real landmarks. "The passing of time in 1844 was a period of great events, opening to our astonished eyes the cleansing of the sanctuary transpiring in heaven, and having decided relation to God's people upon the earth, [also] the first and second angels' messages and the third, unfurling the banner on which was inscribed, 'The commandments of God and the faith of Jesus.'

"One of the landmarks under this message was the temple of God, seen by His truth-loving people in heaven, and the ark containing the law of God. The light of the Sabbath of the fourth commandment flashed its strong rays in the pathway of the transgressors of God's law. The nonimmortality of the wicked is an old landmark. I can call to mind nothing more that can come under the head of the old landmarks" (*ibid.*, pp. 30, 31).

For more than 100 years critics have accused leaders of removing the old landmarks. The critics come and go, but the landmarks remain. Critics are never the kind of people who are doing constructive work to enlarge the cause of God.

"God has not passed His people by, and chosen one solitary man here and another there as the only ones worthy to be entrusted with His truth. He does not give one man new light contrary to the established faith of the body. . . . Let none be self-confident, as though God had given them special light above their brethren" (*ibid.*, p. 45).

Then I heard a loud voice saying in heaven, "Now salvation, and strength, and the kingdom of our God, and the power of His Christ have come, for the accuser of our brethren, who accused them before our God day and night, has been cast down." Rev. 12:10.

Pray for the more than 39 million people of Guangxi (g-wong-she), an autonomous region in China. Its name means "a vast west." The mountains and rivers of this province have been called the most beautiful under heaven.

PRACTICE HIS PRESENCE

Nothing will prove more helpful in living the victorious life than cultivating an awareness of the Lord's constant presence. At conversion we invite Jesus to dwell within us, and each day—and several times a day—we should thank Him that He is willing to make His abode with us.

"As a shield from temptation and an inspiration to purity and truth, no other influence can equal the sense of God's presence" (*Education*, p. 255).

Mark 9:33, 34 tells of an occasion when the disciples were disputing among themselves as to who should be the greatest. If they had stayed with Jesus as they journeyed, they would never have quarreled. Even if they had been conscious of the fact that He knows our thoughts, they would have behaved differently.

When we know Jesus is with us and thank Him for it from morning till night, it makes a difference in our conduct. Conversation would be different in the home, in the car, and even on the way to church if we would practice His presence.

Back in the seventeenth century there lived in France a humble man still remembered as Brother Lawrence. After his conversion at the age of 18, he endeavored constantly to walk as in the presence of the Lord. He worked as a cook and dishwasher, and as he cultivated the habit of thinking of God as ever present with him, his kitchen became a little paradise.

Paradise is where God dwells. In the experience of Moses it was the presence of the Lord in the burning bush that made that place holy ground. It is God's presence in the Sabbath that transforms it into His holy day.

Too often, like Jacob, we have to admit: "Surely the Lord is in this place, and I did not know it" (Gen. 28:16). With only a stone for a pillow, the circumstances were most humble, but God's presence was there.

Brother Lawrence said, "By rising after my falls, . . . I am come to a state wherein it would be as difficult for me not to think of God as it was at first to accustom myself to it."

Then Jacob awoke from his sleep and said, "Surely the Lord is in this place, and I did not know it." Gen. 28:16.

Pray for single parents who are struggling to bring up children in these challenging times. Pray for guidance in supporting them through the love of Christ, according to their needs.

GOD HAS A PLAN

A shoemaker in England learned about the Bible Sabbath through attending evangelistic meetings. He said to his wife, "I've barely made a living working seven days a week; now, if we must keep the Sabbath, I don't know how we'll come out. But it's right, and I'm going to do it."

Then he learned about the tithe being holy and belonging to the Lord. "We have barely made it when I kept all I earned," he told her. "Now I've learned that a tenth of all I get belongs to God. It's true, and we'll do it, but I don't know how we're going to make it."

Soon after his decision to obey the truth, the man received the largest order he had ever received. A firm in London wanted him to make 5,000 pairs of boots. He had to find larger quarters and hire help. This started a manufacturing business that has prospered greatly.

Many times people delay their decision to obey the truth because they fear the circumstances. The truth is that when God sees He can trust us, He can improve our circumstances as He did for the English shoemaker. Never forget that they are under His control.

Inspiration reminds us that "no one is so situated that he cannot be a true and faithful Christian. However great the obstacles, all who are determined to obey God will find the way opening as they go forward" (*Testimonies*, vol. 5, pp. 182, 183).

"There was once a man, anxious in mind, wavering between doubt and hope; till a time came when he could bear his troubles no longer, and he threw himself before an altar in the church; and he said again and again: 'If I could only know that I should always remain faithful!' And all of a sudden he heard an answer in his heart, as if from God: 'And if you did know, what would you do then? Do it now, and your care will be gone.' " (Thomas a Kempis, *Imitation of Christ*).

Now to Him who is able to keep you from stumbling, and to present you faultless before the presence of His glory with exceeding joy . . . be glory and majesty, dominion and power, both now and forever. Jude 24.

Pray for the people living in the area of India known as Meghalya, or "abode of the clouds." Situated in the northeast corner of India, it occupies a mountainous plateau of great scenic beauty, bounded on the south and southwest by Bangladesh.

THE LORD WILL PROVIDE

One of the pioneers of the Seventh-day Adventist movement was a sea captain named Joseph Bates. Bates retired from his maritime career at the age of 35 and spent his savings helping to launch this movement.

Bates was a man of faith and action. On one occasion when he was just about to begin a journey on foot to preach the gospel in a neighboring state, a woman came to him with a gift of enough money to enable him to buy a train ticket.

On yet another occasion he felt called to go to a certain place, and by faith he took his seat on the train although he had neither money nor ticket. He told no one of his need except the Lord, and of course God can impress the minds and hearts of men and women. Within minutes an absolute stranger walked up to Captain Bates and presented him with a gift for his work that was more than enough to pay for the journey.

One day when Bates was writing a tract, his wife told him she was out of flour. He inquired how much she needed and in a short while returned home with just the amount she had mentioned—four pounds. They always bought flour by the barrel, and when Mrs. Bates saw the small four-pound bag, she broke into tears. She was faced with the stark reality that their small fortune was indeed completely gone. "What are we going to live on?" she sobbed.

"The Lord will provide," came the smiling response of the former sea captain. However, at that moment he felt a strong impression to go to the post office. There he found a letter addressed to Captain Bates, but the sender had forgotten to pay the postage, and Bates had no money to pay the charges. He asked the postmaster to open the letter, and inside was money!

The letter contained enough money to restock the pantry, buy a barrel of flour, and of course, pay the postage due.

When the groceries were delivered, Mrs. Bates asked, "Where did it come from?"

"The Lord sent it," answered her husband. And truly He did! Remember, friend, the Lord will provide.

"And it will be that you shall drink from the brook, and I have commanded the ravens to feed you there." 1 Kings 17:4.

Bhutan is a small kingdom in the eastern Himalayan Mountains. Pray for the 1.5 million people of Bhutan, who are among the least evangelized on earth.

HINDRANCES TO PRAYER

During an evangelistic series a mother spoke to me about her great burden for her children, all of whom she had reared in the church. The parents had sacrificed to send them to church school, but now all of them had left the church. "Please do what you can to win them back," their mother pleaded tearfully.

Later in the same series of meetings, the woman's husband came to me with a burden for his wife. "She has never been able to give up the reading of immoral novels," the man explained.

When we are not living right, it is difficult to pray. Consciousness of unforgiven sin makes us feel guilty and uncomfortable at family worship. And of course, the only reason sins are unforgiven is that we cling to them, unwilling to give up our pet indulgences and ask for forgiveness.

If our children know that we are not living as we should, and if we make no attempt to change, how can we expect the church school and Sabbath school to make up for the negative influence in the home.

Any unconfessed sin will prove a hindrance to our prayers. Prayer is no substitute for obedience. The Bible actually tells about one man whom the Lord told to stop praying. God could not answer the prophet Jeremiah's prayer for the people of Jerusalem because they had turned to idolatry. They continued to go through the outward forms of religion, but they had dared to set up idols in the house of God.

Instead of being a positive influence on the nations around them, the people of Israel copied the customs of the pagans, even going so far as to sacrifice their little children to idols.

We sacrifice our children and hinder our prayers for them when we live as hypocrites in their presence.

He who covers his sins will not prosper, but whoever confesses and forsakes them will have mercy. Prov. 28:13.

South Yemen is located on the strategic southeastern coast of the Arabian Peninsula. The country is little more than a desert. All speak the same dialect of Arabic. The population of more than 2.4 million consists of 1,300 clans or tribes. South Yemen is a secular state that recognizes its Islamic cultural heritage, but Communism steadily erodes the influence of all religion on national life. There is no organized Seventh-day Adventist activity there.

THE DECEITFULNESS OF RICHES

The ruins of old Pompeii tell a grim story of the deceitfulness of riches. Looking across the Bay of Naples, you see this volcanic mountain that erupted on August 24 in A.D. 79, pouring cinders and hot ashes over the city to a depth of twenty to thirty feet.

Pompeii's sudden destruction did not come without warning. Since mid-July the volcano had been active. The volume of smoke increased daily, and many of the city's 20,000 inhabitants fled for safety.

As the days passed and nothing happened, some returned and resumed their normal daily routines. And then one day when the people had accustomed themselves to living in the path of danger, the end came, and 16,000 people were suffocated by the volcanic mud and ash that rained destruction upon the city.

We can observe some significant parallels between conditions preceding the destruction of Pompeii and the state of affairs in our day. Some of us have heard since we were children that Jesus was coming soon. At times world conditions have become so serious that people with some knowledge of Bible prophecy have concluded the end was near. They have thought seriously of getting their lives in order. But then the crisis passes, and they forget their good intentions.

Wealth and pleasure seem to have been major pursuits of the people of Pompeii. When the ruins were excavated, all the world was able to see what was of most value to the people who perished there. A young woman had gone back to get her pearl earrings, but she got only to the threshold and perished clutching an earring in each hand. A man returned to rescue a little treasure chest containing gold, silver, and precious stones. Clutching it to his chest, he was overcome as he tried to escape the fumes.

They and many others might have escaped if they had not been lured to delay by the deceitfulness of riches. Someday all the universe will be able to look on and see what you and I counted most valuable in life.

"The cares of this world, the deceitfulness of riches, and the desires for other things entering in choke the word, and it becomes unfruitful." Mark 4:19.

Pray for Buddhist monks and priests and clergy of other world religions who are studying the Adventist message.

BEWARE OF SELF PITY

Many great battles have been fought on land, on the sea, and in the air, but the greatest battles of all are fought against self in the hearts of men and women. Fallen human nature is naturally rebellious and perverse, demanding its own way even when it conflicts with God's will.

It is extremely disappointing to see a person's experience turn sour and bitter. Jeremiah 42-44 relates a story dealing with a group of God's people who indulged in self-pity. Their excuse was that He had given them a bad deal, and they reasoned that they were better off before they began serving the Lord.

From this story we can identify four steps that lead in the direction of apostasy and bitterness. First is that of self-pity, perhaps dwelling on negative thoughts such as the fact that some church member has hurt us. Second is the step of hypocrisy. The delegation listened to the advice of Jeremiah and indicated they would follow his counsel, but their words concealed their real attitude. Hypocrisy insulates us from the very help that could benefit us if we would be completely honest.

The third step is one of defiance, and the fourth and final step is deliberate disobedience. The people went to Egypt, the very place God told them not to go.

A fine young woman was engaged to a young man who was active in the church. Suddenly the young man broke the engagement. Now, it is very possible that he was in the wrong—I don't know the details—but I do know the heartbroken young woman indulged in self-pity. She stopped attending church, and as she continued to feed her resentment, she turned against most of the doctrines she had once so fervently believed.

A former pastor who had to surrender his credentials because of bad conduct allowed resentment to fill his heart, and he also came to the place where he claimed to find errors in the doctrines he once preached with fervor.

Don't let your experience turn sour. Beware of self-pity.

But if you have bitter envy and self-seeking in your hearts, do not boast and lie against the truth. James 3:14.

Remember the work in Namibia today. Namibia, in southwest Africa, is one of Africa's most Christianized lands, and 6,212 Seventh-day Adventists live there.

ALWAYS ASKING FOR MONEY

President Pearson of Miami Christian College observes that people complain that the church is always asking for money. He goes on to tell an experience involving their little boy—their firstborn. Although he was the delight of their hearts, at the same time he was always creating expense for them. He needed clothing, shoes, food, as well as other items that the parents were always glad to provide for their son—in spite of the cost.

Pearson goes on to tell of a dramatic change that brought an end to the ever-increasing demands for more money. The little boy died!

As long as the work of God is alive and growing, there will be increasing demands because of the escalating expenses involved in supporting it.

Every need is a certain sign of life and growth. A dead ministry has no need, but a ministry that is constantly requiring funds is alive and growing.

Dr. A. T. Pierson said, "There is enough jewelry, gold, and silver plate buried in Christian homes to build a fleet of 50,000 vessels; ballast them with Bibles; crowd them with missionaries; build a church in every destitute hamlet in the world; and supply every living soul with the gospel in a score of years. Only let God take possession [of our possessions], and the gospel will wing its way across the earth like the beams of the morning" (quoted in Clay Cooper, *Nothing to Win but the World,* p. 103).

The pioneers were not at all concerned about gathering material things. They gave generously to the work of God. Their minds and hearts centered on the kingdom of heaven. Frequently they sang, "A tent or a cottage, O why should I care? They're building a palace for me over there!"

The pioneers practiced what they sang and preached. The blessing of God was upon them, and their lives were powerful witnesses for the truth. They believed there could be no spiritual progress without self-denial.

The pioneers of the Advent movement set their faces to go forward in spite of trial and suffering, ready to give their lives for the advancement of God's cause. Nothing could stop them, for they knew they were His agents fulfilling prophecy at the appointed hour.

> **"The people who know their God shall be strong, and carry out great exploits." Dan. 11:32.**
>
> *Pray for workers, open hearts, and the planting of new groups of believers.*

SENSE OF SIN

The church member who expresses regret that growing up in the church has deprived him or her of a dramatic conversion experience is really admitting that he or she has never faced the reality of being a sinner. Such an attitude develops out of a faulty understanding of what sin really is.

When Simeon stood with the Infant Jesus in his arms, he said, "This Child is destined for the fall and rising of many in Israel" (Luke 2:34). Nothing can rise again until it has had a preliminary fall. There must be misery because of sin before there can be the true joy of sins forgiven. The only thing that is going to drive a person to the Saviour and make him/her rely upon Christ alone is the true conviction of sin.

When God asked Adam the question "Where are you?" God knew the answer, but He could not help Adam until he faced up to where he was. Likewise, God cannot help us until we admit that we are lost.

When you lose your way and phone for directions, the first question asked is "Where are you?"

The lost sinner will never reach his destination until he admits that he is lost and tells God where he is. The turning point in the experience of a former alcoholic came when he admitted that he was an alcoholic and that he needed help. Soon after, he said, "For the first time in 18 years I quit blaming my wife, my mother-in-law, and my boss for the mess that was me."

The Bible says: "For there is no difference; for all have sinned and fall short of the glory of God" (Rom. 3:22, 23). If admission into heaven was by $1 million tickets, the man with $900,000 would not be able to enter any more than would the man with $100. Both would fall short of making it on their own resources.

We must come to God emptyhanded before we can receive the gift of eternal life.

Sins are the things that we do as a result of living apart from God. Therefore, our primary focus should be on establishing a relationship with Jesus.

But he who doubts is condemned if he eats, because he does not eat from faith; for whatever is not from faith is sin. Rom. 14:23.

Father, strip the prideful sins from our hearts and stir us to share Your last-day truths.

THE BEST INVESTMENT

The widow of Zarephath provided for a prophet and received a prophet's reward. Perhaps there is such a thing as helping a missionary and receiving a missionary's reward. In the case of the widow, the Lord told Elijah, "I have commanded a widow there to provide for you" (1 Kings 17:9).

Unaware of the unusual recompense that would be hers, the nearly destitute widow became worried about what might happen if she shared her meager amount of food. She was down to her last handful of meal, and yet she fed the prophet, and a miracle supply lasted throughout the remaining lean years. Not once during the famine did she see the bottom of the barrel, nor did the oil jar fail (verses 10-16). She received a second blessing when Elijah saved her house from calamity by raising her dead son to life.

Similar rewards came to the Shunammite woman at the hands of Elisha. She made one of the best investments of her life that day when she and her husband decided to build a prophet's chamber as an addition to their house. Their hospitality was abundantly rewarded when, during one of Elisha's visits, he restored life to their only child, who had suffered a fatal sunstroke (2 Kings 4:8-37).

It was after Peter had made his fishing boat available to Christ for a pulpit that he experienced such a catch of fish that the boat almost sank (Luke 5:1-11).

God is the Creator and Owner of the silver and gold and the cattle on the hills, yet He grants His people the privilege of exercising their stewardship by making available to His cause a boat, a prophet's chamber, a barrel of meal, or a jar of oil. Whatever God needs to accomplish the mission, the generosity of His people will provide.

The owners of the tethered donkey conscripted by Christ for His triumphal entry into Jerusalem did not protest when the disciples explained: "The Lord has need of them" (Matt. 21:3). Apparently that was reason enough.

Many today both within the church and outside will respond to the challenge of giving sacrificially to support God's cause when they are convinced, "The Lord has need of _____ ."

And my God shall supply all your need according to His riches in glory by Christ Jesus. Phil. 4:19.

Pray for the more than 1 million unreached Muslim Songhay of West Africa: in Burkina Faso, Mali, Benin, Nigeria, and Niger.

TAKING MEN ALIVE

Peter's miraculous catch of fish followed a night of fruitless fishing. After the miracle, Jesus said, "Do not be afraid. From now on you will catch men" (Luke 5:10). The Greek reads, "You will be taking men alive."

A similar phrase appears in 2 Timothy 2:26: "And that they may come to their senses and escape the snare of the devil, having been taken captive by him to do his will."

These are the only two occurrences of the expression in the Bible. One describes Jesus as taking people alive, and the other describes Satan as taking people alive. In the conflict raging for the souls of men and women, all will be taken either by God's people or by the devil.

Weymouth's translation of John 16:8 says that He "will bring conviction." The Holy Spirit literally makes a "convict" of you. It is one thing to be a captive of sin and quite another thing to be a captive of the Lord Jesus Christ. When the Holy Spirit surrounds you with His influence, His only intention is to lead you to forgiveness and happiness. But when Satan and his agents take men and women alive, it is for the purpose of leading them to eternal death.

Taking men and women alive for Christ and thus rescuing them from Satan is the joyful task to which every follower of Christ is called. Jesus gave the promise "Follow Me, and I will make you fishers of men" (Matt. 4:19).

Sometimes church people say that we should serve humanity without any ulterior motive of winning them to Christ. But remember, if we do not fish for men, the devil will.

"I point you to the life of Jesus as a perfect pattern. His life was characterized by disinterested benevolence" (*Testimonies,* vol. 4, p. 218). Disinterested benevolence does not imply that Jesus did not attempt to save them. It simply means His deeds had no selfish interest or motivation.

Jesus was constantly fishing for souls, "for the Son of Man has come to seek and to save that which was lost" (Luke 19:10). We don't have to apologize for the hook designed to catch men and women alive for Christ.

And Jesus said to Simon, "Do not be afraid. From now on you will catch men." Luke 5:10.

Pray for the Seventh-day Adventist radio and television ministries all over the world.

SHOOTING AT THE SAINTS

Sir William Phips led a naval assault on the city of Quebec. The strategy was that Phips would provide artillery coverage for the troops traveling by land.

Phips arrived with the ships earlier than scheduled. While he waited, he took out his spyglass and studied the city. He saw spire after spire after spire, which meant only one thing—churches. As he looked at the spires, he knew without any doubt that they were on churches of a religion that he hated more than anything else. Through his telescope he also saw statues of the saints everywhere. Suddenly he got so angry that he commanded his ships to fire volley after volley at the statues. The cannons blasted away until the ammunition was all gone. It was then that the bugle sounded. General Howe had arrived expecting artillery cover from the ships—but there was none. After that, there was nothing left to do but retreat. Phips had used up all his ammunition shooting at the saints. The lesson is clear. When we squander our energy shooting at the saints, we have nothing left for real aggressive soul winning.

The vocal critics in the church remind me of Sir William Phips. They spend all their energy, their ammunition, on the wrong enemy. The church deserves their support and protection, not their verbal gunfire. The saints need their respect, love, and care, not the fiery darts and lead bullets of criticism, innuendo, and misunderstanding.

The leaders in the church, those most often shot down by "admirals," should be receiving the help and support of all the saints.

When the gospel should be advancing and the good news reaching everyone everywhere, we must not have wasted our talents, time, and resources in a civil war with fellow church members. Instead, we must focus on the real enemy, the real need—the thousands of gospel-starved people in every country on earth. There are more than 12,000 unreached people groups in the world, and millions are dying without hope and without God while the church languishes in inactivity.

We must arouse to a sense of the great responsibility that God has laid upon us to proclaim His last message to a perishing world.

> **Do not be overly righteous, nor be overly wise: why should you destroy yourself! Eccl. 7:16.**
>
> *Pray for emergency room staff people today, that they may be dedicated, skillful, patient, and minister even as Jesus did to the sick and injured.*

THE MESSAGE TO LAODICEA

God directed the Laodicean message to the last segment of the church before the return of Jesus. No messages follow that to the Laodiceans.

Laodicea means "a people judged," or "people's court of justice," and the message applies to the period of the pre-Advent judgment. In the judgment it is only Christ's righteousness that can save us. Everything depends upon our relationship with Him.

A man once said, "God, I thank You that I am not like other men. . . . I fast twice a week; I give tithes of all I possess" (Luke 18:11, 12). But he found no justification with God.

Fasting, tithing, and other good deeds have their place, but merely doing such things cannot save us. We simply cannot save ourselves. Observing the Sabbath, even when it causes inconvenience and sacrifice on our part, will not save us. Our liberality, even if we go so far as to give all our goods to feed the poor, will not save us.

We cannot earn salvation, but must accept it as a gift. Our beautiful system of doctrine, which has withstood every attack of the enemy, will not save us. Doctrine is important only as it affects relationships. What we believe about God and His teachings shapes our relationship with Him, and it is that relationship that saves us.

The trouble with the Laodicean church is not in doctrine or deed, but in heart condition. The Great Physician applies the stethoscope to the body of the Laodicean church and here is His diagnosis: "You are lukewarm. . . . You say, 'I am rich, have become wealthy, and have need of nothing' —and do not know that you are wretched, miserable, poor, blind, and naked" (Rev. 3:16, 17).

But there is hope for Laodicea. The Lord calls her to repent. He prescribes the "gold treatment" of faith and love; the white raiment symbolizing the righteousness of Christ; and the eyesalve of the grace of God, which gives clear discernment of spiritual values.

Jesus isn't calling the people out of the Laodicean church. Instead, He is knocking at the door, asking to come in.

"Behold, I stand at the door and knock. If anyone hears My voice and opens the door, I will come in to him and dine with him, and he with Me." Rev. 3:20.

Pray for the unreached people group of 2.5 million deaf people in the Philippines, that there may be a rich harvest among these receptive people.

255

SALUTE TO TEACHERS

Many years ago a Johns Hopkins University professor assigned a group of graduate students to take 200 underprivileged 12- to 16-year-old boys and investigate their background and environment. The students were then to predict the boys' chances for the future. After consulting social statistics, talking to the boys, and compiling as much data as they could, the graduate students concluded that 90 percent of the boys would spend some time in jail.

Twenty-five years later another group of graduate students received the job of testing this earlier prediction. They went back to the same underprivileged area and finally managed to contact 180 of the original 200 of the study. Strangely, they found that only four of the group had ever been sent to jail.

Why was it that these men who had lived in a breeding place of crime had such a surprisingly good record? The researchers took note of the fact that they had repeatedly heard about the influence of a teacher. The investigators pressed further and found that in 75 percent of the cases it was the same person. Locating the woman, who was then living in a home for retired teachers, they asked her many questions in an attempt to determine the reason for her marked influence on so many underprivileged children.

The retired teacher said that she couldn't shed any light on the subject. And then, thinking back over the years, she said reflectively, more to herself than to her questioners, "Oh, how I loved those boys . . ." And that love and confidence she bestowed upon those boys was, of course, the secret of their success in life. They had tried to live up to her expectations for them.

"The good that a teacher will do his students will be proportionate to his belief in them. And let the teacher remember that it is the most unfortunate, those who have a disagreeable temperament, . . . that most need love, compassion, and help. Those who most try our patience most need our love" (*Counsels to Parents and Teachers*, p. 267).

Think of the teachers who have influenced your life by their words and example, and join in the spirit of today's salute to the profession.

> **That our sons may be as plants grown up in their youth; That our daughters may be as pillars, sculptured in palace style. Ps. 144:12.**
>
> *Pray for teachers and students. Perhaps there will be some specific names and needs that you will want to pray for.*

CHANGED BY BEHOLDING

A young artist once desired to copy a beautiful picture that hung in a palace. He could not obtain permission to paint there, so he determined to reproduce the picture from memory. Hour after hour he would gaze at the picture until it took possession of him. Then he would hurry to his studio and begin to paint.

Each day the artist spent some time looking at the original picture. As he gazed and studied and toiled, his power grew. Finally, there hung in his studio such a wonderful copy that all who saw it said, "We must see the original."

The more time we spend with Him, the more we shall grow to be like Him. The demonstration that this world needs most is that Christianity really changes people. It must be embodied in human lives. "Christ is sitting for His portrait in every disciple" (*The Desire of Ages*, p. 827).

It is the reproduction of Christ in us, His disciples, that will cause those who know us to say "We must see the original—Jesus."

A man was selling a preparation that supposedly grew hair on bald heads. On the bottles a message read: "Guaranteed to grow hair on bald heads." The medicine man was having good sales until a gust of wind blew his hat off his head—and he was bald! His life betrayed his message.

Gustave Dore was painting the face of Christ when a woman entered his studio. As she stood looking at the portrait of Christ, the painter watched her closely. "Mr. Dore, why do you look at me so anxiously?"

Dore responded, "I wanted to watch the impression the face of Christ that I have painted made upon you."

"I was thinking," she said, "as I looked at your painting that you could not paint Christ's face like that unless you love Him."

"Well, I trust that I do sincerely love Him," the artist replied, "but as I love Him more, I shall paint Him better."

But we all, with unveiled face, beholding as in a mirror the glory of the Lord, are being transformed into the same image from glory to glory, just as by the Spirit of the Lord. 2 Cor. 3:18.

Pray for the more than 57 million people of the province of Hebei (huh-bay) in China. Located on the north side of the Yellow River, this province is famous throughout China for peaches, pears, and nuts.

THE GIFT OF HOSPITALITY

One of the most delightful and practical of the spiritual gifts is that of hospitality. Perhaps you can think of many times when you have been blessed because someone exercised it for your benefit.

Our Christian homes can be one of our greatest assets in leading men and women to Jesus. Many who are convinced of the theory of the truth still need to see a practical demonstration of truth being lived in a happy Christian home. In such a setting the blessings of Sabbathkeeping become evident. Entertaining new or prospective members in our homes on Sabbath is certainly the best way to teach them how to honor it.

Many times a simple, wholesome shared meal on Sabbath will do more good than many sermons or Bible studies. People do not join churches simply because of logic and the overwhelming weight of biblical evidence. Few humans make any kind of lifestyle change solely on the intellectual basis of true or false, right or wrong. Instead, people change because the proposed course of action promises to offer them something personal in the form of more effective living. They tend to do those things that will result in satisfaction of needs.

A few hours spent in a happy Christian home will often result in guests leaving with the conviction "This is what I've been looking for. This is what I want for my family." What an opportunity we miss when a person visiting our church, perhaps for the first time, leaves without getting at least one invitation to Sabbath dinner.

The prayer near the door of Waltham Abbey, on the south coast of England, is a fitting one for every Christian home:

"O God, make the door of this house wide enough to see all who need human love and a heavenly Father's care, and narrow enough to shut out all envy, and pride, and hate, and its threshold smooth enough to be no stumbling block to children or to straying feet, but rugged enough to turn back the tempter's power. Make it the gateway to Thy eternal kingdom, through Jesus Christ."

Be hospitable to one another without grumbling. As each one has received a gift, minister it to one another, as good stewards of the manifold grace of God. 1 Peter 4:9.

Pray for the lonely, the seekers, and the first-time visitors who come to your church this Sabbath, and see that each receives an invitation to Sabbath dinner.

LIFT TOGETHER

In the Philippines there is a fascinating custom among certain villagers from which all of us can learn a lesson. If it becomes necessary to move a home from one part of the village to another, the chief calls all the men together. Half then go out into the jungle and each cuts a long, slender yet sturdy pole approximately 4 inches in diameter and 18 feet long.

When all the men of the village meet at the home to be moved, they place the poles under the house, which rests on stilts approximately three feet above the ground. When the men are stationed one on each end of a pole, the chief shouts "*Mabaccah* ["Lift together!"]!" The men raise their poles at the same time, the house rises off its foundation, and they carry it to its new location.

Careful planning, commitment to a united endeavor, and focusing on a specific goal allow those men to accomplish what no villager by himself could. It is a marvelous demonstration of what a group can do when they all lift the burden together.

"If Christians were to act in concert, moving forward as one, under the direction of one Power, for the accomplishment of one purpose, they would move the world" (*Testimonies*, vol. 9, p. 221).

Unity, cooperation, coordination, and lifting together are essential to the fulfillment of the gospel commission. In the church we find people of different opinions, temperaments, personalities, tastes, and backgrounds, but their love for Christ overrides every difference and constrains them to pull together.

Five hundred years before Paul wrote the words "the love of Christ constrains us" (2 Cor. 5:14), the Greeks used the word that is translated "constrain" to describe the action of the oarsmen in the galleys. The word actually meant "to make them pull together."

Christ revealed the great longing and desire of His heart for His people when He prayed "that they all may be one." It is in our power to answer His prayer.

"That they all may be one, as You, Father, are in Me, and I in You; that they also may be one in Us, that the world may believe that You sent Me." John 17:21.

Pray for the 10 million Buddhist Sinhalese of Sri Lanka. The Sinhalese, who are mainly illiterate, fear their countless demons and deities. Pray that they may find joyful deliverance through Jesus Christ.

259

CURE FOR CHURCH STRIFE

Persecuted by both Catholics and Protestants and then racked by internal dissensions, the Moravians at last found refuge and challenge on Count Zinzendorf's large estate in eastern Germany in the year 1722.

When they began to fight among themselves, the count issued a challenge and an ultimatum. He said, "Pray, pray for the world outside of yourselves . . . pray for the lost."

They formed a prayer chain, one that would continue uninterrupted for 100 years. Sparked by prayer, the Moravians sent teams of missionaries to Africa and to the Americas 100 years before William Carey went to India. Pittsburgh, like many places in the New World, started as a Moravian missionary outpost to the Indians.

Whenever the people of God congregate and become preoccupied with internal concerns rather than reaching out redemptively to the lost, strife invariably breaks out. The energy that they should use in battling the enemy dissipates in civil war that destroys the church.

God's messenger to the remnant church said: "The home missionary work will be farther advanced in every way when a more liberal, self-denying, self-sacrificing spirit is manifested for the prosperity of foreign missions; for the prosperity of the home work depends largely, under God, upon the reflex influence of the evangelical work done in countries afar off" (*Testimonies*, vol. 6, p. 27).

We must never lose sight of this reflex principle that has kept the Adventist movement strong at home and abroad. "Our watchword is to be, Onward, ever onward! Angels of heaven will go before us to prepare the way. Our burden for the regions beyond can never be laid down till the whole earth is lightened with the glory of the Lord" (*Gospel Workers*, p. 470).

The vision of Adventism is still a world vision. We must never set our eyes only on our own church, our own conference, our own union, or our own division and feel that it is the measure of our task. No, we dare not rest until every nation, kindred, tongue, and people group have heard the message.

For though I am free from all men, I have made myself a servant to all, that I might win the more. 1 Cor. 9:19.

Spiritism has been a part of Brazilian life since its first settlers arrived hundreds of years ago. Pray for the 30 million spiritists of Brazil, that the Lord will show them the true way of life.

LOVE AND LAW

When you love someone with all your heart, your deepest joy is to know the wishes of the one you love and to make them a reality. It is in just this way that God deals with us, and we show our love to Him by learning and doing His will.

When God created Adam in His own moral image, He wrote His law in Adam's heart. But when the first members of the human family rebelled against God's authority, their hearts and minds no longer reflected His law. Man put his will where God's had been.

In the time of Moses, God recorded His law on slabs of stone, but His ultimate objective is to see His law once again in the hearts of His people. This takes place under the New Covenant as we individually accept the Lord and let Him write His law in our hearts. Jeremiah 31:31-33; Ezekiel 11:19, 20; and Hebrews 8:10 clearly speak of the time when God will inscribe His law in our lives.

God's moral law points out our sinfulness and makes us aware of our need of a Saviour. Paul demonstrates this when he says: "I would not have known sin except through the law. For I would not have known covetousness unless the law had said, 'You shall not covet' " (Rom. 7:7). The apostle clearly identifies the Ten Commandments as the law that gives us a knowledge of what constitutes sin.

Jesus came "to magnify the law and make it honorable" (Isa. 42:21). Although His enemies accused Him of breaking it, He said, "I have kept My Father's commandments and abide in His love" (John 15:10).

A relationship with Jesus turns all the negative commands into positives. Jesus said, "If you love Me [you will], keep My commandments" (John 14:15). In other words, if you love Me, you will not kill, you will not commit adultery, you will not steal, you will honor marital and parental relationships, and so forth.

It is only Christ living in our hearts that makes obedience possible in each of our lives.

I delight to do Your will, O my God, and Your law is within my heart. Ps. 40:8.

Pray for the people in Karnataka (formerly Mysore), India. This state has a population of more than 40 million, made up of 53 individual tribes speaking more than 19 languages.

MAMMON CEMETERY

Let us take an imaginary walk together through what we might call Mammon Cemetery. We come to the grave of Achan. The marker is a mound of rocks, and the epitaph reads: "I saw, I coveted, I took" (Joshua 7:21).

The cause of Achan's death was stealing from God. Before the fall of Jericho the Lord had made it clear to Israel that they were to reserve the spoils of the city for sacred use (Joshua 6:19), but silver, gold, and a beautiful garment provided temptation that he could not resist. He hid the stolen property under his tent floor, but he could not conceal his thievery from God.

The Lord charged Israel with robbing Him, and when they asked "In what way have we robbed You?" He replied, "In tithes and offerings" (Mal. 3:8, 9). Achan's sin consisted of taking something that belonged to God, and that is what we do when we withhold tithes or offerings.

Continuing through Mammon Cemetery, we encounter the tomb of the first treasurer of the Christian church, Judas Iscariot. On the marker we read the words "thirty pieces of silver," reminding us of the price for which he betrayed his Lord.

Next we see the grave of a wealthy prince, with a marker declaring, "He was very rich." When Jesus told him to sell all he had and give the proceeds to the poor and follow Him, the young ruler decided the price was too high, and he went away sorrowfully. Choosing rather to be the richest man in Mammon Cemetery than the poorest man in the kingdom of God, he considered the bankbook of more value than the book of life.

On the marker of the last tomb we shall visit are just two words: "Thou fool." The individual under it had been blessed with bumper crops. There are those who describe with great eloquence what they would do if they had a million dollars, but the true test of stewardship rests with how we are using what God has already entrusted to us.

God gives wealth not to hoard, but to distribute and invest for extending the kingdom of God.

And He said to them, "Take heed and beware of covetousness, for one's life does not consist in the abundance of the things he possesses." Luke 12:15.

Pray for the 11 million inhabitants of the crab-shaped island of Sulawesi in Indonesia.

LOVE THEM FOR MY SAKE

Both good news and shocking news soon become a part of history, but the death of Jesus Christ for our sins is not merely history—it is still current news.

It's not only news; it's good news! The only news that can heal the sin sickness of the world—it's the good news that everybody in the whole world needs to hear.

A 12-year-old boy in India prayed the night before a final examination at school, "Please help me pass that examination tomorrow." Then he realized his prayer sounded somewhat selfish, so he continued: "Lord, I pray that You'll help everybody in my class pass that examination tomorrow." Pausing again, he then added: "I pray, Lord, that You'll help everybody in the whole school pass the examination."

The boy still was not pleased with his prayer, so he continued: "Lord, I pray that You'll help everybody in all the schools pass the examination." Then he seemed to have an enlarged vision, and he burst out, "Lord, I pray that You'll help everybody in the whole world pass the examination."

That's the kind of missionary vision you and I need today. That's global strategy. We need a vision that goes beyond our own selves, beyond our own families, beyond our own nation. We need a world vision.

A ragged, dirty, disheveled young man knocked at the door of a farmhouse in the midwestern U.S.A. The wife, answering the door, thought he was a tramp asking for a handout. "Go away," she said. "We don't have time for tramps here."

By that time the husband had joined his wife at the door. Looking at the unkempt stranger, he said, "Go away from our door. We don't want to be bothered."

Reaching into his pocket, the young man produced a crumpled piece of paper and handed it to the farmer, who read the following words: "Dear Mother and Dad, this is my friend who cared for me as I was dying on the battlefield. Please, love him for my sake." It was signed "Harry."

Jesus is saying, "Love them for My sake. Help them get ready for their final exams."

"I do not pray for these alone, but also for those who will believe in Me through their word." John 17:20.

Seventh-day Adventist publications and the Voice of Hope *broadcasts reach the volcanic islands of Wallis and Futuna in the southwestern Pacific. Favorable contacts have been made. Pray for the church's outreach there.*

LIKE SEED ON FERTILE SOIL

Jorge and Frederick Riffel were Germans who lived in the Stalingrad area of southern Russia. In the mid-1870s the two young married men decided to emigrate to the New World, Jorge to Brazil and Frederick to Kansas. After four years in Brazil, Jorge and his family moved to Argentina, but crop failures led him to join Frederick in Kansas. The move was providential, for the new immigrant family had barely settled onto their farm when L. R. Conradi, a 29-year-old German evangelist from Michigan, began holding tent meetings in their community.

Both Riffel families attended them regularly, and when the evangelist made his appeal for those who would accept Christ and obey all His commandments, they gladly responded.

Jorge wrote letters back to Argentina telling of his newfound faith, and sent tracts and books that were like seed on fertile soil. He was a man of prayer, and in response to his prayers, it seemed that God was saying, "Go back to Argentina. Return to South America as a lay evangelist."

Jorge and his family and three other German families sold out and organized a missionary band dedicated to carrying the Advent message to Argentina. Reinhardt Hetze, a German friend from Russia, met the lay evangelists. As they bumped along the rough road in Hetze's farm wagon, George gave his friend a Bible study on the Sabbath doctrine. Hetze had heard about the Sabbath previously, but had delayed obedience. Now he took his stand, and soon the first Sabbath school in the South American Division was convening regularly. Within a year 20 people were observing the Sabbath. The church sent Frank H. Westphal to shepherd the new believers, and on September 9, 1894, there was born the first Seventh-day Adventist church in Argentina, and the first in the South American Division. Since 1894 that first congregation of 36 members has grown to a division membership of 877,612.

For as the earth brings forth its bud, as the garden causes the things that are sown in it to spring forth, so the Lord God will cause righteousness and praise to spring forth before all the nations. Isa. 61:11.

Pray for Argentina, with a population of more than 32 million and 53,001 Seventh-day Adventists.

THE UNDELIVERED MESSAGE

In 1910 a girl living in a little village in Bedfordshire, England, wrote a postcard to her sweetheart, who lived in Clifton, 15 miles away. On it she told the young man that she would be pleased to have their friendship continue.

That postcard, written in 1910, was delivered in 1969, fifty-nine years later. The young man died in 1929 without ever receiving the encouraging note from the young woman he desired to be his wife.

An undelivered message of love it was, and that's exactly the trouble with the world today. We have the message, and only the ones who have the message can deliver it.

At a district meeting, church representatives were reporting. One said, "We had no apostasies, no deaths, no births, no marriages, no transfers, and no baptisms. Pray that God will help us to hold our own." It is obvious that with no births, no baptisms, and no transfers, a church cannot hold its own.

Another representative said, "We are all perfectly united." As he sat down, he said under his breath, "We are frozen to death." A dead church will not deliver God's message of love.

A number of years ago the captain of a Greenland whaling vessel had a strange experience. Icebergs trapped his ship near the Arctic Circle, and he decided to cast anchor until morning. As the day dawned, he sighted another ship dimly visible through the morning mist. The captain and some of his men in a smaller boat made their way through the lanes of open space to the mysterious vessel. Boarding the ship, he found every member of the crew dead and frozen stiff. Some were in their hammocks, while others lay upon the deck where they had fallen. The captain was sitting at a table as if writing in a logbook. The last entry on the page on which the captain's lifeless finger rested indicated that the ship had been drifting around the Arctic Ocean for 13 years. It was a floating sepulcher manned by a frozen crew. God forbid that this should describe your church or mine.

"I know your works, that you have a name that you are alive, but you are dead." Rev. 3:1.

Ecuador has religious freedom. Ninety-eight percent of the population of more than 10 million are Christians, with 91 percent being Roman Catholics. Pray for the advance of the last warning message in Ecuador, where we have 13,747 church members.

GOD AND MAMMON

A picture depicts a man picking up gold in the street. He is putting it into bags, and there is a long row of sacks behind him already filled with money. His shoulders are stooped, and his back is bent from the toil of securing the gold. In front of him is a graveyard, and across the picture appears the words "It all ends here."

The world offers money to some, and money is all right if properly used. But when death comes, money cannot stay the cruel hand of the grim reaper. It has little value after death. When a rich man dies, no one asks "How much did he take with him?" but rather "How much did he leave?" At death the wealthiest man living becomes a pauper, and without Christ there is no hope of eternal salvation.

An old Indian chief, when told of the Saviour, said, "The Jesus road is good, but I have followed the old Indian road all my life, and I will follow it to the end." A year later he was on the border of death. As he was seeking a pathway through the darkness, he said to the missionary, "Can I turn to the Jesus road now? My road stops here. It has no path through the valley." And that's the way it is—man's plans and purposes stop here, but the Jesus road goes on. It goes on into eternity.

Both God and Mammon make a totalitarian demand upon us—that is why we cannot serve both.

Depression years tend to put God back on His throne and man back on his knees. We are living in a day in which man has gotten up off his knees and is bursting with newfound pride in his ability to do things.

Money is a demanding god and exacts a demanding worship, but that road ends here in this world. It offers no path through the dark valley. Don't let the glitter of gold get your eyes off that which is of infinitely greater value—the souls of men and women.

"No one can serve two masters; for either he will hate the one and love the other, or else he will be loyal to the one and despise the other. You cannot serve God and mammon." Matt. 6:24.

Seventh-day Adventism in Ghana began in 1888 with a tract given by a ship's captain. Today we have 121,341 Seventh-day Adventists in this large African country. Pray that the final message may soon penetrate every unreached group there.

LITTLE CAN BE MUCH

The story of the feeding of the 5,000 illustrates the principle "Little is much when God is in it." An indication of the event's importance is that it is the only miracle of Jesus that is related in all four Gospels.

The disciples failed to see the possibilities in their limited resources. We might say they lacked "church-growth eyes." They looked at the task in relation to their meager supplies and concluded it was impossible, forgetting that Jesus can take natural elements and do supernatural things with them.

The disciples failed to understand the power of Jesus' presence. He touched the food, and there was more than enough for everyone. When we invite Jesus into our lives, He touches us, and through us, as His modern-day disciples, He is able to bring spiritual bread to the multitudes. Not only is He with us as we study the Bible with others; He is with us in all our daily contacts. His plan is to reach out and touch others through us.

The miracle of the feeding of the 5,000 began when a boy was willing to make available to Jesus the little that he had—a little lunch of five loaves and two fish. Jesus worked with what was available, and He does the same today. Miracles begin in our day when by faith we offer to Him the little that we have.

Then He took the five loaves and the two fish, and looking up to heaven, He blessed and broke them, and gave them to the disciples to set before the multitude. So they all ate and were filled, and twelve baskets of the leftover fragments were taken up by them. Luke 9:16, 17.

Please pray for Mauritius, an island situated about 500 miles east of Madagascar, in the Indian Ocean. It is 790 square miles in area. The population is more than 1 million, with 2,658 Seventh-day Adventists.

Rose Le Meme, who visited Switzerland in 1912 in the interest of her health, introduced Seventh-day Adventist teachings to the island. In Lausanne she attended Adventist lectures and became a convert. Upon returning to Mauritius, she won her two sisters and awakened a great interest in her neighborhood. On September 12, 1914, 77 years ago today, the first 25 converts were baptized and the first church on the island was organized.

A VARIETY OF TEMPERAMENTS

We are all conscious of the fact that the human family consists of a variety of temperaments.

Four hundred years before Christ, Hippocrates, the father of medicine, set forth the theory that there are basically four types of temperaments. Theorizing that temperament types were the result of too much of one of four major body fluids, he named them after the fluids.

According to the Hippocratic theory, too much blood made a sanguine; an excess of yellow bile resulted in a choleric; black bile made a melancholy; and a surplus of phlegm made a phlegmatic.

We now know that we are born with a temperament transmitted from our parents and grandparents by the genes, but many still accept the four basic classifications set forth by Hippocrates.

Although we are all a mixture of temperaments, usually one will predominate. An understanding of the different temperaments will help us to relate more adequately to other members of the human family at home, at work, and in all our social contacts.

God's messenger says: "While parents who have the fear of God in them restrain their children, they should study their dispositions and temperaments. . . . Sometimes everything seems to go wrong. There is fretfulness all around, and all have a very miserable, unhappy time. The parents lay the blame upon their poor children and think them very disobedient and unruly, the worst children in the world, when the cause of the disturbance is in themselves" (*Testimonies*, vol. 1, p. 384).

Life will be happier and more productive if we understand something about our own temperaments and of those with whom we closely associate. The Lord Himself does so. "Not all can be helped in the same way. God deals with each according to his temperament and character, and we must cooperate with Him" (*Gospel Workers*, p. 208).

You will probably recognize yourself and some other people whom you know well in one of the next four readings as we consider Hippocrates' four basic temperament types.

And He said to me, "My grace is sufficient for you, for My strength is made perfect in weakness." Therefore most gladly I will rather boast in my infirmities, that the power of Christ may rest upon me. 2 Cor. 12:9.

Pray that the burgeoning spread of the gospel may continue among the more than 3.2 million people of Puerto Rico. We have 29,950 Seventh-day Adventists on the island.

THE SANGUINE

Today we focus on the first of the four basic temperaments. As you read the characteristics, you will think of people you know who are sanguines. They are of the fun-loving, happy-natured, optimistic temperament.

When the sanguine enters the room, he/she lifts the spirits of everybody. Sanguines are natural-born storytellers, and they will soon have a circle of listeners around them. With them, imagination mixes with memory in such a way that what matters most is the story and not the facts!

Those with this personality type are warm, genial, and outgoing, with a natural charisma. They like to be with people.

Having a genuine love for people, they make so many friends that they have difficulty keeping up with all of them.

Because of their naive, spontaneous enthusiasm, sanguines sometimes are insensitive to the feelings of others. They may come on too strong or as unreal. Sanguines often speak before thinking, but their lovable disposition and transparent sincerity usually get them over the rough spots sometimes created by their blustery, impetuous nature.

This personality type often makes decisions impulsively, basing them more on feelings than analytical thought. Detail work does not appeal to sanguines. Often they are not well organized, and are subject to financial problems. They are better at starting projects than completing them. Restless, lacking discipline, they tend to procrastinate and are sometimes weak-willed. They are inclined to interrupt when others are talking because they are more gifted at talking than listening. Their enthusiasm sometimes expresses itself in a form of verbal shorthand.

If you recognize yourself to be a sanguine, you will see areas of weakness in your life that the indwelling Christ can strengthen. If your spouse or other close family members are sanguine, be thankful for their happy, cheerful spirit. Should they worry about details, deadlines, and accuracy, as some of the other temperaments do, they would not have the carefree qualities you admire and appreciate.

Happy are the people who are in such a state; happy are the people whose God is the Lord! Ps. 144:15.

Papua New Guinea is a land of earthquakes, high mountains, torrential rainfalls, and thick jungles. God has blessed the Seventh-day Adventist Church with a 419 percent increase in membership in the short span of 20 years, growing from 20,871 in 1969 to 108,308 in 1989. Pray for our church leaders and lay members as they evangelize its 3.6 million receptive people.

THE CHOLERIC

If we were to choose one word to describe each of the four temperaments, we might choose the words *lively, active, sensitive,* and *stable.* Yesterday we dealt with the lively, or sanguine, temperament. Today we deal with the active, or choleric.

The choleric is the born leader. This type makes good executives, generals, or dictators, being strong-willed, opinionated, practical, and decisive. Such ambitious idea persons tend to be workaholics.

Having dogged determination, cholerics do not discourage easily. They tend to be loners, and others who are less motivated tend to get in their way. Goal-oriented, they sometimes appear to run roughshod over the feelings and rights of others in pursuit of their goals.

The choleric is an opportunist and comes across as one who uses people to further his own ends. Thriving on activity, cholerics are assertive, independent, and self-sufficient. They often do not give sympathy or compassion.

Cholerics will take a firm stand on issues. Argumentative and ulcer-prone, they get bored by details and are people of action who often come across as bossy. They give advice not asked for and are sometimes abrasive.

Able to make quick decisions, they are optimistic and do not see the pitfalls and potential problems that those of other temperaments may spot.

Unconverted cholerics can be vengeful and inclined to carry grudges. Of the four temperaments, they are the most difficult to lead to conversion as adults because of their self-sufficiency.

It seems to be a law of nature that opposites attract, and yet while that may be true, the characteristics of opposite temperaments can also irritate.

The different temperaments each have strengths and weaknesses, but the power of God can transform the weaknesses. "When Christ is formed within, the hope of glory, then the truth of God will so act upon the natural temperament that its transforming power will be seen in changed characters" (*Counsels to Parents and Teachers,* p. 194).

And Moses chose able men out of all Israel, and made them heads over the people: rulers of thousands, rulers of hundreds, rulers of fifties, and rulers of tens. Ex. 18:25.

The church still faces many challenges in the well-evangelized but suffering land of Uganda. Pray for the partially reached nomadic peoples and the communities of Muslims scattered throughout the country. Pray that evangelism may be the priority. In this land of 16.8 million there are 48,292 Seventh-day Adventists.

THE MELANCHOLY

No one temperament type is better than another. Each has its strengths and weaknesses. Today we consider the melancholy temperament. It is the gifted, self-sacrificing perfectionist with a sensitive and emotional nature. Analytical in nature, this type of person appreciates the fine arts.

With melancholies, feelings predominate, so they experience a variety of moods. Many of the world's great geniuses belong to this temperament. Sensitive to the world's suffering and pain, they are compassionate, and the hurting find themselves attracted to them.

Melancholies are extremely dependable. While they will not push themselves forward to meet people, they value quality friendships and are loyal. Melancholies are highly organized. They are precise and exacting and tend to have unrealistic perfectionist expectations.

The melancholy is a born worrier and deliberates at great length before making decisions. Analyzing himself and others too much, he tends to have a persecution complex and easily jumps to conclusions when trying to discern motives. If he sees two people talking in hushed tones, he is sure they are discussing him.

Severe in judging themselves, melancholies struggle for a sense of personal worth. They are easily offended or insulted, and are sometimes gloomy and depressed. Their moods respond easily to their environment. While they need much affirmation, at the same time they sometimes lack appreciation for the feelings of others.

Through the transforming miracle of the gospel, it is possible for the melancholy to find joy and happiness and still retain the many positive strengths of his/her sensitive and gifted temperament.

Therefore humble yourselves under the mighty hand of God, . . . casting all your care upon Him, for He cares for you. 1 Peter 5:6, 7.

Sri Lanka is a large island southeast of the southern tip of India. There are 1,754 Seventh-day Adventists among a total population of 17.5 million. Buddhism, the state religion, is protected and promoted. Although freedom exists for other religions, there has been some discrimination against minority religions. In this century Sri Lanka is the only non-Muslim Asian country in which the Christian church has steadily declined in numbers and influence.

Pray we may reach out to the many unevangelized villages throughout this island.

THE PHLEGMATIC

The four different temperaments seem to exist in fairly equal proportions. In the colder climates we appear to find more phlegmatics, but this is balanced by the fact that the warmer climates seem to contain more sanguines. Phlegmatics are the calm, easygoing persons who seldom get disturbed. They keep their emotions under control and are patient and soft-spoken, seldom getting excited.

Dependability personified, phlegmatics are practical and efficient—the meticulous-type worker. They are reluctant to take leadership roles, but make good leaders when drafted.

The typical phlegmatic avoids involvement beyond his daily routine. With him there are not too many critical issues, and he will have strong convictions on few matters. Offering advice only when asked, he wants to please and rarely gets disturbed. He is a born peacemaker and a good diplomat.

Phlegmatics don't start out with great expectations, so they seldom get disappointed. Studiously avoiding conflict and easy to get along with, they may even compromise in order to avoid conflict or confrontation. Among the negative qualities sometimes in evidence, we might list timidness, fearfulness, and laziness. They are often weak in communicating and slow in making decisions. As a rule, they resist change and like tradition and routine.

Good listeners, phlegmatics are consistent and predictable. They have a natural dry sense of humor that enables them to see the funny side of things. In addition, they like to tease and are often good imitators.

An understanding of temperament differences gives us an insight into some real-life situations. For example, a melancholy husband is not likely to entrust the keeping of financial records and balancing the family checkbook to his sanguine wife. When she proposes moving the furniture, a sanguine wife should not expect an enthusiastic response from a phlegmatic husband.

He who is slow to wrath has great understanding, but he who is impulsive exalts folly. Prov. 14:29.

New Zealand, with two main islands, has a population of only 3.4 million. Having freedom of religion and no established church, the nation's prevailing trend is secular materialism and a turning away from God. Pray for an outpouring of the Holy Spirit on God's remnant church so that the 9,661 Seventh-day Adventist members there will bring revival and renewal to New Zealand.

WEAKNESS CAN BE MADE STRONG

Now that we have taken a brief look at each of the four temperaments, you probably see which one you most resemble. There will always be some characteristics that do not fit, because we are all products of hereditary and environmental influences. A choleric, for example, may have inherited some of the characteristics of the other three temperaments.

It is human to judge others by ourselves and to feel that those who are different from us are odd, or perhaps have something wrong with them. Our study of the temperaments helps us to see that being different does not necessarily mean being inferior.

No one temperament is better than another. Certain temperaments might appeal to you more than others, but especially as Christians, we should seek to see the strengths in each one. In some cases this will call for a generous measure of God's grace.

The orderly, systematic melancholy may feel frustrated by the disorganized, happy-go-lucky ways of a sanguine spouse or workmate. But it would be a drab world if we were all melancholies, and it would be an unpredictable world if we were all sanguines. We need the balance that we provide each other.

The curiosity of a melancholy might be offensive and seem like an invasion of privacy to someone who fails to perceive that such inquisitiveness is a manifestation of the attribute of caring that makes the melancholy such a devoted friend and effective researcher. The same basic qualities that produce our weaknesses also give rise to our strengths, and often the line between is extremely thin. For example, the persistence of a choleric, which often makes him appear to be overbearing and obnoxious, can make him an effective evangelist.

Identifying and understanding our temperaments can help us see ourselves as others do. When you discover weaknesses, take courage, because God provides strength for them if we ask Him.

Therefore I take pleasure in infirmities, in reproaches, in needs, in persecutions, in distresses, for Christ's sake. For when I am weak, then I am strong. 2 Cor. 12:10.

The Netherlands has complete freedom of religion, but there is also a strong and steady secularization of society. Pray for a revival in this beautiful land of tulips, windmills, and wooden shoes. Pray especially that the Seventh-day Adventist witness may be strong in the power of the Holy Spirit, that this country may return to a vital, biblical Christianity.

LIGHT ON PEOPLE PROBLEMS

A clearer understanding of the temperaments should shed some light on our people problems. In most cases people don't act the way they do to deliberately irritate you—they are just that way by nature.

If your mother was a melancholy, she was probably a good support person. She would patiently assist you with your projects, anticipating your needs and helping you according to your directions. However, if you married a choleric, don't expect her to have the qualities of your melancholy mother. The choleric might try valiantly to give you support when you work on a project together, but it will not be an easy role for her to fill, because a choleric is not by nature a support person.

Instead of passively helping, the choleric will soon be giving the orders and directing the project. That is the choleric's nature, since she is a born leader. When looking for a support person who will be thoughtful and careful, you should probably search among the melancholies or the phlegmatics.

The melancholy will have a place for everything, and everything will be in its place. Melancholies often find themselves frustrated and threatened by the brash self-confidence of the sanguine and the choleric. The easygoing phlegmatic lets the rest of the world go by and doesn't let the conflicts between the other temperaments disturb his enjoyment of life.

The human personality is a complex combination of many factors, of which temperament is only one. But it is an important one. With God's help we can cultivate desirable personality traits, and we can subdue or eliminate undesirable characteristics.

If you recognize yourself to be a phlegmatic, you can cultivate the quality of industriousness so that even though you are easygoing, no one will be able to accuse you of being lazy.

As a choleric, you should qualify yourself for a leadership position of some kind. Your temperament has the ability to boss, but conflict and frustration will result if the choleric starts directing others before being appointed to do so.

"A new commandment I give to you, that you love one another; as I have loved you, that you also love one another." John 13:34

Pray for the United Kingdom today, including England, Scotland, Wales, Northern Ireland, the Isle of Man, and the Channel Islands.

ADJUSTING OUR VALUES

David Livingstone made a resolution that not only shaped his own life of service, but helped mold his generation. He said, "I will place no value on anything I have, or may possess, except in relation to the kingdom of Christ. If anything will advance the interests of that kingdom, it shall be given away, or kept, just as by the giving or keeping it shall most promote the glory of Him to whom I owe all my hopes for time and for eternity. May grace and strength sufficient to enable me to adhere faithfully to this resolution be given me so that not in name only, all my interests may be identified with His cause."

Andrew Fearing used to tell of an elderly isolated couple of church members. They lived on a farm, and sometimes winter storms made it impossible for them to attend the nearest church, which was a considerable distance away. When Pastor Fearing would visit, they would always have an envelope waiting for him with their tithes and offerings. On one such visit the elderly father asked Fearing to come with him to one of the outbuildings. Inside the building were two simple pine caskets that the farmer had made with his own hands. As the man opened the lids, Pastor Fearing saw the white material with which the farmer's wife had lined the homemade coffins. "If one or both of us falls asleep in Jesus before the Saviour returns, we have prepared our final resting places, and the money that might have been spent to buy coffins can go into the Lord's work."

Now, I'm not saying that we must all build our own coffins, but if we would be willing to live simply in the spirit of the pioneers, there are many ways we could save money that we could channel into God's cause.

When at last we give an account of our stewardship, we would experience a sense of disappointment and loss should it be disclosed that we did less than we might have done with what God entrusted to our care.

Moreover it is required in stewards that one be found faithful. 1 Cor. 4:2.

Ninety-three percent of the population of 5 million in Finland is Christian, with most belonging to the Evangelical Lutheran Church. Pray that Seventh-day Adventists, with 6,181 members, may continue their strong evangelistic outreach.

WE REALLY MEAN IT

Picture with me a scene in Singapore. Smoke fills the air. All day long the wood has burned, and now all that remains is a 30-foot-long bed of coals—red-hot coals ready for the Hindu fire-walking ceremony.

In preparation for this ceremony, a Hindu devotes an entire week to purification, praying and performing acts of penance. At night he leaves the comforts of home for a bed on the temple floor; he eats only vegetables, and does not smoke or drink alcoholic beverages.

Now the ceremony is about to begin. The men, with their backs bare and holy powder smeared over their bodies, stretch forth their hands. With a rope whip the temple priests lash the outstretched arms of the fire walkers, deepening their trance. The crowd goes wild as the first devotee runs across the bed of red-hot coals. At the far end of the bed of coals is a milk bath, where the men step into a pool of milk from sacred cows.

Why do these people walk through the fire? Let's ask them. A young mother explains: "Our baby was ill, and my husband vowed to go through the fire if the child lived. He is fulfilling his vow."

"If you want help to pass an examination, or need to get work, or want to get well," three schoolboys tell us, "you must believe that you will get what you asked for. Run through the fire three times, and then you will have it."

Finally we ask a tax collector employed by the Singapore government. "Just as you Christians go to church and ask your God's forgiveness, so we Hindus ask our gods and goddesses to forgive our mistakes and help us. Then we show them that we really mean it by running through the fire. This is how we show that we really mean it."

The apostle Paul points to the sacrifices of ancient Israel as an illustration of what the followers of Christ are to become. In Romans 12:1 he challenges Christians to present their bodies a living sacrifice to God. In other words, we are to give our lives in service to Christ. This is how we show that we really mean it.

> **"Behold, to obey is better than sacrifice, and to heed than the fat of rams." 1 Sam. 15:22.**

> *Pray that the gospel may once again find entrance to North Korea, where all religions have been harshly repressed.*

MARKS OF OUR ALLEGIANCE

While Paul was a prisoner of Caesar in Rome, he noticed that everything around about him bore the mark of Caesar. The bricks of the wall had brands stamped into the clay. The chain links that circled his wrists bore the forger's identity, and the jailer wore the insignia of Caesar's service.

But we can hear Paul say to himself, "I too am marked." The apostle bore in his body the imprints of his allegiance. They were the scars he had received when stoned at Lystra and beaten at Philippi.

We too, as Christians, have marks that declare to others whom we serve. In these days of international unrest and uncertainty, the one virtue that stands out above all others is the virtue of loyalty.

The church needs the loyalty of its members today as never before. Some would make a distinction between their loyalty to Christ and their loyalty to the church. But we do well to remember that Christ is the head of the body—the church.

Let us think of four ways in which we can demonstrate our loyalty to the church. First, by faithful attendance at the services in the house of God.

A second way involves our willingness to accept the duties and responsibilities assigned to us. The work of the church is God's—the greatest task in all the world—and its success depends upon our willingness to serve without monetary reward.

The third way in which we can reveal genuine loyalty to the church is by defending its name and refraining from destructive criticism.

The fourth way consists of giving our means for the church's support. Loyalty in giving is measured not by the amount we give as compared to any other member, but rather in proportion to what we ourselves possess. This is the lesson taught by the widow's two mites.

Loyalty in giving leads to systematic benevolence, which adjusts itself to fluctuations in income and periods of unemployment. It requires little of those who have little, and much of those who have much.

"How then can I do this great wickedness, and sin against God?" Gen. 39:9.

Pray for the 200,000 Gypsies of Spain, known as Gitanos, that they may hear the gospel soon.

TOO STRICT

A woman came to D. L. Moody and complained, "Mr. Moody, I don't like your religion; it's too strict. You say we can't dance, go to the theater, play cards, or drink alcoholic beverages. We can't have any fun."

"But madam, you misunderstood me. I drink and smoke and dance and play cards and go to the theater all I want. I do all these things any time I want to. You see, since Jesus came into my heart, I just don't want to do any of these things anymore."

Many people have never seriously investigated the Adventist faith because it seems to be too strict. They say, "There are too many things you can't do and too many things you can't eat!" But the informed Seventh-day Adventist would say as Moody said, "I just don't want to do any of these things anymore."

A heart full of love for Jesus makes the difference. Furthermore, when I learn that the Adventist lifestyle will add seven to nine years to my life expectancy, I don't want to do the things that would deprive me of that benefit.

Research shows that cigarette smoking increases the risk of death from coronary heart disease by 70 percent, so I certainly don't want to smoke. Scientific study also indicates a link between the use of tobacco, alcohol, tea, and coffee and the risk of various types of cancer.

We constantly hear about the relationship of animal fats to cardiovascular diseases, and I am thankful for a religion that brings such information to the attention of its members.

A trainer had a snake for 18 years, having caught it when it was about nine inches long. It was no thicker than his little finger. At any time he could have crushed it to death between his finger and thumb. He could have dropped it and had an empty hand, but he kept it and played with it as a pet. The trainer thought he was in control, but one day a circus crowd watched in horror as this huge boa constrictor crushed the life out of the trainer.

I'm thankful for a religion that's too strict to let me play with snakes!

At the last it bites like a serpent, and stings like a viper. Prov. 23:32.

Pray for the 3.9 million people of Laos, most of whom are Buddhists. Laos is strategically located between China, Thailand, and Vietnam.

THE CHILDREN OF THE WORLD

A beautiful church building was under construction, and the building committee had hired the best artist in the land to paint a mural of Christ blessing the children. On this particular day the artist had labored late to put the finishing touches on his painting because the committee would meet the next morning to inspect his work.

Noises in the night disturbed the artist. When he rushed to the wall containing his mural, he found a stranger painting on his picture. "Stop! Stop! You're ruining my picture!" the artist cried.

Slowly, calmly, the stranger spoke. "No, I'm making it right. Who told you that the faces of all the children in the family of God are white?" He continued kindly, "Do you see how mistaken you were? You used only one color, and you had five colors on your palette. I have made some faces yellow, some brown, others black, and still others red. You see, these children have come from many lands in answer to My call."

"Your call?" the artist questioned. "What call is that?"

The answer came in words strangely familiar: "Let the little children come to Me, and do not forbid them; for of such is the kingdom of heaven" (Matt. 19:14). And with those words the Stranger, who was the master artist, disappeared.

Looking at the picture, the artist liked it better all the time. Then all of a sudden he awakened to find the early-morning sun streaming through the window, and he was still in bed. It had been only a dream, but it inspired him so that he rushed to the church and transformed the dream into reality.

The committee members were delighted with the mural. With deep feeling one of them said, "Why, it's God's family at home with Him."

And that's what global strategy is all about—helping to hasten the day when all God's family will be home with Him.

Let the redeemed of the Lord say so, whom He has redeemed from the hand of the enemy, and gathered out of the lands, from the east and from the west, from the north and from the south. Ps. 107:2, 3.

Pray for the more than 55 million citizens of Thailand, nearly all of whom are Buddhists. Adventists number 12,905. It is the headquarters for the World Fellowship of Buddhists, and the state religion is Buddhism. However, there is religious freedom.

COPING WITH STRESS

The symptoms of stress are familiar to most people—headache, stiff neck, a tight feeling in the chest, indigestion, and pain between the shoulder blades. All of us have so many voices calling for our attention, so many things demanding to be done.

Unresolved guilt also produces stress. The Bible contains so many promises regarding the forgiveness of our sins that no Christian should have any reason to go through life bearing a burden of guilt.

A violation of basic health principles can produce stress. We should periodically check ourselves by these eight basics: fresh air, sunshine, proper food, pure water, adequate exercise, adequate rest, temperance, and the right mental attitude. Neglect or violation in any of the eight areas will bring on stress.

Nothing is more stressful than indecision. Indecision can drain us of vital energy, and prolonged cases of indecision can actually produce illness.

Certain basic issues in life must be resolved decisively once and for all. These far-reaching decisions will relieve us of the pressure of many minor decisions that will then be unnecessary.

A failure to set priorities on things correctly will lead to stress. The Bible offers some priceless principles for coping with stress. Jesus said: "But seek first the kingdom of God and His righteousness" (Matt. 6:33). What are you seeking for more than anything else?

We have looked at four sources of stress: feelings of guilt, violations of health principles, indecision, and failure to set priorities.

The remedy for stress is faith and trust in the goodness of God. When we trust God and rest in His love, we will avoid inner conflicts that produce stress.

If you would be free from stress, walk in the light of God's Word each day. Put into action what you know to be right.

For I am persuaded that neither death nor life, nor angels nor principalities nor powers, nor things present nor things to come, nor height nor depth, nor any other created thing, shall be able to separate us from the love of God which is in Christ Jesus our Lord. Rom. 8:38, 39.

Pray for the 1.6 million inhabitants of the state of Manipur in India, made up of 28 different tribes. Large numbers of the tribal people have become Protestant Christians within the past 100 years.

ALL TO THE GLORY OF GOD

Phillips Brooks prayed, "God, grant me this day some new vision of Thy truth. Inspire me with the spirit of joy and gladness, and make me the cup of strength to suffering souls." May that prayer be answered for each of us today.

We could summarize the principle that guides Christian conduct in the following words: "Therefore, whether you eat or drink, or whatever you do, do all to the glory of God" (1 Cor. 10:31).

In the realm of diet, dress, recreation, and entertainment, the Christian will sincerely seek to know God's will for him and will say as Jesus did: "Not My will, but Yours be done."

As we mature in Christian experience and realize His will is always for our best good, our will and His become one. In the earlier stages of our experience we will do well to accept God's will as children accept the word of their parents, even when they may not understand all the underlying reasons.

Research reveals that Adventists who follow a vegetarian diet and abstain from alcoholic beverages and nicotine live seven years longer than the average of the general population. Certainly this demonstrates that God's health principles are designed for our good. But a healthful lifestyle includes much more than diet. Recognizing our bodies to be the dwelling place of the Holy Spirit should give us a desire to keep our bodies strong, clean, and healthy. We should cultivate natural health habits, such as getting balanced amounts of exercise and rest, safe exposure to sunlight, six to eight glasses of water a day, breathing deeply of fresh air, and temperance in all good things.

Our desire to exalt Jesus and not self will lead us to choose for ourselves the highest standards of modesty in dress, and to avoid adornment with gaudy cosmetics and jewelry worn basically for display. In all things our desire should be to reveal Christ, not human pride.

The violence and immorality portrayed by the media is clearly incompatible with a Christian lifestyle. We will apply the same high standards to our choice of reading matter and music, and to every other aspect of our Christian lifestyle. Our motive will always be love for our Lord.

For you, brethren, have been called to liberty; only do not use liberty as an opportunity for the flesh, but through love serve one another. Gal. 5:13.

Pray for the northern African nation of Libya. In its 4.2 million people, Christians number more than 45,000, although the government does not tolerate any form of Christian witness. We have no established Seventh-day Adventist activity there.

281

GOD'S MESSENGERS

In South Africa I met a Christian woman who had spent 17 years in a Christian organization known around the world for its humanitarian work. Through reading the Bible, she discovered the fact that the seventh day of the week is the day that our Lord claims as His holy time. When she asked an officer of her church about the Sabbath, he handed her an 1889 issue of the *Review and Herald* that contained doctrinal studies. He cautioned her not to show the magazine to anyone else.

Later a Seventh-day Adventist evangelist came to town, and she attended his meetings. When he presented the message on the Spirit of Prophecy, she had difficulty believing that an author in our time could truly be inspired of God. Then she recalled a small book she had purchased in a local bookshop. She had read it many times and had felt that it was indeed inspired. "If the writer of this little book was inspired, I suppose this Ellen White, referred to by the evangelist, could also have been inspired," she admitted to herself.

When she picked up the treasured volume that she believed bore the marks of inspiration, to her surprise and delight, she discovered the author was Ellen White.

Ever since the entrance of sin interrupted direct communication between God and man, the gift of prophecy has been in operation. God has called men and women to be His special messengers to His people, and Satan has invariably tried to discredit the messenger or the message. When God chose Moses, Miriam and Aaron experienced feelings of jealousy, saying, "Has the Lord indeed spoken only through Moses? Has He not spoken through us also?" (Num. 12:2).

As one reads the entire chapter, it is quite clear that God was not pleased with their attitude. Miriam was smitten with leprosy, and the onward journey of Israel halted until she made things right by accepting her brother's prophetic gift. Miriam was healed, and God's people moved forward.

Then He said, "Hear now My words: If there is a prophet among you, I, the Lord, make Myself known to him in a vision, and I speak to him in a dream." Num. 12:6.

Pray for the Kolamis, a tribe in the state of Maharashtra in India. Numbering more than 60,000, the Kolamis are one of the few remaining tribes in central India that still offer human sacrifices.

REST

Jesus said, "Come to Me, . . . and I will give you rest" (Matt. 11:28). Unfortunately lots of church members do not have rest. Having your name on the church books will not give it to you if you have not first come to Christ. Jesus didn't say "Come to the church, and you will find rest." The church can't give you rest except as you find Jesus through it.

Jesus didn't say "Come to the doctrines, and you will find rest." Doctrines can't give you rest except as they introduce you to Jesus as your personal Saviour. Doctrines about Jesus are not enough. No knowledge about Jesus will take the place of knowing Him whom to know is life eternal.

Nor did Jesus say "Come to the Bible, and the Bible will give you rest." We love the Bible, and certainly we are blessed in reading it, but the Bible didn't die for you and me. Its purpose is to lead us to the One who did. He alone can give rest to the soul.

Jesus didn't say "Come to church activities, and you will find rest." Such things are good and vital—they have their place—but they cannot substitute for coming to Jesus. Working for the Lord is the outgrowth of rest and not the means by which we attain it.

An artist, invited to paint a picture of his concept of rest, placed upon the canvas a thundering waterfall over a bare and jagged rock. A tempest was raging. The rain was being dashed in torrents against the rock. But there, in a little cleft, protected from all that storm, sat a mother bird on her nest, calm, contented, and unharmed by the raging elements all about her. He labeled his picture *Rest*.

Now, this rest aptly describes the turbulent times in which we live. The winds of strife are breaking loose from the hands of the withholding angels, and we need a soul-rest in the midst of the great battle between good and evil.

The need of the hour is for a practical demonstration that spiritual rest is possible in spite of the storms around about us.

For he who has entered His rest has himself also ceased from his works as God did from His. Heb. 4:10.

Pray for the small Adventist membership in the landlocked state of Mali, in northwest Africa, with a population of 8.6 million, 81 percent of whom are Muslim. The nation has freedom of religion.

ANSWER SOMEONE'S PRAYER

A wife who became a Christian decided to have family worship with the children in spite of her husband's lack of interest. When worship time approached, he quietly went elsewhere. But one night he said to himself, "What's the sense of my going off just because Mother wants to go through this silly ritual every night? It's my house. I'll just stay here and read the paper."

So he hid behind his newspaper while his wife gathered the children to her knee, read a Bible story, and then knelt with them in prayer.

The father paid no attention until his boy began to pray a simple, short prayer that ended: "Bless Papa, and help him to know the truth, and to keep the Sabbath. For Jesus' sake, amen."

The father got up and tiptoed to the door, but he had not closed it behind him before he heard his baby girl lisp, "An' bless Papa, an' help him to keep de troof."

He wandered around outdoors until bedtime. The next day his mind was even more disturbed. At worship that evening he laid down his paper and listened. When his son began to pray, that father slipped to his knees for the first time in his life. But he managed to get up before anyone saw him.

The next day was Sabbath, and after the morning chores were done, he put on his best clothes. When his wife inquired about it, he replied, "Why, my dear, I thought I'd go to Sabbath school with you, if you don't mind."

Of course she didn't mind! It was an answer to her prayers and the prayers of the children. That father never missed a Sabbath after that, and he became active in the church.

This experience should encourage those who have been praying for some family member to come to Jesus. Years may pass with no evidence that our prayers will ever be answered, but we should never give up, because prayer does change things.

Perhaps someone reading this page could provide the answer to the prayer of a spouse, a child, a parent, or a brother or sister.

And let us not grow weary while doing good, for in due season we shall reap if we do not lose heart. Gal. 6:9.

Pray for the gospel outreach to professional people such as architects, researchers, engineers, physicians, and lawyers.

BITHYNIA OR TROAS

Paul had his heart set on going to Bithynia, the richest province of Asia, but instead he landed in lowly Troas. So far as his plans were concerned, going to Troas seemed to represent a detour in his life's journey. But it was in Troas that Paul saw the vision of the man from Macedonia pleading, "Come over and help us." The apostle obeyed that call, and it opened the greatest opportunity for ministry of his entire career.

A young couple were looking forward to serving as missionaries in Africa, but the wife failed to pass the medical examination. Severely disappointed, they determined to make all the money they could to extend the kingdom of God in the earth.

The young man's father, who was a dentist, had an interesting sideline of making unfermented wine for the Communion service. The young couple took over and developed the business, which prospered under the blessings of God. Hundreds of thousands of dollars have gone into missionary enterprises as a result of the project. The grape juice still carries the family name, Welch. They had their hearts set on Bithynia, but God saw that Troas would be a better destination for them.

These words were reputedly scribbled a century ago by an anonymous soldier of the Confederacy:

"I asked God for strength that I might achieve;
I was made weak, that I might learn humbly to obey.

I asked for health that I might do greater things;
I was given infirmity that I might do better things.

I asked for riches that I might be happy;
I was given poverty that I might be wise.

I asked for all things that I might enjoy life;
I was given life that I might enjoy all things.

I got nothing that I asked for, but everything I had hoped for.

Despite myself, my prayers were answered. I am among men most richly blessed."

After they had come to Mysia, they tried to go into Bithynia, but the Spirit did not permit them. So passing by Mysia, they came down to Troas. Acts 16:7, 8.

Pray for the 24 million Hindus in the state of Orissa in India, that they may be open to the gospel, and for the very few Christians there who have suffered much persecution for their faith.

A FISH STORY

What does the mention of Jonah bring to your mind? Thoughts of big fish, digestive juices, or arguments about the inspiration of the Bible?

The book of Jonah has been a favorite target for the attacks of skeptics. Can we believe the story of the great fish that swallowed Jonah? Perhaps the real question is: Is there a big enough God to make a fish big enough to swallow a man?

Faith rests ultimately upon the character of your God. The size of your God determines the size of your faith. An atheist asked a Christian girl, "Do you really believe that Jonah spent three days and three nights inside a whale?"

"I don't know what kind of sea creature it was," she replied. "When I get to heaven I will ask him."

"But suppose he isn't there?" the skeptic countered.

Quick as a flash came her reply: "Then you can ask him!"

A Norwegian sea captain told of finding a shark 16 feet long inside a sperm whale. Other objects as much as eight feet in diameter have been discovered in sea creatures. Now Jonah may have been a portly prophet, but it is doubtful that he was eight feet around the waist!

Encyclopedias cite several instances in which a huge fish has swallowed men and women who have survived. The temperature inside a fish's stomach would be 104 to 106 degrees Fahrenheit. The digestive juices do not destroy the inside of the fish's stomach, which is living tissue, and evidence suggests that human skin, which is also living tissue, can likewise survive exposure to digestive juices.

It is easy to become so absorbed in the exciting details of the book that we miss the point of it all. G. Campbell Morgan said, "Men have been looking so hard at the great fish that they have failed to see the great God."

The book of Jonah does not primarily have to do with the fish or Jonah, but God. This little Bible book, with only four chapters and 48 verses, gives more detail about God reaching out to Jonah than Jonah reaching out to Nineveh.

The conversion of the pagans on the ship and in Nineveh was a greater miracle than the fish.

Now the Lord had prepared a great fish to swallow Jonah. And Jonah was in the belly of the fish three days and three nights. Jonah 1:17.

Pray for the more than 30 million people of Guizhou (g-way-joe), "expensive state," a province of China.

SHIPS TO TARSHISH

Jonah's home was in the northern kingdom of Israel at a little place called Gath Hepher. The time was about 786 B.C.

One day a message came from God to him. It was brief, imperative, and commanding: "Arise, go to Nineveh, that great city, and cry out against it; for their wickedness has come up before Me" (Jonah 1:2).

Apart from his visit to Nineveh, we have only one other reference to Jonah's work as a prophet, and that is in 2 Kings 14:25. On that occasion God told him to bear the good news to Israel that certain long-lost territory would be restored to the kingdom. The Lord had sent him with a message of good news to his own people, but now He commanded the prophet to bear a message of doom to a faraway nation of sinners.

Jonah's first mistake was his refusal to do what God asked him to do. The longer the prophet hesitated to obey, the greater the chance the devil had to work on him. And the same is true in your experience and mine today.

The prophet had his eyes on circumstances, problems, evil, and man instead of keeping his focus on God. It appears from the Bible record that he had previously consecrated his life to the Lord and accepted His call to service, but now he did not want to obey, especially when it meant salvation to a hated enemy.

So Jonah found a ship going to Tarshish. It almost seemed providential until we stop to consider that it isn't God who arranges things contrary to His will. The devil always helps us find an excuse when we look for one.

We buy tickets for Tarshish when we turn away from God, from the church, from the family altar, and when we go contrary to the will of God in any matter. The greatest test of a person's Christian experience is a willingness to go all the way in harmony with the commands of God—particularly when it will bring the good news of salvation to another.

Every time we neglect or reject the call of God we are buying a ticket to Tarshish.

But Jonah arose to flee to Tarshish from the presence of the Lord. He went down to Joppa, and found a ship going to Tarshish; so he paid the fare, and went down into it, to go with them to Tarshish from the presence of the Lord. Jonah 1:3.

Pray for the more than 80 million people of the province of Shandong (shahn-doong), "mountain east", in China. Shandong was the birthplace of Confucius.

287

WHAT IS YOUR OCCUPATION?

Jonah paid the fare in order to board the ship bound for Tarshish. We always pay a price when we try to run away from God. The price of the ticket was only a small part of what it cost him for his disobedience.

From the time Jonah decided to go in a direction opposite from the way God was calling him, he went down, down, down. He went down to Joppa, down into the ship, and down into the belly of the great fish.

God allowed a storm to come in order for Jonah to learn to obey. Perhaps there have been times when the Lord has permitted "storms" to sweep over our lives in order for us to learn lessons for our eternal good. How many such storms might we have avoided if we had kept closer to our Lord?

During this terrible tempest God's man was asleep! Do you think Jonah was embarrassed by the sailors' questions? "What do you mean, sleeper? Arise, call on your God" and "What is your occupation?" (Jonah 1:6, 8). Do we ever get ourselves into situations in which others might ask humiliating questions of us?

"If we have been following Jesus step by step, we shall have something right to the point to tell concerning the way in which He has led us. . . . This is the witness for which our Lord calls, and for want of which the world is perishing" (*The Desire of Ages*, p. 340).

It was now apparent that Jonah's unfaithfulness was bringing trouble to those around him. God's people should be part of the solution, not part of the problem, and it is especially sad when the preacher has to be thrown out in order to solve a problem and restore tranquility.

God wants us to excel in our occupations. But related to it is a spiritual calling to use our vocation as an opportunity for witnessing and glorifying God in the workplace.

> **Then they said to him, "Please tell us! For whose cause is this trouble upon us? What is your occupation? And where do you come from? What is your country? And of what people are you?" Jonah 1:8.**

Pray for the progress of the work in Peru, where self-supporting missionaries from Chile first introduced Adventism. Peru today has a population of about 22 million, including 187,151 Seventh-day Adventists.

NOTHING TAKES HIM BY SURPRISE

One of the best ways to learn to pray is to study the prayers of the Bible. Jonah's prayer in chapter 2 of his book contains confession, praise, and at least partial repentance. As you relate this to your prayer life, how much time do you spend in confession, praise, and repentance?

Something else we can learn from his prayer experience is that you can pray anywhere. Jonah prayed inside the fish! Even more important than position or posture is the motive behind the praying.

Thoughtful leaders in worship service often announce, "As far as it is possible, let us kneel in prayer." For accident victims and the elderly with painful arthritic joints, the pain created by kneeling on a hard floor might largely destroy the blessing of the prayer.

Try to imagine Jonah's emotions as the sailors were picking him up to throw him into the angry sea. Do you think he had any hope of surviving, or did he expect this to be the end?

Try to capture his sensation as he fell from the railing of the ship into the turbulent waters. He hit the water and went under. If he inhaled, it was not air, but water that entered his nose and mouth. Was Jonah praying during these hectic moments? We don't know.

One of the greatest needs in the Christian experience is to find your way to God in the light, so that when the crisis comes, you will know your way in the darkness.

When you enter your home in the dark, you can find your way because you have learned to do it in the light.

"Now the Lord had prepared a great fish to swallow Jonah" (Jonah 1:17). Think about this! God had made provision for the emergency. Actually, while we face many emergencies and accidents, God does not. Sovereign over all, He knows the end from the beginning. Nothing takes Him by surprise. God was still in control of circumstances when the sailors cast Jonah into the sea.

Remembering that there are no emergencies with God should give you a quiet confidence that whatever today might bring your way, the Lord will have made advance provision for you to cope with it.

Then Jonah prayed to the Lord his God from the fish's belly. Jonah 2:1.

Pray for the people in war-torn Lebanon, with its population of more than 2.8 million, 600 of whom are Seventh-day Adventists.

A SECOND CHANCE FOR SERVICE

While we have no second chance in terms of salvation beyond this life, we do have a second chance in terms of service during this present life. God offered Jonah another opportunity to go to Nineveh, and He will give you a second chance for service too.

After his double sin of murder and adultery, David wrote many of his most beautiful psalms, including the twenty-third. Peter preached his Pentecost sermon and wrote both of his Epistles after he had denied the Lord three times. John Mark was useful in the ministry after he gave up in discouragement on his first missionary journey. He later wrote the Gospel that bears his name.

God gave Jonah a second chance to preach in Nineveh, and great were the results. Perhaps a key to his success was the fact that he preached God's message and not his own ideas. "Preach . . . the message that I tell you," the Lord instructed him (Jonah 3:2). God has to speak to us before He can speak through us.

In chapter 1 Jonah was running from God. Chapter 2 portrays him as running to God. By chapter 3 he was running with God, and in chapter 4 he was running ahead of God.

Chapter 1 tells of Jonah the disobedient prophet. Chapter 2 depicts him as the praying prophet. In chapter 3 he is the preaching prophet, and in chapter 4 he is the pouting prophet. The little book closes abruptly, leaving us to learn the rest of the story when Jesus returns. The open-ended closing provides for each of us the opportunity of benefiting from Jonah's experience and having the story of our lives end as we would choose.

Consider some of the lessons to be learned: the path of self-will always leads downward; it is futile to resist God's will; one usually runs into a storm when one flees from God; and eternal values are of more worth than transitory material benefits.

Try to add to the list of lessons to be learned.

Now the word of the Lord came to Jonah the second time, saying, "Arise, go to Nineveh, that great city, and preach to it the message that I tell you." Jonah 3:1, 2.

Remember those who live in the frozen north—the Laplanders in Europe, with a population of more than 200,000, almost 200 of whom are Seventh-day Adventists. Also remember the outreach to the Eskimos in North America, of whom we have a membership of more than 100, with about 100 children.

IS IT RIGHT
FOR YOU TO BE ANGRY?

From a human point of view the book of Jonah should have ended with chapter 3, especially if it could have had one more verse: "And Jonah spent the rest of his days in follow-up and nurture, discipling the new converts at Nineveh." It would have been a happy, satisfying ending, and the prophet would have been an undisputed hero.

Unfortunately Jonah was not satisfied with events. When his mission succeeded, he felt disappointed and angry. The prophet could understand doomsday better than he could forgiveness.

When he should have been rejoicing over the conversion of the people of Nineveh, he instead indulged in selfish pride. "He allowed his mind to dwell upon the possibility of his being regarded as a false prophet. Jealous of his reputation, he lost sight of the infinitely greater value of the souls in that wretched city" (Prophets and Kings, p. 271).

It was at this point that Jonah admitted the reason he had tried to flee to Tarshish. He knew God was merciful and forgiving, and feared that his prediction regarding the destruction of Nineveh would not be fulfilled. His own reputation as a prophet seemed more important to him than the fate of a city.

Retreating to a hill outside the city, he made himself a shelter from the sun and sat to watch what would happen to the city.

God prepared a vine to give Jonah shade and comfort, and he was pleased. But the next day a worm ate through the vine, and it died. The prophet's anger returned, and for the second time he asked the Lord to take his life. For the second time the Lord asked, "Is it right for you to be angry?" Jonah affirmed that it was.

The prophet was angry because God spared the city and destroyed the plant. If He had spared the plant and destroyed the city, Jonah would have been happy. His attitudes and priorities were all mixed up.

You can evaluate the quality of a person's life by the things that make them happy or angry. Perhaps some of us caught a glimpse of ourselves in the book of Jonah!

Then the Lord said, "Is it right for you to be angry?" Jonah 4:4.

Pray for the more than 27 million people of the Chinese province of Fujian (foo-jee-en). Fujian, which means "prosperity found," lies across the Taiwan Strait, facing the island of Taiwan.

291

WATCH OUT
FOR WOODEN SHOES

The word "worry" derives from the Anglo-Saxon *wyrgan,* meaning "to choke, to strangle." If an enemy were to put his fingers around your neck and press as hard as he could, he would be doing to you essentially what you do to yourself when you indulge in worry or fear.

William R. Inge said, "Worry is interest paid on trouble before it becomes due." Satan tries to crush our spirit by getting us to bear tomorrow's problems with only today's measure of grace. If we are worrying about tomorrow, it will rob us of our enjoyment of today. Worry will not empty tomorrow of its problems, but it will deplete us of our reserve of strength we need to face tomorrow.

Sabot is the French word for a wooden shoe. Our word "sabotage" originated from the practice of throwing a wooden shoe into the machinery to stop the work. It has come to mean any attempt to hinder production or spoil a product. Worry is the wooden shoe that Satan would cast into our lives to hinder us in the work of God. It paralyzes the spirit, sours the disposition, and effectively hinders us in our Christian service.

How can we overcome the worry habit? Here are some practical suggestions. Write down precisely what you are worrying about. Then add what you think you can do about it. Consider what God can do if you ask Him to. Decide what course of action to follow. Start immediately to carry out your decision.

An early manuscript records the name of a man called Amerimnos, which may be translated "without worry." It is thought that the man was a pagan Greek who had been known as a perpetual worrier. After his conversion to Christianity, he stopped worrying, and so was named Amerimnos, the man who never worried.

As God gives us victory over the worry habit, may we come to be known as men and women who do not worry. And may others, through our witness, also come to trust the heavenly Father who cares for us all and wishes to relieve us of our burdens of worry.

"Therefore I say to you, do not worry." Matt. 6:25.

Only 37 miles from the coast of England, Belgium is a land that is very much a mission field. The Protestant witness is very small. Pray for the 1,565 Seventh-day Adventist members in Belgium.

THE BOW OF PROMISE

Speaking of the Bible promises, the servant of God wrote: "They are leaves from that tree which is 'for the healing of the nations' (Rev. 22:2). Received, assimilated, they are to be the strength of the character, the inspiration and sustenance of the life" (*The Ministry of Healing*, p. 122).

Have you ever tried to imagine the experience of Noah and his family as they walked out of the ark after their voyage of more than a year? The ark had no outer deck for recreational activity, no deck chairs for basking in the sunshine. It was an enclosed cabin, below-deck experience.

Can you imagine the landscape left by the Flood—rocks, boulders, and buried forests? You wouldn't need colors to paint the picture, because it was all shades of gray. Noah was thankful to be alive and to have his family with him. He gathered them together for worship, and just as they were rededicating themselves, God put the color into the picture. A beautiful rainbow appeared in the heavens, a token or promise that He would never again allow a flood to come and destroy the earth and its people.

Sometimes we pass through prolonged stormy experiences that seem to leave our little world a desolate wilderness, but when we take time to be alone with God, He reminds us through the rainbow of His loving promises that He has not forsaken us, that there will be a brighter tomorrow.

"To every promise of God there are conditions. If we are willing to do His will, all His strength is ours. Whatever gift He promises is in the promise itself. 'The seed is the word of God' (Luke 8:11). As surely as the oak is in the acorn, so surely is the gift of God in His promise. If we receive the promise, we have the gift" (*Education*, p. 253).

God's promises are sure. He will not deceive, forget, or change—and He is able to fulfill them! "Then grasp His promises as leaves from the tree of life" (*The Ministry of Healing*, p. 66).

Therefore, having these promises, beloved, let us cleanse ourselves from all filthiness of the flesh and spirit, perfecting holiness in the fear of God. 2 Cor. 7:1.

Pray for the 400,000 Malays of Singapore. They strongly resist Christianity, and although they have had access to the Bible since 1733, only 1 percent are Christians. Pray for the house church ministries that are reaching out to them.

THE CHRISTIAN WASTEPAPER BASKET

Every business requires some provision for waste disposal. A business office would soon cease to function efficiently if it had no wastepaper baskets in which to throw junk mail, mistakes, and other useless materials. If one allowed such articles to occupy desk space, the office would soon become cluttered to such an extent that efficient operation would be impossible.

A carpenter's shop or a mechanic's bench would be in the same condition if one did not discard mistakes and waste materials. No businessman, professional man, or laborer is likely to succeed if he keeps all his past mistakes on display around the walls of his work place.

In the Christian life we are destined for defeat if we dwell constantly on the mistakes of the past. Too many Christians let their minds center on unpleasant events of the past. What the mind concentrates on is what we talk about, and the more we speak about unhappy experiences, the more they become embedded in our memories. Such talk makes us unwelcome to those who have to listen to our morbid recitations of past problems.

Just as "a merry heart does good, like medicine" (Prov. 17:22), so a negative and complaining disposition can actually bring on sickness. We would do well to treat our memories as the human body treats food—assimilate what we can use constructively and discard the rest. Retaining wastes in the physical body, or mentally in the mind, results in sickness.

In the life of the Christian the equivalent to a wastepaper basket is the ability to forget. When it comes to memories we need to decide what to keep and what to throw away. Many people are miserable not because of present circumstances, but because they dwell on unhappy events of the past.

We should forget our forgiven sins. God does, and we should too! There is good news in this promise to the penitent sinner: "None of his sins which he has committed shall be remembered against him" (Eze. 33:16).

Thank God for His willingness to forgive and forget. Let's not spend our time sorting through the "wastebasket."

"I, even I, am He who blots out your transgressions for My own sake; and I will not remember your sins." Isa. 43:25.

Pray for the gospel outreach to office workers, such as secretaries, managers, custodians, treasurers, and business executives. Pray for a specific office worker whom you know personally.

GOD KNOWS BEST

God's promises fall naturally into four distinct groups: (1) promises of spiritual blessings; (2) promises of material blessings; (3) promises of deliverance and preservation; and (4) promises of wisdom and guidance.

Under the category of promised spiritual blessings would come cleansing, comfort, forgiveness, joy, mercy, overcoming power, pardon, and peace. Such spiritual blessings are precious jewels in His storehouse.

Too often when we read of promised blessings, we think primarily in terms of material benefits, such as health and wealth, and when they are not immediately forthcoming, we feel that God has forsaken us. If we would seek first for spiritual blessings, most of our problems would be solved.

When we pray for spiritual blessings and for wisdom and guidance, we may be sure that God will grant our request, because He has revealed in His Word His will regarding such matters. He instructs us to seek first the spiritual blessings of the kingdom and His righteousness. And if we ask for wisdom, He promises to respond liberally.

When we pray for material blessings, deliverance, and preservation, we must always add the words "Not my will but Your will be done." God knows that some of us would lose our souls if we had too much of our world's wealth. When we pray for deliverance from danger or an extension of our earthly life, sometimes God has in mind a better plan for us.

Moses prayed that he might live a little longer and be permitted to go into the Promised Land, but he died on lonely Mount Nebo. Elijah prayed that he might die, but he lived. God planned for Moses a special resurrection, and He intended for Elijah to go to heaven without experiencing death.

The Lord had purposes for Moses and Elijah that were far beyond what they could ask or think!

Now to Him who is able to do exceedingly abundantly above all that we ask or think, according to the power that works in us, to Him be glory in the church by Christ Jesus throughout all ages, world without end. Amen. Eph. 3:20, 21.

The Bosnians are the largest of a number of Muslim groups in Yugoslavia. Of the almost 1.5 million Bosnians, 99 percent are Muslims, and they are extremely resistant toward Christianity. Pray that the Christians there will be filled with a new spirit of boldness to witness to the Bosnians.

BE OF GOOD CHEER

Today let us think about three different occasions when Jesus used the expression "Be of good cheer." They provide a basis of hope for the sick, courage for the fearful, and peace for the perplexed.

First is the story found in Matthew 9:2 of a young man who was the victim of a terrible disease, doubtless brought on by his own sinful indulgences. Four friends carried him on a cot to the feet of Jesus, who, "seeing their faith, said to the paralytic, 'Son, be of good cheer; your sins are forgiven you.' "

The young man's basic problem was sin, and his healing followed forgiveness. The story also teaches us that our faith can unite with that of others to produce wonderful results. If you know your sins are forgiven, you may "be of good cheer."

Second is the experience when the disciples found themselves caught in a fierce storm on the Sea of Galilee. Jesus, walking on the water, approached their boat, and the disciples, thinking He was a ghost, reacted with fear. "But immediately Jesus spoke to them, saying, 'Be of good cheer! It is I; do not be afraid' " (Matt. 14:27).

The storms of life can prove to be blessings in disguise if we meet Jesus in them. The greatest danger is when we lose sight of the Saviour. But the Lord's response to the sincere cry "Lord, save me" is always immediate. Often overlooked is the fact that Peter evidently walked on the water back to the boat with the support and companionship of his Master. When we walk with Jesus, there is no need to be afraid.

The third occasion when Jesus said "Be of good cheer" was at the close of one of His greatest sermons (embracing chapters 13 to 16 of John's Gospel). Jesus makes it clear that His true followers will face hatred and persecution, even as He did. But even in times of tumultuous persecution He assures true believers: "You may have peace."

Christ defeated the great enemy on every battlefield on which we will ever have to fight, and His victory becomes ours through faith. Though conflicts may rage around us, we may have a peace of mind beyond understanding.

And the peace of God, which surpasses all understanding, will guard your hearts and minds through Christ Jesus. Phil. 4:7.

Pray for the Chuang, the largest ethnic group in China. Concentrated in the autonomous region of Guangxi (g-wong-she), they are basically animistic. Pray that a witness for Christ will develop.

THE LITTLEST TOE

Christ established the church in order to provide a family for all who are born into His kingdom. The church should be a loving fellowship. It should be warm and caring—not a refrigerator to preserve perishable piety, but an incubator to nurture the newborn of the kingdom.

The church is the only organization that Christ Himself instituted. He formed it to be a redemptive agency. It is through redeemed men and women that He purposes to evangelize the world—the real business of the church.

Many of us are spending precious time and funds doing good things that could be done equally well by those who are not blessed and entrusted with a knowledge of the third angel's message of Revelation 14. Only those who have a personal relationship with Jesus and an understanding of the messages of those three angels of Revelation can give "the witness for which our Lord calls, and for want of which the world is perishing" (*The Desire of Ages,* p. 340).

It is time to lay aside what others can do and devote our energies to the most essential work—witnessing to the power of our Lord who came to "save His people from their sins" (Matt. 1:21).

There are no perfect congregations today because there are no perfect people. But our Lord has a plan to transform His church by His sanctifying power and the influence of His Word into the perfect and glorious church described in Ephesians 5:26, 27.

Christ is not ashamed to be connected with the church as its head. We may all be part of His body. Martin Luther said he was "Christ's littlest toe." It is important for the "littlest toe" to be connected to the foot and thus to the body.

Obviously Satan will do everything in his power to cause hurt and separation in the church. He will try to bring discouragement and doubt so that members will be tempted to sever their connection with it. Never forget that Christ is the head of the church, and the church *will* triumph.

Christ also loved the church and gave Himself for it . . . that He might present it to Himself a glorious church, not having spot or wrinkle or any such thing, but that it should be holy and without blemish. Eph. 5:27.

Pray for the church in the troubled country of Chad in north central Africa. The nation has 50 unreached people groups. We have 412 members in this country of more than 5.7 million.

RELIGIOUS BOREDOM

There are people even in the church who long for a joyful religious experience and don't know how to find it. Some consider religious services monotonous. To them sermons are dull, and they enter into prayer and Bible study only out of a sense of duty.

Their attitude is like that of a small boy suffering from a severe case of spring fever, dragging himself to school with utmost reluctance. His heart just isn't in it.

We become dissatisfied and bored with religion when it doesn't produce the results that we expect. Or it can be unproductive and ineffective when we hold on to certain reservations and fail to make our surrender complete. When we stop short of a full surrender, we leave ourselves susceptible to double-mindedness, crowd-mindedness, negative-mindedness, and guilt-mindedness.

The double-minded person wants to be religious yet have the pleasures of the world also. We cannot serve two masters. Our attitude must be "This one thing I do."

Saul gave evidence of crowd-mindedness when he admitted, "I feared the people" (1 Sam. 15:24). Many cringe before public opinion. They are more concerned about what the neighbors are going to say today than about what God will say in the day of judgment. Such a state develops inner conflicts, as with the 10-year-old who was summoned by his friends to come out and play baseball, while at the same time called by his mother to stay in and look after his little sister. He is divided between two loyalties.

The Pharisees were an example of negative-mindedness. Some of them made religion an austere tyrant instead of a way of joy. Closely related to this state is guilt-mindedness. Such people dwell on their mistakes. They cannot forgive themselves, and they think God has not forgiven them.

In summary, the cause of religious boredom is self, and the solution is Jesus Christ.

> **"I have been crucified with Christ; it is no longer I who live, but Christ lives in me; and the life which I now live in the flesh I live by faith in the Son of God, who loved me and gave Himself for me." Gal. 2:20.**

> *Pray for the more than 2 million people of Tibet, now known officially as Xizang (she-dzong), meaning "western treasure house." Its capital city of Llasa is the spiritual home of Buddhism. Ethnically the Tibetans are not Chinese, but are related to the Burmese.*

HOW BEAUTIFUL UPON THE MOUNTAINS

Guyana, formerly British Guiana, was the first country on the South American continent to receive the Adventist message. In 1883 a member of the staff at the International Tract Society office in New York, gave a bundle of Seventh-day Adventist papers to the captain of a ship bound for Georgetown, requesting him to distribute them when he arrived there. When the ship arrived in port, the captain scattered the material on the wharf, saying, "I have fulfilled my promise." A man standing by gathered some of the publications, read them, and lent them to his neighbors. Soon there was a group observing the seventh-day Sabbath.

These new converts contacted the International Tract Society, and a colporteur went to British Guiana. Canadian-born colporteur George King, who developed the idea of subscription sales of Seventh-day Adventist books, labored for a time in British Guiana and sold many books there. The first Seventh-day Adventist church and Sabbath school in the country organized in 1887.

Some years prior to the arrival of O. E. Davis, who pioneered among the Indians in the interior, an Indian chief in a vision had gained knowledge about the seventh-day Sabbath, clean foods, and temperate living. Pastor Davis, after having made some converts, suffered repeated attacks of malaria and died. Some 14 years later two missionaries went in search of the tribe he had worked with. They found them still singing "Jesus knows all about our struggles" and other hymns that Davis had taught them. Pastor Davis was loved and long remembered by these people, who are known among Adventists as the "Davis" Indians.

One layman who lives near the Venezuela border told of walking seven days through the jungle on two occasions to clear the grave of Elder Davis, who is buried at the foot of Mount Roraima.

Think about our pioneer missionaries who, in spite of extremes of climate, poisonous snakes, fierce animals, and unfriendly people, have made lonely journeys to bring the good news of the gospel to unentered territories.

How beautiful upon the mountains are the feet of him who brings good news, who proclaims peace, who brings glad tidings of good things, who proclaims salvation, who says to Zion, "Your God reigns!" Isa. 52:7.

Pray for the church in Guyana, where the population is 989,000 and the Seventh-day Adventist membership is 23,105.

MAKING RESTITUTION

From my many years spent in public evangelism I have numerous memories involving acts of restitution. I know of no greater evidence of the genuineness of Christianity than when a person under conviction by the Holy Spirit will return stolen property. When repentance is genuine, it will lead to restitution.

In a number of cases I have had men and women ask me to go with them for moral support as they confessed dishonesty and offered to make restitution. I think of a man who stole gasoline from the company pump, another who took tools from the place where he worked, a young woman who stole money from the cash register when she worked as a checker, and another young lady who had never been caught by the store detective for shoplifting, but now her conscience had caught her.

In some cases the thefts were serious enough that the offender could have been sent to jail if the victim had pressed charges. In many cases the person wronged was not a Christian, and yet in every case they were visibly moved by the fact that the new Christian would risk the consequences in order to make things right. I'm sure we will meet many in the kingdom who first became interested when a convert came to them to confess a wrong and to make restitution.

Sometimes it is a longtime Christian who has a lapse in his or her religious experience and needs to make restitution.

"You cannot make every case right, for some whom you have injured have gone into their graves, and the account stands registered against you. . . . The best you can do is to bring a trespass offering to the altar of the Lord, and He will accept and pardon you. But where you can, you should make reparation to the wronged ones" *(Testimonies,* vol. 5, p. 339).

Bringing an offering will not take the place of making restitution to the person wronged if that person is still alive. When things are made right, the burden of guilt rolls away and a great peace of mind results.

"If the wicked restores the pledge, gives back what he has stolen, and walks in the statutes of life without committing iniquity, he shall surely live; he shall not die." Eze. 33:15.

El Salvador is the smallest and most densely populated mainland state in the Americas. In a population of over 5.5 million, Seventh-day Adventists are the second-largest Protestant denomination, with 38,396 members.

IT WAS VERY GOOD

At the end of Creation week, when God looked upon the works of His hand, He was able to say that it was very good, or just right. The earth is the right size. A change by as little as 10 percent either way in the size of our planet would, according to scientific findings, make life on earth impossible.

The atmosphere is exactly right for our breathing apparatus and exactly right to keep the earth from scorching by day and freezing all life by night. The ozone in the atmosphere is exactly right for filtering out the deadly rays from space. The temperature of the earth is just right. If the average temperature of our planet were to increase by as much as three degrees, most major land areas would be flooded from melting ice.

The distance of the earth from the sun is exactly right to supply us with undiminishing light and heat.

Let us take an imaginary sightseeing trip through starland at the speed of light, 186,000 miles a second, or about 11 million miles a minute. If we started from the center of the sun, it would take us three seconds to reach the sun's surface. About three minutes of travel would hurl us to Mercury, and almost another three minutes to Venus. About two more minutes would bring us to the orbit of Earth, and an additional four and a half minutes to Mars

It would require another half hour to reach Jupiter, and beyond that, a 36-minute flight to Saturn. From Saturn to Uranus would be an 81-minute flight, with another hour and a half to reach Neptune. Finally, an additional one and a quarter hours would transport us to Pluto.

All of this travel at a speed of 11 million miles a minute would have covered a total distance of 4 billion miles from our starting point.

As we head back toward the sun, contemplating everything we have seen, we think of the remarkable evidence of an all-wise Designer, and we remember the words recorded in Genesis:

Then God saw everything that He had made, and indeed it was very good. So the evening and the morning were the sixth day. Gen. 1:31.

East Germany is the only Protestant country in Eastern Europe. The German Democratic Republic Union Conference, with head-quarters in East Berlin, has prospered and has a membership now of 9,174. Pray that the Seventh-day Adventist Church may make evangelism its primary concern.

THE TIDES OF LIFE

During World War II when the Allies drove the Italian forces out of Eritrea in North Africa, the Italians tried to make the harbor unusable to the Allies. They filled great barges with concrete and then sank them, effectively blocking the entrance.

To solve the problem of the blocked harbor, the Allies chained large, empty oil storage tanks to the sunken barges at low tide. When the tide came in, the buoyant power of the floating tanks freed the barges from the sucking sand of the bay, allowing the Allies to clear the harbor.

In the fourth act of Julius Caesar, Shakespeare has Brutus saying: "There is a tide in the affairs of men, which, taken at the flood, leads on to fortune." In other words, certain times of opportunity occur when circumstances are just right for action.

God's plan is for each person to have at least one opportunity to know and follow truth. That opportunity might come through reading a book, hearing a program on radio or television, listening to a sermon, or through contact with a friend, relative, neighbor, or even a stranger. It could come through the ring of the telephone or doorbell or something in the mail.

The Holy Spirit uses many and varied agencies to give each of us our opportunity for decision. And the Holy Spirit wants to use us as agents in providing others their flood-tide opportunity. When these golden opportunities come, it is important that we love Jesus so much that we will not delay in sharing the gospel.

It is said that Satan once called together the emissaries of hell for a consultation on how to bring about the ruination of the men and women of earth. Satan called for volunteers to undertake this evil mission, and he questioned them regarding the strategy they intended to use.

One proposed: "I will tell the people of earth that there is no heaven." Another said he would announce that there is no hell. Others presented different plans, but no demon was dispatched to earth until one said, "I will tell the people of earth that there is no hurry!"

And Satan said, "Go!"

> **And the Lord said, "My Spirit shall not strive with man forever." Gen. 6:3.**

> *Tribal peoples occupy the mountain regions of Taiwan. Seventh-day Adventists have entered 7 of the 10 tribes. Please pray for the Sediq, an animist tribe as yet unreached by the gospel.*

GOD MOVES IN MYSTERIOUS WAYS

The hymn writer William Cowper penned these lines:

"God moves in a mysterious way
His wonders to perform."

A German youth named Burchard hit a companion during a fight at a party. The man fainted, and in the excitement someone shouted that he was dead.

Thinking that he had committed a crime that could send him to prison, Burchard made a hasty decision to flee the country. This drama took place in Brazil's beautiful Itajaí Valley, in the state of Santa Catarina.

Burchard went to the port of Itajaí and stowed away on a ship bound for Europe. During the voyage he met some Adventist missionaries on board who were eager to get addresses of German families living in Brazil that might be interested in receiving Christian publications.

It was in 1879 that the first package of Adventist printed materials arrived at Itajaí, addressed to a storekeeper whose name Burchard had given to the missionaries on board the ship. The storekeeper wasn't interested in them, so he used the papers to wrap soap for his customers. In this way the publications spread across the countryside.

The Word of God is like seed, and so it was with the books and tracts sent from Germany to Brazil. The wife and son of the storekeeper to whom that first package was addressed were among those who read, believed, and were baptized.

Blown by the wind of the Holy Spirit, the gospel seed spread to many places, including the town of Gaspar Alto, where in 1887 a German immigrant, Guilherme Belz, read Uriah Smith's Thoughts on the Book of Daniel. As a child in Pomerania, Belz had learned that according to the Bible the seventh day is the Sabbath. His mother and their pastor told him that Christ had changed the day of rest, but reading the book in Brazil revived his interest, and he began observing the Sabbath even though he did not know that anyone else in all the world was keeping the seventh day. As far as is known, he became the first Seventh-day Adventist in Brazil.

"Now the parable is this: The seed is the word of God." Luke 8:11.

Only 5 percent of the Masai tribe in Kenya, Africa, belong to any Christian denomination. The Masai culture offers no hope for eternity. Please pray for the Masai people and continue to support world missions by regularly giving a percentage of your income.

THE LORD WILL DO WONDERS

Only the Jordan River lay between the children of Israel and the Promised Land, but it was flood time when melting snows had made the river deep and wide. And there were enemy giants on the other side. At this seemingly inopportune time God challenged His people: "Arise, go over this Jordan" (Joshua 1:2).

Joshua's response was immediate, and the people followed their leader. "Then Joshua rose early in the morning; . . . he and all the children of Israel, and lodged there before they crossed over" (Joshua 3:1).

People usually reflect the spirit of their leader. "Those who occupy positions of influence and responsibility in the church should be foremost in the work of God. If they move reluctantly, others will not move at all" (*The SDA Bible Commentary,* Ellen G. White Comments, vol. 6, p. 1104).

Special preparation was necessary before the people could go into the Promised Land. Recognizing this need, Joshua said to the people, "Sanctify yourselves, for tomorrow the LORD will do wonders among you" (Joshua 3:5).

God wanted to do marvelous things for His people, but first they had to accept His assignment and make individual spiritual preparation. There are striking parallels between their experience and ours. Canaan, the Promised Land, was a type of the heavenly Canaan. Before Jesus takes us there, we have an assignment to complete and a spiritual preparation to experience.

"I was shown God's people waiting for some change to take place—a compelling power to take hold of them. But they will be disappointed, for they are wrong. They must act" (*Testimonies,* vol. 1, p. 261). The first step is for us to accept the assignment God has given to us—the gospel commission.

God wants to do wonders for your congregation, your family, and for you personally. Accept the assignment He has for you. Make an entire, wholehearted consecration to the service of Christ.

And Joshua said to the people, "Sanctify yourselves, for tomorrow the Lord will do wonders among you." Joshua 3:5.

Please pray for the republic of Djibouti, a hot, dry desert enclave located between Ethiopia and Somalia. In 1989 arrangements were made to establish a dental clinic that would be the first Adventist activity in this country.

LORD, SEND A REVIVAL

"A revival of true godliness among us is the greatest and most urgent of all our needs. To seek this should be our first work" (*Selected Messages,* book 1, p. 121). I suppose we have all prayed many times for revival, and the longing remains in our hearts to see it come.

The Bible is a history of revivals, and from its accounts we see that the basic prerequisites for them are prayer, repentance, and obedience. We find the promise of revival in Genesis 50:24: "God will surely visit you."

As we open the book of Exodus we find revival as a nation of slaves return to the true God and forsake the idolatry of Egypt. They turn from doubt and despair to liberty and the Promised Land.

David's psalms are largely prayers for revival and praise to God for blessings received. "Revival" is the message of every prophet of the Bible. The task of the prophets was to turn the people back to God. And that is revival!

Think of the work of Elijah and Elisha and Nehemiah. Isaiah describes his own personal revival experience when he says: "I am undone. . . . for my eyes have seen the King, the Lord of hosts" (Isa. 6:5).

The need of revival was the burden of Jeremiah, and Ezekiel also called for revival. The spirit of revival is evident in the book of Daniel, and as we come to the minor prophets, it seems as though with one voice they cry: "O Lord, revive Your work in the midst of the years!" (Hab. 3:2).

The New Testament begins on a note of preparation for revival: "Repent, for the kingdom of heaven is at hand!" (Matt. 3:2). In the book of Acts we find that laypeople went everywhere preaching. Even the deacons were out holding meetings!

How can we prepare for the promised revival in our day? Put away all idols. Make a full and complete surrender to Jesus Christ. Devote time each day to strengthening that relationship through prayer and Bible study. Share the love of Jesus with others. Be willing to pray, "Lord, send a revival and let it begin in me." Remember: "When churches are revived, it is because some individual seeks earnestly for the blessing of God" (*Christian Service*, p. 121).

Will You not revive us again, that Your people may rejoice in You? Ps. 85:6.

Pray that revival, growth, and outreach may become part of the life of every Seventh-day Adventist church.

BATTLE OF THE MIND

How can we gain victory over sins of thought? Sometimes we forget that we are what we think. True it is that you "sow a thought, and you reap an act; Sow an act, and you reap a habit; Sow a habit, and you reap a character; Sow a character, and you reap a destiny."

The thought of sin is just one step from the act of sin. It may be possible to play with sinful thoughts with no apparent harm, but eventually the devil will spring his trap, and you will be his victim.

The decisive battles for human souls are fought in the thought life. It is there that we win or lose.

We are shocked and saddened when a spiritual stalwart falls into sin. In such cases invariably the mind has played with sinful thoughts, never intending for them to become actions. Though apparently sudden, such falls are not really so. "For as he thinks in his heart, so is he" (Prov. 23:7).

It is sometimes a fine line, a delicate matter, to determine just where sin begins. Satan will take God's blessings and by cunning perversion turn them into temptations. The devil will corrupt a wholesome friendship by idle imaginings and illegitimate daydreams.

God must work a miracle in our lives to give us victory, but He does not interfere with our power of choice. Our personal choice will be the deciding factor for victory or defeat.

"Everything depends on the right action of the will. . . . God has given us the power of choice; it is ours to exercise. We cannot change our hearts, we cannot control our thoughts, our impulses, our affections. We cannot make ourselves pure, fit for God's service. But we can *choose* to serve God, we can give Him our will; then He will work in us to will and to do according to His good pleasure. Thus our whole nature will be brought under the control of Christ" (*The Ministry of Healing*, p. 176).

We gain the victory over sins of thought through surrender to Jesus Christ.

Let this mind be in you which was also in Christ Jesus. Phil. 2:5.

In 1987 two literature evangelists commenced work on the tiny island of Nauru, occupying eight square miles in the western Pacific Ocean. It is the world's smallest republic, with a population of only 8,100. Please pray for the people of Nauru. Pray also for the outreach of Adventist World Radio to densely populated cities, sparsely settled rural areas, and dwellers on remote islands.

TO BUILD OR TEAR DOWN?

In the great struggle raging over human souls, Satan is ever alert to see those who will allow unfaithful leaders and inconsistent conduct to get their eyes off Jesus. If the devil sees that we can be swayed by his diversionary tactics, he will point to weaknesses and mistakes on the part of leaders.

Satan can cite King David, who committed adultery and murder; Hophni and Phinehas, two extremely wicked men who were priests in Israel; Judas Iscariot, who was a thief and a traitor; and Ananias and Sapphira, who lied to God—to mention only a few.

One of the strong evidences for the inspiration of the Bible is that it does not try to hide the sins of some of its leading characters. But our experience would certainly be morbid if we were to dwell on the accounts of the Bible personalities who failed to the exclusion of the far greater number who lived lives to the glory of God.

Because of God's patience and mercy, many sinners who at first failed later gained victory and were forgiven. What was true in ancient times is true today. If we look for scandal, we will find it, but thank God, if we look for sincere, honest-hearted, committed Christians, we will discover them in far greater numbers.

While some spend their time, energy, and resources tearing down God's church, the majority keep their eyes on Jesus and give of their time, talents, and means to advance the work of the Lord.

When Elijah lamented "I alone am left" (1 Kings 19:14), God informed him that He knew of another 7,000 who were faithful (verse 18)!

Satan has the title "accuser of our brethren" (Rev. 12:10), a title he would gladly share with you or me. But that is the work he has chosen, while you and I must choose to prepare for God's question "What did you do about the Great Commission?"

"Yet I have reserved seven thousand in Israel, all whose knees have not bowed to Baal, and every mouth that has not kissed him." 1 Kings 19:18.

The republic of Indonesia, with its more than 187 million people and 3,000 inhabited islands, and its great diversity of culture and economies, is a challenge to Christian outreach. Indonesia has 114,454 Adventist Church members. Pray that the last warning message will spread throughout this vast area.

ASK THE LORD FOR HELP

Leonard Lee tells how as a youth of 19 he was trying to run away from God. He was working his way through northern Canada to Alaska when he got caught in a blizzard while attempting to reach a trading post on the Liard River.

At last his food supply ran out, and he became completely lost in a blinding blizzard. As he trudged along on his snowshoes he heard a voice say, "Turn to the left." When he looked around, there was no one in sight. He kept going straight ahead until again he heard that voice say in pleading tones, "Turn to the left." Finally, although he could see no reason for turning to the left to face the full fury of the storm, he obeyed the voice.

Lee walked many miles until he came to a creek bed and decided to turn right, hoping the creek would lead him to the river. But again he heard that voice saying, "Turn to the left," and again he obeyed.

A short distance up the creek he saw a cabin half buried under snow. Using his snowshoe for a shovel, he dug his way to the door and went in. Out of the darkness came a groan that startled him. There he found an old man in a sleeping bag lying on a bunk. His beard and eyebrows covered with ice from his breath, and his leg broken, the man was weak from lack of food.

He had been lying there for a week, and finally in desperation he had asked God to send help. Young Lee now knew that the Lord was using him to answer the old man's prayer.

Leaving the warm fire he had started to heat the cabin, Lee set out on the 20-mile journey to a trading post where he could find food and help for the old man. He himself was hungry and exhausted, but he forgot his own needs in the face of the greater needs of another.

Through this experience the lives of both were saved, and the faith of both strengthened. Perhaps someone today is praying a prayer that God can use you to answer.

> **"Call upon Me in the day of trouble; I will deliver you, and you shall glorify Me." Ps. 50:15.**

Pray for the more than 110 million people of Pakistan. About 97 percent are Muslim, but Pakistan is one of the most open Muslim lands for the gospel. The Afghan refugees in Pakistan may be more receptive to the gospel also. Pray for the advance of God's cause in this land.

THE EXPERIENCE
OF CONVERSION

Most readers of this page are very well acquainted with the theory of conversion, but perhaps some still lack the reality of the experience.

When we believe in the Lord Jesus Christ, we are converted. But for many the questions remain: What does it mean to believe? And how do we believe?

Augustine describes his conversion in these words: "I continued my miserable complaining. How long, how long shall I go on saying, tomorrow and again tomorrow. Why not now? Why not have an end of my uncleanness this very hour?

"Such things I said weeping in the most bitter sorrow of my heart and suddenly I heard a voice from some nearby house. . . . It was a sort of sing-song repeated again and again: 'Take and read, take and read, take and read.'

"I arose interpreting the incident as quite certainly a divine command to open my book of Scripture. . . . I opened the Scripture and in silence read the passage Romans 13:13, 14. I had no wish to read further and no need. With the very ending of the sentence it was as though a light of utter confidence shone in all my heart and all the darkness of uncertainty vanished away."

From all outward appearances John Wesley seemed to be a Christian. But for more than 10 years he experienced a struggle between nature and grace. His cry of desperation was "How to perform what is good I do not find" (Rom. 7:18).

That miracle moment came in Wesley's life as he was listening to the reading of Luther's preface to the Epistle to the Romans, which described the change that God works in the heart through faith in Christ. Wesley always looked back to that moment as the hour of his conversion.

Most of us have grown up hearing that Jesus died for our sins. It seems that our familiarity with the theory makes the experience more difficult.

The miracle of conversion becomes a reality in our individual lives when the theory is transferred into experience. While it may seem elusive, this transforming experience is available to each one of us.

But put on the Lord Jesus Christ, and make no provision for the flesh, to fulfill its lusts. Rom. 13:14.

Pray for the more than 3 million people of Hainan Tao, the rubber-producing center for China.

WHAT IS MAN?

The psalmist, contemplating the wonders of creation, asked: "When I consider Your heavens, . . . What is man that You are mindful of him" (Ps. 8:3, 4)? In our reading today we want to consider God's heavens.

Every 24 hours our galaxy travels 1 1/2 million miles through space at more than 66,000 miles an hour. The 200-inch Hale reflector telescope on Mount Palomar can see as many as 1 million galaxies inside the bowl of the Big Dipper alone. The human mind cannot comprehend the vastness of the universe. Our planet is part of a galaxy of 100 billion stars. There are estimated to be more than 100 billion galaxies in the universe, each with its complement of stars and planets.

At the other end of the scale, the electron microscope and biochemical research have enabled investigators to examine the images of cells magnified as much as 200,000 times. There are so many molecules in one drop of water that if they could be transformed into grains of sand, there would be enough sand to pave a road from Los Angeles to New York!

One astronomer said that if you could count all the grains of sand at all the seashores in all the world, you would have approximately the same number of grains of sand as there are stars in the heavens!

Aside from the sun, the star nearest our earth is Proxima Centauri. It is more than four light-years away, or more than 24 trillion miles from earth. Traveling in a rocket ship at the speed of 25,000 miles per hour, it would take us more than 100,000 years to reach this star!

If there were a railroad to the sun, a train traveling 90 miles per hour would have to travel without stopping for almost 120 years to reach the sun. But an airplane traveling 600 miles per hour would have to fly nonstop for more than 4.5 million years to reach Proxima Centauri!

On the one hand, we view the miracle world brought to view by the microscope. And on the other hand, we view the staggering vastness of the universe revealed by the telescope. And in between are you and I, causing us to exclaim, "What is man?"

When I consider Your heavens, the work of Your fingers, the moon and the stars, which You have ordained, what is man that You are mindful of him, and the son of man that You visit him? Ps. 8:3, 4.

Opportunities for proclamation of the gospel in Chile have never ᵕⁿ greater. Pray for our 61,468 members in Chile as they ᵕᵒ to evangelize this South American country.

THEY WILL SEE HIM COME

Many of us have had friends or family members who cherished the hope that they might have been able to see the glorious event of the second coming of Christ. But now these loved ones sleep in their graves. Did they hope in vain for this privilege? We read in the Bible that "all things are possible to him who believes" (Mark 9:23). Could God make it possible for those who died with this hope to actually see the return of our Lord?

Today, by comparing scripture with scripture, we will make a discovery that will strengthen your faith and bring joy to your heart. As you know, the Bible mentions some special resurrections in addition to the resurrection of the righteous and the resurrection of the impenitent.

When Jesus died on Calvary, there was an earthquake. "The graves were opened; and many bodies of the saints who had fallen asleep were raised; and coming out of the graves after His resurrection, they went into the holy city and appeared to many" (Matt. 27:52, 53).

We have reason to believe that these resurrected ones were taken to heaven with Christ at His ascension as trophies of His power over the grave and death. Ephesians 4:8 reads: "When He ascended on high, He led captivity captive." In the margin of the KJV we read: He led "a multitude of captives."

Daniel speaks of a time when "many of those who sleep in the dust of the earth shall awake, some to everlasting life, some to shame and everlasting contempt" (Dan. 12:2). It is not the general resurrection because it will involve "many," not all, and will include some righteous and some unrighteous.

Revelation 1:7 indicates that those who had a part in the Crucifixion will be in this resurrection. Now, here's the good news: "All who have died in the faith of the third angel's message come forth from the tomb glorified, to hear God's covenant of peace with those who have kept His law" (*The Great Controversy*, p. 637). They will see Jesus come!

Behold, He is coming with clouds, and every eye will see Him, and they also who pierced Him. And all the tribes of the earth will mourn because of Him. Even so, Amen. Rev. 1:7.

Liberia is a small coastal state between Sierra Leone and the Ivory Coast. While the country has freedom of religion, Adventist mission advance has been difficult and slow. There are 9,355 Seventh-day Adventists in this country of more than 2.5 million.

JESUS ONLY

There are many great names in the world—names that almost any man, woman, boy, or girl can identify—but the name of Jesus stands above every one, because He is our Saviour.

In the field of religion Moses is known as a great deliverer of God's people. Confucius has renown for his wise sayings. Mozart is a great name in the world of music, Rembrandt in the world of art, and Einstein in the field of science. All great people, but not one of them could save anyone from sin.

Imagine a person who has been bitten by a poisonous snake. Well aware of the ultimate results of that poison, he helplessly awaits his fate, without an antidote or a ray of hope. And then he hears that there is an antidote within reach.

Each of us has been infected with the deadly poison of sin, and our only hope lies in a Saviour who has the antidote.

As the glorious scene of Christ's transfiguration, described in Matthew 17, faded away, the disciples lifted up their eyes and saw no man except "Jesus only."

Peter had had an up-and-down experience, and it was probably more down than up, until he witnessed the character of Jesus under suffering and persecution. The disciple then began to see the true significance of that wonderful name. He saw it also in that look of pity cast upon him by the Saviour in the judgment hall in which he had denied the name of Jesus. The multitudes at Pentecost felt that a name that could change a denier into an orator for the cross of Christ was one they also needed in order to change their lives.

Perhaps you have gone through an experience that makes it easy for you to imagine the hopelessness, shame, and frustration that Peter felt after denying his Lord. In such moments of discouragement "Jesus only" is the answer.

"To all who are reaching out to feel the guiding hand of God, the moment of greatest discouragement is the time when divine help is nearest" (*The Desire of Ages*, p. 528).

And when they had lifted up their eyes, they saw no one but Jesus only. Matt. 17:8.

Pray for the more than 37 million people, mostly Hindus, in the state of Gujarat in India. This state was the birthplace of Mahatma Gandhi.

312

GOD GUIDES HIS WORK

Someone has said there are three stages to Bible study. First is the cod liver oil stage—you take it like medicine because you're told it's good for you. The second is the shredded wheat stage—dry but nourishing. Third is peaches and cream. How sad it is that many never persevere to the peaches and cream experience.

Leopoldina was born in the little Portuguese colony of Guinea on the coast of West Africa. In her early 20s she reached the peaches and cream stage of Bible study, even though the church of her family did not encourage Bible study.

As Leopoldina compared what she found in her personal Bible study with what her church taught, she discovered discrepancies. Her questions embarrassed and annoyed church leaders.

From her Bible study she discovered that salvation is a gift from God, received by grace through faith, and not something earned by good works. She questioned why the church was observing the first day of the week when the Bible repeatedly states that the seventh is the day our Lord blessed as His holy day.

Irritated by questions they couldn't answer, church leaders accused the girl of being demon-possessed. She prayed that God would guide her in her study of His Word. Leopoldina gathered together several young people who were also interested in Bible study. Eventually the group began observing the seventh-day Sabbath.

When a Seventh-day Adventist pastor arrived in Portuguese Guinea and asked for authorization to establish an Adventist mission in the country, he was told that the government would grant permission only if there were at least two members resident there.

The pastor didn't know about Leopoldina and her group of Sabbathkeepers, and they didn't know about the Seventh-day Adventist Church, but providentially a literature evangelist found Leopoldina. He discovered she was a Seventh-day Adventist in belief just from her study of the Bible.

God used this girl who had implicit faith in His Word to open the way for the beginning of the Seventh-day Adventist church in the country that since 1973 has been known as Guinea-Bissau.

Behold, the eye of the Lord is on those who fear Him, on those who hope in His mercy. Ps. 33:18.

Pray for the 1.5 million animist Tung-chia (dong-jaw) of southeast Guizhou and west Hunan provinces and north Guangxi in China. It is likely the gospel has not touched any of the Tung-chia.

313

WHAT IT MEANS TO WORSHIP

All people worship something. You don't choose whether to worship or not—you simply choose whom, or what, you worship.

A woman leaving church with tears in her eyes exclaimed to the pastor, "I have never worshiped before! I've been to hundreds of services, but today I worshiped for the first time."

What does it really mean to worship? Do you personally worship God daily? weekly? more often? less often? How do you know when you have worshiped, or do you?

Someone suggests, by way of definition, that worship is offering our lives and all that we are to God each day. Is it possible to sit through a well-organized service with impressive liturgy and eloquent prayers and yet not worship?

Here's another suggested definition of worship: "Worship is honor and adoration given to God." Do you go to church to give or to get? Do you go to give worship or to get a blessing? It is as we give worship that we receive the blessing. If you do not feel blessed by attending church, perhaps it is because you have not learned to give worship.

Worship begins with meditation. As you focus on the Word of God, you discover spiritual truth, and out of the discovery comes meditation, and out of the meditation worship. Meditation leads to praise, and giving praise to God is worship.

The theme of worship runs throughout the Bible. The fall of the human race occurred when Adam and Eve failed to worship God. The first murder occurred when Cain failed to render to God acceptable worship. The climax of the struggle between good and evil is an issue over true and false worship.

True worship can take place anywhere at any time, but human beings like to confine God to a building because then they can enter His presence when they wish to and leave His presence when they wish. What does worship mean to you? And how often do you really worship?

Give unto the Lord the glory due to His name; worship the Lord in the beauty of holiness. Ps. 29:2.

Pray for the suffering Vietnamese. Pressures on Christians there continue to be severe. The communist occupation of South Vietnam ended the war, but brought great hardship to the population. All open missionary activities closed in 1975. Pray especially for our 3,873 believers that their lives may be spared, their faith maintained, and their love multiplied.

THOSE WHO SEARCH WILL FIND

A literature evangelist was working in the town of Balikpapan, on the island of Borneo, when to his surprise he met a group of Chinese who were observing the Sabbath. They had belonged to a certain Protestant church, but when they discovered in the Bible that the seventh day must be kept holy, they formed their own group, calling themselves "Christ's true church." They believed that they were the only ones in the world who were honoring the seventh-day Sabbath.

In 1860 a German pastor in Elberfeld, North Rhine-Westphalia, began to observe the Sabbath based on his personal study of the Bible. At the time he knew of no other Christians doing so. Several years later an itinerant beggar who had been given shelter by one of our believers in Switzerland told of a group of Sabbathkeepers in Germany, for by this time the pastor had made some converts. In 1875 when J. N. Andrews journeyed there from Switzerland, he found a group of 46 Sabbath observers in Elberfeld.

In 1909 one of our pastors in Norway contacted a woman whose brother was a pastor of the state church. She had discovered the seventh-day Sabbath from reading her Bible, and had kept it for 15 years, not knowing whether anyone else in all the world was observing that day.

South African Pieter Wessels was such a conscientious youth that he questioned whether it was right to allow his windmill to run on Sundays. His brother John suggested that if he was going to take the Bible literally, he should observe the seventh-day Sabbath according to the Ten Commandments.

Pieter searched his Bible for proof of Sunday sacredness, and as a result, he began observing the seventh-day Sabbath in 1885 even though he knew of no other Sabbathkeeping Christians in the world.

The discovery of diamonds on Wessels' farm brought a fortune into their hands, which they generously shared to build up Seventh-day Adventism in South Africa.

"All over the world men and women are looking wistfully to heaven. Prayers and tears and inquiries go up from souls longing for light, for grace, for the Holy Spirit. Many are on the verge of the kingdom, waiting only to be gathered in" (*The Acts of the Apostles*, p. 109).

O God, You are my God; early will I seek You. Ps. 63:1.

Pray for parents who are contemplating divorce that they will consider the welfare of their children.

HE ORDERS WHAT IS BEST

We live in an age of turmoil, confusion, and stress. Often we find our most carefully laid plans and cherished hopes dashed to destruction. Sometimes we feel we can no longer cope. At such times we need to remember:

"Above the distractions of the earth He sits enthroned; all things are open to His divine survey; and from His great and calm eternity He orders that which His providence sees best" (*The Ministry of Healing*, p. 417).

At the beginning of each day, and frequently through it, we need to pause long enough to remember that God is in control of our lives if we have asked Him to be. He will not let anything happen that will not ultimately prove to be for our best good. Many times what at first seems the worst that could happen proves later to be the best, as illustrated by the following experience.

The only survivor of a shipwreck made his way ashore on an uninhabited island. After building a crude hut to shelter himself from the elements, he prayed to God for deliverance and scanned the horizon in vain each day in search of a passing ship.

One day as he returned home after searching for food, he was horrified to find his hut in flames. The little that he had was going up in smoke! The worst had happened—or so it appeared.

To the man's limited vision it was the worst, but to God's infinite wisdom the man's loss was for the best, because the very next day a ship arrived. "We saw your smoke signal," the captain announced.

Sometimes we are helped by being hurt. A skilled physician about to perform a delicate operation upon the ear said reassuringly to the patient, "I may hurt you, but I will not injure you." If we would only listen through our hurts, how often we would hear the Great Physician speak the very same message to us.

Be still, and know that I am God; I will be exalted among the nations, I will be exalted in the earth! Ps. 46:10.

Pressures on Christians have been severe in Communist Ethiopia, but we have seen thrilling growth over the past 25 years. Pray for an unabated vision for the lost, courage in suffering, and patience to love when misrepresented.

A SPECIAL WEEK AHEAD

On Sunday, December 6, 1885, at the General Conference session held in Battle Creek, the committee on finance gave its report. It pointed out that many phases of God's cause were suffering because of lack of funds, and suggested that our people everywhere make a Christmas donation to the cause. They recommended that the week between the holidays, including Sabbath, January 2, be set aside as a Week of Prayer and that the General Conference Committee suggest suitable subjects for consideration each day, preparing addresses to be read at the beginning of this Week of Prayer and at appropriate intervals during it. The report appears in the *Review and Herald* of December 8, 1885.

This same issue of the *Review* carried a back-page note from the president of the General Conference, George I. Butler, calling the attention of our churches to this Week of Prayer. Then the next issue had an article by the president of the General Conference entitled "The Week of Prayer and Humiliation," in which he pointed out the carelessness and indifference of many Seventh-day Adventists, many of the members being spiritually asleep, or "drowsing over the brink of a precipice." He stated, "Our General Conference has appointed this Week of Prayer, hoping it will bring many of our people to their senses."

We do not know what materials went out to the members, or how, but we find in the *Review and Herald* of January 19, 1886, an article by Elder Butler on the Week of Prayer and its results. He was gratified with the reports that had already come in and with the upturn in the financial outlook because of the sacrifices of the Adventist people.

With this as a beginning, the session of the General Conference meeting in 1886 appointed a Week of Prayer for December 25, 1886, to January 1, 1887, and with this, it has become a custom.

This year's Week of Prayer begins tomorrow. May it be a blessing to you.

"Watch therefore, and pray always that you may be counted worthy to escape all these things that will come to pass, and to stand before the Son of Man." Luke 21:36.

How we need to dedicate this week to prayer and study! Pray that the special blessing of Heaven will be upon His church during this week dedicated to seeking after God.

WEEK OF
PRAYER AND SACRIFICE

The year was 1922. World conditions were beginning to return to normal after the upheaval of the First World War. Missionaries who had been forced to return to the homeland were now making plans to get back to their mission posts.

At the General Conference Autumn (Annual) Council in Kansas City that year the leadership was studying the church's world budget. They estimated that our total mission income for the year would fall short of meeting the requirements by a quarter of a million dollars. If they could not make up the lack, they would have to cut back the missionary program. New missionary families would have to be held up, and in all likelihood many already serving in the mission fields might have to return home. What could be done? The council delegates sought the guidance of heaven through prayer.

The answer came through the conference presidents, who were closest to the churches. They said, "Let us make next Thanksgiving week a week of sacrifice for making up this need."

The council met in October, and with Thanksgiving coming in November, they had little time to promote the plan, even in North America. Overseas they could spread the word only by brief cable messages to conferences and mission offices. The hand of providence seemed evident as the word sped to and fro through the earth, and a wave of conviction put the urgency of the case into every heart, it seemed. In all lands and languages members cheered one another on in preparing for an offering of sacrifice that would keep the line of advance steady. "No retreat" was the watchword among our people around the world.

And what was the result? In that one week they made up the deficiency of funds. That is how the Week of Sacrifice began. Later the Week of Sacrifice merged with the annual Week of Prayer.

The pioneer spirit of sacrifice lives on in Adventism. Our readings for the next week will be focusing on the Week of Prayer, and we will be especially blessed if it is also a week of genuine sacrifice.

> **Confess your trespasses to one another, and pray for one another, that you may be healed. The effective, fervent prayer of a righteous man avails much. James 5:16.**
>
> *Pray for our missionaries and members who are experiencing hardship, danger, and sacrifice.*

318

WEEK OF PRAYER

When the church called for a Week of Sacrifice in 1922, it had no thought of making it an annual appeal, but two factors led to its becoming that: The blessings of God resulting from sacrificially giving one week's salary to the support of the world mission program, and the ever-increasing financial demands of a rapidly growing worldwide work.

The 1924 Autumn (Annual) Council marking the fiftieth anniversary of our foreign mission program recommended that the concept of the Week of Sacrifice be adopted in all lands as a yearly plan until the Lord returns.

Denominational employees attending the Annual Council led the way by pledging a week's salary for missions, and pastors and members willingly followed their example. Some postponed the purchase of needed clothing, others cut back on the household budget, while some skipped meals. One woman gave up a pleasure trip, another donated a $1,000 bond. A doctor gave the money he had saved to buy a new home. The motivation behind such sacrificial gifts was to avoid a cutback in our world mission program.

When the Week of Sacrifice combined with the Week of Prayer, added blessings resulted. An annual tradition developed that has blessed the lives of many through the years. The *Adventist Review* puts out a special Week of Prayer issue. The reading for the first Sabbath is compiled from Spirit of Prophecy writings, and the one for the last Sabbath of this special week is written by the president of the General Conference. There is a reading prepared for each day by one of our spiritual leaders as well as special children's features. Congregations around the world meet in churches or in homes to share the readings and to pray. The annual Week of Prayer is a unifying and revivalistic factor in the experience of church members.

Times of comparative affluence weakened the emphasis on sacrificial offerings in some parts of the world, but economic conditions in recent years have reawakened us to an awareness of our need to give sacrificially so that the work may expand.

Then He said to His disciples, ''The harvest truly is plentiful, but the laborers are few. Therefore pray the Lord of the harvest to send out laborers into His harvest.'' Matt. 9:37, 38.

Pray that each believer might see clearly his or her responsibility in relation to the spiritual harvest in progress.

PRAYER POSSIBILITIES

Several years ago two young businessmen in Australia told me of the blessing that had come to them as the result of spending an hour a day in prayer. The method they used could be varied, of course, but at least it stimulates ideas. They spent approximately five minutes on each of 12 aspects of prayer: praise, waiting, confession, Scripture reading, watching, intercession, petition, thanksgiving, singing, meditation, listening, and praying for reapers.

Even after several years have elapsed, I still remember the excitement of those two Australian businessmen who found a deepening, enriching, and rewarding experience in prayer as the result of finding and following a plan that caught their imagination and gave new meaning to their prayer experience.

During the next 12 days we will discuss these points one at a time. I can assure you we have a blessing in store that could change your life.

Someone else shared with me a weekly prayer plan that he follows. On Sunday he prays for pastors and churches; on Monday for working people, servants of the community, city officials, policemen, firemen, social workers, and public health nurses; Tuesday for heads of nations and for world peace, remembering especially areas of war and strife.

Wednesday is health day, when he remembers those in hospitals and nursing homes, doctors, nurses, administrators of health institutions, researchers, patients, and visitors.

Thursday's prayers focus on Christian education and the media. This would include teachers, students, parents, and those engaged in Christian radio and TV, as well as Christian publications, Bible translation, and radio and TV personalities.

Friday's prayers are for families, the newly married, the bereaved, those in trouble, loved ones, friends, and acquaintances.

On Sabbath the prayer focuses on praise, thanksgiving, and witnessing.

Many Christians go through life without really learning to pray. They speak words and phrases that they have used over and over again, but there is no real communication with the Lord. May many look back on this week as the time when their prayer experience became more meaningful.

And it came to pass, as He was praying in a certain place, when He ceased, that one of His disciples said to Him, "Lord, teach us to pray, as John also taught his disciples." Luke 11:1.

Pray for your own experience in prayer, that something may take place this week that will bless all your remaining days.

PRAISE THE LORD!

Praise marks the beginning of the model prayer that Jesus gave, "Hallowed be thy name" (KJV). Prayer and praise grow out of relationship, so the prayer begins with a statement of relationship, "Our Father."

Praise shifts the emphasis from self to God. If we trace the origin of the word *praise,* we find it is derived from *prize.* To praise God is to prize God, to value, cherish, and esteem Him—to recognize His worth.

We will do well to cultivate an attitude of praise. "Then let us educate our hearts and lips to speak the praise of God for His matchless love. Let us educate our souls to be hopeful and to abide in the light shining from the cross of Calvary. Never should we forget that we are children of the heavenly King, sons and daughters of the Lord of hosts. It is our privilege to maintain a calm repose in God" (*The Ministry of Healing*, p. 253).

The glories of each new morning will give us reasons for praising the Creator as we behold the beauties of nature and hear the songs of the birds.

"Accustom yourselves to speak the praise of God. Make others happy. This is your first work. It will strengthen the best traits of character. Throw the windows of the soul wide open heavenward, and let the sunshine of Christ's righteousness in" (*Welfare Ministry*, p. 79).

In other words, form the habit of praising God. "If more praising of God were engaged in now, hope and courage and faith would steadily increase" (*Prophets and Kings*, p. 202). Not only does praise bring joy to our heavenly Father, but it results in positive benefits to us.

"Nothing tends more to promote health of body and of soul than does a spirit of gratitude and praise. It is a positive duty to resist melancholy, discontented thoughts and feelings—as much a duty as it is to pray" (*The Ministry of Healing*, p. 251).

Psalm 45 begins, "My heart is overflowing . . ." The Hebrew term for "overflow" is "to boil over," and that is what praise is. Praise comes from a heart so warmed by God's love and goodness that it is boiling over. It can be manifest individually or corporately. When God's people come together with warm hearts, the praise that breaks forth is true worship.

Let everything that has breath praise the Lord. Praise the Lord! Ps. 150:6.

Pray a prayer of praise.

WAIT UPON THE LORD

What does it mean to wait upon the Lord? Basically, it is the silent surrendering of the soul to God. To wait upon the Lord is to enter into a trust relationship with Him. It is to rest in the Lord, surrendered to His will for our lives because we know we can have complete confidence in Him. We trust Him on the basis of our personal acquaintance with Him, the promises of His Word, and His dealings with us in the past. As God's messenger reminds us, "We have nothing to fear for the future, except as we shall forget the way the Lord has led us, and His teaching in our past history" (*Life Sketches*, p. 196).

Our time of waiting upon the Lord may be one of wordless worship as we review in our minds the way the Lord has guided our lives in the past. A little boy whose daddy was a pastor knew that he was not to disturb his father's study time. The little fellow pleaded, "Daddy, I will sit still and won't say a word if you will only let me be here with you."

Prayer is relationship, and our waiting time is a time of contact with God. Someone has said that waiting is the bridge that takes us away from a carnal world to a spiritual world.

In sitting at the feet of Jesus, Mary demonstrated the "one thing" that many of us must cultivate. "The 'one thing' that Martha needed was a calm, devotional spirit, a deeper anxiety for knowledge concerning the future, immortal life, and the graces necessary for spiritual advancement. She needed less anxiety for the things which pass away, and more for those things which endure forever. Jesus would teach His children to seize every opportunity of gaining that knowledge which will make them wise unto salvation. The cause of Christ needs careful, energetic workers. There is a wide field for the Marthas, with their zeal in active religious work. But let them first sit with Mary at the feet of Jesus" (*The Desire of Ages*, p. 525).

But those who wait on the Lord shall renew their strength; they shall mount up with wings like eagles, they shall run and not be weary, they shall walk and not faint. Isa. 40:31.

Pray for a patient, trusting spirit to wait upon the Lord.

CONFESSION

What is confession? It is admitting that I have sinned. Human pride does not make it easy to say, "I am a guilty sinner." But unconfessed sin can separate us from God. Isaiah says, "Behold, the Lord's hand is not shortened, that it cannot save; nor His ear heavy, that it cannot hear. But your iniquities have separated you from your God; and your sins have hidden His face from you, so that He will not hear" (Isa. 59:1, 2).

"Those who have not humbled their souls before God in acknowledging their guilt have not yet fulfilled the first condition of acceptance. If we have not experienced that repentance, . . . and have not with true humiliation of soul and brokenness of spirit confessed our sins, abhorring our iniquity, we have never truly sought for the forgiveness of sin; . . . we have never found the peace of God. The only reason why we do not have remission of sins that are past is that we are not willing to humble our hearts and comply with the conditions of the word of truth" (*Steps to Christ*, pp. 37, 38).

In Christ's model prayer He teaches us to pray, "Forgive us our debts," meaning our trespasses or sins. But God can forgive us only when we are willing to confess--to admit—our sins. "He who covers his sins will not prosper, but whoever confesses and forsakes them will have mercy" (Prov. 28:13). "True confession is always of a specific character, and acknowledges particular sins. They may be of such a nature as to be brought before God only; they may be wrongs that should be confessed to individuals who have suffered injury through them; or they may be of a public character, and should then be as publicly confessed. But all confession should be definite and to the point, acknowledging the very sins of which you are guilty" (*ibid.*, p. 38).

The reluctance to admit having done a wrong usually rests on a deeper problem than the specific act. It generally stems from the vanity of self-righteousness or the moral conceit of thinking ourselves better than we really are. Very few have the moral dignity to confess a wrong willingly and sincerely.

If we confess our sins, He is faithful and just to forgive us our sins and to cleanse us from all unrighteousness. 1 John 1:9.

Pray for the courage to confess specific sins and for the faith to believe God and accept His forgiveness.

READ PRAYERFULLY

Prayer is talking to God, but any relationship is strengthened by two-way communication. By listening for His voice as we read His Word, we make it possible for Him to speak to us.

As we read, or hear a recording of, a chapter of the Bible, often a particular verse impresses a truth upon our mind. It is well to stop at that point and meditate on God's Word. Perhaps the verse will suggest something that you should pray about. In this way you can pray your way through the Bible one day at a time.

The Bible reading done in our prayer time should be a time when we listen for what God has to say to us on a personal level. It should be for the purpose of becoming better acquainted with Him.

Many reading these words have heard or read the suggestions of Pastor Glenn Coon regarding the ABCs of prayer. First, you find a specific Bible promise related to your prayer need. On the basis of Matthew 7:7, which says, "Ask, and you will receive" (NEB), you ask God to fulfill this promise in your life. Next, in harmony with Mark 11:24 ("when you pray, believe that you receive"), you believe that God is answering your prayer. Finally, you claim by faith the answer and thank God for it, in harmony with 1 Corinthians 15:57 and Matthew 21:22. The latter verse promises us, "Believing, you will receive."

Let's take a specific example. I want to be a soul winner. With the help of a concordance, I find an appropriate Bible promise: "Follow Me, and I will make you fishers of men" (Matt. 4:19). With my Bible open to that verse I kneel down with my finger on the text and claim God's promise, in turn promising to follow Jesus in everything. I believe He will answer because I know I can trust Him, so I begin thanking Him for those He will help me lead to Christ.

> **For this reason we also thank God without ceasing, because when you received the word of God which you heard from us, you welcomed it not as the word of men, but as it is in truth, the word of God, which also effectively works in you who believe. 1 Thess. 2:13.**

> *Pray for the gospel outreach to blue-collar workers such as builders, masons, landscapers, and road laborers.*

WATCH AND PRAY

Watching implies staying awake spiritually and keeping on guard against the subtle attacks of the enemy. We need to be aware of the various ways in which Satan seeks to hinder our prayers. For example, he tries to keep us busy with less important things. The cares of life consume our time. Pet sins rob us of spiritual power. Preoccupation with television steals our desire to pray. And the list could go on endlessly.

One of the most common hindrances to prayer is wandering thoughts or drowsiness. You will remember we suggested a prayer journal as a good means of counteracting such problems. Writing your prayer in a journal will keep your mind from wandering.

Praying out loud is another aid to watchfulness. Some have found it helpful to pray and walk at the same time, making objects along the way subject matter for prayers. One obvious example is praying for our neighbors. Another is giving thanks for the beauties of nature. You can also watch for subject matter for your prayers as you read the *Adventist Review* and even the daily news.

We have a good example of watchfulness, or the lack of it, in the experience of the disciples during Christ's agony in Gethsemane. "But they had not heeded the repeated warning, 'Watch and pray.' At first they had been much troubled to see their Master, usually so calm and dignified, wrestling with a sorrow that was beyond comprehension. They had prayed as they heard the strong cries of the sufferer. They did not intend to forsake their Lord, but they seemed paralyzed by a stupor which they might have shaken off if they had continued pleading with God. They did not realize the necessity of watchfulness and earnest prayer in order to withstand temptation'' (*The Desire of Ages*, p. 688).

Then He came to the disciples and found them asleep, and said to Peter, "What, could you not watch with Me one hour? Watch and pray, lest you enter into temptation. The spirit indeed is willing, but the flesh is weak." Matt. 26:40, 41.

Pray for God's continued blessings on the proclamation of the three angels' messages in Switzerland, where M. B. Czechowski, a Polish ex-Catholic priest who had joined the Adventist Church in 1857, first preached Seventh-day Adventism in 1865. Switzerland has a church membership of 4,067 in a population of more than 6.5 million.

INTERCESSION

Intercessory prayer is praying to God for the needs of another person. Perhaps it is someone who could not or would not pray about a matter, but the Lord has placed the burden on our heart to bring the matter to Him. Remember, "It is a part of God's plan to grant us, in answer to the prayer of faith, that which He would not bestow did we not thus ask" (*The Great Controversy*, p. 525).

Dr. J. G. McClure tells of an invalid woman in Springfield, Illinois, who had been bedridden for 17 years and was almost helpless. For many years she had been praying to God in a general way about evangelism. But one day she asked for pen and paper and wrote down the names of 57 acquaintances.

Three times a day she prayed for each of the 57 people by name. Besides writing letters to them telling of her interest and concern, she also contacted Christian friends in whom she knew these persons had confidence and urged them to speak a word for Christ as they had opportunity. She had unquestioning faith in God, and in her humble dependence upon the Lord she interceded for the unsaved. Eventually every one of the 57 individuals professed faith in Jesus Christ as his or her personal Saviour.

Does intercessory prayer destroy man's free will? God will not coerce a person's will because we pray. People whom God created to be free have become slaves to sin, selfishness, and prejudice, and it is for freedom from this enslavement that we pray, so they will be free to choose Christ.

"In times past there were those who fastened their minds upon one soul after another, saying, 'Lord, help me to save this soul.' But now such instances are rare. How many act as if they realized the peril of sinners?" (*Gospel Workers*, p. 65).

> **Therefore I exhort first of all that supplications, prayers, intercessions, and giving of thanks be made for all men, for kings and all who are in authority, that we may lead a quiet and peaceable life in all godliness and reverence. 1 Tim. 2:1, 2.**
>
> *Pray that you will "fasten your mind" on some specific persons, and pray until you see results.*

PETITION

Petition is asking God for the help we need. It expresses our dependence on the Lord. Christ's model prayer contains seven petitions, and like the Ten Commandments, they naturally divide into two parts. The first three recognize God's greatness and authority, and the last four deal with human needs and our dependency.

1. "Hallowed be Your name."
2. "Your kingdom come."
3. "Your will be done."

4. "Give us this day our daily bread."
5. "Forgive us our debts."
6. "Do not lead us into temptation."
7. "Deliver us from the evil one."

It is interesting that every sentence in the Lord's Prayer has its basis in an Old Testament quotation. As we read the Bible, we find good subject matter for prayer. Our Lord drew the subject matter for His model prayer from Scripture.

When we analyze our prayers, we will probably find they largely consist of asking and thanking. God invites us to ask and promises we will receive if we meet the conditions of answered prayer. We must ask in faith and in Jesus' name. Our requests must harmonize with God's will, and we must ask them with unselfish motives.

Sometimes it seems we do not receive the things we request, and there are various reasons for this. Sometimes God knows the timing is not right, so He says, "Wait awhile." Other times the thing we have in mind would not be for our good. And sometimes we have the wrong motives. "You ask and do not receive, because you ask amiss, that you may spend it on your pleasures" (James 4:3). It was not so with George Mueller, who asked God to provide daily food for more than 2,000 English orphans. His motives were unselfish and his prayers produced results. During his lifetime he received nearly $1 million in answer to believing prayer.

But let him ask in faith, with no doubting, for he who doubts is like a wave of the sea driven and tossed by the wind. James 1:6.

Pray for Adventism in Guatemala, which E. L. Cardey and C. A. Nowlen introduced in 1908. They acquired an English language school and converted it into a missionary enterprise. The seven teachers at the school became the nucleus of the first Sabbath school in Guatemala. Church membership now stands at 35,243 in a total population of more than 8.4 million.

THE PRAYER OF THANKS

What a wonderful experience it is to take at least five minutes every day to count our many blessings, naming them one by one, as we sing that familiar old gospel song.

We take so many things for granted. How long has it been since you really stopped to thank God for a place to live, food to eat, a warm bed, eyes to see the beauties that surround you, and freedom to worship? Millions of people do not enjoy such privileges.

The Bible says, "In everything give thanks; for this is the will of God in Christ Jesus for you" (1 Thess. 5:18). I remember an elderly man who told me he thanked God for water every time he took a drink and thanked God for air every time he stepped outside. It is easy to complain when we have a pain, but do we remember to thank God for its absence on those days when we are not hurting? Cultivating a thankful spirit and taking time on a regular basis to express appreciation for all the good things that come our way does something for our mental attitude, and brings added joy into our lives.

Fulton Sheen makes this observation about children: "Gratitude or thankfulness comes relatively late in their young lives. They almost have to be taught it; if not, they are apt to grow up thinking that the world owes them a living."

We can even thank God for apparent adversity, knowing that He allows nothing to befall us that will not ultimately prove to be for our best good. "God never leads His children otherwise than they would choose to be led, if they could see the end from the beginning, and discern the glory of the purpose which they are fulfilling as coworkers with Him" (*The Desire of Ages*, pp. 224, 225).

There is so much for which to be thankful, so let us take time every day to count our blessings. Above all things, we should thank God that there is Someone to thank. Be thankful not only for the gifts, but most of all for the Giver.

We give thanks to You, O God, we give thanks! For Your wondrous works declare that Your name is near. Ps. 75:1.

Pray a prayer of thanksgiving for what you feel especially thankful for today.

SINGING

"As a part of religious service, singing is as much an act of worship as is prayer. Indeed, many a song is prayer" (*Education*, p. 168).

Speaking of the practice of Jesus, the Lord's messenger says, "Often He expressed the gladness of His heart by singing psalms and heavenly songs" (*The Desire of Ages*, p. 73).

An Ellen White comment in the *Youth's Instructor* of September 8, 1898, mentions that Christ often sang Psalms 66, 68, and 72. Their common theme is praise and thanksgiving

What possibilities do you see of spending five minutes of devotional time in singing? You could sing some of the psalms or other portions of Scripture that lend themselves to singing. Or you could sing from the hymnal, or even simply read the words of some of the hymns that are really prayers. Whether or not you have ever done it before, you will find a great blessing in taking time to read and meditate upon the words of some of the less-familiar songs in your hymnal. Perhaps you could meditatively listen to songs on tape or record.

A few evenings ago we had a visit from a former neighbor who is a university science professor with two doctorates. He told us of the influence on his early life of a neighbor who, having recently lost her husband, would sing through her tears, "What a Friend We Have in Jesus." He credits the witness of this Christian widow as the major factor motivating him to become a Christian.

God is worshiped with song and music in the courts of heaven and in our assemblies here on earth, but perhaps some of us have not been experiencing the joy that can come to us individually or as families as we make a joyful noise to the Lord by praising Him in song. As we do this, we are entering into the worship experience of heaven.

Make a joyful shout to the Lord, all you lands! Serve the Lord with gladness; come before His presence with singing. Ps. 100:1, 2.

Pray for Adventism in the beautiful Samoan islands in the South Pacific, about 1,600 miles northeast of New Zealand. Seventh-day Adventism began there in 1895 when Dr. and Mrs. F. E. Braucht arrived on the mission ship Pitcairn, to establish medical work. The population of the islands is 200,000, including 5,677 Seventh-day Adventists.

MINUTES OF MEDITATION

Perhaps one reason that Eastern meditation cults have attracted many adherents in the Western nations is the fact that with our busy pace we have not taken time for meditation.

Consider these words of counsel written to a preacher: "You will receive more strength by spending one hour each day in meditation, and in mourning over your failings and heart corruptions and pleading for God's pardoning love and the assurance of sins forgiven, than you would by spending many hours and days in studying the most able authors" (*Testimonies*, vol. 1, pp. 433, 434).

Eastern meditation seems to emphasize an empty mind, but Christian meditation recommends a focus on specific themes. Profitable themes for meditation include Christ's sacrifice, God's truth, the plan of redemption, God's love and goodness, the Word of God, the beauties of nature, and sermons you have heard. "The words and the character of Christ should be often the subject of our thoughts and of our conversation, and each day some time should be especially devoted to prayerful meditation upon these sacred themes" (*The Sanctified Life*, p. 92).

Christ's habits of meditation provide a good model for us: "Whenever it was His privilege, He turned aside from the scene of His labor, to go into the fields, to meditate in the green valleys, to hold communion with God on the mountainside or amid the trees of the forest. The early morning often found Him in some secluded place, meditating, searching the Scriptures, or in prayer" (*The Desire of Ages*, p. 90).

Meditation counteracts stress, reduces blood pressure, and elevates our thoughts. Above all, it draws us closer to God. Paul suggests thoughts for meditation in Philippians 4:8: "Finally, brethren, whatever things are true, whatever things are noble, whatever things are just, whatever things are pure, whatever things are lovely, whatever things are of good report, if there is any virtue and if there is anything praiseworthy—meditate on these things."

"This Book of the Law shall not depart from your mouth, but you shall meditate in it day and night, that you may observe to do according to all that is written in it. For then you will make your way prosperous, and then you will have good success." Joshua 1:8.

Pray for Seventh-day Adventist work in Morocco, which began in 1925 when a European Seventh-day Adventist layman opened a Sabbath school. Church membership stands at 31 in a total population of more than 23 million.

PRAY FOR REAPERS

All of us pray for the harvest—the individuals for whom we have a burden that they will be ready for Christ's return. We have been praying for the people of all the countries in the world because we believe in the effectiveness of intercessory prayer, and we know that God "desires all men to be saved and to come to the knowledge of the truth" (1 Tim. 2:4).

As our example, consider Paul, who prayed for the nation of Israel. "Brethren, my heart's desire and prayer to God for Israel is that they may be saved" (Rom. 10:1).

While it is natural and good that we pray for the unsaved, it seems that our Lord commanded prayer for the harvester rather than for the harvest. Real evangelism begins by talking to God about men before talking to men about God. It pleads with God to send laborers into His harvest. As we pray for reapers, often the Holy Spirit reminds us that in God's plan every believer is a reaper. Everyone works at harvesttime!

"All over the world men and women are looking wistfully to heaven. Prayers and tears and inquiries go up from souls longing for light, for grace, for the Holy Spirit. Many are on the verge of the kingdom, waiting only to be gathered in" (*The Acts of the Apostles*, p. 109).

While some religious leaders saw the common people as chaff to be destroyed, Jesus saw them as a harvest to be gathered in.

While you are praying for some Christian to cross the path of your loved one, another believer somewhere is praying for a loved one within your sphere of influence—in your corner of the harvest field. By praying for reapers, you make yourself vulnerable to the call of God. At no time is the conscience so sensitive as at the moment of heart-to-heart communion with God in prayer.

As we pray for reapers to reach the unreached people groups, the hidden peoples, and our own unsaved loved ones, it could well be that we will hear the Lord asking, "Who will go?" Who will go to your corner of the harvest field?

Then He said to His disciples, "The harvest truly is plentiful, but the laborers are few. Therefore pray the Lord of the harvest to send out laborers into His harvest." Matt. 9:37, 38.

Pray for reapers to gather in the final harvest.

STORE THE TREASURES

As you faithfully spend time alone with God in prayer each day, whether it is one hour or something less, you should have that prayer journal we talked about some months ago in which to store your treasures. The treasures will include mountain top experiences with the Lord that will come from praise, singing and meditation; answers to prayer that will result from those minutes of intercession and petition; victories that will originate in confession; and new thoughts and nuggets that you will discover during prayer time with God's Word. Take the final moments of your prayer time to record these treasured experiences so that you can enrich your life by reviewing them in the future.

Let's just give a little more thought to scheduling your quiet moments. It helps to have a definite time. If you decide to dedicate one hour, the five-minute segments may vary. Some days you might spend 10 or 15 minutes on some portion of God's Word and less on other segments of your prayer time. You can be flexible. If an hour seems unrealistic for you, start with a shorter period, and maybe you will want to increase it in the future.

Most of us have to make the time by getting up earlier, but the effort will be well rewarded, especially if we store our experiences in a journal. God has His book of remembrance, and we should have one too.

It helps also to have a definite place for meeting with the Lord. It might be a certain room of the house or a secluded site in the garden or in the woods. Wherever it is, it will become a hallowed spot, especially if you record the blessings you find there.

Then those who feared the Lord spoke to one another, and the Lord listened and heard them; so a book of remembrance was written before Him for those who fear the Lord and who meditate on His name. Mal. 3:16.

Pray for the more than 7,000 islands making up the Republic of the Philippines. Seventh-day Adventism began there in 1905 with one man, when R. A. Caldwell arrived from Australia to sell Adventist publications. Today the church has grown from that small beginning to a membership of 438,329, making it, with the exception of an indigenous religion, the largest Protestant denomination in this country, which has a total population of 62 million.

332

I AM WITH YOU ALWAYS

It was November 17, 1840. At 5:00 on that bleak winter morning the Livingstone family knelt for family worship on the day that David was to leave his parental home in Blantyre, Scotland. By lamplight David read from the Psalms: "The Lord shall preserve your going out and your coming in from this time forth, and even forevermore" (Ps. 121:8).

After prayers came the anguish of farewells, and then father and son started out together on the long walk to Glasgow.

Livingstone married Mary Moffat, daughter of missionary Robert Moffat, and repeatedly he tried to settle down to the life of an ordinary mission station for the sake of his wife, but it was impossible. The smoke of a thousand native settlements in which no White man had ever been seen kept drawing him onward. His indomitable courage came from the promise of God, "Lo, I am with you always, even to the end of the age" (Matt. 28:20). Commenting on this text in his journal, he wrote on January 14, 1856, "It is the word of a Gentleman of the most strict and sacred honor, so there's an end of it."

When the University of Glasgow conferred the Doctor of Laws degree upon David Livingstone, even the students showed unusual respect for this man who bore upon his person the marks of his struggles and sufferings in Africa. His left arm, crushed by a lion, hung helplessly at his side, and a hush fell upon the great assembly as David Livingstone announced his resolve to return to Africa.

In another journal entry echoing the sentiments of the Apostle Paul in Philippians 4:13 ("I can do all things through Christ who strengthens me"), Livingstone wrote, "If You will be with me, I can do anything, anything, anything."

David Livingstone died in Africa on his knees talking with his God. In the truest sense, the Lord was with him to the very end.

"Teaching them to observe all things that I have commanded you; and lo, I am with you always, even to the end of the age." Amen. Matt. 28:20.

Do you know someone who has caught the vision and is serving God in some faraway, difficult area of earth, perhaps having left a promising career, family, friends, and comforts to give self in service to God? Pray for that specific person just now.

WRITE IT DOWN

This will be the third time this year that I have referred to the value of keeping a journal to preserve good ideas that otherwise would be lost. An administrator friend of mine frequently used an interesting play on words, saying, "If you don't write, you're wrong!" You will be surprised how much more you get out of a sermon if you take notes on those points that really impress you. Jotting down ideas helps to clarify them, and it certainly helps us to remember.

With a little effort you will be able to form the habit of having pen and paper close by at all times. Many have learned the value of having writing equipment beside the bed for recording inspiration that may come during wakeful moments through the night. It is much safer to trust thoughts to paper than to memory.

Among the greatest benefits of keeping a journal are spiritual self-discovery, spiritual reflection, and a deepening of spiritual experience. You can record insights gleaned from personal Bible study and preserve the thrill of those prize moments of illumination.

Your journal can include prayer requests and answers, problems and hurts, and hopes and plans for the future, including both personal long-range and short-range goals and objectives.

Writing crystallizes issues and helps in problem solving. When you feel unclear concerning God's will, or as to the solution of a particular problem, you can talk it over with the Lord in a journal. As specific details come into focus with the passing of time, prayer and careful thought often open the door to decisions and progress.

Record feelings and perceptions. Be completely honest. Discipline yourself to write positively. When you experience an answer to prayer or an exciting evangelistic encounter or an insight into Scripture, write it down. This record will provide for you a new appreciation of God's interest and involvement in the details of your life.

Then the Lord answered me and said: "Write the vision and make it plain on tablets, that he may run who reads it." Hab. 2:2.

Pray for the progress of the work in Sierra Leone, which began in 1905 when J. M. Hyatt, a Black American layman, arrived in Freetown and began work by holding prayer meetings in his home. Present Seventh-day Adventist membership is 8,959 among a population of 3.8 million.

THERE IS HOPE IN YOUR FUTURE

The Bible says, "For in the resurrection they neither marry nor are given in marriage, but are like angels of God in heaven" (Matt. 22:30). But the Bible also says there will be children in the world to come. "The wolf also shall dwell with the lamb, the leopard shall lie down with the young goat, the calf and the young lion and the fatling together; and a little child shall lead them" (Isa. 11:6).

Evidently the only parents privileged to bring up children in this coming perfect world will be those who have experienced the sadness of losing a child in our present life of sin, sickness, and disease. Our God of justice and love does not always intervene to prevent sickness and death now, but He has marvelous ways of compensating in the life to come for those heartaches and sorrows we have borne in the present world.

There is hope for bereaved parents in this description of the resurrection: "Little children are borne by holy angels to their mothers' arms" (*The Great Controversy*, p. 645). "All come forth from their graves the same in stature as when they entered the tomb" (*ibid.*, p. 644).

The prophet Malachi says, "But unto you that fear my name shall the Sun of righteousness arise with healing in his wings; and ye shall go forth, and grow up as calves of the stall" (Mal. 4:2, KJV).

Jeremiah, speaking prophetically of those babies of Bethlehem destroyed at Herod's command, says, "They shall come back from the land of the enemy. There is hope in your future" (Jer. 31:16, 17).

The anticipation of meeting in the resurrection that baby who died in infancy will strengthen the determination of the parents to be there.

A shepherd who wants his flock to cross a stream will often pick up a little lamb in his arms and walk across, knowing that the sheep will follow. In many cases, little children will literally be the means of leading their parents and brothers and sisters into the kingdom of heaven.

Thus says the Lord: "Refrain your voice from weeping, and your eyes from tears; for your work shall be rewarded," says the Lord, "and they shall come back from the land of the enemy. There is hope in your future," says the Lord, "that your children shall come back to their own border." Jer. 31:16, 17.

Pray for the 4.2 million inhabitants of the province of Qinghai (ching-hi) in China. Qinghai means "blue sea."

GOD'S FOREKNOWLEDGE

Many people confuse God's foreknowledge with predestination. Foreknowledge means to know the future in advance, and this ability belongs to God alone. He appeals to His possession of this ability as one of the evidences that He is the true God.

Let us imagine for the sake of illustration that I possess the ability to know the future. Because of my foreknowledge, I know without a doubt that the sun will be in the heavens tomorrow. Does that mean that I personally am responsible for the rotation of the earth? Not at all! The fact that I know the sun is going to appear does not necessarily mean that I cause it to do so. Likewise, the fact that God can see ahead and knows a certain thing will happen does not necessarily mean that He makes it happen.

While God knows in advance who will reject salvation, that does not mean that He causes these people to be lost. On the contrary, God is "not willing that any should perish but that all should come to repentance" (2 Peter 3:9). It is only because He respects our freedom to choose and does not impose His will upon us that some will be lost.

God foreknew that Judas would betray Jesus, but God didn't cause it to be that way. Jesus said, "Woe to the world because of offenses! For offenses must come, but woe to that man by whom the offense comes!" (Matt. 18:7).

The Lord foresaw the drama that would be enacted in the struggle between good and evil, between Christ and Satan, but we choose the part we play in it.

There is definite predestination in God's plan for dealing with the problem of sin. He determined beforehand what would be the means and the conditions whereby sinners might be saved. But in all of this predestination, the Lord has left every individual free in the exercise of his own will to choose whether he will let the God-given Saviour save him according to the conditions set forth in the Bible.

I am God, and there is none like Me, declaring the end from the beginning, and from ancient times things that are not yet done. Isa. 46:9, 10.

Pray for the more than 35 million people of the province of Yunnan (yu-oon-non), which borders Vietnam, Laos, and Burma.

PREDESTINATION AND FREE CHOICE

What a pity it is for men to miss the beautiful biblical teaching that all men have a chance to be saved. This doctrine stands in sharp contrast to the fatalistic teaching of some other world religions that "what is to be, will be." Some proclaim that all disasters are the will of God.

Predestination claims that God planned every action of our lives before we were born, and that we have no choice but to follow the pattern—we are merely puppets. The implication of such a teaching is that God is responsible for evil.

First Corinthians 15:22 is the key to a correct understanding of predestination: "For as in Adam all die, even so in Christ all shall be made alive." The Bible declares that the family of Adam is all predestined to be lost, while the family of Christ is all predestined to be saved. We are all members of the family of Adam by birth into this world. In order to be saved, we must change from the family of Adam to the family of Christ. To get into the family of Christ, we must be born again. On this basis any person who chooses to be saved can be saved.

Paul applies this principle in reference to Israel. He says, "And so all Israel will be saved" (Rom. 11:26). The apostle explains that the literal Israelites who do not believe are pruned like branches off a tree. Gentiles, or non-Israelites, who do believe are grafted in to take their place. In being grafted in they become part of Israel, and in this way "all Israel will be saved."

Peter makes it clear that we have to do something in regard to our salvation. "Therefore, brethren, be even more diligent to make your calling and election sure" (2 Peter 1:10).

We decide our own election. God is voting for us to be saved. The devil is voting for us to be lost, and we cast the deciding vote.

Not one individual will be lost because of an act of God. We decide as individuals whether we will be saved or lost.

And the Spirit and the bride say, "Come!" And let him who hears say, "Come!" And let him who thirsts come. And whoever desires, let him take the water of life freely. Rev. 22:17.

Pray for the more than 27 million people of the province of Shenxi (shun-she) in China. Shenxi means "west of the mountain passes."

337

CONDITIONS OF ANSWERED PRAYER

One of the first conditions of answered prayer is to sense our need. It is the vacuum of our need that siphons blessings from heaven's reservoir through the channel of prayer into our lives.

The exercise of faith is another condition of answered prayer. God longs for us to develop trust in Him not only because it is an evidence of our love for Him, but also because He knows it will contribute to our happiness and peace of mind.

We must be willing to live in harmony with God's law if we expect Him to answer our prayers. "One who turns away his ear from hearing the law, even his prayer shall be an abomination" (Prov. 28:9).

Prayer should be in harmony with God's will. We should study to know His desires for us, and even then should pray as did Jesus, "nevertheless, not as I will, but as You will" (Matt. 26:39).

To be "on praying ground" we should make matters right not only with God but with our fellow human beings. "But if you do not forgive men their trespasses, neither will your Father forgive your trespasses" (Matt. 6:15).

Our prayers should be rightly motivated to glorify God and benefit others. "You ask and do not receive, because you ask amiss, that you may spend it on your pleasures" (James 4:3).

There must be perseverance in our prayers. "Our prayers are to be as earnest and persistent as was the petition of the needy friend who asked for the loaves at midnight. The more earnestly and steadfastly we ask, the closer will be our spiritual union with Christ. We shall receive increased blessings because we have increased faith" (*Christ's Object Lessons*, p. 146).

In addition, we are to ask in Jesus' name. When you apply for a loan at the bank, it is important to have good references. Jesus invites us to give His name as our reference. His name is His character, implying that our prayers must harmonize with the character of Christ.

When you pray, keep in mind the conditions of answered prayer, and having met those conditions, trust God to answer in the way He sees best.

"And whatever you ask in My name, that I will do, that the Father may be glorified in the Son." John 14:13.

Pray for the more than 80 million people of the Chinese province of Henan (huh-non), which lies south of the Yellow River.

TRUST THE LORD

Psalm 112 describes some of the characteristics of a righteous person. Among other things, the psalm mentions how such a person will deal with adversity. For our meditation today let's look at some of the phrases in this chapter.

"There arises light in the darkness" (verse 4). To the upright person, there will appear light even during the darkest experiences of life, because Jesus is the light, and He is always with His people. And the Scriptures are light also. When it seems that darkness surrounds you, hold on, because eventually some ray of light and hope will break through the gloom.

"He will never be shaken" (verse 6). For a short time it might seem adversity overwhelms the follower of God, but he can say, "I have set the Lord always before me; because He is at my right hand I shall not be moved" (Ps. 16:8).

"He will not be afraid of evil tidings; His heart is steadfast, trusting in the Lord" (verse 7). Many people past middle age know the anxious suspense of waiting for the results of a biopsy or diagnostic X-ray. Usually the news is good, and a feeling of relief and gratitude floods over the person waiting for test results. But sometimes the tidings indicate a serious problem. Even then the righteous person will trust the Lord knowing that:

"God never leads His children otherwise than they would choose to be led, if they could see the end from the beginning, and discern the glory of the purpose which they are fulfilling as coworkers with Him. Not Enoch, who was translated to heaven, not Elijah, who ascended in a chariot of fire, was greater or more honored than John the Baptist, who perished alone in the dungeon. 'Unto you it is given in the behalf of Christ, not only to believe on him, but also to suffer for his sake' (Phil. 1:29). And of all the gifts that heaven can bestow upon men, fellowship with Christ in His sufferings is the most weighty trust and the highest honor" (*The Desire of Ages*, pp. 224, 225).

He will not be afraid of evil tidings; his heart is steadfast, trusting in the Lord. Ps. 112:7.

Pray for the church on the tiny peninsula of Macao on the coast of the province of Guangdong (gwong-doong) in China. Pray for the thousands of refugees from Vietnam and Burma now in Macao. Macao is one of the most open fields for missions in Asia.

HER SPECIAL MINISTRY

Hattie Johnson found it difficult to go to church after her husband died. They had always sat together in church, and now it seemed so terribly lonely to sit by herself. She felt tempted to stay home—that is until she found her special ministry. Let me tell you about it.

Hattie would look for a seat on the aisle near the back of the church. As the people gathered for worship, she would silently pray for the visitors who would visit their congregation that day. When she recognized a visitor sitting all alone, she would leave her seat and find a place beside her. There would be a handshake, a smile, and a few quiet words of welcome. Upon leaving the sanctuary after the worship service, Hattie and the visitor would have an opportunity to get better acquainted. If the woman had no other plans, usually Hattie would invite her home for lunch. Hattie made many wonderful friends over the years through her ministry to those who found their way to the services of her church. Because of her special concern for others who were lonely, the pain of her own loneliness turned into the joy of service.

"Those who give their lives to Christlike ministry know the meaning of true happiness. Their interests and their prayers reach far beyond self. . . . Such ones receive wisdom from heaven. They become more and more identified with Christ in all His plans. There is no opportunity for spiritual stagnation" (*Testimonies,* vol. 9, p. 42).

If loneliness is one of your problems, find a special ministry that will bring you into contact with other people. In ministering to others, you will yourself be blessed.

The basic cause of loneliness is separation. It may be separation from friends or it may be caused by travel or by death. The cause gives us a clue to possible remedies. Mankind will always be lonely when separated from God. Cultivating a sense of God's presence is the ultimate cure for loneliness. Henry Martyn's diary contains this sentence: "My chief enjoyment was the enjoyment of God's presence."

For if they fall, one will lift up his companion. But woe to him who is alone when he falls, for he has no one to help him up. Eccl. 4:10.

Pray for the Seventh-day Adventist outreach in Austria, where in a population of more than 7.5 million we have about 3,000 church members.

PITCAIRN ISLAND

Pitcairn Island, located in the central Pacific Ocean, is 2,868 miles from Wellington, New Zealand. A young officer named Pitcairn who was on watch aboard the sailing ship *Swallow* discovered the island in 1767. In 1790 nine mutineers from the *H.M.S. Bounty* with a group of Tahitians arrived on the island.

By 1800 John Adams was the only man who had survived the drinking, debauchery, and fighting. Reading the *Bounty* Bible that he had discovered in his sea chest transformed his life and one by one the lives of all the others on the island. John Adams used the Bible as a textbook to teach the children to read.

Nearly 20 years passed before another ship visited lonely Pitcairn Island, where the coastline is such that vessels must anchor far from shore and passengers must come ashore in small native boats. Sailors aboard the visiting vessel were amazed by what they found on Pitcairn. Soon the world heard the strange story of the survivors of the *Bounty* mutiny and their remote island colony.

In 1876 James White and J. N. Loughborough sent Adventist publications to Pitcairn. They had no indication that the printed material had reached this remote island until 10 years later, in 1886, when John I. Tay, a Seventh-day Adventist ship's carpenter, spent five weeks on Pitcairn teaching the inhabitants Seventh-day Adventist doctrines. Unanimously the islanders accepted the Sabbath. When the bell rang for church at 10:00 the next Sabbath morning, everyone on the island attended

Tay returned to America, and gradually the story of Pitcairn reached most of the 50,000 Adventists of that day. The Sabbath schools undertook to raise the money to build a mission ship to transport missionaries to Pitcairn and other islands of the South Seas.

On November 25, 1890, 101 years ago today, John I. Tay returned to Pitcairn aboard the missionary ship *Pitcairn*. Eighty-two persons were baptized and organized into a church. ❦

Sing to the Lord a new song, and His praise from the ends of the earth, you who go down to the sea, and all that is in it, you coastlands and you inhabitants of them! Isa. 42:10.

Pray for the people on lonely Pitcairn Island and for those who will be attracted to the message of Christ through the story of these islanders and their faith. Pray also for the conversion of people living on other remote islands.

WALK IN A WORTHY WAY

Two men walking together saw a stranger approaching. The one said to the other, "Here comes an old army man." "How do you know?" his companion asked. "By the way he walks," the friend replied.

Someone has said that we talk more by our walk than in any other way. In his letter to the church at Ephesus, Paul speaks of seven different walks.

The walk of disobedience (Eph. 2:2) characterizes the natural man in a state of rebellion against God. When Christ was here on earth, He commanded the angry waves, and the sea became calm; He rebuked the wind, and it ceased; but when He spoke to the human race, they did not obey.

The walk worthy of our spiritual vocation appears in Ephesians 4:1. Regardless of what we do to pay expenses, the real vocation of every Christian is to serve as an ambassador of Jesus Christ and a winner of souls.

The third walk is that of love (Eph. 5:2). Love is one of the fruits that gives evidence of the Spirit's indwelling. Walking in love is walking with God, for God is love.

Next, we come to the circumspect walk. An old-time preacher, trying to illustrate what it means to walk circumspectly, described a cat navigating a brick wall that had sharp pieces of broken glass embedded in the cement. The cat puts each paw down very carefully to avoid injury.

The Christian will walk not as other Gentiles do (Eph. 4:17). Too often, like the Israelites of old, we are influenced rather than exerting an influence. The church and the world expect Christians to be different. And God expects us to be different.

We are to walk as children of the light—following God's Word in all things (Eph. 5:8).

The seventh walk is that of good works (Eph. 2:10) resulting from Christ living out His life within us.

May God help us to walk worthy of our vocation.

> **I, therefore, the prisoner of the Lord, beseech you to have a walk worthy of the calling with which you were called. Eph. 4:1.**
>
> *Pray for the 102.5 million people of one of the world's poorest nations. Bangladesh is 87 percent Muslim, and the vast majority of the people have never heard the gospel. Pray that it may spread more rapidly in this needy land.*

SPECIAL
PRAYER AND ANOINTING

Our loving Lord has made marvelous provisions for His people's needs that we often overlook. He has provided baptism by immersion to make real the concept of forgiveness and the removal of guilt; foot washing to periodically renew that experience; and the Lord's Supper to remind us of His death and His return.

God has also offered us the privilege of special prayer and anointing in times of serious illness. You can read about it in James 5:14-18. Here God invites the sick person to "call for the elders of the church, and let them pray over him, anointing him with oil in the name of the Lord." The initiative is to come from the person who is ill.

More than one elder offers prayer so that no human instrument will get the credit if healing takes place. God alone is the Healer. All taking part in such a service must prepare themselves by confessing and forsaking every known sin.

The promise is threefold: "The prayer of faith will save the sick, and the Lord will raise him up. And if he has committed sins, he will be forgiven" (verse 15).

Sometimes healing takes place immediately, sometimes gradually, sometimes God heals through physicians and surgeons, and sometimes the illness may prove terminal, but still the promise is sure, and the Lord will raise that person in the resurrection of life. He will be saved. If all sins have been confessed, they will be forgiven. And that is what matters most.

When we follow the scriptural instructions regarding prayer and anointing, a peace of mind comes to the person prayed for. He or she will want to live in harmony with all the light God has given, and can then rest in the assurance that God's will shall prevail.

"God is too wise and good to answer our prayers always at just the time and in just the manner we desire. . . . Because we can trust His wisdom and love, we should not ask Him to concede to our will" (*The Ministry of Healing*, p. 231). It is always safe to pray "Thy will be done."

Is anyone among you sick? Let him call for the elders of the church, and let them pray over him, anointing him with oil in the name of the Lord. James 5:14.

Pray that the work of our church may continue to spread throughout the Caribbean islands of Antigua and Barbuda.

BREAD FROM HEAVEN

Three energetic, growing children came home from school, puffing and panting from their run up the hill. Desperately hungry, they called out, "What's for supper?"

"God hasn't sent it yet," Mother responded. And that evening Father, Mother, and three children gathered by faith around the table to thank God for food that had not yet arrived.

Now it so happened that this very afternoon two women from their church felt concerned and decided to visit this very family. As they walked along the country road, each carrying a basket of food, a bakery truck passed them, and just as it did, the back door flew open and a nicely wrapped loaf of bread fell out.

Then the truck hit a bump, and more loaves fell out in all directions. Not realizing what had happened, the driver sped on. The women discussed what to do. If they left the bread in the road, cars would run over it or dogs would devour it. They decided to gather the bread and see if the driver would return. He didn't, so the women carried all they could and made their visit.

Can you imagine the scene in that home? The table was set, and a family of five was sitting around a table. Thanks had been returned. The only thing missing was food! And then there was a knock at the door. When one of the children opened the door, she exclaimed, "Jesus has sent us bread—bread from heaven."

Please, dear Lord, send us bread from heaven today. We must share the bread with a hungry world. Sharing the bread of life with a spiritually hungry world is what global strategy is all about.

Many marvelous resources are available to help us locate the people groups who still do not have the spiritual bread. But in addition, we have the thrilling privilege of cooperating with the Holy Spirit who will give us providential guidance as He did for the two women in our story. "The Holy Spirit will come to all who are begging for the bread of life to give to their neighbors" (*Testimonies*, vol. 6, p. 90).

> **And Jesus said to them, "I am the bread of life. He who comes to Me shall never hunger, and he who believes in Me shall never thirst." John 6:35.**

> *Pray for the more than 65 million people of the province of Jiangsu (jeeong-su), located on the lower portion of the Yangtze River.*

PROVIDER AND PROVISION

The name Jehovah appears in many different compounds in the Bible to reveal different characteristics of God in His relationship to us. The story of Abraham and Isaac on Mount Moriah contains our first example. When Isaac asked his father about the lamb for a burnt offering, Abraham answered, "Jehovah-jireh," which means "God will provide." The old King James Version says, "God will provide himself a lamb" (Gen. 22:8). In other words, the Lord was both the provider and the provision.

Abraham called the place where this great lesson of God's grace was revealed to him Jehovah-jireh, "The Lord will provide" (verse 14). Do you have places in your experience that you could call Jehovah-jireh?

Twenty centuries later the heavenly Father brought His Son to another mountain to be the sacrificial offering. This time no ram appeared as a substitute, and no angel held back the instrument of death. Our Lord was the substitute. He was the lamb.

God provided the sacrifice for us in the person of His Son, and only a parent can begin to understand the implications of such a sacrifice. Sometimes God rewards our faith in a seemingly miraculous way, as in the case of Abraham on Mount Moriah. In other instances we pray and exercise faith, but our experience echoes the cry of Christ on that other mountain called Calvary, and it seems that God has forsaken us.

Perhaps we have had special prayer and anointing, but the pain and illness continue. We have prayed earnestly, but the problem remains.

The very fact that God spared not His own Son is also the assurance that He will, in His own good time, "freely give us all things" (Rom. 8:32). We must leave the timing with Him.

The Jehovah of the Old Testament is the Christ of the New Testament. Therefore Jesus is our Jehovah-jireh, and He will provide. In some cases, He will give the answer to our cry "at the last trump"—when He comes again—but what He provides will endure forever!

"Therefore do not worry. . . . Your heavenly Father knows that you need all these things. But seek first the kingdom of God and His righteousness, and all these things shall be added to you." Matt. 6:31-33.

Pray for the more than 25 million Muslim population of Algeria. Situated in northern Africa, with the Sahara Desert occupying 80 percent of the country, this land, where Christians number about one per every 125 of the population, does not permit proselytism.

THE
EXPLOSION OF KNOWLEDGE

In Daniel's day, 500 years before the birth of Jesus, the horse was the swiftest means of travel. No doubt King Nebuchadnezzar had the fastest horse in the realm, but its speed would not exceed 35 miles per hour.

Six hundred years later when Emperor Nero's horse ran around the old circus in Rome, the speed was the same. And it remained the same until the nineteenth century. It took some 6,000 years for man to go from a speed of 35 miles per hour to 200 miles per hour. But it required only 25 years to advance from 200 miles per hour to 18,000 miles per hour!

Twenty-five hundred years ago Daniel spoke of the time of the end when knowledge would increase (Dan. 12:4). If a time machine could take us back just 200 years, we would find a strangely different world. There would be no electric lights--not even kerosene lamps, just tallow candles.

Two hundred years ago life was pretty much the same as 2,000 years ago. There were no automobiles or trains, and certainly no airplanes—not even bicycles! Electrical appliances of any kind did not yet exist. That means no radio or television and no movies.

Humanity had not yet invented gas stoves, refrigerators, or freezers. Photographs, telephones, and indoor plumbing were still in the future. You could not yet find rubber, celluloid, or plastic goods on the market. If you needed surgery, there was no anesthetic.

This explosion of knowledge included knowledge of the Scriptures. The book of Daniel was to be sealed until the time of the end. The unsealing of Daniel's prophecy helped in the study of Revelation because those two prophetic books deal with many of the same prophecies.

The increase of knowledge has put within our reach insights into Bible teachings that were not so clearly available to earlier generations.

Before Jesus returns, the gospel is to go to all people everywhere. The explosion of knowledge makes this possible through modern methods of printing and transportation. But the dedicated individual Christian is still the key!

"But you, Daniel, shut up the words, and seal the book until the time of the end; many shall run to and fro, and knowledge shall increase." Dan. 12:4.

Pray for the more than 7,000 people of Anguilla in the British Antilles. Seventh-day Adventists have a membership of about 1,000 on this small island of the Caribbean.

YOUR INHERITANCE

When God created the Earth, He intended for it to be inhabited (see Isa. 45:18). If sin had not intruded, perfect people would have dwelt forever on our planet in a perfect environment. We may be sure that God will not allow Satan to thwart His plans for our world permanently.

God promised Abraham that he would be "the heir of the world" (Rom. 4:13). Jesus, in the Sermon on the Mount, stated, "Blessed are the meek, for they shall inherit the earth" (Matt. 5:5). In His model prayer Jesus taught His followers to pray, "Your kingdom come. Your will be done on earth as it is in heaven" (Matt. 6:10).

Heaven is where God is. His presence makes it heaven. At the end of the millennium, when the New Jerusalem comes down to rest upon the earth, a loud voice from heaven declares, "Behold, the tabernacle of God is with men, and He will dwell with them, and they shall be His people, and God Himself will be with them and be their God" (Rev. 21:3). Thus heaven will have come to earth with real people in a real world.

"In the Bible the inheritance of the saved is called 'a country' (Heb. 11:14-16). There the heavenly Shepherd leads His flock to fountains of living waters. The tree of life yields its fruit every month. . . . There are ever-flowing streams, clear as crystal, and beside them waving trees cast their shadows upon the paths prepared for the ransomed of the Lord. There the wide-spreading plains swell into hills of beauty, and the mountains of God rear their lofty summits. On those peaceful plains, beside those living streams, God's people, so long pilgrims and wanderers, shall find a home. . . . And the years of eternity, as they roll, will bring richer and still more glorious revelations of God and of Christ" *(The Great Controversy,* pp. 675-678).

No wonder Satan tries to cheat us out of the inheritance that he himself forfeited. Do you have the assurance that through the merits of Christ you will be there? If not, settle it this very day.

Come, you blessed of My Father, inherit the kingdom prepared for you from the foundation of the world. Matt. 25:34.

Pray for the more than 6 million people of the Yemen Arab Republic. Pray that this land where Islam is the state religion may open wide for the gospel.

MANNA

The manna represented Jesus, and its lessons for us are many. Providing it involved a series of miracles every week. Through Jesus, the Living Bread, our lives can be a series of daily and weekly miracles too.

Manna came from heaven to satisfy man's physical hunger. Jesus came among us to satisfy man's spiritual hunger. Both arrived in a miraculous way. There is much about each that we cannot understand. When the manna appeared, people asked, "What is it?" Of Jesus people asked, "What manner of man is this?" (KJV). There hovers about Him an element of mystery hard for us to comprehend, for we are finite, but He is infinite God.

The people of Israel didn't need to understand the manna to be fed—they simply needed to eat it. To be fed spiritually what we really must do is to receive Christ (see John 1:12). By the process of assimilation physical food within us sustains our bodies. Christ within us sustains us spiritually. Paul speaks of this mystery: "To them God willed to make known what are the riches of the glory of this mystery among the Gentiles: which is Christ in you, the hope of glory" (Col. 1:27).

The manna was small, and Jesus arrived as a small baby. It was round, and the one who felt its circumference could find neither beginning nor end, just as Jesus is without beginning or end. Its whiteness represented the purity of Christ. As it was sweet, the psalmist invites us to "taste and see that the Lord is good" (Ps. 34:8).

God provided the manna daily, and the people gathered it early in the morning. We should daily, in the early hours, make time to feed on spiritual bread. The supply of manna was sufficient to meet each person's needs, and Christ's grace is sufficient to meet our needs. The manna was God's gift, as is Christ. In neither case could man earn or pay for what God alone gave freely. But we can share God's gift with others and that's what Global Strategy is all about.

For the bread of God is He who comes down from heaven and gives life to the world. John 6:33.

Pray for the more than 260,000 people of Brunei, two small enclaves in Sarawak on the island of Borneo. The government allows free practice of religions but does not allow missions to operate. Adventists have no established activity in the area.

MORE ABOUT MANNA

In the grinding, beating, and baking of the manna we have a graphic portrayal of Christ's sufferings. When the Israelites baked manna, they exposed it to the action of fire, which speaks to us of God's wrath toward sin. Christ was sinless but He took upon Himself our sins, represented by the leaven. In the baking process fire checks the action of the leaven.

The manna rested upon the earth for only a short time. Jesus' life upon earth lasted only 33 years. Once lying on the ground, the manna was lifted up, providing a beautiful symbol of the resurrection. Some of it was placed in a golden pot and carried into the presence of the Lord in the tabernacle, symbolic of the Ascension.

God made no other provision for food except the manna, just as there is no other means of salvation. The people were to both gather and eat. A preacher must teach the people how to go to the Word, gather spiritual food, and feed themselves.

The manna was free and came in sufficient supply to meet the needs of all. "So when they measured it by omers, he who gathered much had nothing over, and he who gathered little had no lack. Every man had gathered according to each one's need" (Ex. 16:18). Likewise, Christ's righteousness is available to all.

Although Scripture describes manna as angel's food, yet the people tired of it and complained. When we tire of the food God provides, we need to ask ourselves, "Is there something wrong with the food or with me?"

As we feed upon Christ we receive strength to serve Him and others. The manna lasted to the end of Israel's journey while Christ has promised He will be with us always, "even unto the end of the world" (Matt. 28:20, KJV).

I am the living bread which came down from heaven. If anyone eats of this bread, he will live forever; and the bread that I shall give is My flesh, which I shall give for the life of the world. John 6:51.

Pray for the 30,000 people on the famous rocky peninsula on the south coast of Spain—Gibraltar. We have only recently established a Seventh-day Adventist church there.

WHAT IS GOD LIKE?

Some have pictured God as a cosmic policeman whose only interest is to force us to obey His law. Others portray Him as a heavenly grandfather who loves us but is too feeble to help us much.

How wonderful it is that the God whom we worship is pictured for us as a loving, caring parent. The pastor whose son missed three days of school revealed something of God's compassion. The father didn't know anything about his son's absence until the boy's teacher called at the home to see if the boy was ill.

When Steve arrived home, father and son had a serious talk behind closed doors. "I can't tell you how bad I feel," the father said. "I've always trusted you implicitly, but here you've been living a lie for three days."

After the quiet talk, the father suggested they kneel down and pray. Steve listened to the prayer of his heartbroken father, and it was more painful than a whipping. Following prayer the father explained that you can't separate sin and suffering. "For the wrong you have done," he said, "you must spend three days and three nights in the attic. I'll prepare a place for you to sleep, and we'll bring you food three times a day."

When suppertime came the parents had no appetite, and when bedtime came, they couldn't sleep. Finally the father said, "I'm going up in the attic to sleep with Steve." The boy was wide awake even though it was very late, and something glistened in his eyes. The father got in between the sheets with Steve, and soon their tears mingled on each other's cheeks.

The next night when bedtime came, the father said, "Good night, Mother, I'm going to the attic to be with Steve." And again the third night the father slept in the place of punishment with his son. This for me is a helpful picture of God. In the person of His Son He came down and slept in the place of our punishment. Jesus said, "He who has seen Me has seen the Father" (John 14:9). In other words, the Father is just like Jesus.

The Lord God, merciful and gracious, long-suffering, and abounding in goodness and truth, keeping mercy for thousands, forgiving iniquity and transgression and sin. Ex. 34:6, 7.

Pray for the more than 9 million people of Beijing (bay-jing), a provincial name meaning "northern capital." It has been the seat of central government in China for a thousand years, and the famous great wall of China begins nearby.

350

GOD THE HOLY SPIRIT

Our minds, chained as they are to clocks and calendars, often find it difficult to comprehend the eternity of God. God the Father, the Son, and the Holy Spirit have always existed and always will.

Referring to Creation, God said, "Let Us make man in Our image, according to Our likeness" (Gen. 1:26). God the Father, Son, and Holy Spirit cooperated in Creation. As early as Genesis 1:2 the Holy Spirit is referred to: "And the Spirit of God was hovering over the face of the waters."

At Jesus' baptism God clearly manifested Himself in three persons — the Father spoke from heaven, Jesus stood in the river Jordan being baptized, and the Holy Spirit descended in the form of a dove (Matt. 3:13, 16, 17). Baptism is to be administered in the name of the Father, Son, and Holy Spirit (see Matt. 28:19, 20).

Let us think of the characteristics of the Holy Spirit. He is more than a power or an influence — He is a Person. For example, He can be grieved. Ephesians 4:30 says, "And do not grieve the Holy Spirit of God, by whom you were sealed for the day of redemption."

It is possible to lie to the Holy Spirit. Acts 5:3 reports, "Ananias, why has Satan filled your heart to lie to the Holy Spirit?"

Speaking of the Holy Spirit, Christ comments, "He will teach you all things" (John 14:26). It is our privilege to know Him. "But you know Him, for He dwells with you and will be in you" (verse 17).

The Holy Spirit knows both the things of man and of God (see 1 Cor. 2:11). He exercises His will in the distribution of spiritual gifts (see 1 Cor. 12:11). The characteristics we have listed — the capacity to be grieved, lied to, to teach, to know and be known, and to will — are those of a person and not of a mere abstract influence.

In the outworking of the plan of salvation we might see God the Father reaching out to lost humanity as a loving Father. Subsequently we see the Son of God reaching out to us as a brother, and finally Father and Son send the Holy Spirit to plead with us to repent and accept eternal life. There is nothing more God can do!

And do not grieve the Holy Spirit of God, by whom you were sealed for the day of redemption. Eph. 4:30.

Pray for the 1.6 million people in Lesotho, a small landlocked country completely surrounded by South Africa. Seventh-day Adventists number 2,073.

SPIRITUAL RENEWAL

Life and wholeness in the church can never come by simply redirecting human efforts. They are only found in God Himself, His Son, and His Spirit.

The first step to renewal is when I see the need for it and do something about it. "When churches are revived, it is because some individual seeks earnestly for the blessing of God. He hungers and thirsts after God, and asks in faith, and receives accordingly. He goes to work in earnest, feeling his great dependence upon the Lord, and souls are aroused to seek for a like blessing, and a season of refreshing falls on the hearts of men" (*Christian Service*, p. 121). What a tremendous encouragement it is to know that revival in the church can begin with just one person. That person could be you!

You cannot merely teach me principles of renewal. Renewal comes from a new life within. Nor can you set me afire by simply showing me a picture of a flame. Instead you must put me in contact with the Living Fire, so that I can see the light and feel the warmth.

When a person is willing to accept the blame for the church being as it is, that person is a candidate for renewal. He or she realizes that the problems with the church are the very kinds of problems in his or her individual life.

A hunger for something better so intense that the person is willing to pay whatever price is necessary to have a new life for himself and for his church makes a person a candidate for renewal.

When one sees that the only hope for renewal and life is to rest solely on God the Father, the Son, and the Holy Spirit, then that person too is a suitable candidate.

I cannot renew anything. I cannot bring new life to a dead church. Only He who had the power to raise Christ from the dead can do that.

> **O Lord, I have heard your speech and was afraid; O Lord, revive Your work in the midst of the years! In the midst of the years make it known; in wrath remember mercy. Hab. 3:2.**

> *Pray that God will start a revival in your church, and pray humbly that it might begin with you.*

AN OWNER'S MANUAL

God reveals His will to us in at least three ways—through the Scriptures, through the Holy Spirit making impressions upon our minds, and through providential circumstances.

We must first of all consult the Scriptures in order to discover God's will on any given subject. Until we have done this, to ask for a special sign or personal revelation would be to open ourselves to Satanic deceptions.

When we purchase sophisticated equipment, we expect to receive an owner's manual from the manufacturer. If human beings feel it necessary to supply an owner's manual with machines of metal and plastic that can be replaced, how much more necessary it is that God should provide a guide to accompany the crowning work of His creation. We need some standard of authority to govern our lives unless we want to be totally dependent on our own judgment. In that case our own intellect becomes our God.

We do not have space enough to list all the reasons for accepting the Bible as our source of authority, but we can mention a few. The message of the Bible transforms lives in a miraculous way. Profligates become pure, criminals become kind, and infidels become believers.

The accuracy of Bible prophecy proves that its writers were inspired. If the prophecies of the Bible are true, then we certainly have good reasons to believe the other parts of the Bible are also.

Nearly 40 human writers authored the Bible over a period of nearly 1,600 years. Actually the Bible is a collection of 66 books bound in one volume, and yet they all agree and complement each other.

The Bible provides answers to life's most insistent questions: Where did I come from? Why am I here? Where am I going? And best of all, Scripture leads us to Jesus Christ, the source of life and happiness. As the Bible is the written Word of God, so Christ is the living Word of God. Although Satan has waged relentless warfare against both Christ and the Bible, both live on.

We believe the Bible is indeed God's book. Let's use it as the guide of our lives.

"All Scripture is given by inspiration of God, and is profitable for doctrine, for reproof, for correction, for instruction in righteousness." 2 Tim. 3:16.

Pray for the more than 1 million Jains living in the state of Maharashtra in India. This prosperous community with its own religion has scarcely been touched with the gospel.

ONE WAY

According to legend the ancient city of Troy had but one entrance, and from whatever direction travelers approached the city they could not enter except through that one legally appointed entrance. Likewise, only one way leads to heaven, and that is the Jesus way.

No one can enter heaven by good works or the strength of human will, by philosophy, or by arousing the good traits of human nature.

It is only by coming to Jesus that we can obtain eternal life. He is the door into the kingdom. May the sentiment of our hearts be "Live out Thy life within me, O Jesus, King of kings!" This—and only this—is the "one way" to victory in the Christian life.

A man once gave directions to another who stopped to ask the way to a certain street. "Is that the best way to get there?" the questioner inquired a little doubtfully.

"It's the only way," came the quick reply. "The other road will lead you right back to where you started." In a world of confusion how good it is to know that the connecting link between earth and heaven is still there. Jesus is the way.

Jacob's dream of a ladder reaching from earth to heaven with angels ascending and descending it was actually a representation of Jesus as the connecting link between earth and heaven.

Some years ago on Lincoln's birthday a cartoon pictured a ladder reaching from a humble log cabin to the White House on the top of a high mountain. The caption declared "The ladder is still there." The ladder that reaches from earth to heaven is still there too. Jesus has made clear that the way from earth to heaven is through accepting Him as our Saviour and Lord. Jesus is the one who links earth with heaven. He came down to earth to show men and women that God loves them. Then He went back to heaven bearing man's flesh that He might plead His sacrifice as an atonement for sin.

And He said to him, "Most assuredly, I say to you, hereafter you shall see heaven open, and the angels of God ascending and descending upon the Son of Man." John 1:51.

Pray for firemen, painters, interior decorators, and others who work with ladders, that their ladders might point them to Jesus, the way from earth to heaven.

A RELIGION OF JOY

The death of Jesus provides forgiveness for our sins, but the fact that He ever lives enables us to gain victory over temptation and sin.

Many Christians are like the boy whose mother told him not to go swimming. After a while he came home with all the telltale marks of having been in the water. "Why did you disobey me and go swimming?" the mother asked.

"Mother, I got tempted," he replied.

"But I notice you took your bathing suit along," she observed.

"Well, I guess I expected to get tempted," the boy admitted.

Too often we make provision for temptation and deprive ourselves of the joy of victory through the living Christ.

Romans 5:10 says, "For if when we were enemies we were reconciled to God through the death of His Son, much more, having been reconciled, we shall be saved by His life." The death of Jesus would not have paid the price of our sin if His life had not been spotless and blameless.

On the other hand the death of Jesus would not have saved us if He had not risen from the grave to intercede for us and to live out His life of victory within us. How true it is that we are saved by His life as well as by His death.

The universe rests on the principle of justice. "The wages of sin is death," and justice demands the life of the sinner, or a sinless substitute. Jesus had to die so that we could live. Do we really grasp the truth of it?

The resurrection of Jesus is the assurance of our resurrection. It is the miracle of history on which the Christian faith is built.

The evidence for the Resurrection was so convincing that the Jewish leaders didn't even visit the tomb to verify the disciples' claim. If a massive search could have produced the body of Jesus or other evidence refuting the Resurrection, it would have put an end to Christianity before it began.

The Roman soldiers saw it all and were too excited to tell anything but the truth. "He was seen by over five hundred brethren at once" (1 Cor. 15:6), as well as smaller groups and by individuals.

His death assures us that our guilt is canceled. His life shows us how to live, and thanks to the Resurrection, gives us power to live as we should. Ours is a religion of joy!

But now Christ is risen from the dead, and has become the firstfruits of those who have fallen asleep. 1 Cor. 15:20.

Pray for the 8.3 million people of Tianjin (te-en-jin) City ("heavenly ford"), and independent city in China.

DRESSED FOR CHURCH

Can you imagine the sight at church next weekend if everyone were to come dressed according to the age of his or her spiritual maturity? Some old in years would have the garments of children or infants, because they have not grown spiritually since being born again.

Lovable little babies are the object of approving looks and words, but an infant that does not grow up is a source of worry and concern.

Peter urges us to "grow in the grace and knowledge of our Lord and Savior Jesus Christ" (2 Peter 3:18).

Paul spoke to believers in Corinth as babes in Christ (see 1 Cor. 3:1). If they had assembled for worship dressed according to their spiritual maturity, they would have come in baby clothes!

One thing that promotes growth is the food we eat. Paul said, "I fed you with milk and not with solid food; for until now you were not able to receive it" (verse 2).

The same problem of spiritual immaturity surfaces in the letter to the Hebrews. Converts who should have grown so that they would be capable of teaching others were still babes (see Heb. 5:11-14).

As we read on into chapter 6 of Hebrews, it seems clear that milk represents the gospel. Solid food would symbolize deeper Bible study, including the doctrines, prophecies, and Christian duties. As long as we are willing to be nursed, the milk diet will suffice. But if we want to grow spiritually and share with others the gospel that has given life to us, we must partake of solid spiritual food.

Spiritual growth requires the spiritual exercise of sharing our faith with others in harmony with the gifts that God has given us. One exercise definitely not conducive to growth is church hopping. We need to be faithful to our home church and the duties assigned us there.

Plants, in order to grow, need to send down their roots. Likewise we, in order to grow to Christian maturity, must be "rooted and grounded" (Eph. 3:17) not only in love but also in our home church.

For though by this time you ought to be teachers. Heb. 5:12.

Pray for the approximately 60 million people of West Bengal in India, where more than 36 tribes speak 85 languages and dialects.

CHOICES
WE DON'T HAVE TO MAKE

We don't have to choose between upholding Christian standards and offering acceptance to the wayward who do not measure up to those standards. Jesus associated freely with persons of doubtful reputation, but He kept His personal standards high. We have no authority to lower the standards set forth in the Word of God. If our motive in mixing with non-Christians is redemptive ministry, we should do so as long as we are strong enough in Christ to influence others for good without evil influencing us.

Of Jesus it is written, "With Him external distinctions weighed nothing. That which appealed to His heart was a soul thirsting for the water of life. . . . Upon their thirsty hearts His words fell with blessed, life-giving power. New impulses were awakened, and the possibility of a new life opened to these outcasts of society" (*The Desire of Ages*, p. 274).

Jesus made a clear statement regarding the responsibility of the church to maintain discipline. This is necessary to safeguard the children of the church who are at an impressionable age and to rightly represent the character of Christ to those both inside the congregation and out. It is interesting that in our permissive society the denominations that are growing fastest are the conservative churches that uphold a strict discipline.

What, after all, is the difference between the saint and the sinner? Not that the saint has no sin in him. Nor that the sinner never has a thought about God. The difference is that the saint is overcoming his sin through the power of Christ, but sin is overcoming the sinner.

We can never reach sinners with the gospel if we shun them. They deserve an opportunity to see Christian compassion demonstrated whether their sins are external like smoking, drinking, and drugs, or "respectable" internal ones like pride, envy, or selfishness.

The immoral woman at Jacob's well, the Christ-persecuting Saul of Tarsus, and Zacchaeus, the tax collector, did not appear outwardly to be good prospects, but in each case they had an inner longing for the water of life.

For the Lord searches all hearts and understands all the intent of the thoughts. 1 Chron. 28:9.

Pray for East and West Malaysia, consisting of the Malay Peninsula and the northern third of the island of Borneo, that God's cause may enjoy true freedom of religion.

357

THE GREAT CONTROVERSY

All humanity is now involved in a great controversy between Christ and Satan regarding the character of God, His law, and His sovereignty over the universe.

There was once a perfect universe, and then sin originated in the heart of the angel who occupied the highest position of any created being. Lucifer was the covering angel who stood by the throne of God.

Filled with a spirit of self-exaltation, Lucifer said, "I will ascend into heaven, I will exalt my throne . . . I will also sit on the mount . . . I will ascend above the heights of the clouds, I will be like the Most High" (Isa. 14:13, 14).

The roots of rebellion trace back to Lucifer's pride over his beauty and wisdom. Although holding the highest angelic position, he envied the honor and adoration given to Christ (see Eze. 28:12-15).

It is incredible to think that spiritual warfare began in a perfect heaven. Sadly, though, it did, and from there it spread to earth with the expulsion from heaven of Satan and his followers. Eve, deceived by Lucifer disguised as a serpent, believed that she could transgress God's law without experiencing the wages of sin—death.

The moral law, the foundation of God's government, is the pivotal point at issue. Lucifer charged that God's law—the transcript of His character —was unreasonable and could not be kept. In other words, He meant that God was Himself unreasonable.

It was at Calvary that the cosmic controversy reached its climax. During its early stages the intelligent beings of other worlds had not had a chance to see the fruit of rebellion against God and His law. However, the sinfulness of sin stood revealed to all the universe in the suffering of the Son of God on Calvary.

In our day the controversy focuses on the deity of Christ and the authority of His Word. The great controversy theme gives new significance to Bible doctrines, vindicates God of any responsibility for the cruelty and suffering in the world, and teaches us to hate sin but love the sinner. It assures us of final victory through Christ.

For we have been made a spectacle to the world, both to angels and to men. 1 Cor. 4:9.

Pray for the approximately 100 Indian tribes of North America and the outreach of the gospel to each one. On this continent many thousands of Indians need to hear of Jesus' soon return.

AN UNUSUAL BURIAL

In one of the countries on the continent of Africa a young man of a certain village announced that he would be buried in the yard at the back of his house at 3:00 that very afternoon.

The man appeared to be strong and healthy, but as the curious villagers gathered around his house early that afternoon, they found the young man digging a large hole in the back yard. Some of his friends had brought shovels and were helping him.

After they finished the hole, the man and his friends began carrying pails of water to fill it. At 3:00 the pastor came and buried the young man in the waters of baptism.

Baptism is the grave between an old life of sin and a new one in Christ Jesus. Before the burial there must come death to that old life of sin, and death usually does not occur without a struggle.

Baptism by immersion fittingly represents the experience of death as the candidate momentarily stops breathing before going under the water. The immersion represents burial, and coming up out of the water symbolizes resurrection to a new life in Christ.

If we are sure we have had an inner experience, how important is the outward ceremony? To witness the joy of the candidate on the day of baptism provides a good part of the answer. Baptism is a public testimony.

Baptism signifies our decision "that we should no longer be slaves of sin" (Rom. 6:6). The cleansing connotation of water makes very real the deliverance from the dominion of sin and the beginning of a new "clean" life. Like the wedding ceremony, baptism is a decisive act symbolizing a love relationship. The one who may have been tossed to and fro by many winds of doctrine has now made a final decision.

In baptism we give ourselves to Jesus, and for that reason many choose to be baptized during that season that places special emphasis on giving gifts to Jesus. It is certainly a most appropriate way to begin a new year.

And now why are you waiting? Arise and be baptized, and wash away your sins, calling on the name of the Lord. Acts 22:16.

Pray for the more than 51 million people of the state of Tamil Nadu at the southern tip of India.

TALK FAITH

As a young Christian I became a colporteur, or literature evangelist—one who sells Bibles and other Christian publications from home to home. After a time I seemed to be surrounded by mountains of difficulties. The territory assigned to me was economically depressed, it rained all the time, my car developed problems, and the people had every conceivable excuse for not buying.

Deciding to visit the publishing department director who had started me, I had a long list of reasons that books would not sell in my territory. When I arrived at the office he was busy with another appointment. While waiting in the reception area, I picked up the book *Christ's Object Lessons*, and it fell open to pages 146, 147: "When perplexities arise, and difficulties confront you, look not for help to humanity. Trust all with God. The practice of telling our difficulties to others, only makes us weak, and brings no strength to them. It lays upon them the burden of our spiritual infirmities, which they cannot relieve. We seek the strength of erring, finite man, when we might have the strength of the unerring, infinite God. . . .

"Never allow yourself to talk in a hopeless, discouraged way. . . . By looking at appearances, and complaining when difficulties and pressure come, you give evidence of a sickly, enfeebled faith. . . . The Lord is rich in resources; He owns the world. Look heavenward in faith."

I said nothing about my doubts and difficulties to the director, and in a few minutes I was driving back to my territory with a new confidence and courage that had come to me from my Lord.

If you are facing doubts and difficulties, look to the Lord for your help. Give Him an opportunity to speak to you by spending time with His Word. Focus your thoughts on the source of your faith, and do not allow yourself to dwell on doubts and difficulties. The exercise of faith is like that of a muscle—it grows stronger with use.

> **Looking unto Jesus, the author and finisher of our faith, who for the joy that was set before Him endured the cross, despising the shame, and has sat down at the right hand of the throne of God. Heb. 12:2.**

> *Pray for the attempts being made for God's last-day message to find entrance in Somalia, which borders Ethiopia and Kenya. It has a population of 8.5 million.*

CLEAN FOR COMMUNION

As the disciples assembled for the Last Supper they argued about which of them was the greatest. They were not ready for communion with their Lord.

From the words and example of Jesus we know that He instituted a service of preparation for the Lord's Supper. Jesus the Master fulfilled the role of a servant as He washed the feet of each of His disciples. They needed a lesson in humility, and knowing that needy humanity in every generation would require this same lesson repeated, Jesus said, "If I then, your Lord and Teacher, have washed your feet, you also ought to wash one another's feet. For I have given you an example, that you should do as I have done to you" (John 13:14, 15).

Taking part in this meaningful ordinance has a marvelous way of causing us to search our hearts, make things right, and thus prepare ourselves for the blessing of the Lord's Supper.

We may take a shower in the morning, but by lunchtime we have been exposed to contamination in many forms, and we feel the need of washing our hands before we eat. Likewise, following baptism we encounter the defiling influences of this world, and in preparation for the Lord's Supper we wash each other's feet to restore the "cleanness" that we experienced following baptism. "Jesus said to him, 'He who is bathed needs only to wash his feet, but is completely clean; and you are clean, but not all of you ' " (John 13:10). In a sense, foot washing is a miniature baptism.

The unleavened bread and unfermented wine of the Communion service are extremely meaningful symbols. The kernels of wheat had to be crushed and ground into flour before we could derive life-giving nourishment from the bread. Likewise, the body of Jesus had to be broken before His death could give us life.

The wine was unfermented because fermentation is a form of spoiling and deterioration, which could not fittingly represent the blood of a pure and perfect Saviour. The grapes must be bruised and crushed in order to produce juice. So it was with the Saviour's shed blood.

How deeply meaningful is the Communion service!

If you know these things, happy are you if you do them. John 13:17.

Pray for the more than 430,000 Muslim people of Bahrain in the Persian Gulf, where evangelism is forbidden and where Seventh-day Adventists have no established work.

FIND A MINISTRY

"Christ intends that His ministers shall be educators of the church in gospel work. They are to teach the people how to seek and save the lost" (*The Desire of Ages*, p. 825). God calls believers not to be spectators but to be participants in the mission of the church.

The decisive act of enlisting to become a soldier in the Roman army in the time of Christ was formalized by a military oath called a *sacramentum* from which we derive the word "sacrament." All who by their vows and baptism pledge to take an active part in the warfare between Christ and Satan become part of the *laos* ("laity"), the people of God.

In a sense baptism is also an ordination for service. "All who receive the life of Christ are ordained to work for the salvation of their fellow men" (*ibid.*, p. 822). "All are alike called to be missionaries for God" (*The Ministry of Healing*, p. 395).

The clergy are part of the *laos*. The difference is only a matter of function. The clergy are full-time specialists with the responsibility of training the laity for ministry. Every member of the body then becomes a minister. To equip us for our ministry God gives each believer spiritual gifts.

One of the Christian's greatest experiences in this life is to discover his or her gifts and to find a ministry. You may remember that we discussed spiritual gifts in our readings from February 9 to 15. Perhaps this week you will want to turn back in this book and review some of those thoughts.

The main chapters dealing with spiritual gifts are Romans 12, 1 Corinthians 12, and Ephesians 4. Some things that will help you to discover your spiritual gifts include studying the Scriptures, being open to providential guidance, and the confirming by other members of the church body of your own feelings about your gifts. Also spiritual gifts seminars and tests designed to help you in the discovery of your gifts will help you determine what special abilities God has endowed you with.

To avoid the frustration of not having an outlet to use the gifts you have discovered, prayerfully consider the needs for ministry that exist in the area where you live. Such awareness along with consultation with your pastor will help you to the fulfilling experience of discovery and ministry.

As each one has received a gift, minister it to one another, as good stewards of the manifold grace of God. 1 Peter 4:10.

Pray for Albania's more than 3 million people. Pray that God will open the way for the liberating gospel to be proclaimed freely in that country.

PERFECT IN HIM

Christ is Prophet, Priest, and King. When He finishes His intercessory ministry in behalf of sinners, we will live without an intercessor, but there will never be a time when we will live apart from Christ, because "in Him we live, and move and have our being" (Acts 17:28).

Many feel overwhelmed when they read Christ's admonition to be perfect. Based on our day-to-day experience, perfection seems beyond our reach. But in a most remarkable manner Christ has provided a way so that the seemingly impossible becomes possible.

"It was possible for Adam, before the fall, to form a righteous character by obedience to God's law. But he failed to do this, and because of his sin our natures are fallen and we cannot make ourselves righteous. Since we are sinful, unholy, we cannot perfectly obey the holy law. We have no righteousness of our own with which to meet the claims of the law of God. But Christ has made a way of escape for us. He lived on earth amid trials and temptations such as we have to meet. He lived a sinless life. He died for us, and now He offers to take our sins and give us His righteousness. If you give yourself to Him, and accept Him as your Saviour, then, sinful as your life may have been, for His sake you are accounted righteous. Christ's character stands in place of your character, and you are accepted before God just as if you had not sinned" (*Steps to Christ*, p. 62).

When we enter into a saving transaction with Christ whereby He takes our sin and gives us His righteousness, we are perfect in Him. His demonstration of His unconditional love wins our love and loyalty in response. "We love Him because He first loved us" (1 John 4:19).

Because we love Jesus we want to please Him, so as we learn His will, we do it. His love demonstrated to us motivates our obedience. But because our "life is hidden with Christ in God" (Col. 3:3), when the Father looks at us He sees Jesus and His perfection. As long as we abide in Him, we are perfect—perfect in Him.

For you died, and your life is hidden with Christ in God. Col. 3:3.

Two million members of the Arakanese tribe dwell in the high mountainous teak forests of western Burma. Pray that the gospel of God's saving love may reach them.

THE GREEN-EYED MONSTER

One of the devices the devil has to rob us of peace of mind and contentment is envy. Envy, jealousy, and covetousness are all related. Envy originated in heaven when Lucifer became jealous of Christ. The green-eyed monster of envy continues to rear its ugly head in unexpected places and in the best of circles.

Two young couples were holding an evangelistic crusade together. The young men preached on alternate nights. All went well until Charles perceived that the attendance was consistently better on the nights when Frank preached. For days waves of jealousy washed through Charles' mind. He felt troubled because he knew God couldn't bless him with the feelings he had.

Determined to get victory over his envy, he went through an experience somewhat like Jacob's night of wrestling with the Lord, but in the end he triumphed.

When they came to the final night of the meetings, Frank put his arm around Charles as they met in the little prayer room. He said, "Charles, I have a confession to make. All during these meetings it has seemed to me as if you always had the larger crowds, you preached the better sermons, and you had the greater response. Charles, I have been terribly jealous, and I want you to forgive me and pray for me."

The green-eyed monster distorts our vision. Envy also warps our reason. Saul began to feel jealous of David when the musicians sang, "Saul has slain his thousands, and David his ten thousands." It was just too much for the first Israelite king to have the people say that David was ten times as good a soldier as he.

Brooding over the comparison with David, Saul became so angry that he threw a javelin at the younger man.

"The envious man diffuses poison wherever he goes, alienating friends and stirring up hatred and rebellion against God and man. He seeks to be thought best and greatest, not by putting forth heroic, self-denying efforts to reach the goal of excellence himself, but by standing where he is and diminishing the merit due to the efforts of others" (*Testimonies*, vol. 5, p. 56).

Do not fret because of evildoers, nor be envious of the workers of iniquity. Ps. 37:1.

Pray for the more than 26,000 "Water People" of Zaire who live in about 60 villages along the swamplands of the Zaire River.

A CHURCH IN YOUR HOME

Nymphas lived in Laodicea about 12 miles from Colosse. The Christian church in those early days had no church buildings as we have today. They met on a regular basis in certain homes.

When Paul composed the letter to the Colossians he sent salutations to the believers in nearby Laodicea. He wrote, "Greet the brethren who are in Laodicea, and Nymphas and the church that is in his house" (Col. 4:15).

Aquila and Priscilla had a church that met in their home when they lived in Rome (Rom. 16:3-5), and a congregation also met in their house when they lived in Ephesus (1 Cor. 16:19). Philemon had a church that met in his house (Philemon 1:2).

Some of you who are reading this page could advance God's cause if you would dedicate a room in your house as a place where a small congregation could meet. You might begin with a Branch Sabbath School, a Revelation Seminar, or a Bible study.

On one of my visits to the Philippines, I met a husband and wife who were literature evangelists. As they found interested people in the course of their work, they invited them to a Sabbath service in their home. I visited this house church when it had grown to more than 40 members. The Lord's blessings were evident.

Another couple in Manila, who own an electroplating business, started a church on the flat roof of their factory, which is several stories high. When we visited the Rooftop Church the membership had reached 60, and they had built a roof and walls to enclose the congregation. Churches met in houses, factories, medical offices, warehouses, even roof tops! Think of the possibilities in these days when small groups are so effective.

Through the years as I've seen fields struggle to help new congregations provide houses of worship, I've wondered what would we do when large numbers join us during the outpouring of the latter rain. Now I believe I know a possible answer—house churches.

If you live in an area without a church, pray about the possibility of one in your house.

Greet the brethren who are in Laodicea, and Nymphas and the church that is in his house. Col. 4:15.

Pray for an increase in house churches and a blessing on existing ones.

A UNIQUE PARTNERSHIP

On his last birthday, spent far away from friends at home, in the wilds of Africa, David Livingstone wrote these words in his diary: "My Jesus, my King, my Life, my All; I again dedicate my whole self to Thee." Livingstone recognized that God has entrusted each of us with time, talents, and material possessions. His response was to trust the Lord with all he had and was.

One of the greatest practical blessings of Christianity is the ever-increasing awareness that our God is not distant and intangible, but close and personal. This personal relationship develops confidence so that we are willing to trust Him with all we have and are.

The Lord in turn accepts the responsibility of ownership, but He makes us His stewards. This results in a unique partnership in which the Lord bears all the responsibilities involved in ownership, and we get to enjoy all the benefits as stewards or managers of what we have entrusted into His hands.

Our Lord takes the initiative in this arrangement by placing in our hands 100 percent of the benefits from this partnership even though 10 percent is His on the basis of the ancient biblical principle of the tithe. "And all the tithe of the land, whether of the seed of the land or of the fruit of the tree, is the Lord's. It is holy to the Lord" (Lev. 27:30).

We are to bring our tithe to the "storehouse," or church, and it is to be used exclusively for the support of gospel outreach and nurture, and the ministry responsible for directing such activities.

The words of Jesus clearly indicate that the principle of tithe, or tenth of our increase, belongs to God carries over into New Testament times. In Matthew 23:23 Jesus upheld the practice of tithing.

If we are systematic in our stewardship, our giving, like our tithing will be proportionate to the Lord's blessings.

One of the greatest lessons of truth for the new Christian is to really believe the Bible promise in our text for today.

> **"Bring all the tithes into the storehouse, that there may be food in My house, and prove Me now in this," says the Lord of hosts, "If I will not open for you the windows of heaven and pour out for you such blessing that there will not be room enough to receive it." Mal. 3:10.**

> *Pray for the more than 6 million people in Guinea, Black Africa's least evangelized country. Guinea is now open to the gospel, but there are only a few Christians, and no organized Seventh-day Adventist program.*

FROM FEAR TO COURAGE

We are often defeated not so much by our actual experiences as by our fear of what might happen. Of all the emotions that influence human action, fear is one of the most forceful.

We may struggle with the fear of recession, fear of accident or some terrible catastrophe, fear of national disaster, fear of crime or terrorism, or the fear that death may snatch our family or friends away from us.

What will give us freedom from such fears? The answer lies in learning to know God so that we can confidently trust His plan for our lives. When we recognize that God is all-powerful and that because of His love for us He will always act in our best interest, we can set aside our fears.

Courage is born of the conviction that God is with us and will never fail us, a conviction that will bless us in every aspect of our lives, including our participation in God's cause.

"Obstacles to the advancement of the work of God will appear; but fear not. . . . He can remove all obstructions to the advancement of His work. He has means for the removal of every difficulty, that those who serve Him and respect the means He employs may be delivered" (*Testimonies*, vol. 8, p. 10).

If mountains of difficulties seem to rise up ahead of you, don't be afraid. Trust the God who is able to change the most forbidding circumstances. "When in faith we take hold of His strength, He will change, wonderfully change, the most hopeless, discouraging outlook. He will do this for the glory of His name" (*ibid.*, vol. 8, p. 12).

The fundamental roots of courage and fearlessness are faith and devotion. The man who is afraid has lost his faith. Among Jesus' favorite expressions were "Courage"; "Be of good cheer"; "Don't be afraid."

God is by the side of every man or woman battling to advance the Lord's cause, or who strives for personal victory over evil. Draw strength from the promise in our text for today.

Have I not commanded you? Be strong and of good courage; do not be afraid, nor be dismayed, for the Lord your God is with you wherever you go. Joshua 1:9.

Pray for the 12.7 million people of Shanghai City. Shanghai, a name meaning "on the sea," is China's largest city, and this great seaport is the outlet for the Yangtze River basin.

UNITY IN THE BODY OF CHRIST

The church is one body with many members, called from every nation, kindred, tongue, and people.

In Ephesians 4 Paul describes the gifts of ministry placed in the church "till we all come to the unity of the faith" (verse 13). The chapter emphasizes unity. The Holy Spirit is the one essential element for Christians to have it. Paul counsels, "walk worthy of the calling . . . with all lowliness and gentleness, with longsuffering, bearing with one another in love, endeavoring to keep the unity of the Spirit in the bond of peace" (verses 1-3).

There is "one body." Like the various parts of the human body, each member of the church has a function to perform. Remembering that Christ is the head of the body will produce a harmony that will discourage dissident and offshoot tendencies.

There is "one Spirit." One Spirit indwelling and controlling each individual believer will produce unity.

There is "one hope." The Bible speaks of the return of Jesus as "the blessed hope" (Titus 2:13).

There is "one Lord." The pagan religions had many gods, but by contrast Christianity has one Lord.

There is "one faith." Paul is here making the point that Christians achieve unity when all embrace the same body of biblical beliefs.

There is "one baptism." Baptism by immersion into the body of Christ beautifully emphasizes the unity that should characterize the Christian church.

There is "one God and Father of all." Our heavenly Father is the source of all unity in the family of God, although the family consists of many diverse elements. Think of the time of Christ when there were slave and master, Jew and Gentile, rich and poor. In our day we have many cultures, customs, and colors. To see such diverse elements blending together in unity is a powerful testimony to unbelievers.

Behold, how good and how pleasant it is for brethren to dwell together in unity! Ps. 133:1.

Pray for the more than 7 million people of Kalimantan, the Indonesian portion of the island of Borneo.

THE LAMB AND THE PRIEST

The sanctuary in heaven is the tabernacle that the Lord set up and not man. In it Christ ministers on our behalf, making available to believers the benefits of His atoning sacrifice offered once for all on the cross.

The sanctuary service of ancient Israel beautifully prefigured Christ's sacrifice and mediation. The daily service in the holy place depicted God's day-to-day provision for the forgiveness of sin, and the annual service in the Most Holy Place foreshadowed the final judgment and the eradication of sin from the universe.

Moses constructed the earthly sanctuary after a pattern based on the true sanctuary in heaven (Heb. 8:2; Ex. 25:9). Just as the earthly sanctuary was cleansed annually on the Day of Atonement, so the heavenly sanctuary was to be purified prior to the return of Jesus. Remember that this cleansing of the records of sin represents the judgment.

God completes this phase of the judgment before the Second Advent because just before He comes, the decree goes forth, "He who is unjust, let him be unjust still" (Rev. 22:11).

The Lord doesn't need to conduct an investigation, for He knows the details of our lives. Rather it is for our sake and for the benefit of other intelligent beings in the universe who look on. Everyone must know that He has done everything possible to save the lost.

As long as freedom of choice remains, an investigation at the end is absolutely essential. It is our decision that determines the verdict in the final judgment. God's decision is based on ours. It is a question of our relationship with Christ. "He who has the Son has life; he who does not have the Son of God does not have life" (1 John 5:12).

Atonement has two aspects—Christ's death for us, and His intercession for us. In the symbols of the sanctuary both the slain lamb and the high priest represent Christ.

For Christ has not entered the holy places made with hands, which are copies of the true, but into heaven itself, now to appear in the presence of God for us. Heb. 9:24.

Pray for the 7.2 million people of the secular state of Niger in north central Africa. Although the government provides freedom of religion, Christians number only .4 percent of the population, or one per every 250. Pray that the remnant church may find entrance to this country.

FULLY GOD AND FULLY MAN

The babe born in Bethlehem's manger was not half human and half divine. He was fully God and fully man.

One of the most profound truths of the Bible common to both Judaism and Christianity appears in Deuteronomy 6:4, 5: "Hear, O Israel: The Lord our God, the Lord is one! You shall love the Lord your God with all your heart, with all your soul, and with all your might."

As Seventh-day Adventists we worship one God who created all things, and who has revealed Himself to mankind as Father, Son, and Holy Spirit. He is not three gods, or one God with three heads, but one God manifest in three persons, and this is what the word "trinity" describes. This is the "Godhead" spoken of in the Bible.

The Father, Son, and Holy Spirit are equal in nature, but Christ voluntarily subordinated Himself to the Father in order to become a part of the human family. Philippians 2:5-11 describes Christ's condescension. Christ humbled Himself and took the form of a servant.

A misunderstanding of some statements referring to Jesus' earthly life has caused some to believe that He was a created being and not God. While a created being might conceivably be able to give his earthly life in exchange for one other created being's, only one equal with God could offer His life to make possible the eternal salvation of the entire human race.

The name Yahweh (the pronunciation "Jehovah" was unknown prior to the late Middle Ages) clearly applies to the Son as well as the Father. We know, for example, that Jesus is the Saviour. Isaiah 43:11 says that it is Jehovah who is our Saviour. In other words, Jesus is Jehovah. Jesus is the Rock, and Jehovah is also the Rock (see Deut. 32:3, 4). Jesus is the Branch, and Jehovah is the Branch (see Jer. 23:5, 6).

Because we are finite human beings trying to comprehend an infinite God any illustration we use to depict Him must fall short, but consider the light that illumines your room at night. The bulb might represent Jesus whom men could touch. The filament could symbolize the Father, who is "in Christ." The electric current might stand for the Holy Spirit everywhere present. And yet all three are the light.

And Thomas answered and said to Him, "My Lord and my God!" John 20:28.

Pray for the province of Assam in India, with a population of 22.3 million and 60 different languages. The population is 71 percent Hindu and 24 percent Muslim.

THE CHILD OF BETHLEHEM

Most thoughtful adults, if they had a wish list, would put near the top something like this: to live a happy and secure life with my family and friends, with no sickness, old age, or death.

"The gift of God is eternal life" (Rom. 6:23), and this is the day when people around the world think of gifts. Our heavenly Father's greatest gift to this world was Jesus, and Jesus' gift is eternal life—a gift that cost Him His life.

Many reading these words have laid to rest a loved one this year, and have had special occasion to think of death and resurrection. The death of a loved one makes the promise of the resurrection intensely real.

God's plan for a great family reunion centers in the Babe of Bethlehem whose birth we celebrate today. It does not matter that no one knows the exact date of His birth—the very fact that He was born itself calls for celebration and rejoicing. Because the Child of Bethlehem was born and fulfilled His mission, there will be a resurrection, and those who sleep in Jesus will then be part of the family circle again, forever!

Why should Jesus come again if He was here 2,000 years ago? The Bible and our own personal needs provide us with many answers to that question. One of the very evident answers is that the resurrection depends upon His second coming.

As we await the resurrection at the return of Jesus, how wonderful it is to know that the dead are peacefully sleeping, unconscious of the passing of time. From Genesis to Revelation the Bible teaches that "the dead know nothing" (Eccl. 9:5).

A biblical understanding of death takes away the fear created by uncertainty. It removes the basis for belief in spiritualism and purgatory.

When Jesus returns, we will put on immortality and will be caught up together with our resurrected loved ones to meet our Lord. Today as we celebrate the Saviour's birth, let us also rejoice that soon He will come again and make an end of death.

Then the angel said to them, "Do not be afraid, for behold, I bring you good tidings of great joy which will be to all people." Luke 2:10.

Pray for the more than 31 million people of the province of Shanxi (shahn-she), which means "west of the mountains." This is one of the poorest provinces in China, with coal mines occupying more than 80 percent of its territory.

WAITING AND WATCHING

Although Joseph and Mary lived in Nazareth, unusual circumstances brought them to Bethlehem, and as prophecy foretold, Christ was born in Bethlehem.

At this season of the year the thoughts of men and women around the world focus on the first advent of Jesus in Bethlehem's manger nearly 2,000 years ago. Strangely, some of the religious leaders of Christ's generation were not the ones who were looking for His coming. They were preoccupied with rules, liturgy, and selfish interests. But devout believers like Anna and Simeon were waiting and watching for the coming of the Redeemer (Luke 2:34-38).

Prophecy pinpointed the time when the Saviour would appear. Sixty-nine prophetic weeks or 483 literal years from the decree for the rebuilding of Jerusalem in 457 B.C. would reach to the anointing of the Messiah, according to Daniel 9:24, 25. The prophet Micah foretold the place of His birth in Bethlehem.

In addition, prophecy also gives many signs pointing to the time of our Lord's second coming. How many such signs do you see being fulfilled before our eyes today? Your list might include the great increase of prophetic knowledge, the increase of crime and violence, wars and rumors of wars, destructive earthquakes, the gospel being preached in all the world, pleasure lovers with a form of godliness, moral revolution, famines, natural disasters, and financial instability.

In spite of all the signs, the Second Coming will take most people by surprise, just as did the Flood in Noah's day. His second advent will be like the visit of a thief in the night, not invisible, but unexpected.

The New Testament alone has more than 300 references to the return of Jesus. He promised, "I will come again" (John 14:3).

God is not waiting primarily for prophecy to be fulfilled. Rather He wants men and women to have the chance to make their decisions and to share Jesus with others so they too can accept Him. Everything is ready for that hour. The question is, Are you? Am I?

He who testifies to these things says, "Surely I am coming quickly." Amen. Even so, come, Lord Jesus! Rev. 22:20.

Pray for the more than 11.3 million people of Syria, a secular state with Islam recognized as the religion of the majority. We no longer have any established Adventist organization there.

LOVE HIM MORE

Perhaps you've heard someone say "It doesn't matter what you believe just as long as you have love in your heart." Doctrine divides us, but love unites us, they say. Fortunately, we don't have to choose between doctrine and love.

Every doctrine of the Bible rightly understood will reveal another aspect of the love of Jesus and cause us to love Him more. God takes such a personal interest in His people that He has even given us dietary suggestions to help us enjoy optimum health Like a loving parent He counsels us against entertainments and indulgences that might be destructive to our spiritual or physical life, and encourages instead wholesome pursuits that will truly re-create our vital forces.

Jesus takes away our fear of death by reminding us that He experienced death and is alive again. Death is just like being asleep with no consciousness of the passing of time. He further reassures us by stating that He has the keys of the grave and of death.

The weekly Sabbath not only reminds us of Creation and the Creator, but is a foretaste of heaven. Stewardship principles offer us a partnership relationship with God. The ordinances of baptism and the Lord's Supper both represent a relationship with Jesus.

As Christians we become part of a wonderful church family that seeks to provide love and acceptance. It is a family in which the most prized possession of every member is the robe of Christ's righteousness.

In the church our Lord has placed gifts for our nurture and growth. Gifts like the gift of prophecy and the gift of pastors and teachers. One of His greatest gifts is the promise that He will come again and take us to the heavenly paradise He's gone to prepare.

Our Lord has dealt patiently with the problem of rebellion and is allowing every individual to weigh the evidence in the great controversy and make an intelligent decision.

Most likely you are a part of His church. If so, rejoice and share Him with others. If not, decide to join it today, and before you go to sleep tonight, tell someone about your decision.

And the Spirit and the bride say, "Come!" And let him who hears say, "Come!" And let him who thirsts come. And whoever desires, let him take the water of life freely. Rev. 22:17.

India has 26,000 castes. Christianity has made converts among only 100 of them. Remember India in your prayers today.

WHAT A DAY TO BE ALIVE

Readers of this page are living in times of change. It seems natural to resist change, especially if one is past middle age. But all changes are not necessarily bad. To illustrate that point, consider the fact that the experience of conversion is a matter of change. Even though it is a change for the better, we usually have a tendency to hold back and resist.

God is not the initiator of all changes, but God does use change to His advantage in spreading the gospel. And the people of God should do likewise.

Islam, Buddhism, Hinduism, and Judaism have been almost impenetrable so far as the gospel is concerned, but secularism is breaking their traditional holds and making them accessible. The old authoritarianism and social control of the group is gradually giving way and creating a receptivity to new ideas.

Think of the changes that have taken place in recent years in the Soviet Union and in China. Only a decade or two ago it was hard to see how the gospel could reach the people of some of earth's most populous countries. But all the while God is at work.

"In the annals of human history, the growth of nations, the rise and fall of empires, appear as if dependent on the will and prowess of man. . . . [But] above, behind, and through all the play and counterplay of human interest and power and passions, the agencies of the All-merciful One [are] silently, patiently working out the counsels of His own will" (*Prophets and Kings*, pp. 499, 500).

The words of God through Habakkuk, which appear as today's text, seem appropriate again in our day. What a day to be alive!

Look among the nations and watch—be utterly astounded! For I will work a work in your days which you would not believe, though it were told you. Hab. 1:5.

Pray again for the great cities. Population projections for the year 2,000 show two cities with more than 20 million (see prayer suggestion for January 5). Among those with more than 10 million will be: Greater New York, 15.5; Seoul, 13.5; Shanghai, 13.5; Rio de Janeiro, 13.3; New Delhi, 13.3; Buenos Aires, 13.2; and Cairo, 13.2.

IS ANYONE THIRSTY?

The Feast of Tabernacles was a joyous festival at the end of the harvest. The feast began on the fifteenth day of the seventh Jewish month and continued for seven days. The people were well established in the Promised Land. They could plant their crops and reap their harvest. Springs, wells, and cisterns provided them with a dependable supply of water. This feast was a memorial of their wilderness wanderings when they did not have such material benefits. During the Feast of Tabernacles, the people lived in tents and other temporary structures as a reminder of how God had sustained their ancestors and met their needs during their desert journeys for 40 years.

Going up to the Temple at the morning hour of worship, the people, carrying branches of willow in their hands, marched joyfully around the altar of burnt offering. In connection with the morning sacrifices, a priest brought to the Temple a vessel filled with the water that flows from the spring Gihon, accompanied by the Levites chanting the words of Isaiah 12:3, "Therefore with joy you will draw water from the wells of salvation." A priest poured the water out beside the altar into a conduit through which it flowed down to the Kidron Valley. This part of the ceremony commemorated the water that God provided from the rock in the wilderness. That rock was a symbol of Jesus who by His death would cause living streams of salvation to flow to all who were thirsty.

On the last day of the feast, as the priest carried the pitcher of water to the altar as a part of a ceremony whose true meaning so many had forgotten, Jesus invited those with spiritual thirst to come to Him. Many of those people were seeking to meet their restless longings with things of this world, which can never truly satisfy, and many are in such a state today. If you are in a similar spiritual experience, He invites you to come to Him today.

On the last day, that great day of the feast, Jesus stood and cried out, saying, "If anyone thirsts, let him come to Me and drink." John 7:37.

Pray for Mauritania, an Islamic republic in the northwestern part of Africa. With an area of 419,231 square miles, the population is 1.8 million, and the nation has no Adventist presence.

SQUARE-UP TIME

The Chinese used to have an unwritten law that they must settle all accounts by New Year's Day. Those who ignored this law could expect to be severely dealt with. As we approach the end of the year, it is appropriate that we review our financial obligations to our fellow human beings as well as to God.

One of the responsibilities a person accepts when he or she takes the name of Christian is the financial support of the church program through tithe and offerings. The prophet Malachi records God's promise of abundant blessings to the faithful steward.

Such blessings include satisfaction, happiness, and the knowledge that we are active participants in God's work. In the final day we will not regret any amount of money, time, or talent we have given to advance His cause.

As we review our stewardship, think about the two little children who entertained themselves by acting out the story of the Flood.

The bathtub seemed the the logical place for their flood, and an old box became the ark. They turned on the shower, and the floods descended. Finally they pulled the plug, and the ark rested on dry ground.

Remembering that Noah offered a sacrifice to God, the children decided the kitchen stove would be the place to burn it. Reaching into the ark, the little boy found one of his sister's animals and said, "Let's burn this."

"Oh, no," she objected, and she reached into the ark to find one of her brother's animals. "Let's give this to God," she suggested. Now it was his turn to protest. Finally, she solved the dilemma by a trip to the attic. She came back with a little toy lamb so dirty that they couldn't identify its original color. One leg was missing, its head was bashed in, and it had no tail.

"Let's give this for our sacrifice," she said. "We'll never want it again anyway."

We smile at the children, but what does the record of our stewardship say about our love for God? Do we love the Lord enough to give Him our best, or do we give Him only what's left after we have satisfied the gods of this world?

So let each one give as he purposes in his heart, not grudgingly or of necessity; for God loves a cheerful giver. 2 Cor. 9:7.

Pray for the 400,000 Italians living in Toronto, Canada.

LOOKING BOTH WAYS

Potato harvests marked the cycle of the year to the Swedish peasant. Koreans dated events by the ripening of cucumbers, while American Indians marked the annual cycle by "snows."

The Jews have always reckoned their civil year from the first day of the month Tishri in the autumn. The ancient Egyptians, Phoenicians, and Persians also began their year at the autumnal equinox. The Romans designated January 1 as the beginning of the new year. January is named for Janus, the Roman god of gates and doors, represented as having two faces looking in opposite directions.

The end of an old year and the beginning of a new one is indeed a time to look both back and ahead. We glance back to review the lessons learned and to recount the blessings that have come our way.

As we look forward, we are thankful for a God who knows the future and has promised to walk with us all the way. The new year marks the passing of time. Many regard time as a monster that steals our youth, dims our sight, grays our hair, slows our step, and saps our vitality. They view time as an enemy with whom we must forever wrestle in mortal combat. But for the Christian, time extends beyond an earthly lifetime into the countless ages of eternity.

The passing of time carries the Christian nearer and nearer to the shore of a better land where we shall see our Saviour face to face.

As the children of Israel came to the Jordan and faced an unknown future, God promised to show them the way they should go. For us as for them, the important thing is to walk with the Lord through the days of the coming year.

M. Louise Haskins wrote:

> "I said to the man who stood at the gate of the year:
> 'Give me a light, that I may tread safely into the unknown!'
> And he replied: 'Go out into the darkness, and put your hand into the hand of God,
> It shall be to you better than light, and safer than a known way.' "

For you have not passed this way before. Joshua 3:4.

Pray that the gospel of Jesus Christ may penetrate the Islamic state of Kuwait, a wedge of desert at the northeast end of the Arabian Gulf.

SCRIPTURE INDEX